The Forgotten Front

Foreign Military Studies

History is replete with examples of notable military campaigns and exceptional military leaders and theorists. Military professionals and students of the art and science of war cannot afford to ignore these sources of knowledge or limit their studies to the history of the US armed forces. This series features original works, translations, and reprints of classics outside the American canon that promote a deeper understanding of international military theory and practice.

Series editor: Joseph Craig

An AUSA Book

The Forgotten Front

The Eastern Theater of World War I, 1914–1915

Edited by Gerhard P. Gross

Translated by Janice W. Ancker

UNIVERSITY PRESS OF KENTUCKY

The present translation is based on the original German edition published in 2006 and represents the state of research at that time.

The University Press of Kentucky is scholarly publisher for the Commonwealth, serving Bellarmine University, Berea College, Centre College of Kentucky, Eastern Kentucky University, The Filson Historical Society, Georgetown College, Kentucky Historical Society, Kentucky State University, Morehead State University, Murray State University, Northern Kentucky University, Transylvania University, University of Kentucky, University of Louisville, and Western Kentucky University.

Editorial and Sales Offices: The University Press of Kentucky
663 South Limestone Street, Lexington, Kentucky 40508-4008
www.kentuckypress.com

Library of Congress Cataloging-in-Publication Data

Names: Gross, Gerhard Paul, 1958- editor. | Ancker, Janice W., translator.
Title: The forgotten front : the Eastern Theater of World War I, 1914-1915 / edited by Gerhard P. Gross ; translated by Janice W. Ancker.
Other titles: Vergessene Front—der Osten, 1914/15. English
Description: Lexington, Kentucky : University Press of Kentucky, [2018] | Includes index.
Identifiers: LCCN 2018012011| ISBN 0813175410 (hardcover : alk. paper) | ISBN 0813175445 (online) | ISBN 0813175437 (pdf) | ISBN 0813175429 (epub)
Subjects: LCSH: World War, 1914-1918—Campaigns—Eastern Front. | Collective memory—Germany.
Classification: LCC D551 .V3813 2018 | DDC 940.4/22—dc23

This book is printed on acid-free paper meeting the requirements of the American National Standard for Permanence in Paper for Printed Library Materials.

Manufactured in the United States of America

Member of the Association of University Presses

Contents

Foreword

Over a century after it began, the First World War, the first global conflict of the past century, has once again captured public attention. In Germany, in contrast to France and Great Britain, where the "Great War" has been continually present in political culture and historical research, interest in the First World War has lingered in the background, overshadowed by the Second World War.

The academic debate over what has been called the seminal catastrophe of the twentieth century was for a long time dominated by the casting of blame. In the Fischer Controversy during the 1960s, the First World War was viewed primarily from the perspective of revisionist political history. In the 1970s, it was approached from the angle of structural and social history. In the 1990s, a boom in German World War I research reflected the coming of age of a younger generation of historians who were not directly affected by personal experience of the war. Using multiple approaches and incorporating the personal and everyday recollections of participants, the history of mentalities, and cultural history, new ground has been broken and a path has been forged out of what historian Gerd Krumeich has called the "*cul de sac* of structural historical-normative interpretations."

The Military History Research Office (Militärgeschichtliches Forschungsamt, MGFA) has contributed to the research debate in recent years with its own articles and by presenting new issues for research. On the occasion of the eightieth anniversary of the outbreak of the war, an initial survey of the current status of research was presented in *Der Erste Weltkrieg: Wirkung, Wahrnehmung, Analyse* (The First World War: Effects, Perceptions, Analysis) on behalf of the MGFA, published by Wolfgang Michalka in 1994. Another project, *Kriegsende, 1918: Ereignis, Wirkung, Nachwirkung* (War's End, 1918: The Event, Impact, and Aftereffects), published on behalf of the MGFA by Jörg Duppler and Gerhard P. Gross in 1999, analyzed the war's end on the western front in 1918 in an approach that combined cultural history, the history of mentalities, and the history of events. This was a comparative study of the "era of world wars" incorporating both structural history and experiential history. A third study, *Erster Weltkrieg–Zweiter Weltkrieg: Ein Vergleich* (First World War–Second World War: A Comparison), published under the auspices of the MGFA by Bruno Thoss and Hans-Erich Volkmann in

2002, put this manner of research to the test, in a sense, in an effort to resolve deficiencies in traditional analyses and develop a new approach to research. The chapters in this present volume reflect these newer perspectives.

In the coming years the research interests of the MGFA will focus on the era of world wars as a whole. In doing so, we will integrate the First World War to a greater extent and in a way that will reach beyond the mere acknowledgment of the war's centennial in 2014. We have received encouragement on this path by recent reviews of our research papers from a series of professional publications.

On the occasion of the ninetieth year after the outbreak of the war, the German Historical Museum staged an exhibit called *Der Weltkrieg, 1914–1918: Ereignis und Erinnerung* (The World War, 1914–1918: Event and Remembrance). The intensive and positive cooperation between the MGFA and the German Historical Museum before the creation of the exhibit provided the opportunity to combine military historical expertise with the capabilities of the museum. The result was the genesis of this book, the Forty-Sixth International Conference for Military History by the MGFA, *Die vergessene Front—Der Osten, 1914/15: Ereignis, Wirkung, Nachwirkung* (The Forgotten Front—The East, 1914–1915: The Event, Its Impact, and Aftereffects), which was held in the portion of the German Historical Museum called the Zeughaus, an arsenal in former times. We wish to expressly thank the museum's general director, Professor Dr. Hans Ottomeyer, for his cooperation. The positive reception from the public, the media, and the academic sphere helped to draw positive attention to the themes of the conference and exhibit.

I also wish to thank our professional colleagues from both home and abroad who, as presenters and discussion participants, presented their research and made it available for publication.

In the original German edition of this book, the editorial staff of the MGFA supervised the publication project all the way to the setting of the print: Michael Thomae was in charge of coordinating the articles, Rüdiger Bergien (Berlin) handled the copyediting; Antje Lorenz was responsible for the layout, and Bernd Nogli prepared the accompanying maps for the volume. Ulrike Lützelberger (Brandenburg) prepared the index. She also handled the transliteration of locations and personal names from the Cyrillic alphabet. Our thanks to them for the commitment they all demonstrated, and especially to Oberstleutnant (Lieutenant Colonel) Dr. Gerhard P. Gross, who was not only responsible for the academic supervision of the conference but edited the resulting volume as well. The book is a cooperative effort introducing the new series Zeitalter der Weltkriege (Era of the World Wars), which is published by the MGFA and the Ferdinand Schönigh publishing house in Paderborn. I wish this volume a positive reception in the academic sphere.

Dr. Hans Ehlert
Colonel and Bureau Chief of the Military History Research Office
(Foreword to the German edition, 2006)

Translator's Note

I wish to thank the Association of US Army (AUSA) Book Program for the opportunity to translate this volume, which I believe offers valuable perspectives and new avenues for further research. I specifically want to thank Roger Cirillo, now retired from his post with AUSA, for his ability to find amazing material for translations. Thanks also to Joseph Craig, the present director of the book program at AUSA, for continuing the project.

Many experts were essential to this translation. My deepest thanks go to my husband, COL (Ret.) Clinton J. Ancker III, for his expertise in military history and military terminology. Thanks also to the very helpful research librarians at the Combined Arms Research Library (CARL) at Ft. Leavenworth, Kansas, and to Russian linguists Associate Professor Benjamin Tromley at the University of Puget Sound and LTC (Ret.) William Connor. Many thanks to the excellent staff at the University Press of Kentucky and superb copyeditor Robin DuBlanc.

The issue of the capitalization of military organizations and military and political titles is governed by *The Chicago Manual of Style*. Thus, the Great General Staff of the German Forces is capitalized, but the general staffs of subordinating organizations are not.

For the occasional foreign words and expressions that resist smooth translation into English, I have provided a brief explanation either in translator's notes or parentheses.

Janice W. Ancker

Introduction

On 2 August 1914, the following appeared in an article in the *Frankfurter Zeitung* under the heading "On Weapons":

> With an evil unsurpassed, at the same moment the czar was issuing an appeal for the friendship of the German Reich, the leading men of Russia were sharpening the very weapons with which they planned to attack Germany behind its back. . . . Truly, the German soldiers who are presently on the way to the borders have a difficult but also great and heroic task. It is not just a matter of protecting homeland, parents, mothers, and children against half or completely Asiatic hordes, rather, it is foremost about defending western European ethos against the deception of self-seeking abusive despots, who are also courtiers and grand dukes.[1]

With these words, one of the leading newspapers of the Kaiser Reich, fully in the name of the German government, propagandized the imminent war as a war of defense against czarist Russia. The topoi of betrayal and defense of European culture from Asian hordes and czarist despotism, the same themes that would be taken up anew in the Second World War by the National Socialists, were employed here to ignite national unity in the hour of danger. This was completely in line with the thinking of the Great General Staff of the Field Army's Generaloberst Helmuth von Moltke the Younger, who for years had warned against danger from Russia because of the Russian arms buildup and the French-financed accelerated expansion of the railway system in the Russian western provinces.

It may seem paradoxical that in the face of the propagandized and real perception of military threat, barely 15 percent of the German military was mobilized on the eastern front, while over two-thirds of the army were mobilized along the western front against France. This deployment, however, was completely in keeping with the military logic of the Great General Staff. As the solution to the strategic dilemma of having to fight a war on two fronts, against France and Russia, the military leaders of the Kaiser Reich had planned since the time of Generalfeldmarschal Alfred Graf von Schlieffen to first attack France with the bulk of the German military. After the presumed victory, units would then be available to defeat the Russian Army. Thus, in the strategic calculations of the military leadership of the Kaiser Reich, the eastern front was only a secondary theater of war. But on the eastern front, unlike on the western front, the Kaiser Reich had to conduct a coalition war. As an alliance partner, Austria-Hungary, like Bulgaria and the Ottoman Empire, was not always as compliant as the Germans wished. This was because in Vienna there was doubt about the often repeated dogma from the Army High Command (OHL) that "the fate of Austria would not be decided on the Bug River, but on the Seine."[2] Along with significant differences of mentality among the allied armies, from the beginning of the war on, political, strategic, operational, and tactical problems had to be overcome. That the allies were successful despite all the differences that arose is demonstrated in the success of the offensives they undertook together in the summer of 1915.

In the collective German memory, the idea of the First World War is pervaded by the trauma of the modern technologized war on the western front, whereas since the Second World War, the events and battles on the eastern front of 1914–1915 (other than the battle of Tannenberg) have shifted into the background. Thus, the phrase "all quiet on the eastern front" offers a succinct description of the scholarly research over the course of many years on the first two years of the war. This is due to the fact that, despite the major military victories against Russia, it was in the east that the war was decided in favor of the Entente. After 1945, the eastern front of 1914 to 1918, overwhelmed by the shadows of the Wehrmacht's *Vernichtungskrieg* (war of extermination) against the Soviet Union and against the backdrop of the discussion about war guilt in the Fischer Controversy, fell victim to a collective amnesia. Even in the 1980s, amid the growing orientation of some of the younger generation of historians toward *Alltagsgeschichte,* or the history of everyday life in the First World War, and the new thematic, theoretical, and methodological research that went hand in hand with it, the eastern front was seldom studied.

Against this background, the Military History Research Institute, in conjunction with the German Historical Museum, took the opportunity of the ninetieth anniversary of the outbreak of the war to devote itself to the eastern front, an area that had previously been rather neglected by research. The conference took place within sight of the exhibit titled *The World War, 1914–1918: Event and Remembrance* in the Zeughaus of the German Historical Museum in Berlin. In view of the success of the previous conference on the end of the war on the western front in 1918, this conference chose as its central theme the eastern front of the years 1914–1915.[3] Professional historians from eight countries researched the eastern theater of war in terms of operations, mindset, and cultural-historical issues. Also discussed were current issues concerning the representation of the war on the internet, in exhibitions, and in museums.

The conference covered three interconnected thematic complexes:

- The operations on the eastern front in the first two years of the war.
- The reality of war as it was experienced at the front and in the homeland in terms of both *Erlebnis* (direct experience) and *Erfahrung* (learning experience).
- The representation of war experience and the reality of war in museums, memorial sites, and modern media.

The papers from this conference, supplemented by an article on the subject of prisoners of war, are presented in this volume by the Military History Research Institute in three thematic sections reflecting the structure of the conference itself.

Hew Strachan (Oxford) introduces the subject in his chapter, "The Eastern Front: Geopolitics, Geography, and Operations." The eastern front, he believes, has long been unjustifiably neglected by researchers. This stems from the fact that for a long time prior to the start of the First World War, the Great General Staff considered Russia the main enemy. The paradox that Germany, because of its central role in a war against Russia and its French ally, intended to attack first in the west and then in the east he explains in light of the thesis of British geographer and geopolitical theorist Halford Mackinder as it applied to the geographical conditions of Russia. Mackinder's thesis led German leaders to believe that a quick victory in the east would be impossible. Strachan underscores the fact that there were also structural weaknesses in the German Empire that prevented the German military and political elite from solving the strategic dilemma presented by geography, whether in peace or war.

Because collective experience and the processing of group-specific experiences are bound to military realities, military analysis of the conduct of war on the eastern front has taken precedence over analysis of cultural and societal history. Stig Förster (Bern) introduces a complex of themes underscoring the historically factual operational level of the conduct of war that are addressed in part 1, "The Battles on the Eastern Front, 1914–1915." Gerhard P. Gross shows that the operational conduct of the war by the German military in the east corresponded to the overall strategy of the leadership. In addition, he points to the tensions between the second Army High Command (OHL) and the commander in chief of the combined German military in the east. Gross demonstrates that the campaign in the east, in contrast to that of the west, was conducted as a mobile war in many areas, and cites some essential differences between the western and eastern fronts in tactics and operations. But the operational victories and the resulting political victories did not obscure the reality that ultimately Russia was not going to be defeated militarily, or that the wished-for separate peace would be accomplished only through the revolutionizing of the Czarist Empire.

Boris Khavkin (Moscow) represents the traditional military historical interpretation, viewing Russia as the "steamroller" of the Entente that fought the war "down to the last Russian soldier." The Western Powers, according to this view, used the Russian military as a counterbalance to the German offensive in France, and the Russian East Prussia Operation had been the prerequisite for the victory on the Marne. In the same vein, Khavkin ascribes the Russian defeats to the Russian Army's material inferiority and to the fact that the Russian leaders had been repeatedly obliged by their allies to enter into unprepared offensives.

Günther Kronenbitter (Augsburg) demonstrates that prior to the beginning of the war, cooperation between the army leaders of Austria-Hungary and Germany had been quite satisfactory. It was not until the July Crisis and the first months of the war that failings in this area became apparent. While the Austrians complained about the lack of support from Germany, the Germans complained about the weaknesses of the army and the supposed lack of ability among its leaders. Ultimately, Kronenbitter points out, the Germans demanded strength ratios commensurate with their own leadership role in the conduct of the war. He views the mutual resentments that grew out of this to be the result of poor planning for military cooperation, German high-handedness, and a lack of unity of political aims in the east. Kronenbitter argues that the divergent war aims associated with the national futures of Ukraine or Poland were the consequence of structural differences between the German Empire and the economically underdeveloped, multiethnic Habsburg Monarchy.

Part 2 of this volume addresses direct experience with the realities of war, the war experience as a learning process, and how the war is depicted in literature. Introduced by Jörg Baberowski (Berlin), the focus of this section is reflected in its title, "The Battlefields of Concepts / Concepts of the Battlefields: The Eastern Front of the First World War and Perceptions of the Enemy."

Piotr Szlanta (Warsaw) points out that at the beginning of the war all participating powers sought to gain the sympathies of the Poles for themselves, and in the process they fed the Poles' hopes for independence. The outbreak of the war split the political elite of Poland into two camps: one pro-Austrian and one pro-Russian. The lines dividing these camps were fluid, however. In the first years of the war, the Polish population professed loyalty to all three partitioning powers. Due to the tough occupation policy of Russia in Galicia, that of the Central Powers in Congress Poland, the falling standard of living, and the lack of a credible and binding assurance of a Polish nation after the war, the Poles broke away from the occupying powers and avoided any definite taking of sides.

Hubertus F. Jahn (Cambridge) and Peter Hoeres (Münster) examine the way in which the enemy was perceived by the Russian side and how they, in turn, were perceived by the Central Powers. Jahn writes that in prerevolutionary Russia, both self-perception and perception of the enemy were very strongly determined by various ideologies, by the views of societal groups, and even by individuals. Moreover, before and over the course of the First World War, perceptions changed. Thus, the fascination that German culture had held for the Russians even at the end of the nineteenth century was replaced during the First World War by an emotionally charged rejection of the German enemy and the German cultural sphere. Jahn illustrates the changes in Russian popular mass culture up to the time of military defeats of 1915, citing as an example the image of Kaiser Wilhelm II, who was depicted as a laughable puppet and turned into an object of derision, ridicule, and hatred.

According to Peter Hoeres, there was a clear hierarchy in the Austrian and German perceptions of the enemy. Slavs were considered dull, dirty, lacking independence, and lazy, while the British and French, despite their alleged "degenerate nature," were thought of as being on an equal level. Before the war began, the concept they had of the east was of impoverishment, desolation, and absence of culture. When they invaded Russia, this concept was confirmed. The most significant experiences were of filth, boundless expanses, and an unimaginable mixture of ethnicities. Encouraged by the German military government, the idea rapidly spread of protecting one's own population from what was perceived as chaos, and at the same time of engaging in a cultural mission in the east. Hoeres emphasizes, of course, that the perception of the Slavs and the east during the First World War can hardly be compared with the "war of annihilation" in the east after 1939, since during the Second World War, a crucial role was played by Bolshevism, the notion of the *Untermensch,* or subhuman, and radical anti-Semitism.

The literary approach to the eastern front is the focus of chapters by Eva Horn (Basel) and Birgit Menzel (Mainz). According to Horn, in contrast to the literature of the western front, that of the eastern front did not deal with the trauma of technologized mass war. Instead, it reflected the chaotic, exotic, and "primitive" side of the war. In Horn's view, although the war experience of the eastern front did not impact the concept of the First World War in Germany in a crucial way, it affected how the Russian enemy was seen during the Second World War and this had serious consequences. As Menzel explains, unlike Russia's other major wars, the First World War did not emerge as a prominent theme in Russian literature. Overshadowed by Russia's Civil War and the Second World War, the First World War was acknowledged only marginally and selectively in the literary sphere.

Igor Narskij (Chelyabinsk), whose chapter deals with the reality of war and the experience of Russian soldiers in the first years of the war, also addresses the Russian culture of remembrance. His conclusion is that the First World War, displaced by the Russian Revolution and the Civil War, has been forgotten, scrubbed from the collective memory of the Russians. The few personal testimonials of Russian officers from the first years of the war appeared for the most part after the fact and are often influenced by later experiences. The reality of war of the first years, he finds, is clearly different from the reality of the war between 1916 and 1917. The morale reports from the military censors showed that the soldiers did not find the supply situation in the years of 1914–1915 to be extremely burdensome, and massive dissatisfaction did not rise dramatically until early 1916. Narskij sums up by saying that paradoxically, what the Russian soldiers experienced during the war had a civilizing and disciplining effect on Russian society as a whole. For the first time, its peasant soldiers, pulled away from their primitive agrarian living environments, experienced being part of a modern social entity. Narskij sees the socialization of millions of Russian soldiers as precursor to the expansion of the social basis for Bolshevism.

Hans-Erich Volkmann (Freiburg) examines the experiential world of German military leaders in the era of the world wars. Surprised by the unexpectedly high degree of mobilization of the Russian Army and its quick advance, leaders in the German General Staff learned that although they could defeat the Russian enemy tactically and operationally, ultimately the wide expanse of Russia's territory prevented the Germans from achieving a decisive victory. Looking back on this experience from the postwar era prior to the Second World War, these front officers realized that in the future Russia could be beaten militarily only with modern war technology (such as tanks and air power). Volkmann also points out that at the outset of the war German soldiers had not had any particular preconceptions about the enemy, which meant that initially they lacked sufficient motivation. As a remedy, during the Second World War, the National Socialists used propaganda against "Jewish Bolshevism" in their war against the Soviet Union.

In his chapter on German occupation policy in the east, Vejas Gabriel Liulevicius (Knoxville) explores the extent to which later developments under National Socialism were defined by the policy in the land of Ober Ost and the experience of the German occupation. He demonstrates how the experiences of the occupation government during the First World War, such as the control of large levels of the population in a quasi-colonial manner and the perception of the population as dirty, lazy, and dangerous, became a rallying point for the National Socialists. The German occupation policy during the First World War, he writes, although it was aimed toward ethnic manipulation, stood in sharp contrast to the murderous "war of extermination" conducted by the Wehrmacht beginning in 1941, characterized as it was by anti-Semitism and a radical biological racism.

The depiction of war experience and war reality in museums, memorial sites, and the modern media is the central focus of part 3, "The Culture of

Remembrance of the First World War," introduced by Rainer Rother (Berlin). Christine Beil (Tübingen) addresses the subject of German war exhibits, which were a special form of presentation of the war for the home front. The war exhibits were not perceived by the public as propaganda sites but were thought of instead as occasions for enjoyment and learning. They were designed in an entertaining way (with mockups of trenches for people to experience) or in the style of large major expositions, using every opportunity to strengthen the home front in its will to persevere. The depiction of the eastern front and dirty Russian soldiers also solidified the impression of German cultural superiority over "Russian barbarism" while legitimizing the German claim to parts of the occupied eastern territories.

Kristiane Janeke (Berlin) examines the suppressed memory of the First World War as it is exemplified in the Moscow City Fraternal Cemetery, which was originally intended as a pan-Russian memorial site. For Janeke, the cemetery, which was founded in 1915, redesigned as a recreational park in 1925, and almost completely destroyed in 1940, offers an opportunity to trace the cycles of world war remembrance in Russia. Officially, only the fallen "heroes of the Revolution," the Civil War, and later of the Second World War, or "Great Patriotic War," are remembered here, not the dead of the First World War. Janeke interprets the current revitalizing of the cemetery as a first step on the path to Russians' remembrance of the history of the First World War. On the other hand, there is also evidence that the cemetery site is being exploited politically for the sake of pan-Russian interests.

The memorializing of the Unknown Soldier, as Rainer Rother (Berlin) shows, can be considered a success story. Originating after the First World War as special form of collective memory, this ritual embodies a cultivated and politically useful form of remembrance of the dead and the war, particularly in western Europe and the United States.

Gundula Bavendamm (Berlin) turns our attention to the internet as a medium of world war remembrance. As Bavendamm illustrates, over the last twenty years in the west and for several years in the east as well, a virtual forum of memories of the world war has come into existence on the internet. Various virtual museum activities and memorials have evolved, as well as differences specific to each nationality.

In his overview of the essays in this volume on the German conduct of war on the eastern front in the First World War, Rüdiger Bergien (Potsdam) addresses the issue of continuities in "Prologue to the 'War of Annihilation'? The Eastern Front of the First World War and the Problem of Continuities." In his view, the new approach that alleges continuities in the German conduct of war in the east from the First World War to the Second World War should also be examined in the context of the chapters presented in this volume. So far, he believes, there is still an insufficient empirical basis for addressing the question of what German soldiers actually experienced during the First World War. Further, which developments and experiences from the two world wars can be viewed as parallel? According to Bergien, to address this question fairly, research on the other countries involved in the war in the east needs to be included. Only by comparing the occupation practices of all participating warring parties can one identify national characteristics that affected the conduct of war in the east. Only then can the question of the inner unity of the two world wars be answered.

The Forty-Sixth International Conference for Military History has provided an inventory of scholarly work on the "forgotten eastern front" of 1914–1915. The linking of historical research with aspects of museum expertise has uncovered a gap in research into such areas as the interaction between the partners of the Central Powers and in the systematic analysis of individuals' war recollections. Further clarity is needed on the strategic impact of the transport capacities of both sides and on the situational interaction at the level of tactics and operations. It was also determined at the conference that scholarly approaches such as the history of mentalities and experiential history, if they are not accompanied by due consideration of the operational environment and military actions, run the danger of losing sight of the reality of war. In such cases, traditional approaches to military history appear indispensable. In the process it becomes possible to uncover falsifications that may have concealed the preliminary stages of the racially based war of extermination. Research and discussion are still needed in this area.

The present volume also shows that so far, in Poland and Russia, the war in the east has at best been researched as a part of their respective national histories. In the German-speaking realm, research methods, outcomes, and special subject matter interests pertaining to eastern European history (such as research of stereotypes, the culture of violence, the meaning of the Russian defense system for the societal order in Russia, and the Revolution of 1917) only slowly found their way into research on the First World War.

Still, attempts to decipher mutual patterns of perception among the hostile parties might in the future accord the First World War its due significance as a European war and a "seminal catastrophe" of the twentieth century. The conference and *The Forgotten Front* have furthered opportunities for discourse in international comparative perspectives and at the same time revealed that Western historiography can profit from the new level of international cooperation with young historians from the former Eastern Bloc and their new methodical approaches and modern formulation of issues. The credit belongs to the presenters and section leaders as well to the numerous historians who contributed to the Forty-Sixth International Conference for Military History and enriched it with their expertise and research. The publisher extends a special thanks to all of them.

Notes

1. *Der Grosse Krieg. Eine Chronik von Tag zu Tag. Urkunden, Depeschen und Berichte der Frankfurter Zeitung,* no. 1, *Vorgeschichte des Krieges. Der Krieg bis zum Fall von Lüttich,* Frankfurt 1914, 42.

2. *Der Weltkrieg 1914–1918,* revised at the Reichsarchiv, vol. 2, *Die Befreiung Ostpreussens,* Berlin 1925, 12.

3. The research papers from the conference addressing the end of the war on the western front are found in the volume *Kriegsende, 1918: Ereignis, Wirkung, Nachwirkung.*

1

The Eastern Front

Geopolitics, Geography, and Operations

Hew Strachan

Just over one hundred years ago, on 25 January 1904, Halford Mackinder delivered a lecture at the Royal Geographical Society in London that geographers in Britain regard as the founding moment of geopolitics. Mackinder, who had read natural sciences and history at Oxford before qualifying as a lawyer, was the pivotal figure in the establishment of modern geographical studies in British universities. A serial pluralist, he was never happy doing one job when he could be doing several. In 1904 he was reader in geography at Oxford University, a student (that is, fellow) of Christchurch, and director of the London School of Economics. He would later become a member of Parliament, and he was the British high commissioner in south Russia in 1919.[1]

His 1904 lecture, which was attended by Spenser Wilkinson, appointed Oxford's first professor of military history in 1909, and Leo Amery, the strongest advocate of Britain's war aims in the Middle East in 1917–1918, was called "the geographical pivot of history." Mackinder sought "a formula which shall express certain aspects . . . of geographical causation in universal history. If we are fortunate, the formula should have a practical value as setting into perspective some of the competing forces in current international politics."[2] As the leaders of the European Union today struggle to define their continent and wonder whether to draw a line at the Bosphorus or the Caucasus, it is worth remembering that for Mackinder Europe and Asia were not two continents but one. He called it Euro-Asia. A continuous landmass of 21 million square miles, it embraced, he calculated, half the world's land surface if the deserts of Arabia and the Sahara were excluded. He defined Euro-Asia as the world's "heartland" and Russia, placed at its center, as the "pivot state." "The most remarkable contrast in the political map of modern Europe," he declared, "is that presented by the vast area of Russia occupying half the continent and the group of smaller territories tenanted by the Western Powers."[3]

Mackinder drew attention to the succession of invaders who had moved from east to west, the horse-mounted warriors of the steppes—Mongols, Tatars, and Cossacks. He argued that thus far in the world's history Russia's latent potential had been restrained by the problems of communication: road building across such a vast area had been too challenging a task. Instead, sea power had provided the basis for global economic links. Although his own country, Britain, a landmass on the periphery of Euro-Asia, had been the most conspicuous beneficiary of sea power, Mackinder reckoned that era was now drawing to a close. Alfred Thayer Mahan's theory of maritime supremacy drew on evidence from the eighteenth and early nineteenth centuries; it would not prove applicable to the twentieth. "Trans-continental railways are now transmuting the conditions of land-power, and nowhere can they have such effect as in the closed heart-land of Euro-Asia."[4]

In 1904 Mackinder feared an alliance between Russia and Germany. Such a relationship would give the pivot state of the Eurasian heartland direct access to the oceans in the west. It would place the divide between east and west not on the Bug or the Vistula but on the Atlantic seaboard. Britain's maritime supremacy would be directly challenged by a state whose eastern extremities would also abut the Pacific. After the First World War, in 1919, when Mackinder wrote a text designed to influence the peacemakers at Versailles, *Democratic Ideals and Reality,* he was more explicit about geopolitical probabilities and their likely impact on immediate policy. "Who rules East Europe commands the Heartland: who rules the Heartland commands the World Island: who rules the World Island commands the World."[5] He feared that Russia, after the Bolshevik Revolution of 1917, would be too weak to resist German penetration, and that Germany would therefore dominate eastern Europe and also—following his own logic—the world.

The consequence for a geopolitician like Mackinder was that the eastern front could never be "the forgotten front." Geopolitics implied exactly the opposite—that it was the front from which all other outcomes would flow. Moreover, he was quite clear that, although the democratic powers of the west, Britain and the United States, did not think geographically, Germany did. "We have had for a byword in these times the German war map," he wrote in *Democratic Ideals and Reality.* "It may be questioned, however, whether most people in Britain and America have fully realised the part played by the map in German education in the past three generations. Maps are the essential apparatus of Kultur, and every educated German is a geographer in the sense that is true of very few Englishmen or Americans. He has been taught to see in maps not merely the conventional boundaries created by scraps of paper, but permanent physical opportunities—'ways and means' in the literal sense of the words. His Realpolitik lives in his mind upon a mental map."[6]

What Mackinder was doing with geography when he developed his ideas about geopolitics was using it as a basis for what in the 1920s British thinkers like J. F. C. Fuller and Basil Liddell Hart would call grand strategy, the incorporation of social, political, economic, and military means in one all-encompassing approach to national policy. For Mackinder geography was the determinant of strategy, and he believed that that conviction also shaped the outlook of Germany. However, he was not quite right, because Realpolitik, as Mackinder called German policy, could also expose problems and obstacles as well as "ways and means."

Mackinder's sense of the opportunities and tensions in the relationship between Germany and Russia before 1914 was hardly new to the Germans in general or to the German General Staff in particular. On the one hand, the possibility of cooperation flickered in 1904 itself. In October Germany offered Russia a defensive alliance, and in July 1905 the kaiser and the czar reached an agreement at Björkö. It was the Russians, not the Germans, who broke off these contacts. The belief that a Russo-German pact made sense continued to fuel the long-term designs of many Germans, including Erich von Falkenhayn, the chief of the General Staff in 1914–1916.[7] On the other hand, the awareness of latent conflict took a number of forms. Racially it was characterized by the clash between Teuton and Slav. Culturally—and consequently—Germany saw itself as the outer bastion defending European civilization against Asiatic backwardness. The rapidity of Germany's modernization in the decades after unification made it more aware both of progress as a force in its own right and of the contrast between itself and a neighbor that was medieval and even primitive. Politically, Germany in this context was not a monarchy dogged by arrested constitutional development but the representative of political enlightenment. Possessed of universal male suffrage and the largest Socialist party in Europe, it was the very opposite of Russia, an autocracy and a police state that sent its Socialists to Siberia or into exile.

However, Germany could not afford to be self-confident in its superiority. Mackinder's views were widely shared: given its landmass, its natural resources, and its population, Russia had the potential to dominate not only Germany but all Europe. Germans, like others, saw Russia as the coming power. Its gross domestic product before 1914 was greater than that of any other European state, including both Germany and Britain, and its annual growth rate between 1908 and 1913 ran at 3.25 percent. Over the same period its output from its metal industries rose 88.9 percent.[8] This was the key sector of the economy in terms of raw military power. In 1914 the Russian Army mustered 1.4 million men before mobilization, as opposed to 800,000 men in the German Army. Russia's so-called grand program of 1913 aimed to increase the army's annual recruit contingent from 455,000 to 585,000. By 1917 the Russian Army would be three times the size of Germany's.[9]

To successive chiefs of the German General Staff between 1871 and 1914, therefore, Mackinder's insight was hardly novel. Moltke the Elder was convinced of Russia's potential as a result of his visit there in 1856. In 1871, even before the war with France was concluded, he turned his thoughts to Russia, identifying between it and his own country "an unmistakable mutual aversion in faith and custom, a conflict in material interest."[10] Schlieffen told his sister in 1892 that Russia was "our special enemy."[11] Moltke the Younger shaped his own attitude to preventive war around the growth of the Russian threat. Although it was Britain that prompted the kaiser to convene the notorious "war council" of 8 December 1912, it was Russia that caused Moltke the Younger to declare at that meeting that the sooner the war came the better.[12]

It was not just the nature of the threat that made Germany's eastern front so central to German policy. It was also the nature of Germany's response. Both the elder and younger Moltkes reckoned that, if war came in Europe, it would be long, and the one reason for this was it would be a war fought by coalitions. In 1866 and 1870 single campaigns had won wars in short order because they were fought by single powers. But in 1914 no power stood alone: each, if defeated, could be rescued by an ally. In Germany's case that ally was Austria-Hungary.

This was the second geopolitical or grand strategic reason why the eastern front was so pivotal to Germany. The First World War began in the Balkans, and it was triggered by Austria-Hungary's need to reassert itself as a Balkan power. The state that could deter it from doing so was Russia, and it was to bolster Austria-Hungary's resolve against Russia that Germany issued the so-called blank check at the beginning of July 1914. Germany entered the war as a consequence of its alliance obligations. Moreover, it was on the eastern front, not the western, that the German-Austrian alliance was played out. Vienna had no interest in what happened in France and Belgium.

In the days of Moltke the Elder, he and his Austrian counterpart as chief of the Great General Staff, Friedrich von Beck-Rzikowsky, had reflected these geopolitical and grand strategic assumptions in an operational solution. The German Army from the north and the Austro-Hungarian Army from the south, the one moving from East Prussia and the other from Galicia, would aim to envelop a portion of the Russian Army by converging east of Warsaw in what is today Poland.[13] But, extraordinarily, in February 1913, with war being fought in the Balkans, Moltke the Younger told his Austrian counterpart, Franz Conrad von Hötzendorf, "The main impact of the entire European war, as well as the fate of Austria, will not be decided on the Bug, but ultimately on the Seine."[14] Thus by the eve of the First World War the operational solution was out of step with the geopolitical, grand strategic, and alliance imperatives. It was so above all for geographical reasons—and herein is the relevance of Mackinder.

Moltke the Elder had planned an offensive into Russian Poland, but Schlieffen progressively abandoned such thinking. He set little store by the Austro-Hungarian Army and so let the two armies' joint planning fall into abeyance. He focused his attention on the northern sector of Germany's eastern front, on East Prussia rather than the middle Vistula. If the Germans advanced at all, their axis was more likely to be due east rather than southeast. Instead of staying close to the Austro-German frontier, they would move away from it, lengthening their lines of communication as they did so. Russia's ability to trade space for time by withdrawing into Asia would increase the danger of overextension. When the German advance passed beyond Warsaw and entered Russia proper, it would be shouldered north once more. The Pripet marshes divided the front at its center, forcing any army deployed on a broad front in two divergent directions. The Pripet River, into which the marshes drained, flowed eastward to the Dnieper. The latter was one of a series of rivers, running north-south, that seemed to form natural lines of defense. Schlieffen concluded in 1894: "The expanse of the country, the great distances of Russia, cannot be defeated."[15]

A British military commentator, Colonel A. C. Macdonnell, in *The Outlines of Military Geography,* published in 1911, itemized the waterways of the Nemen, the Augustów canal, the Vistula, the Wartha, and the Prosna as natural defenses in west Russia, and those of the Pruth, Dniester, Bug, and Pripet in southwest Russia. He characterized Warsaw and Novo Georgievsk as "one huge entrenched camp." Furthermore, he appreciated, as Schlieffen had done, that getting to Warsaw was only the beginning; from there to Petrograd or Moscow was still 650 to 700 miles. "This long distance over difficult and inhospitable regions," Macdonnell warned, "still presents as formidable an obstacle to the advance of the invader as it did in the time of Napoleon."[16] However, Macdonnell then added a rider to his historical analogy: "if we exclude the increase to railway communications." Here was the rub. Mackinder had reckoned that railways were transforming the geopolitics of Euro-Asia.[17]

There is no reason to imagine that Schlieffen or the younger Moltke read Mackinder's 1904 lecture. It is more probable, even if by no means certain, that they were familiar with the work of Friedrich Ratzel, the founder of geopolitics in Germany. Mackinder was right: Germany took geography seriously. By 1914 the German General Staff's land survey section had a complement of over five hundred officers. The trigonometric, topographic, and cartographic sections each contained ten subsections. It had seven map series in production.[18] Ratzel published the first edition of his great text, *Politische Geographie,* in 1897. He saw states as organically linked to the soil on which they found themselves, and argued that their cultural influence radiated out from their centers, compelling smaller neighbors to cluster under their suzerainty: "Culture created an increasing basis and means for the cohesiveness of the national group and also continued to expand the circle of consciousness of political solidarity."[19] He traced this process of cultural development and expansion over two millennia, placing Rome at its beginning and Russia at its end. For him, as for Mackinder, Russia was a potential world power that would in due course bring the landmass stretching from the Pacific to the Atlantic under its sway.[20]

Ratzel said nothing in his 1897 edition about war itself, but he remedied the omission in the second edition, published in 1903. However, this was not a polemical tract concluding that Germany would have to fight Russia for possession of the heartland. Geography was a constraint, not an opportunity. He warned against campaigns of overextension, quoting as examples Napoleon's campaigns of 1807 in Poland and 1812 in Russia, and citing Jomini to support his case. "The conditions for a normal field campaign were not present. Reconnaissance was almost impossible; orders sent out were not received. The distances, the dirt, the ice, the snow, [and] random incidents played a main role. These had a power that took control of the dice, and won sway over human genius."[21] Ratzel disagreed with those who were inclined to say that railways had changed the balance between offense and defense (and Mackinder was one of them, albeit to show how the Russians, like the Mongols, might break through to the west). Ratzel believed that railways favored the defense—allowing the power that had been attacked to concentrate to meet the threat and to deliver a counterstroke. Events on both the eastern and western fronts in 1914 would prove him right.[22]

Ratzel confronted his military readers with a conundrum. Too large a theater of operations and the effort would disappear into thin air; too small and the objective of the war would not be achieved. In his view the optimum was to seek a theater of war that was restricted enough to enable a decision, but not so small that that decision was minor in its effects.[23] The German General Staff therefore confronted a paradox—the threat lay to the east, but the operational possibilities were greater to the west. It took counsel of its geopolitical fears and the geographical possibilities. Its review of the terrain went no further across the frontier than Poland. The conclusions it drew were pragmatic. It planned a defensive battle only in East Prussia, exploiting the shield of the Masurian Lakes and using its own railway network not just for deployment but also for operations themselves. In August 1914 its thinking on the defensive counterstroke was duly carried into brilliant effect at Tannenberg. Here was the fruit of Schlieffen's legacy, of staff rides and map exercises.[24]

The Great General Staff favored the offensive in the west for very similar operational reasons—the geography meant its goals were closer and its highly developed railway network facilitated the movement of mass armies. Sigismund von Schlichting, a veteran of the campaigns of 1866 and 1870 and an interpreter of the legacy of the elder Moltke, observed in his *Taktische und Strategische Grundsätze der Gegenwart* (1897–1899; Tactical and Strategic Foundations of the Present), "Civilization, which offers the means to peaceful intercourse, also opens the gates to enemy invasion."[25] His books laid down principles that made it clear that he, like Ratzel, never countenanced the possibility of Germany invading Russia. His general rule was that the more civilized and cultivated a country, the more it favored invasion. Its landscape, shaped by roads and railways, prompted movement, and its agriculture fed the army. He did not mention Russia by name, in itself perhaps an example of how inconceivable he considered a German attack on that country to be. But he was clear that operations in uncultivated land (he took Bulgaria as his example) would require totally different strategic measures and methods from those used by the German Army hitherto, and stressed that large rivers would be the greatest obstacles to the armies of the future. It is worth adding in parentheses that he thought waging war in two different theaters would expose Germany's war leadership to contradictory strategic pressures.[26]

Geography was therefore the key determinant as to where the army would fight—because geography shaped operational possibilities regardless of political considerations or the wider strategic context. Schlichting's assumptions about the benefits of fighting in the more developed parts of Europe rested on the primacy of transport and supply. He was unusual: despite their importance, logistics were not a fashionable topic. In 1913 the German General Staff's historical section published a tactical and strategic examination of army supply. It proceeded by way of case studies drawn from nineteenth-century wars. One of these was Napoleon's 1812 invasion of Russia, which it declared had "opened a new epoch in the development of supply of armies. It demonstrates clearly that the growth of the armies has increased the difficulties involved in feeding them, especially in countries that have few means to support the operations needed to prevent the masses [of soldiers] from melting like snow in the sun."[27] It concluded that Napoleon's supply system could not cope with the strains of invading Russia, which required a totally different approach to logistics. The only feasible solution to such challenges was the railway.

However, in 1913 the railway network of eastern Europe and Russia was insufficient to sustain an invasion. Moreover, the German Army still planned, despite the General Staff study's observation about the growth in army size, to feed off the land. The text's relevant passage revealed not only that the German Army had failed to develop a new approach to supply but also how cavalier it was regarding the possible consequences: "Since the Revolutionary War it has been one of the most important principles of the army supply primarily to make use of local resources. That must apply to our own or our allied territories just the same as for the enemy, even though the forms of exploitation are of a different manner. It is always a matter of getting along with as few supplies as possible in order to keep the army mobile. Undue regard for the country's population must not hamper this. They have often inflicted heavy damage on our own troops and then, in some cases, handed over the country's crops to the enemy."[28]

Herein is one further explanation for the atrocities visited on the civilian populations of Belgium and northern France in 1914.[29] For the German Army struck west when the war came. It could not go east, not least because it planned to feed off the land. In this respect it obeyed the logic spelled out by Schlichting. But events proved Schlichting wrong and Ratzel right. Railways, and indeed the level of industrialization enjoyed by western Europe in general, favored the defensive at the Marne and continued to do so during the "Race to the Sea."

Now time—along with space, the other standard imperative in the formation of operational concepts—kicked in. Before the war successive chiefs of the German General Staff had confronted a paradox. They knew that a major European war was likely to be long. This was not just a consequence of the alliance blocs. It was also the result of tactical developments: defensive firepower, delivered by breech-loading rifles, machine guns, and quick-firing artillery, was likely to cause attacks to bog down. But once nations had gone to war their peoples would be unlikely to accept compromise. The incipient clash between Teuton and Slav, once evoked in German public consciousness, played on popular prejudices sufficiently deep for them not to be easily defused. The challenge that confronted Schlieffen and then the younger Moltke was that Germany could not live with the consequences of those insights. It was not economically strong enough to sustain a long war. In the first place it was outnumbered. The German Army could not match the combined strengths of France and Russia. Britain's entry to the war did not make this equation much worse, at least not immediately, but it had massive economic consequences. London became the Entente's arsenal and financier, and its strategy in 1914, using sea power to impose a blockade, underlined its readiness to engage in a long war. Germany therefore needed a quick operational success so that what happened on the battlefield could overturn the inevitability of defeat in the long term. In other words, Germany had to fight a short war because it could not—it seemed—sustain a long one.[30] In Belgium and northern France its armies pillaged to feed themselves, but they also used terror to speed their advance. In 1870 the campaign in France had achieved rapid success on the battlefield at Sedan, but the war had been prolonged into 1871 by the *francs tireurs* (French irregulars). In 1914 the Germans tried to combine both phases in one, acting preemptively against civilians as they advanced and using the argument of military necessity to justify the ethical consequences.

In the event, however, the outcome of the fighting on the western front in 1914 reversed Germany's original conundrum. Before the war, geopolitics and alliance considerations pointed Germany to the east, but operational considerations took it west. By November 1914 grand strategy—if we can use a phrase that the Germans not only never used but also did not comprehend—pointed Germany to the west, because Britain had become the mainstay of the enemy coalition and therefore had become the logical focus of their main effort. But the operational possibilities seemed greater in the east.

In the winter of 1914–1915 this imbalance manifested itself in a bitter feud between Falkenhayn at OHL, and Hindenburg and Ludendorff at what became Ober Ost. Falkenhayn saw Britain as the enemy's center of gravity and therefore the proper goal for German strategy, but he could not marshal the operational means to fulfill the strategic ends. Germany lacked a navy big enough to take on the British Grand Fleet, and it lacked the military punch to finish off France, Britain's principal ally on land. Hindenburg and Ludendorff extrapolated from the defensive victory at Tannenberg to argue along Schlieffenesque lines. Envelopment battles were achievable in the east because the force to space ratio was more favorable, and therefore strategy should be bent to the operational possibilities.

Broadly speaking, that was what Germany did in 1915. It adopted the defensive in the west in November 1914, digging deep trenches so that it could create a *masse de manoeuvre* for use in the east. It overran Poland in the summer of 1915, and it precipitated Russia into the "great retreat." On 25 June 1915, Hans Delbrück wrote in the *Preussische Jahrbücher* (Prussian Yearbooks): "Even standing on the outskirts of Przemyśl, Lwów (Lemberg) is already in our hands. It is a field campaign for which there is no comparison in world history. The pursuits of Alexander the Great stretched across enormous areas and were carried out with all assembled resources to the point of exhaustion. But the battles of this campaign that had yet to be fought were no longer needed; the strength of the enemy was completely broken and drained by the battle."[31] On 27 August 1915, his comparison was not with Alexander but with Napoleon. He recognized that the Russians could trade space for time as in 1812. But, he went on, "it is all very different today. The land itself will have more to give because it is more densely settled and better cultivated than in 1812. Acts of destruction, as are now seen in Poland, are easier ordered than accomplished; there always remains much left over."[32]

These were the greatest German and Austro-Hungarian victories of the war—in terms of armies broken, cities captured, and ground conquered. But the operational possibilities still did not march in step with strategic goals. Many of the reasons for that were geographical. The German Army was designed to fight close to its frontiers. It was now engaged on something that exceeded its geographical range—in terms of transport and supply, in terms of operations, and in terms of grand strategy.

Logistically, Delbrück was wrong. Hindenburg's and Ludendorff's plans for massive envelopments in the east exceeded the reach of the German Army's transport systems. Falkenhayn modified their scale, but Polish *panje* (one-horse) wagons were no substitute for railways. Moreover, the Russians adopted a scorched-earth policy as they fell back. The armies of the Central Powers plunged forward across a land stripped bare.

Operationally, Hindenburg and Ludendorff failed to recognize that envelopment was not the panacea that Schlieffen and his followers maintained it was. Envelopment battles made sense where there were fixed points that were also reasonably proximate—frontal positions where the enemy could be pinned, frontiers against which he could be driven. But on the eastern front space for maneuver allowed space for the Russians to retreat. The geography enabled envelopment on paper but invalidated it in practice. In October 1915, Falkenhayn wrote to Hindenburg, "One cannot hope to deal a fatal blow by means of a large-scale encirclement to an enemy who is superior in numbers, who brazenly declines to put up a fight regardless of sacrificing territory and people, and who also has the breadth of Russia and good railroads to back him up."[33] Russia's geography undermined Germany's operational competence in 1915.

Strategically, the war Germany now waged required it to develop a new conception that went beyond operational possibilities, that recognized its political, economic, and social aspects, and that united these into what later observers would call grand strategy. Germany in 1914–1918 lacked the institutional structure to develop such a broad approach to strategy. The powers to do so were vested in the kaiser, who was not equal to the challenge, and OHL was essentially no more than an operational headquarters. This lack of an institutional and conceptual base for the development of grand strategy was far more significant on the eastern front than it was on the western for two reasons. The first was the size of the theater of war. Issues of supply and manpower were intimately connected with the war's political and economic direction. Significantly, Ludendorff was one of the first to advocate for the independence of Poland. His reasons were military: he wanted it to raise men. But it soon became clear that the independence he had in mind was notional, albeit again for narrowly military reasons. He wanted Poland to form a protective buffer for Germany in the east. But the real charge behind the Polish question was not military but political. A commitment to Poland's independence would undermine efforts to seek a separate peace with Russia, and the establishment of any form of Germany suzerainty would prejudice relations with Germany's ally Austria-Hungary. Vienna wanted Poland, or a large chunk of it, to be subordinated to the Dual Monarchy.

Such considerations brought into relief the second consideration. The war on the eastern front was a coalition campaign in a way that was not true of any other major front for the Central Powers. Germany ran the western front, Austria-Hungary the Italian, Bulgaria the Macedonian, and the Ottoman Empire the Caucasian and Arabian. But all four powers had stakes in the war against Russia. OHL proved itself totally unable to work out command structures appropriate to the conduct of coalition warfare. The Austro-Hungarians felt that they had been let down from the very start of the war because the Germans had not honored the plan to envelop Warsaw. Their anger was deepened by the humiliation of 1914–1915: that winter, as the Russians stood poised to break into Hungary, the Austro-Hungarians were rescued by the Germans. OHL did nothing to pour oil on these wounds. Falkenhayn subordinated Austrian troops to German command. The victories of 1915 were the work of two Germans, August von Mackensen and his chief of staff, Hans von Seeckt, not of Austro-Hungarian commanders. For a whole month at the end of that year, Falkenhayn and Conrad did not speak to each other, instead setting about developing their own plans for 1916. In Falkenhayn's case that meant attacking the French at Verdun, in Conrad's the Italians in the Trentino. Both neglected their common front in Russia.

The logical outcome should have been defeat and collapse for the Central Powers. That of course was what happened in the war as whole. But the Central Powers did defeat Russia and were able to impose a "German victory" at Brest-Litovsk. Crucially, however, they achieved it in spite of military victories, not because of them. Russia collapsed from within. Here was a frightful portent. Brest-Litovsk pointed the way to two conclusions.

First, it suggested that what mattered in war were not operational ideas, let alone grand strategy, but just plain fighting. Tactical capabilities themselves became a device for shaping strategic outcomes. In 1914–1915 Ludendorff had argued in terms of great envelopment battles. In 1917–1918, when planning the offensive in the west, Ludendorff memorably said: "I object to the word 'operation.' We will punch a hole into their line. For the rest, we shall see. We also did it this way in Russia!"[34]

Second, Brest-Litovsk seemed to demonstrate that when victory came it would be because the enemy nation would implode, as Russia had done in 1917. Germany's own defeat seemed to confirm the argument. In the west the allies achieved a series of tactical successes in the so-called hundred days of late 1918, but not a victory that could be explained in operational terms. There was no envelopment or even much of a breakthrough. Instead the German defeat was attributed to revolution, hunger, and governmental instability. When Ludendorff came to reflect on it in 1935 in *Der totale Krieg,* he stressed that the bases for victory in war were national mobilization, totalitarian government, and the subordination of the nation's resources to the waging of war: strategy as defined by Clausewitz—the use of the battle for the purposes of the war—fell into a black hole.

By then this was also a prophecy. In 1941 Mackinder (now an old man) was proven right. His prediction of 1919 that Germany and Russia would clash for control of the heartland came to pass. But he had not anticipated that the geographical constraints on Germany waging war in the east pointed against its succumbing to the geopolitical imperatives. Karl Haushofer, himself a professional soldier who had served with the Bavarian Army in the First World War and who retired as a major general, was Mackinder's greatest admirer and the most obvious exponent of geopolitics in interwar Germany. For him, military geography proved a powerful constraint on geopolitics. His conclusion was not that Germany should fight the Soviet Union but that it should seek cooperation. He welcomed the Russian Revolution as a blow to capitalism, and therefore a greater danger to Britain than to Germany. Russo-German antagonism could only play into Britain's hands. Established not only as professor of geography in Munich but also president of the party-approved association of German academics, he welcomed the Russo-German pact of 1939. In a memorandum of 1940, "Der Kontinentalblock," he declared that the most important task of "our time" was the creation of a Eurasian block: his aim was not to follow Mackinder but to prove him wrong.[35] He welcomed the Nazi-Soviet pact of 1939. If he and others who thought geographically and geopolitically had had their way, it might have been the eastern front of the Second World War that became the "forgotten front."

The conclusions in relation to Germany's invasion of the Soviet Union are self-evident. This was not a campaign to whose operational requirements the German Army had ever given serious consideration, even under Moltke the Elder. Indeed, its rejection of the very idea was a reflection of at least one lesson derived from Clausewitz, who had served in the 1812 campaign and drew many important conclusions from that experience, including the inherent strength of the defensive and the diminishing power of the attack. When the OKH was told to get on with it by Hitler, its solutions, as in the campaigns that had worked in 1939–1941, were tactical-operational—a series of encirclement battles close to the frontier, designed to produce a result before the winter. Its thinking had advanced little since Ludendorff. Nobody asked how these victories were to be related to political objectives. Both space and time were acknowledged to be potential problems—and were of course linked. If the Russian forces could not be annihilated close to the frontier, then they could retreat into the interior and the war would become protracted. The campaign would exceed the geographical reach of the German Army—both logistically and conceptually. Therefore terror would be part of a package designed to get quick victory. Partisans presented the Germans with protracted war, as they knew from 1870–1871 and, as they knew from 1914, brutality could nip such resistance in the bud.

Hitler's own way out of the dilemma was one that temperamentally the army could embrace: Russia would collapse from within. Here were the lessons from 1917–1918. In 1914 the German Army had used terror as a means to aid its achievement of operational success, not as a substitute for it. In 1941 it still pursued operational successes, but such triumphs could no longer be ends in themselves because the Germans knew that they could not themselves produce final victory. The "stab in the back legend" is central to understanding many of the assumptions that underpinned the conduct of the Second World War on both sides. But in adapting its lessons to the eastern front in the Second World War, the German Army neglected one other element in its defeat of Russia in

1917–1918. Its policy on the eastern front after the February Revolution of 1917 had been one of fraternization, not coercion. Moreover, Germany itself had supported the Bolsheviks. On 17 March 1941, the chief of the Great General Staff, Franz Halder, wrote in his diary, "In Great Russia force must be used in its most brutal form. The ideological ties holding together the Russian people are not yet strong enough, and the nation would break up once the functionaries are eliminated."[36] The tensions between geopolitics and geography were to be resolved not by operational excellence but by brutality and terror.

Notes

1. See Brian W. Blouet, *Halford Mackinder: A Biography* (Texas, 1987); W. H. Parkes, *Mackinder: Geography as an Aid to Statecraft* (Oxford, 1982). What follows is part of a bigger study comparing the roles of geography and geopolitics in the German operations and strategy in both world wars, in developing which I have incurred two debts. The first is to Jürgen Förster, who has drawn my attention to relevant sources in German, and the second is to Andreas Rose, who has undertaken research in the interwar German periodical literature on my behalf. I am most grateful to the Faculty of Modern History at Oxford, which has funded Andreas Rose's work. Current military history and much military theory tend to ignore geography despite its self-evidently decisive effect: Hervé Coutau-Bégarie, *Traité de stratégie* (Paris, 1999), is the deeply impressive exception that proves the rule. In English, see also Patrick O'Sullivan and Jesse W. Miller, *The Geography of Warfare* (Beckenham, 1983). Geographical studies of the First World War focus on the western front: see Robert Villate, *Les conditions géographiques de la guerre: Etude de géographie militaire sur le front français de 1914 à 1918* (Paris, 1925); and Douglas W. Johnson, *Battlefields of the World War: Western and Southern Fronts, a Study in Military Geography,* 2 vols. (New York, 1921). Johnson's wartime book did embrace the eastern front: see Douglas W. Johnson, *Topography and Strategy in the War* (US edition 1917; London, 1918). Vejas Gabriel Liulevicius, *War Land on the Eastern Front: Culture, National Identity and German Occupation in World War I* (Cambridge, 2000) is concerned with the geography of the eastern front but not for its operational consequences.

2. H. J. Mackinder, "The Geographical Pivot of History," *Geographical Journal,* XXIII (1904), 422.

3. Ibid., 423.

4. Ibid., 434.

5. Quoted by Blouet, *Mackinder,* 168.

6. Mackinder, *Democratic Ideals and Reality: A Study in the Politics of Reconstruction* (London, 1919), 26, quoted by G. Nicolas-Obadia and C. Guanzini, *Halford John Mackinder: Géographie et politique* (Lausanne, 1988), 49–58.

7. Holger Afflerbach, *Falkenhayn. Politisches Denken und Handeln im Kaiserreich* (Munich, 1994), 11, 294–95, 303–5.

8. Keith Neilson, "Russia," in Keith Wilson, ed., *Decisions for War, 1914* (London, 1995), 98; Dietrich Geyer, *Russian Imperialism: The Interaction of Domestic and Foreign Policy, 1860–1914* (Leamington Spa, 1987), 265; Peter Gatrell, *Government, Industry and*

Rearmament in Russia, 1900–1914: The Last Argument of Tsarism (Cambridge, 1994), 139, 176–78.

9. Norman Stone, *The Eastern Front, 1914–1917* (London, 1975), 35–36.

10. Gerhard Ritter, *The Sword and the Sceptre: The Problem of Militarism in Germany*, 4 vols. (London, 1970–73), 1:228–29; see also his letter of 28 August 1856, in Max Horst, ed., *Motlke. Leben und Werk in Selbstzeugnissen* (Bremen, n.d.), 229–36.

11. Eberhard Kessel, ed., *Generalfeldmarschall Graf Alfred von Schlieffen. Briefe* (Göttingen, 1958), 296.

12. John Röhl, "An der Schwelle zum Weltkrieg. Eine Dokumentation über den 'Kriegsrat' vom 8. Dezember 1912," *Militärgeschichtliche Mitteilungen*, I, no. 21 (1977), 77–134.

13. Scott Lackey, *The Birth of the Habsburg Army: Friedrich Beck and the Rise of the General Staff* (Westport, CT, 1995), 114–17, 161–62; Graydon Tunstall Jr., *Planning for War against Russia and Serbia: Austro-Hungarian and German Military Strategies, 1897–1914* (Boulder, CO, 1993), 16–48; Günther Kronenbitter, *"Krieg im Frieden." Die Führung der k.u.k Armee und Grossmachtpolitik Österreich-Ungarns 1906–1914* (Munich, 2003), 293–96.

14. Jehuda Wallach, *Das Dogma der Vernichtungsschlacht. Die Lehren von Clausewitz und Schlieffen und ihre Wirkung in zwei Weltkriegen* (first published 1967; Munich, 1970), 139, fn 27.

15. General Staff Ride (East), 1894, quoted by Robert Foley, ed. *Alfred von Schlieffen's Military Writings* (London, 2003), 14.

16. A. C. Macdonnell, *The Outlines of Military Geography* (London, 1911), 76–77. For Mackinder's own reflections on this front, see Halford Mackinder, *The World War and After: A Concise Narrative and Some Tentative Ideas* (London, 1924), 36–39.

17. Mackinder, "Geographical Pivot," 434. As early as 1899, T. Miller Maguire, *Outlines of Military Geography* (Cambridge, 1899), 151–52, made the same point.

18. Arden Bucholz, *Moltke, Schlieffen and Prussian War Planning* (New York, 1991), 184–85.

19. Friedrich Ratzel, *Politische Geographie* (Munich and Leipzig, 1897), 193.

20. Ibid., 322.

21. Ibid. (1903 edition), 374.

22. Ibid. (1903 edition), 471.

23. Ibid. (1903 edition), 375.

24. Terence Zuber, *Inventing the Schlieffen Plan: German War Planning, 1871–1914* (Oxford, 2002), is the most recent and most revisionist discussion of these issues; see especially 63, 102, 181. On the origins of the Tannenberg maneuver, see Dennis Showalter, *Tannenberg: Clash of Empires* (Hamden, CT, 1991).

25. Sigismund von Schlichting, *Taktische und Strategische Grundsätze der Gegenwart*, 3 vols., (Berlin, 1897–99), 2:26.

26. Ibid., 2:30–33, 47.

27. *Heeresverpflegung*, published by Grosser Generalstab, Kriegsgeschichtliche Abteilung I (Berlin, 1913), 50.

28. Ibid., 290.

29. The explanation is not one given much weight by John Horne and Alan Kramer, *German Atrocities, 1914: A History of Denial* (New Haven, 2001), but the part played by

requisitioning and plundering in promoting clashes between indigenous populations and armies is even more evident on more mobile fronts.

30. Hew Strachan, *The First World War,* vol. 1, *To Arms* (Oxford, 2001), 1005–14; Stig Förster, "Der deutsche Generalstab und die Illusion des kurzen Krieges, 1871–1914. Metakritik eines Mythos," *Militärgeschichtliche Mitteilungen,* 54 (1995), 61–95.

31. Hans Delbrück, *Krieg und Politik 1914–1916* (Berlin, 1918), 114.

32. Ibid., 128.

33. Alfred Franke, "Wehrgeographisches zum Russlandfeldzug Napoleons," *Zeitschrift für Geopolitik,* XI (1934), 459.

34. Quoted by Holger Herwig, *The First World War: Germany and Austria-Hungary, 1914–1918* (London, 1997), 392.

35. Hans-Adolf Jacobsen, *Karl Haushofer-Leben und Werk,* 2 vols. (Boppard am Rhein, 1979), 1:606–33.

36. Franz Halder, *The Halder Diaries, 1939–1942,* trans. and ed. Trevor Dupuy (Boulder, CO, 1975), 833.

Part 1

The Battles on the Eastern Front, 1914–1915

2

Introductory Remarks

Stig Förster

The eastern front is not the only front of the First World War that has slipped into the background of modern memory and been overlooked in the culture of remembrance. Probably even less known are the events in the Balkans and in the Near East. Does anyone still recall that German officers commanded entire sections of the front in the Ottoman Empire, or that an "Asian Corps" of eighteen thousand Germans fought in the Near East early in 1918? The Bolshevik October Revolution occurred right after the war in the east, and for this reason the political aftermath of this part of the war is generally known. But forgotten are the military operations that played out over the course of the war in the east, with the exception of the battle of Tannenberg. In the German culture of remembrance, Tannenberg was highly celebrated for decades. The Russian author Alexander Solzhenitsyn created a literary monument to its memory.[1] But what followed is for most people only a dim memory. Memories of the battles, catastrophes, and pyrrhic victories have long since faded. The western front received more press: it was ultimately decisive, characterized by monstrous battles of annihilation and horrifying trench fighting, and the countries involved represented a dominant mental image for people in the west.

The eastern front was different in that all of the countries that sent their armies to the battlefields of the east were counted among the losers of the First World War. This fact as well as the fundamental political changes that took place at the end of the war have meant that interest in revisiting the history of the events or delving into the mental and cultural conditions on the eastern front has been rather modest outside of Germany. Memories of the battles on the eastern front ultimately became overshadowed by battles in the same areas during the Second World War, which by 1941 had developed into one of the most horrific slaughters in world history.

That said, the current state of research on the operations of the First World War is actually not all that bad. As the essays in part 1 show, in recent decades operations have been researched both in general outline and in some cases in surprisingly rich detail. Certainly there are still some large gaps, such as military history "from beneath," which would include a look at the day-to-day realities of war. Furthermore, the western front has been studied and reviewed in much more detail. But thanks to recent research efforts, the operations of the eastern front can now be well reconstructed. At least for the first two years of the war, which are the main focus of the following chapters, a general outline can be made of the course of the operations. We know exactly at which points decisions were made; we know that the Russian Army was declining gradually; we know that the Austro-Hungarian Army was bleeding out, although it held on for a surprisingly long time; and we know that the German Army was exhausting itself on inconclusive victories.

But much is still either debatable or has yet to be addressed sufficiently. The military planning during the time leading up to the war, for instance, needs to be further researched and discussed. Another issue concerns how the war was perceived by the responsible parties when they began operations in August 1914. How did their concept of war impact the actual operations, and how did this change under the real conditions? What did the military leaders learn from their experiences in the war, and what conclusions did they draw from them?[2] What role was played by political, ideological, economic, and social issues? To what extent did mentalities play a part? These are only some examples of the questions that need to be addressed with respect to operations on the eastern front in the First World War. Future debates promise to be interesting because they will include historians not just from Germany but from the Anglo-Saxon countries, Austria, Russia, and the countries of the former Eastern Bloc. The following essays represent a point of departure for these debates.

Yet this starting point, not enough in and of itself, only underscores the need for further intensive research. Kronenbitter and Khavkin, for example, emphasize that the top military leaders in Austria-Hungary and Russia would not have considered it possible for the war to have lasted as long as it did. The Austro-Hungarian chief of General Staff, Conrad von Hötzendorf, was at least confident of a quick German victory over France.[3] In fact there is evidence suggesting that among the top military leaders of the German Empire, few harbored any illusions of a short war, even though optimism and the belief in a quick victory were widely disseminated. This is evident in Moltke's words to his adjutant Major von Haeften on the night of 31 July 1914: "This war will grow into a world war in which England, too, will become engaged. Very few can envision the breadth, duration, and the end of this war. How it will all end, no one today has any idea."[4]

On 3 August 1914 he also remarked to General Mackensen, who was stationed on the eastern front: "The troops in the west will have it easier than here on the eastern border. . . . Only a quick victory against France can free us from this critical situation. I predict a long duration for this campaign. The existence or nonexistence of the German Empire is at stake and with it that of the German people."[5]

Minister of War Erich von Falkenhayn candidly shared the following with the American diplomat Henry White after the outbreak of the war: "The coming in of England had made all the difference in the world, both to the probable duration of the war (which he thought was likely to last at least three or four years), and possibly even to its outcome."[6]

Many German military officers thought the same. Still, they did not consider it to be a matter of offensive planning; they simply longed for the war to be over.[7] With respect to the duration of the war, were the German officer elite so much more far-seeing than their comrades in the Danube Monarchy and Russia? It may well be that the top leaders in Austria-Hungary entered the war hoping at least for defeat with honor. But did they really expect that this catastrophe would take place after only a few months? And the Russians? Did they really believe that in just a few months they could march into Berlin or Vienna with their incomplete and only moderately trained army? Years earlier, it was a Russian author who rather precisely predicted that if the major European powers clashed with one another, there would be a long-lasting and catastrophic war.[8] Thus, the question of preconceptions about the war must be thoroughly examined, especially as this is of great importance to evaluating the planning and implementation of military operations.

The chapters in this volume focus primarily on the planning and execution of military operations in the east.[9] A recurring topic among the Great General Staff officers was the issue of a possible *schwerpunkt* designation, or main effort, during the deployment of German forces. German planning expected the relatively few troops remaining in the east to operate defensively against the Russians, who had far superior numbers. What was needed in order to halt the Russian steamroller, however, was an offensive approach at the tactical level. At the same time, as Gerhard P. Gross writes in his chapter, the German General Staff faced the Russian Army with a mixture of respect and contempt. In reality, the German Army was superior to its enemy in terms of quality. While this made the operational victory at Tannenberg possible, that victory also played an important part in the German Empire's strategic defeat in the long run, as no decisive victory took place in the west.

Gross also points to the less known events in the east up to the end of 1914. Despite repeated setbacks, the Germans achieved further victories during this phase as well. The egomaniacal Ludendorff used the situation to pressure Erich von Falkenhayn, the chief of the Army High Command, to move the schwerpunkt from the west to the east. In 1915 Falkenhayn partially conceded. With new troops, a larger victory was then achieved in the east. It was primarily the breach near Gorlice-Tarnów that presented a considerable challenge to the Russians, who were finally forced to give up Poland and parts of the Baltic states. Yet with all of the setbacks and despite terrible losses, the Russian Army remained intact. Unable to defeat the Russians decisively, the Germans "nearly victoried themselves to death," as the expression goes. As 1915 drew to a close, there was still no foreseeable end to the war.

At the outbreak of the war in the east, the German General Staff made the decision to maintain the defensive, which placed the Austro-Hungarian Army in an extremely dangerous situation. Its task was to take on the main burden of the battles against the Russians. Combined war efforts were plagued by inadequate agreements, poor coordination, and mutual distrust. There was never an order from higher up that addressed the combined forces. As Günther Kronenbitter points out, those sorts of problems during a coalition war were completely normal. Perhaps, however, one might also add that a hallmark of the Central Powers' conduct of war was the inability to meet the organizational requirements for a large, modern, industrialized war. Nevertheless, any time the two sides stepped up together for a partially combined action, such as Gorlice-Tarnów, they were successful. As Lothar Höbelt writes, this particular victory further demonstrated that the Austro-Hungarian Army was capable of surprising accomplishments.[10] Despite the significant leadership mistakes at the beginning of the war, despite terrible losses in the winter of 1914–1915, and despite heavy defeats, the Austro-Hungarian Army held on, recovered to some extent, and during 1915 was fully able to make life difficult for the enemy. Even Italy's entry into the war had little impact in this area. By the end of 1915, Höbelt shows, the military leadership of the Danube Monarchy was probably surprised by how well it had withstood these sorts of battles. But the most serious tests were still to come, and in the end, the Danube Monarchy did not survive these.

By the end of 1915 the Central Powers had brought to a halt the Russian steamroller that had been so feared before the war. It was even forced into reverse. But what did the events of 1914–1915 look like from the Russian point of view? In his essay Boris Khavkin presents an interesting view of this topic. News of the course of the war on the eastern front, he writes, was largely suppressed in the Russian media as well. At first glance, the Russian Army's numerous setbacks and defeats hardly appear to be glorious chapters of Russian history. At the same time, however, for an understanding of the roots of the October Revolution, it is vital to grasp the extent and results of these disasters. Khavkin shows that poor planning, underqualified leaders, the army's inadequate equipment and weaponry, the miserable logistics, and the limited industrial foundation amounted to crucial weaknesses.

Nevertheless, up to the end of 1915 (and beyond) the Russian soldiers fought brilliantly and won repeated victories. Even under heavy losses the morale of the troops remained intact. The army had not yet been decisively defeated. The troops were constantly faced with impossible missions that had been conceived purely for political reasons. The attack on East Prussia at the beginning of the war, for instance, had to take place much too early and with too few resources, and as a result the Russians were not able to support their French ally against the German invasion. Khavkin stresses that this was the case over the following year and a half as well. Khavkin, therefore, maintains that the Russians took on the main brunt of the battle against the Central Powers and in doing so gradually bled out. One could counter this argument, however, by pointing out that in 1915 the French and the British repeatedly attacked the German position in the west without any sweeping victory. Their losses were also enormous. Furthermore, from the beginning, the Russian leaders were swift to sacrifice their soldiers in pursuit of their own aggressive aims. Ultimately, Khavkin's argument also brings to mind the Soviet claims that the Western Allies in the Second World War consciously delayed the opening of a second European front against Hitler's Germany in order to allow the Red Army to bleed out.

The essays presented in this volume, whatever their critical stance may be, offer interesting insights and material for discussion and provide a potential platform for further research. The dramatic consequences of the numerous battles described here, the horrifying losses, and the devastation of whole regions serve as witness to the necessity of bringing the eastern front of the First World War out of its place in the shadows.

Notes

1. Alexander Solzhenitsyn, *August Vierzehn,* Darmstadt 1972.

2. Leading military officers frequently learn little or nothing at all on the battlefields and instead persist with prefabricated principles and prejudices. Even famous field commanders turn out to be rather narrow minded on closer observation. As an example, see the work by Alan T. Nolan, *Lee Considered: General Robert E. Lee and Civil War History,* Chapel Hill 1991.

3. Terence Zuber, on the other hand, in support of his thesis concerning the defensive mindset of the German General Staff, argues that at least one person, the younger Moltke, did expect a protracted war. See his chapter in the German edition of this book.

4. Hans von Haeften, *Meine Erlebnisse aus den Mobilmachungstagen* 1914, Bundesarchiv-Militärarchiv (Federal Archive–Military Archive) Freiburg i. Br. (BA-MA), N35/1.

5. Quoted in Theo Schwarzmüller, *Zwischen Kaiser und "Führer." Generalfeldmarschall August von Mackensen,* Paderborn 1995, 93.

6. Quoted (in English) in Holger Afflerbach, *Falkenhayn. Politisches Denken und Handeln im Kaiserreich,* Munich 1994, 170f.

7. See Stig Förster, "Der deutsche Generalstab und die Illusion des kurzen Krieges, 1871–1914. Metakritik eines Mythos." In: *Militärgeschichtliche Mitteilungen* 54 (1995), 61–95; Stig Förster, "Der Krieg der Willensmenschen. Die deutsche Offizierselite auf dem Weg in den Ersten Weltkrieg, 1871–1914." In: *Willensmenschen. Über deutsche Offiziere,* edited by Ursula Breymayer, Bern Ulrich, and Karin Wieland, Frankfurt 1999, 23–36.

8. Ivan Bloch, *Der Krieg,* 6 vols., Berlin 1899.

9. Terence Zuber discusses extensively the operational planning by members of the German General Staff before the outbreak of the war. See his chapter in the German edition of this book.

10. See his chapter in the German edition of this volume: Lothar Höbelt, "'So wie wir haben nicht einmal die Japaner angegriffen'. Österreich-Ungarns Nordfront 1914/15." In: *Die vergessene Front,* edited by Gerhard P. Gross, Paderborn 2006, 87–119.

3

In the Shadow of the West

The German Conduct of War on the Eastern Front up to the End of 1915

Gerhard P. Gross

In the collective memory of the Germans the "bloodbath" of Verdun has widely been held as the defining battle of the First World War. When it comes to the question of significant battles on the eastern front, the response is hardly ever Tannenberg, for instance, or Gorlice-Tarnów, but Stalingrad, the German Verdun of the Second World War.

Both Verdun and Stalingrad represent the horror of the war and the failure of military leaders and have had a crucial impact on how Germans view the use of military force. The battles on the eastern front in the First World War, on the other hand, have vanished from our memory. This was not always so. In the postwar period, every child knew about the historical victory of Tannenberg. After Tannenberg, Generalfeldmarschall Paul von Beneckendorff und von Hindenburg and General Erich Ludendorff were hailed as the patrons of German victory, likened to the Dioscuri of Greek mythology, and celebrated as the legendary saviors of East Prussia. In 1916, after the collapse of General Erich Falkenhayn's second OHL (Army High Command) prior to Verdun, it was they who took over as the third OHL.[1]

In order to reconstruct the first two years of the German conduct of the war on the eastern front on the basis of written descriptions or a comprehensive overview in the professional literature, one must rely on publications from the English-speaking countries or content oneself with works published in Germany in the 1920s and 1930s.[2] The reason is that, due to the purpose of the history of operations as it is customarily applied, the subject is an unpopular field of activity for German military historians. For decades, these sensitivities have impeded the development of a modern history of operations as a discipline within the field of military history. Nevertheless, the last several years have seen a shift of opinion, and younger military historians increasingly inquire about the "sense, purpose and aims of the history of operations and its classification within the modern of field military history."[3]

This essay will explore the interdependence between the German conduct of war on the eastern front and the strategic situation of the Central Powers in the years 1914–1915 as well as the differences of opinion within the German military leadership. There will also be an analysis of the essential differences between the tactical and operational conduct of war on the western and eastern fronts. Problems of coalition warfare will be outlined only briefly, as they are treated in more detail in a later chapter in this volume by Günther Kronenbitter.

The Operational Triumphs: Tannenberg und Gorlice-Tarnów

At the beginning of 1914, the schwerpunkt of German land and naval warfare lay on the western front and in the North Sea. While the German Imperial Navy concentrated its High Seas Fleet on the decisive battle in Wilhelmshaven, the Great General Staff had been planning since the time of Generalfeldmarschall Alfred Graf von Schlieffen how to wage a prospective two-front war. First they planned to attack France with the mass of the German Army, and as a result of this presumed war of destruction, more military forces would become available and sent from the western front to defeat the Russian Army.[4] In the strategic calculations of the empire's military leaders, the eastern front was a secondary theater of war. In 1913 the chief of the General Staff of the Field Army, Generaloberst Helmuth von Moltke the Younger, had even discontinued reworking the deployment plan for the east.[5] Thus, in August 1914 seven-eighths of the German land forces deployed in the west, and only one-eighth in the east. There was no coordinated operations plan for the Central Powers to conduct the war against the Russian military forces in case of a multiple-front war, nor was there a supreme command. Each of the allies planned its own war separately and was kept only vaguely informed by its confederates.

Therefore, it was not until 1909 that Moltke presented the proposed German schwerpunkt in the west to the Austro-Hungarian chief of General Staff, Feldmarschall Franz Freiherr Conrad von Hötzendorff. For the planned Austrian offensive in Galicia, he expected Conrad to lead only one relief attack against the Russian Narev Army, depending on the how the situation developed.[6] Until German reinforcements from the western front arrived, the main burden of the conduct of the war lay on the shoulders of the Austro-Hungarian Army. Even before the Russian mobilization was finished, the Germans expected an attack on East Prussia via the Masurian Lake District by two Russian armies with about 360,000 soldiers operating independently. Based on this assessment of the enemy situation, the 8th Army was deployed in the area east of the Vistula for the defense of the over nine-hundred-kilometer eastern border. Commanded by Generaloberst Maximilian Graf von Prittwitz und Gaffron, it was made up of four army corps consisting of six infantry divisions, three reserve divisions, and one cavalry division, with about 120,000 soldiers.[7] The remaining section of the front as far as Silesia was defended by Landwehr and replacement troops that at the beginning of the war were supposed to cover the left flank of the Austro-Hungarian offensive in Galicia.[8] The German units were numerically inferior to the Russian units by about one to three.

With this strength ratio, how did German leaders plan to successfully defend the eastern German border? The Great General Staff confronted the Russian Army with a mixture of respect and disdain. While it recognized that the Russian soldiers were capable of a tenacious defense, it judged the tactical and leadership abilities of the officers as rather modest. Yet at the same time the Russian military appeared in fact to be fully developed in terms of equipment, training, and weapons. The German infantry divisions with thirteen thousand men, however, were slightly superior to the Russians with their seventeen thousand men because they had better cannons, especially for the heavy artillery.[9] A memorandum of October 1913 attests to the methodical slowness of the Russian leaders, their preference for static war, and their limited mastery of the tactics of combined arms. Because Russian troop movements took place very slowly, Russian units were not expected to be able to transition quickly from the defensive mode to the attack. This prompted the following situational assessment: "In the confrontation with the Russians, the German leadership will therefore be able to risk movements that they could not allow themselves against an enemy of equal strength."[10] Based on this appraisal, German leaders, with support from the well-constructed German rail network and through clever exploitation of the interior lines, planned to attack and defeat one Russian force after another, using a clear schwerpunkt in the conduct of offensive and mobile battle.[11]

This scenario had been played through by the Great General Staff since the time of Schlieffen during several general staff rides, but without there ever being a detailed written plan for defense.[12] On the contrary, the deployment instructions for the 8th Army expressly indicated that their commander was to conduct the operations based on his own judgment.[13] The army was supposed to secure the eastern provinces and keep strong Russian units committed there. The Germans sought only an accord with the Austro-Hungarian Army, and the offensive against the Narev Army that had been assigned to Conrad was to be carried out only if the Russians persisted in their defensive operation. Under all circumstances, Prittwitz was to set the terms of action or, as Moltke expressly instructed him: "If the Russians come, simply do not proceed defensively, instead take the offense, offense, offense."[14] East Prussia was only to be given up and the units pulled back to the Vistula under the threat of the destruction of the 8th Army.[15]

On 15 August, earlier than the Army High Command had expected, and under a degree of pressure from the French, the Russian Neman Army under General Paul von Rennenkampf advanced north of the Masurian Lakes.[16] Separated by the chain of lakes, the Narev Army, under General Aleksandr Samsonov, after a few days' delay, marched from the south as far as the East Prussian border.[17] In the face of this situation, Prittwitz decided to first attack the Neman Army with the bulk of the 8th Army. Only the XX Army Corps remained in southern East Prussia near Ordelsburg (now Szczytno, Poland) as flank protection against the advancing Narev Army. The unauthorized attack by the I Army Corps under General Hermann von Francois led to the battle of Stallupönen (now Nesterov, Russia) on 17 August. Having moved forward for an isolated offensive operation, under orders from Prittwitz, Francois had to break off the offensive and pull back his corps.[18] On 20 August 1914, Prittwitz attacked the Neman Army, which had in the meantime advanced as far as Gumbinnen (now Gusev, Russia).[19] Despite a few critical setbacks, the battle appeared to take a favorable course, and Prittwitz received the report that the Narev Army had ceased its advance and had begun to attack further to the west than had been expected. The danger of becoming encircled caused Prittwitz, despite objections from his general staff officers, to break off the battle in progress and pull his army back to the Vistula line.[20] Moltke had been displeased with the hesitant leadership of the 8th Army for quite a long time, and even though Prittwitz's order to pull back to the Vistula was covered in the instructions for deployment, on 22 August Moltke dismissed Prittwitz and his chief of general staff Generalmajor Georg Graf von Waldersee.

It remains outside of the scope of this essay to explore the pros and cons of this decision as it is presented in German military literature.[21] The important point is that the command of the 8th Army was given to Hindenburg and Ludendorff because of differences in opinion with the Army High Command concerning operations. Moltke hoped that Hindenburg and Ludendorff would provide more spirited leadership and above all achieve victory. Thus began the ascent of two very different men who were hardly known outside of the military establishment. This would soon change, however. On 31 August the new commander of the 8th Army reported to the kaiser that the Narev Army had been destroyed.

Considering how the situation developed, with numerically inferior units—191,000 Russian soldiers confronting 153,000 German soldiers—and a second army with about 200,000 soldiers in the rear, how could such a victory come about, and what were the military and political consequences? Building on the deployment already begun under Prittwitz's leadership, and having received the best possible intelligence about the enemy's every step through German aerial and radio reconnaissance, Ludendorff and Hindenburg moved all their forces, save for a thin screen of cavalry, from the area in front of the Neman Army as it slowly advanced toward Königsberg (now Kaliningrad, Russia).[22] From 26 to 30 August, concentrating all reserves, they attacked the Narev Army, surrounding and destroying it.[23] The heroes of Tannenberg and the legend of the battle of Tannenberg were born.

No sooner had the battle been fought than it was already being compared with Cannae, and Hindenburg and Ludendorff were celebrated as the true heirs of Schlieffen.[24] Victorious figures could now be put on display before the German people, the allies, and the enemy, even in the face of the collapse of the German western offensive. Militarily the Russians were dealt a serious defeat, and the Russian steamroller was brought to a halt. The victory, however, also had a deeper long-term strategic dimension in its effect on public mentality. The German soldiers' latent sense of superiority over the Russian soldiers and their leaders, which had been present before the beginning of the war, had now been confirmed. Its aftereffects were felt throughout the Second World War. This triumph at the operational level simultaneously obscured the German Empire's defeat in the area of strategy. Faced with the looming catastrophe in the east, Moltke had summoned two army corps of the right flank in the west to the eastern front.[25] At the time of the battle of Tannenberg they were en route by train and not present for the battles on the Marne. France's calculations had panned out. The early Russian attack had forced the Army High Command to release reserves for the east and prevented the designation of a schwerpunkt that Schlieffen had thought absolutely necessary, and for which Moltke had striven. Even now, in the military literature on this subject, this set of facts tends to be left unstated as a paean to German operations.

How can the situation on the eastern front after the victory at Tannenberg be described? The Neman Army was consolidated for defense, while the German public, roused by scare reports about Russian atrocities, demanded the liberation of East Prussia.[26] Meanwhile, in Galicia, the Austro-Hungarian Army was forced onto the defensive and faced a catastrophe. In the face of this situation, Conrad demanded the promised offensive toward the Narev River. The German side, however, considered this attack too risky, without first having eliminated the threat to the flank from the Neman Army. They decided to accept the risk of annoying Austria and first run Rennenkampf out of East Prussia.

Thus, after meeting up with the reinforcements from the west, the 8th Army deployed against the Neman Army. On 7 September, at the same moment the situation on the Marne was coming to a head, they launched a frontal attack on the right flank, with a strong wing. Although the offensive did not lead to a resounding success, Rennenkampf broke off the battle out of fear of encirclement, pulled his units back without being noticed at first, and retreated. He lost forty-five thousand soldiers and left more than two hundred cannons behind the Neman.[27] With this, the danger to East Prussia was averted for the moment, and portions of the 8th Army became available for further operations.

As an outcome of the battle, however, Ludendorff took note that the Russians knew how to "organize retreats and move the mass through the countryside away from the roads."[28] Amid all their victories, the German leaders had discovered that the Russian Army had the capability of retreating in an orderly manner away from fully constructed streets and road networks.

Given the devastating defeat of the Austro-Hungarian Army in Galicia, Conrad, who felt exploited and abandoned, pressed for direct German support. But because of the "Race to the Sea," it was not possible to transport more units to the eastern front, and therefore the Army High Command decided to create the 9th Army from the bulk of the 8th Army in Upper Silesia. As commander, the kaiser appointed Hindenburg, who would simultaneously take over the overall leadership of all operations in the east.[29] Although there was no unified supreme command over the allied militaries, the 9th Army, in close cooperation with the 1st Austro-Hungarian Army, was to advance against Russian units south of Warsaw to relieve the Austrians in Galicia. In a master stroke of organization, in only ten days, nine divisions, a total of about ninety-five thousand men, were transported by rail from East Prussia to the area of Cracow. On 28 September the attack began.

The operational goal served by this offensive was unclear to Hoffmann, who was the "Ia," or staff operations officer of the 9th Army, even after the start of the attack. "In earlier operations the goal had been clearly given . . . this time everything is still unclear. . . . Where our thrust is supposed to be directed still cannot at all be foreseen."[30] Hoffmann, who was solely fixated on the operational victory, had overlooked the strategic intent of the Army High Command. The goal was not the destruction of a few Russian Army corps but the stabilization of the Austro-Hungarian Army and with it the Danube Monarchy; the objective was to deal with Austrian indignation over Germany's failure to keep its promise—in other words, it was about allied solidarity.

The advance developed into a nightmare for the German troops. As had been predicted by the Great General Staff, after crossing the border the troop leaders were confronted "with new conditions due to the nature of this theater of war."[31] Constant rain had transformed the already bad roads into a muddy wasteland, and for the first time German leaders realized that mobile operations in Russia would be subject to strict limitations. After reaching the Vistula, Ludendorff ordered a decisive attack on Warsaw, while the Austro-Hungarian Army was to cover the southern flank. The Russians, who in the meantime had regrouped and pulled together more than sixty divisions en masse from Galicia for an attack against the German units, had crossed the

Vistula for the counterattack.[32] With this, the Russian advance in Galicia was in fact successfully halted, but now the northern encirclement of the 9th Army by the far superior Russian forces became a threat. On 27 October, after the collapse of the Austrian relief attack at Ivangorod (now Deblin, Poland), the German units, now threatened by encirclement, broke off the offensive amid heavy fighting and pulled back to the German Empire's border.[33] To slow the Russian advance and bring them to a halt at the German border, the Germans systematically destroyed railways, roads, and lines of communication.[34] This was based on the knowledge that at a distance of about 120 kilometers from the nearest rail point, the advance of a modern army would be impeded by logistical challenges.[35]

The difficult strategic situation forced a restructuring of the chain of command in the east. Hindenburg was appointed commander in chief of Ober Ost (Supreme Command of all German forces in the east), and Ludendorff was named as his chief of general staff.[36] Here again, no unified supreme command over the Central Powers' two fronts was established. Because a static defense against the Russians, who were advancing with superior forces, did not appear promising, and because of Falkenhayn's offensive in Flanders, there were few available reserves. Hindenburg and Ludendorff therefore decided to further conduct the defense in a mobile and offensive manner. The approximately ten-day window of opportunity that was won by the halt of the Russian advance was used for reorganizing the German units. All available forces from the 8th and 9th Armies, a total of nine infantry and three cavalry divisions, were concentrated at Thorn (now Toruń, Poland), with the intention of stopping the Russian attack by attacking the enemy's right wing in a southeastern direction. The attack that began on 11 November forced the superior Russian units to retreat to the rail hub at Lódź, where they became partially encircled.

But due to tenacious Russian resistance, the German units, which were inferior in numbers, could not close the encirclement. When the Russian reserves that had been brought in attacked and encircled several German divisions, it was a disaster in the making.[37] The encircled divisions broke through the lines and reached their own front lines, bringing along more than ten thousand prisoners of war. In the following weeks, thanks to the reserves that had been brought from the Flanders front, the Germans succeeded in a frontal attack that pushed the Russians back to Warsaw.[38] During the fighting at Lódź, the Russian military leaders demonstrated for the first time that they too had mastered mobile operations and were not to be underestimated.

A repeated accusation made after the war was that Falkenhayn squandered his chance to destroy the Russian main forces because of his failed formation of the schwerpunkt in the west. But this was an irrelevant argument, as Ober Ost had not planned a strategic offensive from the beginning, and instead had only intended to rectify the critical front situation.[39] Thus, Ludendorff did not consider himself in a position to present his operational planning to Falkenhayn, remarking: "Everything was still in a state of uncertainty."[40] It was not until 4 November that he reported his further plans to the Army High Command. Falkenhayn, the kaiser, and the army high commanders in Flanders were at this time still convinced they could force a victory in the west. Until that victory could be won, fighting was to continue in the east using delay tactics in accordance with Schlieffen's ideas, and only limited goals were to be pursued. With this in mind Falkenhayn wrote to Ober Ost on 26 November 1914: "Any victories in the east that can be achieved at the cost of our position in the west are worthless."[41]

Hindenburg and Ludendorff, in contrast, considered a victory over Russia possible and demanded a clear relocation of the schwerpunkt to the east. This controversy over strategy between Westler (westerners) and Ostler (easterners), which flared up repeatedly during the utilization of the few operational reserve troops, sparked the military leadership crisis of the winter of 1914–1915. It came to a head when Hindenburg and Ludendorff tried to have Falkenhayn dismissed.[42] Wilhelm II, however, categorically rejected this. Falkenhayn's decision to make available the newly formed Reserve Corps of Ober Ost for an offensive in East Prussia only defused the situation on a surface level. Nothing changed with the differing foundational positions, for Falkenhayn, unlike the leaders at Ober Ost, no longer believed in a decisive victory against Russia, but instead expected only "greater local victories." The interpersonal relationships between those involved were so deeply poisoned that when taken together with the fundamental differences in opinion, cooperation was nearly impossible, and it was only a question of time before the conflict would escalate once more.[43]

After the defeat of the Russian 10th Army, which had meanwhile penetrated East Prussia once more, the troops in the east also shifted to static warfare.[44] The grand operational victory that had been announced by Ober Ost had not happened, however, and the Army Reserve was sent in to ensure a tactical victory. Falkenhayn considered himself vindicated in his conviction that Russia could not be beaten completely by military means. This realization was now shared by Hoffmann: "The Russian Army cannot be completely defeated; [it is] something we could do only if we fought solely against Russia."[45]

Despite victories in the east, Russian pressure on the Austro-Hungarian Army did not lessen, and on 22 March, the Przemyśl fortress capitulated. Further defeats for the Danube Monarchy could bring Romania and Italy into the war on the side of the Entente, and therefore, although he would still have preferred a decisive victory in the west, Falkenhayn decided on an offensive in the east to relieve Austria-Hungary militarily and politically. The newly formed operational Army Reserve, which had been internally restructured, was not deployed against Serbia or in the west but brought together en masse at Gorlice-Tarnów, and thereby the schwerpunkt of German conduct of the war was temporarily shifted to the eastern front.[46] At the schwerpunkt of the attack, the Army High Command had therefore gained a slight superiority in infantry at a local level but was burdened by excess cannons, particularly heavy ones.[47] The newly formed 11th Army under Generaloberst August von Mackensen, altogether eight infantry divisions, and the 4th Austro-Hungarian Army were tasked with bringing the Russians to their knees by an offensive in the rear of the Russian Carpathian front.[48]

Parallel to this, Ober Ost was to fix the Russian armies in the north with its units and feign an offensive on Riga by attacking in Courland. But issues related to the chain of command caused difficulties. While circumventing Ober Ost, which was informed of the operation only a few days prior to the beginning of the attack, Falkenhayn and Conrad came to the agreement that the 4th Austro-Hungarian Army was to be subordinated under Mackensen for the duration of the operation.

The overall command over the offensive operation was given to Conrad, who had to contact Falkenhayn before any important decisions.[49] The success of the attack depended on the tactical breakthrough of the enemy's defensive system. But this was exactly what had caused the collapse of the German offensive in Flanders. The success of the attack by the III Army Corps at Soissons in January 1915, which in future would be cited as the model for limited attacks in static warfare, vindicated the hopes of the Army High Command that a breach was possible, even given the deeply echeloned defensive positions. Afterward, Oberst Hans von Seeckt, as chief of staff of the III Army Corps and intellectual father of this operation, was appointed by Falkenhayn as chief of staff of the newly formed 11th Army and tasked with planning the breach. He based these plans on experience gained at Soissons.[50] Along with the necessity of the element of surprise, von Seeckt required smooth cooperation in the battle of combined arms, the deployment of heavy artillery conforming to the schwerpunkt, and freedom of action at all tactical leadership levels. To ensure the cohesiveness of the attack, he demanded "deployment in depth by the attacking infantry and rapid reporting of artillery impact."[51] Moreover, the attack should be carried out quickly in order to hamper Russian resistance in the rear positions and to prevent their bringing in reserves.

On 2 May, after several hours of heavy artillery fire, the German and Austrian units breached the enemy positions at a width of sixteen kilometers in only three days.[52] Although the Russian soldiers put up a tenacious resistance after the initial shock, they could not prevent the tactical breach.[53] Over the next days and weeks this expanded to a major offensive that the Central Powers kept supplied by repeatedly bringing in further reserves, despite Allied relief attacks in Artois and Italy's entry into the war.

On 22 June, after the San-Dniester line was reached and Przemyśl was recaptured, Lwów (Lemberg; now L'viv, Ukraine) fell. Falkenhayn now decided to collapse the Russian Narev-Vistula front in a push by the 11th Army to the north and an attack by Ober Ost across the Narev. The two pincers were supposed to meet up north of Warsaw and encircle the Russian units. The still-simmering conflict between Falkenhayn and Ober Ost broke out anew over this question. Hindenburg and Ludendorff considered the layout of the Army High Command's pincer operation to be wrong. Instead, they proposed a wider encirclement operation by way of Kovno (now Kaunas, Lithuania) and from there to penetrate the Russian Army from the rear and win a decisive victory.[54] Falkenhayn, who had a higher estimation of the Russian ability to resist than did Ober Ost, was still able to win over the kaiser with his plans.[55]

Falkenhayn's skepticism was validated over the following weeks. As had already happened in East Prussia, the Russians pulled back and destroyed the lines of communication as they went. The Russians put up such a tough defense and the resupply situation became so bad due to the overextension of the supply routes that the German attacks proceeded very slowly.[56] The encirclement of the Russian armies failed, and the planned encirclement operation became a frontal pushing back of the Russian units to the east. This changed nothing in the offensive carried out across the Memel in August by Ober Ost, during which Kovno was captured. At the end of 1915, the troops of the Central Powers transitioned to a defensive stance approximately on a line from Riga to Czernowitz (now Cernivci, Ukraine). In total, the Russian armies lost over 2.3 million soldiers during this offensive. The Central Powers had won the largest operational victory of the war, but it was not a victory of total destruction.[57]

The Limitations of Mobile War

The assessment of the Russian Army by the Great General Staff prior to the beginning of the war had proven surprisingly precise. As expected, the Russian soldiers had put up a strong defense, but their leaders executed mobile offensive operations in a slow and somewhat poorly coordinated manner.[58] On the other hand, the Russians showed a mastery of delay actions combined with an orderly retreat deep into their own area. Gallwitz particularly underscores this ability of the Russian officers, noting that they possessed "some distinctive features: along with their inherent calm, a clear sense of the terrain and how to exploit it. Both characteristics enabled the Russians to get out of difficult situations and very cleverly mask their retreat; zeal and agility in the terrain reinforcement were magnificent."[59] These same traits were to confront German soldiers again and again during the Second World War as well.

Yet during their operations planning, Ludendorff and many other German General Staff officers failed to take such known factors into account, just as they had done before the war with regard to the famously poor transport conditions in Russia. The Germans believed that their own superiority in terms of heavy artillery, together with the German leadership skill in tactical mobile warfare, more than made up for Russia's superior numbers. The Russians' inferior artillery was something they were never able to compensate for during the war, although they had previously attempted to correct it through their initiatives to The Hague Land War Convention.

But the Germans had one more important advantage—their experience of static warfare in the west.[60] The Germans quickly absorbed their tactical learning experience from the western front and Gorlice-Tarnów, which gave them an advantage in terms of innovation. In the following years in the east, the new skills in artillery and attack procedures were instilled into the German Army and were further developed and tested, giving the Germans a developmental edge over the French and English in offensives in the early part of 1918.

How can the situation of the German leadership at the end of 1915 be described? The designation of a longer-term schwerpunkt, which would have made a strategic victory possible, was prevented again and again due to the need to employ troops for relief attacks in the west. Reserves were always lacking at the crucial moment. Thus, the Russian Army was defeated but not destroyed and, despite considerable losses, it remained intact.

This had not been Falkenhayn's intent. By means of a victory on the eastern front he had wanted to break Russian offensive capabilities only temporarily, with a view to possibly entering into a peace agreement with the Russians.[61] Although the victories in the east did not force Russia into peace, they nevertheless had considerable effect on the overall conduct of war. The Central Powers had won a slight reprieve that in 1916 enabled the formation of a schwerpunkt in the west.[62] Further, while it did not prevent Italy from entering the war, it did prevent Romania from doing so. Their successes also prompted Bulgaria to enter into the war on the side of the Central Powers. This ensured the victory over Serbia and ultimately the alliance with Turkey.[63]

Nevertheless, over course of the operations in the east, Falkenhayn considered himself vindicated in his conviction that the Russians would avoid decisive battles by retreating into their interior, "where the Central Powers could not pursue them."[64] For this reason both he and von Seeckt were convinced that they would be able to attain victory only in the west.[65] Ludendorff and Hindenburg likewise considered themselves vindicated. They accused Falkenhayn of failure at a strategic level, certain that in having failed to completely defeat and destroy Russia, he had squandered their only opportunity.

These accusations found their way into the official historical writings on the war and posthumously led to a psychological examination of Falkenhayn on behalf of the Reich Archive.[66] But how valid were these accusations? Certainly German conduct of war at Tannenberg and at the fortress of Thorn had shown that temporarily, by winning the initiative, strategic inferiority could be offset by strength in operations. It was also revealed that the conduct of operations involved limitations that even today tend to be ignored. Certainly the German troops, unlike in the static war in the west, carried out largely successful tactical and operational offensives, but in the east narrow limits were placed on the conduct of mobile battle. While the German rail network enabled rapid troop transport and designation of main effort within Germany, mobile operations in Russia were considerably hampered by the country's poorly developed transportation system.[67] The cavalry, condemned to insignificance in the west, did acquire a certain importance during fighting in Courland in 1915, but it was never able to leave its imprint on mobile war in Russia. The mobile war was characterized more by the march-step of the infantrymen and the jogging along of the horse-drawn artillery cannons and *Panjewagen,* or one-horse carriages, on bad roads far away from the final railway debarkation point.[68] In this, the Russian expanses and the crawling pace set narrow limitations on mobile warfare. Rapid, broad area encirclement operations, with their sense of finality, would have been a deciding factor in destroying the Russian Army, but they were possible only on paper and in the minds of a few general staff officers. In reality, a military victory based on the operationally significant environmental conditions combined with the German military's thinking on mobile warfare was not possible. This redirected German leaders to seek strategic victory by means of a political plan. Thus, the limitations on the German conduct of war, which become obvious when following the history of operations on the eastern front, ultimately led to Lenin's journey through the German Empire.

Notes

1. See Bernd Martin, *Masuren. Mythos und Geschichte,* edited by the Evangelischen Akademie Baden, 3rd edition, Karlsruhe 2002 (= *Herrenalber Forum,* 22).

2. Even the *Encyclopedia of the First World War* concentrates on the treatment of the western front and treats the east in a more rudimentary manner. See *Enzyklopädie Erster Weltkrieg,* edited by Gerhard Hirschfeld, Gerd Krumeich, and Irina Renz, Paderborn 2003. See Peter Graf von Kielmansegg, *Deutschland und der Erste Weltkrieg,* 2nd ed., Stuttgart 1980; Sönke Neitzel, *Blut und Eisen. Deutschland und der Erste Weltkrieg,* Zürich 2003; Michael Salewski, *Der Erste Weltkrieg,* Paderborn 2003. There is no more recent, more comprehensive description of the German conduct of war on the eastern front in 1914–1915. Along with individual studies on the battle of Tannenberg, for instance, in Franz Uhle-Wettler, *Höhe-und Wendepunkte deutscher Militärgeschichte,* rev. ed., Hamburg 2000, 201–53, the operations in the east are treated only in connection with biographies of Erich Ludendorff. See Franz Uhle-Wettler, *Erich Ludendorff in seiner Zeit. Soldat, Stratege, Revolutionär. Eine Neubewertung,* Berg 1995; Wolfgang Venohr, *Ludendorff. Legende und Wirklichkeit,* Berlin 1993. See also William C. Fuller Jr., "Die Ostfront." *In: Der Erste Weltkrieg und das 20. Jahrhundert,* edited by Jay Winter, Geoffrey Parker, and Mary R. Habek, Hamburg 2002, 34–70; John Keegan, *Der Erste Weltkrieg. Eine europäische Tragödie,* Reinbek bei Hamburg 2000, 201–47, 324–31; Den-

nis E. Showalter, "Even Generals Wet Their Pants: The First Three Weeks in East Prussia, August 1914." In: *War and Society,* 2 (1984), 60–86; Dennis E. Showalter, "The Eastern Front and the German Military Planning, 1871 to 1914—Some Observations." In: *East European Quarterly,* 15 (1981), 163–80; Dennis E. Showalter, *Tannenberg: Clash of Empires,* Hamden CT 1991; Norman Stone, *The Eastern Front, 1914–1917,* London 1975; Hew Strachan, *The First World War,* vol. 1, *To Arms,* Oxford 2001, 281–373; Hew Strachan, *Der Erste Weltkrieg. Eine neue illustrierte Geschichte,* Munich 2003, 163–86. See also Walter Elze, *Tannenberg. Das Deutsche Heer von 1914. Seine Grundzüge und deren Auswirkung im Sieg an der Ostfront,* Breslau 1928; Hermann von Kuhl, *Der Weltkrieg 1914/1918,* vol. 1, Berlin 1929; *Der Weltkrieg 1914–1918,* edited at the Reichsarchiv (Reich Archive), vol. 2: *Die Befreiung Ostpreussens,* Berlin 1925; vol. 5: *Der Herbstfeldzug 1914. Im Westen bis zum Stellungskrieg. Im Osten bis zum Rückzug,* Berlin 1929; vol. 6: *Der Herbstfeldzug 1914. Der Abschluss der Operationen im Westen und Osten,* Berlin 1929; vol. 7: *Die Operationen des Jahres 1915. Die Ereignisse im Winter und Frühjahr,* Berlin 1931; vol. 8: *Die Operationen des Jahres 1915. Die Ereignisse im Westen Frühjahr und Sommer, im Osten vom Frühjahr bis zum Jahresschluss,* Berlin 1932.

3. Stig Förster, "Operationsgeschichte heute. Eine Einführung." In: *Militärgeschichtliche Zeitschrift,* 61 (2002), 309–13, here 311. On the ongoing discussion, see the controversial articles in: *Was ist Militärgeschichte?* edited by Thomas Kühne and Benjamin Ziemann, Paderborn 2000 (= *Krieg in der Geschichte,* vol. 6).

4. Terence Zuber, in his dissertation "Inventing the Schlieffen Plan: German War Planning, 1871–1914," Oxford 2002, has begun a wide debate on a reevaluation of the Schlieffen Plan. See also Zuber's chapter in the German edition of this book and the discussion in *War in History since 2001* as well as the collected volume *The Schlieffen Plan: International Perspectives on the German Strategy for World War I,* edited by Hans Ehlert, Michael Epkenhans, and Gerhard P. Gross, Lexington, KY, 2014.

5. Annika Mombauer, *Helmuth von Moltke and the Origins of the First World War,* Cambridge 2001, 102–4.

6. See Lothar Höbelt, "Schlieffen, Beck, Potiorek und das Ende der gemeinsamen deutsch-österreichisch-ungarischen Aufmarschpläne im Osten." In: *Militärgeschichtliche Mitteilungen (MGM),* 36 (1984), 7–30; John H. Maurer, *The Outbreak of the First World War: Strategic Planning, Crisis Decision Making and Deterrence Failure,* Westport, CT, 1995; Hans Meier-Welcker, "Strategische Planungen und Vereinbarungen der Mittelmächte für den Mehrfrontenkrieg." In: *Österreichische Militärische Zeitschrift,* 2 (1964), special issue 2, 15–22; Helmut Otto, "Zum strategisch-operativen Zusammenwirken des deutschen und österreichisch-ungarischen Generalstabes bei der Vorbereitung des Ersten Weltkrieges." In: *Zeitschrift für Militärgeschichte,* 2 (1963), 423–40; Gerhard Ritter, "Die Zusammenarbeit der Generalstäbe Deutschlands und Österreich-Ungarns vor dem Ersten Weltkrieg." In: *Zur Geschichte und Problematik der Demokratie. Festgabe für Hans Herzfeld,* Berlin 1958, 523–49; Theobald von Schäfer, "Deutsche Offensive aus Ostpreussen über den Narew auf Siedlec." In: *Militärwissenschaftliche Mitteilungen,* issue no. 11/12 (1930), second printing, 1–16; Gerhard Seyfert, *Die militärischen Beziehungen und Vereinbarungen zwischen dem deutschen und dem österreichischen Generalstab vor und bei Beginn des Weltkrieges,* Leipzig 1934.

7. The 8th Army was organized as follows: I Army Corps with the 1st and 2nd Infantry Division; XVII Army Corps with the 35th and 36th Infantry Divisions; XX

Army Corps with the 37th and 41st Infantry Divisions; I Reserve Corps with the 1st and 36th Reserve Divisions. In addition there was the 3rd Reserve Division, the 1st Cavalry Division, as well as four divisions of Landwehr and fortress troops. Of the thirteen divisions only six were active units. A more detailed description of the deployed German units can be found in: *Der Weltkrieg,* vol. 2, 358–65.

8. The equipping of the German units in personnel and material was very heterogeneous. A reserve division would have considerably less artillery than an active infantry division. The Landwehr and security units were not suited to independence either in terms of personnel or material. Not only did they lack engineering equipment, telegraph equipment, supply and medical units, they also lacked artillery and machine guns. See ibid., 364f.

9. On the organization of German units and on the comparison of battle strength, see ibid., attachment 1.1, 364f., and attachment 1.2.

10. "Geheime Denkschrift des Grossen Generalstabes aus dem Jahre 1913: Mitteilungen über russische Taktik." In: Elze, *Tannenberg,* 165–82, here 168.

11. On the tactical and operational doctrine of the German Army before 1914 and during the war, see Gerhard P. Gross, "Das Dogma der Beweglichkeit. Überlegungen zur Genese der deutschen Heerestaktik im Zeitalter der Weltkriege." In: *Erster Weltkrieg—Zweiter Weltkrieg. Ein Vergleich. Krieg, Kriegserlebnis, Kriegserfahrung in Deutschland,* published under the auspices of the Militärgeschichtliches Forschungsamt, edited by Bruno Thoss and Hans-Erich Volkmann, Paderborn 2002, 143–66.

12. See Alfred von Schlieffen, "Die grossen Generalstabsreisen—Ost—aus den Jahren 1891–1905," *Dienstschriften des Chefs des Generalstabes der Armee Generalfeldmarschall Graf von Schlieffen,* vol. 2, 7, edited by the Generalstab des Heeres (Kriegswissenschaftliche) Abteilung (Army General Staff's military science section), Berlin 1938. "Die grossen . . . 1905," an article or chapter within the larger body of writing by Schlieffen, is a description of the staff ride or staff trip to the future eastern front.

13. "'Der Oberbefehlshaber der 8. Armee hat die Operationen im Osten nach eigenem Ermessen zu leiten.' Aufmarschanweisung 1914/15 für Oberkommando der 8. Armee." In: Elze, *Tannenberg,* 185–97, here 193.

14. *Der Weltkrieg,* vol. 2, 45.

15. See "Aufmarschanweisung 1914/15 für Oberkommando der 8. Armee." In: Elze, *Tannenberg,* 195.

16. See Stone, *The Eastern Front,* 47–49; Strachan, *The First World War,* 195.

17. On the Russian plans, see Stone, *The Eastern Front,* 51–59.

18. See *Der Weltkrieg,* vol. 2, 35–78.

19. For details on the course of the battle, see Elze, *Tannenberg,* 93–110; Showalter, *Tannenberg,* 172–210; *Der Weltkrieg,* vol. 2, 79–102.

20. See Max Hoffmann, *Die Aufzeichnungen des Generalmajors Max Hoffmann,* vol. 2, edited by Karl Friedrich Nowak, Berlin 1929, 51f. Elze, *Tannenberg,* 110–16.

21. In German postwar military publications the firing of von Prittwitz is discussed in detail. For examples of this discussion and the related criticisms of von Prittwitz, see Ernst Kabisch, *Streitfragen des Weltkrieges 1914–1918,* Stuttgart 1924. Kabisch states that Molke had turned down Prittwitz as commander in chief of the 8th Army, but was unable to convince the military cabinet because Prittwitz, who was described as a "casino officer" and yarn spinner, had found favor with the kaiser. Even Moltke's efforts

to have Prittwitz dismissed by Minister of War von Falkenhayn failed because Falkenhayn, who as chief of the General Staff of the XVI Army Corps had suffered under him, refused to have him transferred, with the argument that Prittwitz would then tell tales to the kaiser. Ibid., 65.

22. See Hans Meier-Welcker, "Die Rückendeckung der 8. Armee während der Schlacht bei Tannenberg. Was können wir heute noch daraus lernen?" In: *Militär-Wochenblatt,* 121 (1936), 166–70.

23. For details of the battle, see Elze, *Tannenberg,* 116–48; Erich Ludendorff, *Meine Kriegserinnerungen 1914–1918,* Berlin 1919, 32–44; Showalter, *Tannenberg,* 213–319; Strachan, *The First World War,* 324–34, Venohr, *Ludendorff,* 32–52; Uhle-Wettler, *Höhe- und Wendepunkte,* 201–53.

24. See Hermann Gierl, "Zum fünften Jahrestag der Schlacht von Tannenberg." In: *Militär-Wochenblatt,* 104 (1919), 477–510. See also Holger Afflerbach, *Falkenhayn. Politisches Denken und Handeln im Kaiserreich,* Munich 1994 (= *Beiträge zur Militärgeschichte,* 42), 212. Afflerbach states that according to the general view, Ludendorff was seen as the intellectual heir of the Schlieffen tradition by the Great General Staff.

25. During the first days of September the Guards Reserve Corps, 3rd Guards Infantry Division, and 1st Guards Reserve Division, the XI Army Corps, the 22nd and 38th Infantry Divisions, and the 8th Cavalry Division arrived in East Prussia. These units were deployed by Moltke on the night of 28–29 August 1914. See *Der Weltkrieg,* vol. 2, 207. See also Ludendorff, *Meine Kriegserinnerungen,* 45.

26. See "Russische Greuel." In: *Der grosse Krieg. Eine Chronik von Tag zu Tag. Urkunden, Depeschen und Berichte der Frankfurter Zeitung,* vol. 1, Frankfurt, 1914, issue no. 3, 339f.

27. On the course of the battle see Ludendorff, *Meine Kriegserinnerungen,* 48–52; Venohr, Ludendorff, 53–66; *Der Weltkrieg,* vol. 2, 247–317.

28. Ludendorff, *Meine Kriegserinnerungen,* 51.

29. See *Der Weltkrieg,* vol. 5, 55.

30. Hoffmann, *Die Aufzeichnungen,* 55.

31. "Mitteilungen über russische Taktik." In: Elze, *Tannenberg,* 80.

32. On the Russian operations see Stone, *The Eastern Front,* 97–100.

33. For detailed descriptions of the battle, see Venohr, *Ludendorff,* 67–85; *Der Weltkrieg,* vol. 5, 402–500.

34. See Melzer, "Die Anwendungen von Sperrungen beim Feldzug in Südpolen Oktober 1914." In: *Militär-Wochenblatt,* 122 (1937), 70–77.

35. See Ludendorff, *Meine Kriegserinnerungen,* 74.

36. On the new system of command relationships in the east, see *Der Weltkrieg,* vol. 6, 37f.

37. On the Russian operations, see Stone, *The Eastern Front,* 103–7.

38. For detailed descriptions of the battles, see Venohr, *Ludendorff,* 86–107; *Der Weltkrieg,* vol. 6, 98–226.

39. See Venhor, *Ludendorff,* 92–94.

40. Ludendorff, *Meine Kriegserinnerungen,* 74.

41. *Der Weltkrieg,* vol. 6, 254.

42. On the military leadership crisis of winter 1914–1915, see Afflerbach, *Falkenhayn,* 211–23; Ekkehart P. Guth, "Der Gegensatz zwischen dem Oberbefehlshaber

Ost und dem Chef des Generalstabes des Feldheeres 1914–15. Die Rolle des Major v. Haeften im Spannungsfeld zwischen Hindenburg, Ludendorff und Falkenhayn." In: *MGM,* 35 (1984), 75–111; Gerhard Ritter, *Staatskunst und Kriegshandwerk. Das Problem des "Militarismus" in Deutschland,* vol. 3, *Die Tragödie der Staatskunst. Bethmann Hollweg als Kriegskanzler (1914–1917),* Munich 1964, 63–72.

43. Falkenhayn considered Ludendorff "not normal intellectually." Afflerbach, *Falkenhayn,* 248. Ludendorff stated to the chief of the field railroad system, General Wilhelm Groener: "I can only love or hate, and I hate General von Falkenhayn, I find it impossible to work with him." Quoted in Guth, "Der Gegensatz," 76.

44. For a detailed description of the winter battle in the Masurian District, see *Der Weltkrieg,* vol. 2, 172–242.

45. Hoffmann, *Die Aufzeichnungen,* 64.

46. Through the restructuring of the west army—each division had to give up its fourth infantry regiment—an operating reserve of fourteen divisions was created. See Afflerbach, *Falkenhayn,* 287–92: Erich von Falkenhayn, *Die Oberste Heeresleitung 1914–1916 in ihren wichtigsten Erschliessungen,* Berlin 1920, 62–69; Friedrich Carl Scheibe, "Marne und Gorlice: Zur Kriegsdeutung Hans Delbrücks." In: *MGM,* 53 (1994), 355–76, here 366–68.

47. Approximately 675 light and 4 heavy Russian cannons faced 1,272 light and 334 heavy cannons of the Central Powers. In addition, the Central Powers had over 96 mine launchers, which the Russians could not counter with even a single one. The ratio of machine guns (660 to 607) was almost balanced out. Numerical data according to *Deutschland im ersten Weltkrieg,* edited by the Autorenkollectiv des Zentralinstituts für Geschichte der DDR, vol. 2, 2nd ed., East Berlin 1970, 75. On the Russian armaments problems in the area of artillery, see Fuller, "Die Ostfront," 45f.

48. The 11th Army was organized into four German army corps with a total of eight German infantry divisions: the Guards Corps, with the 1st and 2nd Guards Infantry Divisions; the Kneussl Corps, the 119th Infantry Division and the 11th Bavarian Infantry Division; the X Army Corps, consisting of the 19th and 20th Infantry Divisions; and the XXXXI Reserve Corps with the 81st and 82nd Reserve Divisions. It also included the VI Austro-Hungarian Army Corps, with the 12th Austro-Hungarian Infantry Division, the 39th Honved (Hungarian) Infantry Division, and the 10th Austro-Hungarian Cavalry Division. On the contest over the intellectual credit for the breach at Gorlice, see Afflerbach, *Falkenhayn,* 287–90.

49. See ibid., 291f.

50. For a detailed description of the operation and an evaluation of lessons learned, see *Der Weltkrieg,* vol. 7, 23–25.

51. Ibid., 373.

52. The breach is described in detail in the *War Journal of the 11th Bavarian Infantry Division* (Abschrift des KTB der 11. bayerischen Infanterie-Division, 24.4.–30.6.1915, BA-MA, PH 8I/442), and at the army level it is described in the *War Journal of the 11th Army* (Kriegstagebuch des Oberkommandos der 11 Armee, BA-MA, PH 5II/303).

53. For a detailed description of the battle, see *Der Weltkrieg,* vol. 7, 346–443; *Der grosse Krieg 1914–1918,* edited by Max Schwarte, vol. 2, *Der deutsche Landkrieg. Vom Frühjahr 1915 bis zum Winter1916/1917,* Leipzig 1923, 124–50.

54. A stinging analysis of the prospects for success of both operations is found in

Max von Gallwitz, *Meine Führertätigkeit im Weltkrieg 1914/1916. Belgien-Osten-Balkan,* Berlin 1929, 373–78. Venohr offers a summary of the discussion in *Ludendorff,* 116–33.

55. For details on the differences between Ober Ost and Falkenhayn, compare Afflerbach, *Falkenhayn,* 305–13; Volker Ullrich, "Entscheidung im Osten oder Sicherung der Dardanellen: Das Ringen um den Serbienfeldzug 1915. Beitrag zum Verhältnis von Politik und Kriegführung im Ersten Weltkrieg." In: *MGM,* 32 (1982), 45–63, here 50–52.

56. An example for the harshness of battle is found the description of the crossing of the Narev by the II Battalion of the regiment on 23 August 1915. According to Lieutenant Tröbst, who in July 1915 was adjutant in the "Generalfeldmarschall von Hindenburg" Infantry Regiment (2 Masurian Infantry Division No. 147): "Half an hour later, the companies began to vacate their previous positions and one troop at a time, or one person at a time, returned, beaten to weariness, more of a passive herd than human looking. . . . First off, Kramme ordered the counting of casualties. In dead, wounded, and missing, there were three officers, 261 *Unteroffiziere* (NCOs) and soldiers. In plain words, this meant that over half of the battalion had been taken by the devil." Excerpt from the journal of Hauptmann Hans Tröbst. Kindly provided by Mr. Cord Christian Troebst.

57. A detailed description of the offensive by the Central Powers up to the end of 1915 may be found in *Der grosse Krieg,* 143–228; *Der Weltkrieg,* vol. 8, 103–597.

58. Gallwitz evaluates the accomplishments of the Russian soldiers as follows: "The Russian soldier proved once again to be hard working, unassuming, and inured to pressure and casualties. Even to the end, the enormous number of bloody losses and captives have not been able to break down the bearing of the troops; each section of the terrain found them ready to defend once more; their ability to march was brilliant." Gallwitz, *Meine Führertätigkeit,* 378.

59. Ibid.

60. See Jost Dülffer, *Regeln gegen den Krieg? Die Haager Friedenskonferenzen von 1899 und 1907 in der internationalen Politik,* Berlin 1981, 22–25.

61. See Afflerbach, *Falkenhayn,* 294–305; Ullrich, *Entscheidung im Osten,* 46–48.

62. Afflerbach, *Falkenhayn,* 294f.

63. See Scheibe, "Marne," 366f.

64. Afflerbach, *Falkenhayn,* 307.

65. See also Wolfgang Foerster, *West-oder Ostenentscheidung im Winter 1915?* Ms., BA-MA, W-10/51315.

66. Regarding Falkenhayn's behavior during the winter months of 1914, an indirect diagnosis was undertaken by several psychologists on behalf of the Reich Archives. Their files form a basis for the study by Wilhelm Solger in 1937 on Falkenhayn as chief of the General Staff of the German Field Army. In it the psychologists stated that it was not a matter of Falkenhayn's failed capabilities, "but the fact that at that time he was not fully committed to the war situation due to something lacking inwardly." Further, Falkenhayn's problem "is not one of thinking, but of the will." BA-MA, W-10/50709, fols. 18, 23.

67. Gallwitz states that the fleet of vehicles of the 54th Infantry Division, which had been relocated from the west, could not cope with the transport and weather conditions in Russia and the advance was delayed for this reason. Gallwitz, *Meine Führertätigkeit,* 309.

68. Gallwitz describes the slow pace of the advance and the problems with supply as follows: "In those ten weeks my right flank had covered about 450 kilometers, my left 320: that is, a daily average of only 6.5 to 4.5 kilometers. In this manner, soon the forces of the columns could no longer overcome the increasing demands and could not adjust quickly enough to the new rail system." Ibid., 374.

4

Russia versus Germany

The Eastern Front of the First World War from 1914 to 1915

Boris Khavkin

The Russian Empire's operations during the First World War may be a somewhat unfamiliar topic in the west, but in Russia they have actually been forgotten. As surprising as it may seem, Russian schoolchildren of today know more about the 1812 war against Napoleon, known as the War of the Fatherland, than about the First World War.

The tragedy of the First World War has been pushed from the awareness of Russians by more horrifying, overwhelming events. There were the Revolutions of February and October 1917, and the Civil War of 1918 to 1922; there was the terror of the 1920s and 1930s that led to the destruction of whole social groups such as the Cossacks, the czarist officers and officials, the clerics, and the Kulaks at the hands of the Bolsheviks; and, between 1932 and 1934 there was forced collectivization and mass starvation. Then came the Second World War, and with it the deportation of entire ethnic peoples such as the Volga Germans, the Crimean Tatars, the Greeks, the Chechen, and the Ingush.

The cemeteries of soldiers who fell in the battlefields during the First World War were mostly destroyed, anniversary dates went unobserved, and heroes were forgotten.[1] Even the colloquial term "German War" fell from use, and the world war was renamed "the War of Imperialism." Only among Russian émigrés was the culture of remembrance of the First World War maintained.

In Soviet historiography, the First World War was viewed exclusively from the perspective of social class. The War of Imperialism was seen as having been a kind of prologue to revolution and civil war.[2] After the October Revolution of 1917, the Bolsheviks publicized secret documents that demonstrated the Russian government's share in the responsibility for the outbreak of the war in 1914, casting czarism in a bad light.[3] By this time, there had also been several articles published by eyewitnesses and participants in the war.[4]

In recent years, a number of Russian academic papers on the history of the First World War represent a new approach to this subject, although these efforts are currently little known by the general public.[5] Nevertheless, there is an old saying, "For Europe, the twentieth century began in the year 1914," underscoring the extreme importance of the First World War as a part of the world history of the twentieth century. And in Russia, the political, military, mental, and cultural experiences of the First World War are still waiting to be researched and woven into its historical memory.

Russia's Military Plans

The first visible signs of organized preparations by the Russian Empire for a large European war were in 1880, when the chief of the Russian General Staff, General Obruchev, presented his plans to Czar Alexander II for the conduct of war against its most probable enemies—Germany and Austria-Hungary. This planning was driven by the fact that in 1879, Germany and Austria-Hungary had sealed their military alliance against Russia.

In the decades that followed, the Russian General Staff revised its military plans three times in conjunction with changes in personnel strength of the Russian Army, the relocations of troops, and the development of the railway system. The Mobilization Plan of 1890 already provided for two deployment variations. One was in case Germany launched its main attack against Russia, the second in case Germany attacked France first (in which case Russia would direct its operations against Austria-Hungary). The General Staff's next war plan originated in 1900. This plan is noteworthy because for the first time, an intermediate level of command in the theater of war, that is, a High Command of the Fronts, was created. All armies on the western border of Russia were to be incorporated into one of two groups: the Northern Front (against Germany) and the Southern Front (against Austria-Hungary).

Although the General Staff began drawing up a new mobilization plan at the end of 1913, it was still unfinished at the beginning of the war. Therefore, the Russian armies deployed according to the old Mobilization Plan of 1900. Like the Mobilization Plan of 1890, this one had two variations: if Germany, in alliance with Austria-Hungary, deployed its main forces against Russia, the Russian Army was to follow Variation G (from the Russian word *Germaniia,* Germany). This meant that the larger portion of the Russian troops were to march toward East Prussia in the direction of Königsberg (now Kaliningrad,

Russia), in order to then move offensively against Berlin from the East Prussian and Polish deployment area.

If Germany should make its main attack against France, then Russia was to follow Variation A (from the Russian word "*Avstriia*," Austria), which meant that the Russian Army, after concentrating south of Polesje, was to carry out an offensive against Austria-Hungary. The ultimate aim of the Variation A offensive was to capture Vienna and Budapest. Prior to this it would be necessary to destroy the Austro-Hungarian forces positioned in Galicia. In addition, the troops from the Ivangorod-Kovel front (now Deblin, Poland–Kovel, Ukraine) were to be sent ahead around the Carpathians from the west in the direction of Cracow. These operations would ensure that the Austro-Hungarian troops would be cut off from convenient retreat routes.

For the deployment of the Russian troops in 1914, Variation A was adopted. Acting in accordance with this variation, however, the Russian Army would actually begin with an offensive against Germany, to take place on the fifteenth mobilization day, with a concentration of eight hundred thousand men. The strategic goal was to divert German forces from the western front. In accordance with Variation A, the Russian Northwest Front deployed on the sector that ran through Schaulen-Kovno (Russian Savli, now Siauliai-Kaunas, Lithuania)-Neman-Narev-West Bug. Forces consisted of the 1st and 2nd Armies (nineteen field infantry divisions, eleven infantry divisions of the second echelon, and nine and a half cavalry divisions). Deployed against Austria-Hungary, on the line of the Southwest Front that ran through Ivangorod-Lublin-Cholm (now Chelm, Poland)-Dubno-Proskurov (now Khmelnytskyi, Ukraine), were the 3rd, 4th, 5th, and 8th Armies (thirty-three and a half field infantry divisions, thirteen infantry divisions of the second echelon, and eighteen and a half cavalry divisions). Ultimately the Russian armies had the mission of transitioning to the offensive in order to move the war onto German and Austro-Hungarian territory.

Because mutual tensions had also developed between Russia and Turkey, the General Staff had developed a plan in case of a war against Turkey as well. A separate plan of action for the Russian naval forces was worked out for each fleet.

In the professional literature, the czarist government is traditionally blamed for the poor preparation of the Russian Army and of the arms industry for war. And it was true that in terms of artillery, especially heavy artillery, the army ranked behind Germany; in quantity of vehicles, they were behind France; and the Russian fleet was behind that of the Germans. Over the course of the war, there was found to be a shortage of grenades, cartridges, rifles, clothing, and equipment.[6] In fairness, however, it must be also be pointed out that among the general staffs of the countries that would later enter the war, no one foresaw that the war would last four years, three and a half months. No country owned enough weapons, equipment, or food supplies for such a long period of time. The general staffs of the enemy had calculated they would be able to cease fighting within three to four months, or at the latest in half a year.

Overall, however, despite the fact that the development program adopted for the army and navy shortly before the war could not be realized until 1917 and 1918, the Russian Armed Forces represented impressive fighting power even in 1914. Their fighting power, which had been drained by the Russo-Japanese War and the Revolution of 1905, had been gradually restored by the second decade of the twentieth century.

Russia's Entry into the War

Russia entered the First World War proclaiming it was a war to "preserve Orthodoxy and Slavdom." Participation stemmed from the imperialist aims of czarism and a ruling elite who could not tolerate the very thought of giving up the role of major power, even to the smallest extent. Particularly in the Balkans, no thought was given to alternatives to an offensive Russian policy. The imperialist policy of the state converged with the patriotic national mindset of the general Russian public, whom the government urged into war. This played an important part in the crisis of summer 1914.

On 16 July 1914 (29 July on the Gregorian calendar), after Austria-Hungary had opened hostilities against Serbia, Czar Nicholas II signed the ukase for a partial mobilization.[7] But on the following day the czar rescinded it. A telegram from the German kaiser had arrived that Nicholas construed as a plea to stop war from breaking out. He was ultimately convinced otherwise by Foreign Minister S. D. Sazonov, who argued that it was "better to carefully prepare for this without concern for the war breaking out as a result of our preparations than to fear providing a pretense for war and to be taken by surprise." This impressed Nicholas II, and on 17 (30) July 1914, he therefore signed the ukase for total mobilization.

Germany then issued Russia an ultimatum to suspend its mobilization. The German ambassador in Petrograd was Friedrich Graf Pourtales, who was personally against a war with Russia. On 19 July (1 August) 1914, he presented Sazonov with a written message containing Germany's declaration of war.

Between the beginning of the general mobilization and the preparation of its main forces, the Russian Army conducted border forays to draw attention away from the strategic deployment of its troops elsewhere. For reconnaissance, Cossacks were deployed as mobile groups of light cavalry.

On the forty-fifth day of the war, Russia's military had finished its mobilization. In total, 3,915,000 men had been called up from the reserves. Of this number, 3,115,000 were lower-level military (soldiers), officers, physicians, civilian employees (military bureaucrats with duty in the rear), and Cossacks; along with these were 800,000 soldiers of the first class (members of the Landwehr). Before the declaration of general mobilization, Russia's overall military had numbered 1,423,000 men; by mid-September the Russian Army alone totaled 5,338,000 men. This meant that in terms of personnel strength, the Czarist Empire had the strongest land military in the world. As supreme commander of the Russian Army, the czar appointed his uncle, Grand Duke Nikolai Nikolaevich, and as chief of the General Staff, General N. N. Januskevic.[8]

At the beginning of the war, Russia deployed on two fronts with two independent armies:

- the Northwest Front against Germany;
- the Southwest Front against Austria-Hungary;
- the independent (Petrograd) 6th Army to guard the Baltic Sea coast;
- the independent (Odessa) 7th Army to guard the Black Sea coast.[9]

The Course of Russia's Operations against Germany and Austria-Hungary in 1914

A written report to the czar from the supreme commander of the Russian Army, Grand Duke Nikolai Nikolaevich, shows that at the beginning of the campaign of 1914, pursuant to the supreme commander's operations plan, Russian military leaders intended to conduct an immediate offensive against Berlin with the forces of the Northwest Front (under commander in chief General Jakov G. Zhilinski) and an operation against Vienna with the forces of the Southwest Front (under commander in chief General N. I. Ivanov). On the eastern front at this time the enemy had a relatively small force, consisting of twenty-six German and forty-six Austrian divisions. The French armies on the western front, as is well known, were not planning an immediate offensive but were waiting for the result of the Russian offensive.

The Operation in East Prussia

Between 4 and 7 August 1914, the troops of the Russian Northwest Front, as requested by the French General Staff, pushed into East Prussia. (It will also be recalled that at this same time the German armies were invading Belgium in an attempt to encircle the left flank of the French Army.) As the chief of staff of the Northwestern Front, General V. A. Oranovskij, and others reported, Russia began the East Prussia operation despite the fact that the Russian troops were not yet ready for an offensive.

The 1st Army, under the command of General Paul K. Rennenkampf, and the 2nd Army, under General Aleksandr V. Samsonov, pushed into East Prussia, forced the German 8th Army to retreat in the battle of Goldap-Gumbinnen (now Gusev, Russia), and initiated an attack on Königsberg. In response, German leaders relocated considerable forces (two army corps and one cavalry division) from the west to East Prussia. The French Army took advantage of this change in the situation to mount a counterattack on the weakened German troops and halt the German offensive toward Paris.

Between the end of August and the beginning of September 1914, during the East Prussia operation, a turning point occurred. In the battles of the Russian 2nd Army at Tannenberg (26–30 August 1914) and on the Masurian Lakes (8–11 September 1914), one and a half Russian Army corps were encircled and the survivors captured. The Russian 1st Army was then defeated and pushed back out of East Prussia. The two Russian armies lost a total of 250,000 soldiers and officers (dead, wounded, captured, or missing) along with a considerable quantity of weapons and equipment.

The defeat came about primarily because the Russian soldiers were not prepared for an offensive and the operations were conducted poorly by the commander in chief of the Northwestern Front, General Zhilinski. Another factor was the resolute and professionally skilled operation by Generalfeldmarschall Paul von Hindenburg, who had replaced Generaloberst Maximilian Graf von Prittwitz as commander of the German 8th Army, and his chief of staff, Erich von Ludendorff.[10]

Russia's offensive operations at the beginning of the war, however, were not limited to the East Prussia operation. In August and September 1914, in the Warsaw area and the new fortress of Novo Georgievsk (now Modlin, Poland), the country's forces were concentrated for the main strategic strike against Berlin. In October and November, two large battles were carried out on the Polish territory between Russian and German armies at Warsaw-Ivangorod and at Lódź. Both sides fielded over eight hundred thousand men. Although Russian military historians depict the Russian operations as more successful, neither the Germans nor the Russians achieved their goals.

The Operation at Warsaw-Ivangorod

In September and October 1914, the troops of the Northwestern Front (under their new commander, General N. W. Russkij) and of the Southwestern Front (General N. I. Ivanov) successfully stopped the Austrian and German offensive against Warsaw and Ivangorod. The German and Austrian troops had attempted to throw the Russians across the Vistula in an effort to deflect the danger of invasion into Germany's eastern territory.

To this purpose, on 15 September 1914, the Austro-Hungarian 1st Army and the German 9th Army, numbering 310,000 men, transitioned to an offensive against Warsaw and Ivangorod. For its part, the Russian leadership had planned an offensive operation and had therefore relocated four armies (the

2nd, the 4th, the 5th, and the 9th) to the Vistula. But only scattered units reached their assigned sections of the front, and by the beginning of October the Germans were stronger in numbers. On 25 September, two corps of the German 9th Army pushed into the area of Ivangorod up to the Vistula and began a bombardment of this fortress. But they were unable to achieve anything more. On that day, units of the Russian 4th Army (General A. E. Evert) succeeded in crossing the Vistula in this area and establishing themselves on its left bank. They captured a deployment area at Kozienice, from which point Ivangorod could be secured. In a heavy fifteen-day battle, the Russians were able not only to maintain possession of the deployment area but also to expand it.

On 24 September a German assault group under the command of Generaloberst August von Mackensen launched an offensive in the direction of Warsaw. Three days later in the battles at Grojec, thirty kilometers from Warsaw, Mackensen's troops began to push back the Siberian II Corps, which suffered major losses. At this critical moment, the Siberian 1st Infantry Division arrived to relieve its comrades and blocked the route to the Polish capital. At the end of September, the attacks from the Mackensen group were repulsed at the line of the Warsaw forts.

Russian leaders continually brought new reinforcements to the Vistula line. As of 5 October they increased the pressure on the German 9th Army, which began to weaken. In order to reassemble the scattered units, von Hindenburg, who commanded the German and Austrian troops in the area of Warsaw, sheltered his units in the region of Ivangorod, which belonged to the Austro-Hungarian Army (Generaloberst Victor Dankl von Krasnik). Dankl's persistent attempts between 8 and 13 October to destroy the Russian Kozienice deployment area had failed. On 13 October the Russian 9th Army under General P. A. Lecickij pushed back the advanced Austro-Hungarian units and attacked the flank of the Austro-Hungarian 1st Army. Now the tide had turned, and the entire Austrian-German front stood under threat of a breach by the Russians.

Due to heavy losses (up to 50 percent of their personnel) the German and Austrian troops were no longer able to effectively stop the onslaught of Russian troops, whose numbers in this section of the front had by this time increased to as many as five hundred thousand men. Hindenburg feared a breach by the Russians at Warsaw and Ivangorod, which could have led to defeat and encirclement of the German 9th Army. On 14 October, he ordered German and Austrian troops to retreat.

But the Russian armies were unable to pursue the enemy vigorously and effectively. The Russian rear services had not sufficiently prepared for an offensive, the unpaved roads were impassable in autumn, and further, the retreating troops had destroyed the travel routes. By the end of October, Hindenburg was essentially able to avoid a final defeat and lead the troops back in an organized manner to their starting positions. On 26 October, the Russian counteroffensive on the Lask-Przedborz-Mechow-Kosice line came to a standstill because the troops were unable to advance. Their rear services remained more than 150 kilometers back and were not able to supply the attackers with sufficient food and munitions.

Although the Russians had not managed a complete victory, the operation at Warsaw-Ivangorod represented one of the greatest battles of the First World War and one of the few examples of a successful counteroffensive by Russian troops against the German Army. The battle represents a stage of development in the Russian art of war; it was the first operation in Russian military history in which two fronts cooperated with one another. Also important is the outcome of this battle in terms of foreign policy: the Central Powers' failure at Warsaw and Ivangorod and the defeat in Galicia prevented them from bringing the Balkan countries onto their side in 1914.

The Battles at Lódź and Galicia

During the course of the operation at Lódź between 29 October (11 November) and 11 (24) November 1914, the Russian 2nd and 5th Armies foiled German leaders' plans for encirclement and pushed the German 9th Army back from the area of Lódź. Then the Russian troops themselves had to retreat from Lódź on 9 December 1914 under pressure from the enemy. The Russians' attempt to advance from northern Poland to Germany failed.

In August 1914, the Russian 3rd and 8th Armies of the Southwestern Front began an offensive against the Austrians. It developed successfully and led to the occupation of Galicia. On 21 August 1914 they captured Lwów (Lemberg; now L'viv, Ukraine). In order to ensure the success of this offensive, Grand Duke Nikolai Nikolaevich's troops from the Warsaw area were relocated to the Southwestern Front. This simultaneously meant the end of plans to attack Berlin. The main focus of Russian Army operations now shifted to the south, against Austria-Hungary.

On 12 (25) September 1914, the offensive on the Southwestern Front was discontinued. Within thirty-three days, the Russian troops had advanced between 280 and 300 kilometers, had reached the Wisloka River, and had come within 80 kilometers of Cracow. They lay siege to the powerful fortress of Przemyśl and occupied a part of Bukovina, including its administrative center at Czernowitz (now Cernivci, Ukraine). The Austrians losses reached four hundred thousand men, one hundred thousand of whom became prisoners of war; four hundred of their cannons were now in Russian hands as well. The offensive operation in Galicia was one of the most significant victories by the Russian Army in the First World War.

At the end of November 1914, during a conference in the city of Brest-Litovsk, the Russian Army's commanders made the decision to halt offensive operations for a time. Until January 1915 a kind of armistice reigned on the eastern front.

Thus, none of the warring parties attained their originally intended goals as a result of the battles of 1914. The German plan to defeat the enemy in lightning quick attacks in, first in the west and then in the east, had failed, leaving Germany entangled in a long-term two-front war. The Russian offensive in East Prussia had been defeated by the Germans, and an attack on Berlin never took place. The Russian Army's largest success had been achieved in Galicia.

The Campaigns of 1915

The Russian operations plan for 1915 provided for the preparation and implementation of one offensive in the Carpathians and another in East Prussia. The goal of the campaign was victory in 1915.

Despite the fiasco of 1914, the German Army High Command (OHL) also counted on being able to end the war in 1915. The shortage of forces did not permit the Germans to attack on two fronts, in the west and in the east. It was therefore decided that, while conducting defensive operations in the west, they would launch their main attack against Russia. This would bring the war to an end, and the Russians would be coerced into a peace agreement advantageous to Germany, after which Germany would be able to attack in the west with more strength. The sequence of these operations was also influenced by the difficult situation of Austria-Hungary, which had suffered several defeats in Galicia and Serbia and urgently needed the help of its main ally, Germany. Thus, in 1915 the Russian Army carried the heaviest war burden of all of the Entente countries.

Winter Operations in East Prussia and the Carpathians

The German OHL wanted to preempt a Russian attack. On 25 January 1915, an offensive operation was launched by the German 10th and 8th Armies from the direction of East Prussia. The goal was to defeat the Russian 10th Army under General Sievers, which stood in the area between the Neman River and the Masurian Lakes. The Germans did in fact succeed in encircling and destroying a Russian corps near Minsk, but they did not win a sweeping victory because by 13 February the main forces of the 10th Army were able to pull back to the Kovno-Osowiec section of the border. Nor did the attack by German troops at Prassnysch (now Przasnysz, Poland) succeed against the Russian 12th and 1st Armies.

On 17 February (2 March), the Russian 1st, 12th, and 10th Armies seized the initiative in a coordinated offensive. Their enemy put up a fierce defense, and the battles became protracted. It was not until the later part of the month of

March that the German units fell back to the border of East Prussia. Here they entrenched and transitioned into the defense from positions that had been prepared earlier. Attempts by the Russian armies to breach their enemy's defenses were unsuccessful, and at the end of March, the operation at Przasnysz ended. During the course of the operation, the troops of the Northwest Front were able to push the Germans back to the central section of the Niemen, the Bobr, and the Narev Rivers.

Because of the protracted winter battles, the Russian offensive against East Prussia never took place, nor were the Germans ever able to carry out their plan for a deep envelopment of the right flank of the Russian front.

On the southern flank of the eastern front, Russian leaders initiated an operation in January 1915 in the Carpathians that was greatly hampered by winter conditions. Despite high losses, the Russians were able to push the enemy back but still achieved no significant victories. Then, after a Russian bombardment on 9 March, the Austrian fortress Przemyśl capitulated; nine generals, twenty-five hundred officers, and 120,000 enemy soldiers were taken prisoner, and nine hundred cannons were captured. It was the first such victory the Entente had won. But around 29 March, lacking resources, munitions, and equipment, the Russian offensive in the Carpathians came to a halt.

The Gorlice Operation

The most serious and dangerous event on the eastern front was the breakthrough by Austrian and German troops at Gorlice on 19 April 1915. The direction of the attack had been toward Lwów (Lemberg). Their goal was to defeat the Russian troops on the Southwestern Front and capture Galicia. The breakthrough occurred along a thirty-five-kilometer segment of the front by forces of Mackensen's Army Group. Along with Austrian troops, this army group contained four German Army corps that had been brought in from the French front. Its infantry was twice as large as that of the Russians, and its artillery was five times greater (forty times greater in heavy cannons). Thus, against the Russian X Corps alone, which would have to sustain the main attack by the Germans, the army group deployed fifty heavy cannons and many hundreds of field cannons. The total Russian 3rd Army (under General D. R. Radko-Dmitriev), in contrast, was composed of seven corps but had only four heavy cannons and had to hold a two-hundred-kilometer front. In addition, in defending against the enemy barrage, the artillerymen of the Russian 3rd Army could not fire more than five to ten rounds per day per cannon. In a telegram to the minister of war, the commander of the Russian XXIX Corps, General D. P. Suev, reported: "The Germans riddle the battlefields with a hail of metal and make various trenches and fortifications that resemble the terrain, whereby their defenders are often buried in the earth. They use metal; we, on the other hand, use human lives!

They advance on the wings of victory and because of this, they are bold, while we simply defend at the price of heavy losses and spilled blood and then yield. This has an extremely unfavorable effect on everyone's morale."[11]

The deficiencies in provisions for the army stemmed mainly from the inadequate preparation prior to the war, the irresponsibility of the directors of the War Office, and racketeering by various bureaucrats and contractors. "Nothing but scoundrels everywhere," raged the czar by the beginning of 1915, "no boots, no weapons there—one must attack, but cannot attack at all."[12]

Simultaneously with the breach at the area of Gorlice, the Germans conducted offensives against the northern flank of the eastern front: on 14 April 1915, the army group under Generaloberst Max von Gallwitz began an offensive from the area of Tilsit (now Sovetsk, Russia); ten days later, they took Libau (now Liepája, Latvia) and then proceeded toward Schaulen and Kovno.

The Summer Defensive Operations in Poland and the Baltic Region

In mid-June 1915, the Russian armies still operated in the framework of two combined front units. The Northwestern Front under General M. V. Alekseyev was comprised of eight armies (the 1st, 2nd, 3rd, 4th, 5th, 10th, 12th, and 13th). The border between the fronts ran through the area of Sandomierz.

The enemy forces were also combined into two groups. On the German eastern front was the Niemen Army, the 8th, 9th, 10th, and 12th Armies, and the "Woyrsch" army section under commander in chief von Hindenburg and his chief of staff Ludendorff. The Austro-Hungarian Galician front consisted of the 1st, 2nd, 4th, 7th, 11th, and the South Armies, under the command of Archduke Friedrich and Conrad von Hötzendorf. The border between the two fronts belonging to the Central Powers was formed by the Pilica River.

A peculiarity of the course of the front line was that in its middle section it had the shape of an arc that bowed out toward the German troops. The main bulk of the Russian Army was located inside the area delineated by this arc, an area to which Poland's central territories belonged. This meant that these forces were surrounded on two sides by the enemy, giving them an unfavorable strategic position. The leaders of the Central Powers had the possibility of carrying out two new major operations, one out of the north (from East Prussia) and one out of the south (from Galicia).

In the summer of 1915 the OHL had plans to encircle the aggregation of Russian troops standing in Poland. For this, three major operations would be carried out, one by Mackensen's Army Group between the Vistula and the Bug, one in the area of Riga-Schaulen, and one on the Narev. All operations took place simultaneously and placed the highest Russian unit commanders in a difficult situation.

The Austrian-German Army High Command (AOK, Armeeoberkommando) began implementation of its strategic plan immediately after the arrival of the Austro-Hungarian troops at Lwów (Lemberg), which had been emptied of Russians. From the end of June to early July 1915, the German and Austro-Hungarian troops initiated an offensive along the entire front, and an intense three-month battle erupted. The Russians put up a stubborn defense, and for this reason the enemy was able to advance only slowly, under frequent delays and the necessary reassembling of troops.

The German and Austro-Hungarian Army Group (the Austro-Hungarian 4th Army and the German 11th Army) was under the command of Mackensen, who by this time had been promoted to field marshal. Its task was to move north and conduct offensive operations between the Vistula and the Bug, and repulse the southern flank of the Russians, who had moved into Poland.

The three armies of the right flank (the 2nd, the South, and the 7th) were to continue their offensive and safeguard Mackensen's operation from the east. By this means the Austro-Hungarian AOK hoped to permanently force the Russians out of Galicia.

The offensive by Mackensen's Army Group in the strip of land between the Vistula and the Bug began on 13 (26) June 1915 and developed extremely slowly. Mackensen overcame resistance from the armies of the Russian Southwest Front, but it required great effort and by mid-July he had not gotten across the Lublin-Cholm line.

Nor did the Narev operation, which was carried out between 30 June (13 July) and 20 July (2 August) by the forces of Gallwitz's 12th Army, bring the Germans any notable success. The Gallwitz Army Group covered a strip of more than 140 kilometers from the Rozoga River at Myszyniec to the Vistula at Plock. On its right stood the 9th Army of Leopold von Bayern, and to its left stood Scholz's 8th Army. At the start of the battle, the Russian 12th Army under General Litvinov had 177,000 men and 1,255 cannons. The Russians deployed the 1st Army under General Litvinov and the left flank of the 12th Army (the IV Siberian Corps) against the enemy forces. These totaled 107,000 men and 377 cannons. Left of the Russian 1st Army stood the Russian 2nd Army, echeloned toward the rear, on the west bank of the Vistula.

The Russian fortified positions consisted of two defense lines that were five to six kilometers distant from one another, and a rear defense position that lay fifteen to sixteen kilometers to the rear of the first defense line. Only the first line, which included fully developed trenches, wire barriers, and various shelters, was visible to the enemy. The second line and the rear defense position consisted only of trenches. The 1st Army was tasked with holding its positions until the completion of the evacuation of Warsaw. Great dedication was given to the development of the defense system, which meant digging protective and connecting trenches as well as constructing artificial obstacles. The Russian munitions supply was very low; there was a shortage of artillery rounds (the daily norm had been set at five rounds per cannon) and even of rifle cartridges. Thousands of soldiers were without even a rifle.

General Gallwitz decided to launch the chief attack with the main forces of his army in the direction of Prassnysch. To breach the Russian's fortified strip, the enemy concentrated its seven infantry divisions and 860 cannons in a thirty-five-kilometer–long section in the area of Prassnysch. Each cannon was provided with six hundred to a thousand rounds. The Russians defended the breach with two infantry divisions (the 11th and the 2nd Siberian Divisions). The Army Reserve consisted of the 1st Siberian Division, which was located one day's march behind the front line. The German side once more had an overwhelming superiority in infantry and artillery in the field.

At five in the morning of 30 June (13 July) the Germans began with a massive artillery bombardment of the trenches of the first line of the Russian positions. The intensive artillery preparations lasted five hours and ended with several barrages. Then the infantry attack began. Despite the overwhelming superiority and intensive artillery preparation by the Germans, which cost the defenders extremely high losses (up to 30 percent), the battle over the first line of defense lasted all day. The Russian soldiers displayed such fortitude and persistence that the enemy was stunned. It was not until evening that the German units were able to get close to the second line of defense. On the eve of 1 (14) July, the troops of the Russian 1st Army pulled back to their rear defense position. The enemy resumed the attack the next day, 2 (15) July. The four and a half divisions of the Russian 1st Army were attacked by ten German divisions. Once again, the enemy had to overcome strong resistance from the Russians and fend off counterattacks. Bitter fighting flared up in local villages, where the Germans had to carry on their assault house by house, taking high losses. Alekseyev reinforced Litvinov's army with troops pulled from the 2nd and 4th Armies and the garrison of Novo Georgievsk. The deployment of these forces made it possible for the Russians to come to a halt at the bridgehead positions at the cities of Rozan, Pultusk, and Serock. The Germans' attempt to cross the Narev failed completely, and on 5 (18) July their operation came to a halt. Over the six days of the battle at Prassnysch, the German 12th Army, despite its overwhelming superiority, was able to advance only twenty-five to thirty kilometers, sustaining heavy losses. The Russians were not defeated, only forced from their positions and pushed back as far as the Narev.

The OHL, concerned about the lack of success, insisted on a further offensive across the Narev and southward, on toward Mackensen's Army Group. Feldmarschall von Hindenburg gave the order to the 8th and 12th Armies to finish with their preparations in very short order and resume the operation.

On the eve of 10 (23) July, the Germans attacked the bridgehead at Rozan. With this began the battle at Narev. The attack came as a surprise to the Russians, who had to fall back to their second defensive line. One and a half Russian divisions faced three German divisions. The Germans were able to advance to the river south of Rozan. The danger of a further advance into the Russian rear area forced the Russians to leave Rozan and retreat to the left riverbank of the Narev. Between Rozan and Pultusk, where units of the Siberian I Corps that had been most damaged during the battle at Prassnysch were on the retreat, the Germans crossed the Narev with no difficulty.

The German conquering of the Narev was the most important outcome of the battle at Rozan and Pultusk. Now the route to Siedlce was free, and the conditions were right for an attack by German troops on the retreat routes of the Russian 2nd Army. But the sector at Serock-Novo Georgievsk had well-secured forts that held the crossing points on the Neman River. The position at Serock formed the flank on the Bug and Narev. The terrain between the Narev and the Bug to the west was swampy. All of these conditions saved the Russians from having to organize a defense in this area. The enemy's attempts to cross the Narev below Pultusk failed. The area of Pultusk-Wyszkow was covered by two Russian corps, and the offensive by the German troops was brought to a halt.

The battle at Narev was one of the most instructive engagements from the military historical standpoint. Of great significance was how the occupation of the Osowiec and Novo Georgievsk fortresses influenced combat operations. They secured the flank of the Russian 12th and 1st Armies, thus limiting German leaders' latitude for operations and forcing them to launch their attack against the central sector, which the Russians had secured well with the help of engineering technology. In the context of the conduct of battle, the troops involved gathered worthwhile information about fighting in fortified positions, crossing water impediments, and defending from poorly prepared rear sectors.

The Riga-Schaulen Operation

By 1 (14) July the German Niemen Army consisted of six infantry and five cavalry divisions, two infantry and two cavalry brigades, and two independent detachments (*Abteilungen*) totaling seventeen units. These forces were combined into two groups: the northern, or Lauenstein Corps, and the southern, or Richthofen Cavalry Corps. The Niemen Army had 115,000 to 120,000 men and over 600 cannons.

Opposite them stood the Russian 5th Army, consisting of four infantry and six cavalry divisions along with three infantry and two cavalry brigades, totaling 117,000 men, 10,000 of whom were without weapons. The army owned 365 cannons. Later, two Siberian divisions, the 12th and 13th, located in Mitau (Russian Mitava, now Jelgava, Latvia) and Riga respectively, were brought in. These had as many as 20,000 men. But two divisions previously brought from Galicia could not be prepared in time and had a significant shortage of weapons. They were unable to have any impact on events.

The enemies faced one another across an expansive 250-kilometer front. The Germans had no operational reserves, but their forces were approximately equal to that of the Russians. In the area of artillery, the Germans had almost twice the strength of the Russians, however, and were better stocked with munitions. The initiative lay in the hands of the Army High Command. To exploit the advantage, the Niemen Army was given the task of occupying the area of Mitau-Ponewesch (Russian Poneves, now Panevezys, Lithuania).This was supposed to create favorable conditions for the next operation, which would be an attack against Vilnius by circumventing Kovno from the north. From there, the army would have the possibility of proceeding in the direction of Riga and Dünaburg (now Dvinsk, Latvia).

The Russian military leaders understood how important it was to hold the Riga-Schaulen area. A German victory would be dangerous because it would bring the enemy closer to the front line of what was at that time the Russian capital, Petrograd. But limited resources and means did not permit the Russians to prepare offensive actions. They decided to limit themselves to the defense. Their task came down to ensuring the defense of Mitau and Dünaburg, and defending the Kovno fortress from the north. Particular attention was paid to holding the area of Schaulen which, because it was centrally located, covered the above mentioned areas.

At eight a.m. on 1 (14) July, General von Below began the offensive by crossing the Windau (Russian Vindava) with the left wing of his army in the direction of Mitau. The Germans were twice the strength of the Russians, but still advanced very slowly. Under pressure from the superior enemy forces, the right flank units of the Russian 5th Army drew back eastward. The Russians' main force defended unwaveringly in the area of Schaulen. The Germans planned to encircle the Russian divisions occupying the center. The units of the northern wing received the order to leave a unit behind to cover Mitau and to proceed toward the southeast, while the southern corps was to lead an attack in the northeastern direction. This points to the intention of closing the ring of encirclement east of Sadow. On the morning of 8 (21) July, the Germans launched their pincer attack.

The commander of the Russian 5th Army, General Pleve, analyzed the situation correctly and realized the enemy's intent. He ordered an immediate retreat in order to pull the troops out of the enemy's grasp. This step, as the Russian military historian G. Korol'kov wrote, "underscores Pleve's moral courage as there were few generals who were capable of making a decision that ran against the command from headquarters, which was: 'Not one step back!'"[13] The troops employed delay tactics in the broadest sense of the word. The corps fell back from one line to the next, using short but energetic counterattacks. In this manner they retained their forces and evaded the enemy's flank attacks. On 8 (21) July the Germans took Schaulen and on 12 (25) July they also took Ponewesch. This ended the twelve-day battle at Schaulen. But the Russians had been able to escape the encirclement, and the ultimate goal of the German pincer attack was not achieved.

With the capture of Ponewesch the German troops had reached the boundary between the Russian 5th and 10th Armies. There was the threat of a German breach in the direction of Vilnius, and at the same time Riga and Dünaburg stood in danger. To reinforce the 5th Army, reserves were sent in—two infantry and one cavalry division. The 12th Army was relocated to the area of Riga. The Germans managed to occupy Mitau on 7 (20) August, but further advances in the direction of Riga and Dünaburg were prevented. Nevertheless, the Niemen Army could not be ousted from Lithuania.

The Riga-Schaulen operation lasted over a month, from 1 (14) July to 7 (20) August 1915. The Germans conquered a wide portion of the territory and pushed the Russian 5th Army back to the western Dvina. Both sides suffered heavy losses. Although superior in every respect, the German enemy was not able to accomplish his main goal, the defeat of the Russian 5th Army. The unique aspect of this operation was the expansiveness of the front; an army had a front sector of 250 kilometers, a corps had 50, and a division had a sector of 20 to 25 kilometers.

The result was that the hopes of the German OHL to encircle and destroy the main body of the Russian armies in Poland and in the Baltic region remained unrealized. The Russian troops were not destroyed; instead they retreated, vacated a considerable area, and still retained their deployment capability.

The German offensive between the Vistula and Bug and on the Narev placed the Russian armies, which were assembled in a central area, in danger of being surrounded. At a 22 June (5 July) 1915 meeting held in Siedlce, the supreme commander, Grand Duke Nikolai Nikolaevich, instructed General Alekseyev, commander of the Northwest Front, to withdraw the armies to the Bobr-Upper Narev-Brest-Litovsk-Kovel line.

General Alekseyev successfully withdrew the troops to the Osowiec-Lomza-Lubartow-Kovel, which was a difficult task strategically. This had foiled the intent of the enemy, which had been to surround the Russian troops on the left bank of the Vistula. The chief of the Great General Staff, General Erich von Falkenhayn, had to face the fact that the summer operations had not accomplished their goal.[14] This realization was shared by Field Marshal Paul von Hindenburg, the supreme commander of German forces in the east. As he wrote, despite the excellent execution of the Narev attack, the operation in the east had not destroyed the enemy; the Russians had escaped and conducted a frontal withdrawal in what was for them a desirable direction.[15]

Fall Operations and the Stabilizing of the Russian Front

On 3 (16) August Nikolaevich held a briefing in Wolkowyusk (now Vaukavyst, Belarus) with the highest military officers from headquarters and the Northwest Front commands during which important resolutions were drawn up concerning plans for further operations. Their substance is set forth in a report by the grand duke to the czar and in the directive from headquarters of 4 (17) August 1915. The situation on the Northwestern Front and the high number of units located there made it necessary to divide them into two new fronts—the Northern and the Western Fronts. General N. W. Russkij, previously the commander of the 6th Army, was named commander in chief of the armies of the Russian Northern Front; the Russian Western Front was placed under General M. V. Alekseyev.

The main mission of the Northern Front consisted of securing the routes from Petrograd to East Prussia and on to the Baltic Sea. First, the armies of this front had to hold the area of the middle Neman because it was crucial to the evolving strategic situation north of Polesje. Second, they had to cover the routes that ran along the right bank of the Neman in the area of Vilnius and as far as the Vilnius-Dünaburg section of the rail line. Third, they had to hold the lower reaches of the Düna from Dünaburg up to and including Riga. At the same time the Northern Front troops were to "strive, at the first available opportunity, to transition to a forceful offensive in order to push back the enemy as far west as possible and force him out of his starting position, a position that favored the development of their plan to circumvent the right flank of our entire strategic front."

The main mission of the Russian Western Front was to secure the routes to Moscow. The armies of this front first had to hold the area of Grodno-Bialystok from the upper Narev up to and including the city of Brest and second to cover the right bank of the upper Bug to the Brest-Kobrin (now White Russian Kobryn)-Pinsk-Luninets.

Under pressure from the enemy's superior forces, the Russian troops had to vacate Galicia, Poland, and Lithuania in the spring and summer of 1915. At the end of September, they had fortified themselves along the Riga-Dünaburg-Baronovici (now Baranavicy, Belarus)-Pinsk-Lutsk-Dubno line and further southward as far as the Romanian border. This meant fighting along a long continuous front of over thirteen hundred kilometers. Afterward, the eastern front froze, and the mobile war transitioned into a static war.

Along the German western front in 1915, both sides prepared themselves for a decisive operation in the year 1916 by urging on the mobilization of their industry and strengthening their armies' technological equipment. The entire burden of the battles of 1915 lay on the Russian Army. Their forced retreat and the efforts by German diplomats to enter into negotiations with Russia for a separate peace caused concern for the Russians' allies and prompted them to consider a united combat action in support of Russia. On 7 July 1915 in Chantilly, an inter-allied war council was formed for this purpose. But Russia received no effective help from its allies either in 1915 or in the following years.

Russia's allies were relieved simply because Russia was fighting against Germany, Austria-Hungary, and Turkey and was thus diverting a significant part of the military potential of these countries. Russia spared no resources in this respect. During the war years in Russia, about 16 million men were called up, more than one-third of the total number of soldiers drafted by all the Entente countries put together. Half of the divisions that the Entente had at their disposal were Russian.

War Experiences from 1914 to 1915 from the Russian Perspective

In 1914 the Russian troops were pushed out of East Prussia, and some thirty thousand Russian soldiers became prisoners of war. Nevertheless, the Germans had to draw from their forces on the western front, with the result that the English and French troops brought the German offensive to a halt during the brutal battle of the Marne. In August and September 1914 the Russian troops inflicted a heavy defeat on the Austro-Hungarian troops in the battle of Galicia, in which they lost about four hundred thousand soldiers. The armies of the Russian Southwestern Front advanced a distance of 280 to 300 kilometers and captured Galicia. The attempt by the Germans to inflict a defeat on the Russian troops in Poland in fall 1914 failed. The casualties inflicted by the Russian soldiers in East Prussia and by the English and French troops on the Marne brought the collapse of the German plan of attack in 1914. Germany and its allies saw themselves faced with a long-term war that would allow the Entente to bring into play its superiority in materiel and personnel, the most important source of which was Russia.

In 1915 the German OHL concentrated strong forces along the eastern front in an effort to defeat Russia or to force it out of the war. The Russian troops, suffering from a catastrophic shortage of weapons and munitions, began to retreat toward the east. After the end of the German offensive in the spring and summer of 1915, Russia had vacated Galicia, Poland, and a portion of the Baltic states and White Russia (Belarus). The military failures of 1915 led to a reshuffling of the Russian Army leadership. In June 1915, Minister of War V. A. Suchomlinov was denounced for treason and discharged. His post went to General A. A. Polivanov. In August 1915, Czar Nicholas II dismissed the Grand Duke Nikolaevich from the post of supreme commander. At the same time, the chief of the General Staff, General Januskevic, was also removed from his position. The czar himself (who as field marshal still ranked below his uncle Nikolai Nikolaevich) then became supreme commander. General M. V. Alekseyev, the son of an ordinary soldier, became the chief of General Staff. Thanks to his abilities, he had had a brilliant military career and enjoyed great authority in the active army. After his appointment, General A. E. Evert took over as commander in chief of Russia's western front.

As the war escalated, its conduct became increasingly gruesome. The Germans deployed chemical weapons for the first time on the eastern front in January 1915, bombarding the Russian troop positions with poison gas shells.[16] On 31 May 1915 the Germans at Wola Szydlowska in the area of Bolimow carried out a gas cylinder attack that resulted in the poisoning deaths of over a thousand Russian soldiers and officers on the defensive strip of the Russian 2nd Army.

Overall, the campaign of 1915 was a tragedy for the Russian Army, which suffered enormous casualties.[17] Nevertheless, Germany was still not able to achieve its main goal of forcing Russia out of the war in 1915.

Conclusions

It is not only in Russia that the eastern front of the First World War is a "forgotten war." In the west, it is also at least an unfamiliar war in many respects. Yet the eastern front was of extraordinary significance. For three and a half years, the Russian Army had to hold a 1,934-kilometer front that extended from the Baltic countries to the Black Sea (along with the 1,100 kilometers of the Caucasian front). Russia stood against the combined forces of Germany, Austria-Hungary, and Turkey. The western front, in contrast, from the English Channel to Switzerland (630 kilometers), had the combined militaries of France, Great Britain, and Belgium, which were further reinforced in 1917 by the American Army. In addition, four Russian brigades were sent to support these allies. Although the war broke out at a time when the Russian Empire had not yet finished the reorganization of its military forces, it still made a major contribution to the victory of the Entente Powers. One might even go so far as to say that in an indirect way Russia saved France as early as at the start of the war in East Prussia when General A. V. Samsonov's army was defeated.

The great loss of Russian lives in the years 1914 and 1915 stemmed from the unsatisfactory leadership of the military forces by the commander in chief of the army and the Russian government, as well as dependence on the demands of the Western Allies when it came to Russia's operational and strategic planning. By the end of 1915, the Russian Army had incurred overall losses of approximately 3 million men, including three hundred thousand dead. Yet although Russia gave up extensive territory, it preserved its resources for further battles.

In the first years of the war the significant socioeconomic discrepancy between the industrially developed countries of Germany, Great Britain, and France on the one hand and the agrarian-industrial country of Russia on the other was clearly brought to light. This discrepancy manifested itself in the shortages of material equipment in the Russian Army, particularly with respect to modern weapons, and the low educational level of most of the soldiers. Moreover, 60 percent of the new Russian recruits lacked sufficient military training.

Clearly recognizable even in the first years of the war was the self-serving policy of Russia's allies, who fought the war "down to the last Russian soldier." The Entente used the eastern front as a counterbalance to the German offensive on the western front and repeatedly forced the highest military and political leaders in Russia, against earlier strategic agreements, to send unprepared troops into the fight. In the end, the Russian military played the role of a "steamroller" in the destruction of a significant portion of the war potential of Germany, Austria-Hungary, and Turkey. Nevertheless, at the end of the war, Russia and its army was not counted among the victors.

The war demanded all of Russia's material reserves. Even in 1915 the shortages of many industrial raw materials and fuel was noticeable. In 1916, these shortages developed into an acute crisis which, along with the failures on the front, created the preconditions for the Revolution of 1917.

The military and political victory over the coalition of Central Powers fell to the United States, Great Britain, France, Italy, and Japan. In Russia, however, because of the revolutions of February and October 1917, the army collapsed, as was seen in the massive desertions and the catastrophic disintegration of discipline among the troops.

Thus, for Russia, the experience of the First World War ended with the collapse of the monarchy and the fall of the empire; the Bolshevik overthrow of the government; Russia's "revolutionary" exit from the war on 25 October 1917 (the policy of "neither war nor peace"); the separate peace agreement signed with the Central Powers on 3 March 1918 in Brest-Litovsk; and a brutal civil war which, as a consequence of foreign military intervention, would last until 1922.

Notes

1. See the chapter by Kristiane Janeke in the present volume.

2. D. V. Verzhkovskii and V. F. Liakhov, *Pervaia mirovaia voina 1914–1918 gg.* [The First World War, 1914–1918], Moscow 1964; *Pervaia mirovaia voina 1914–1918 gg. Sbornik statei* [The First World War, 1914–1918. Collection], Moscow 1968; A. A. Strokov, *Vooruzhennye sily i voennoe iskusstvo v pervoi mirovoi voine* [Military and Strategy in the First World War], Moscow 1974; *Istoriia Pervoi mirovoi voiny 1914–1918 gg.* [History of the First World War, 1914–1918], Moscow 1975.

3. Russko-germanskie otnosheniia. Secretnye dokumenty [Russian-German Relations: Secret Documents], Krasnyi archive, Moscow 1922; *Perepiska Vil'gel'ma II s Nikolaem II 1894–1914 gg.* [Letters between Wilhelm II and Nikolai II, 1984–1914], Moscow, Petrograd 1923;

Finansovye soveshchaniia sojuznikov vo vremia vojny [Financial Briefing by the Allies during the War], Krasnyi archive, Moscow 1924; *Mezhdunarodnaia politika noveishego vremeni v dogovorakh, notach i deklaratsiiakh* [The International Policy of the New Era in Lectures, Notes, and Declarations], vols. 1 and 2, Moscow 1925–1926; *Evropeiskie derzhavy i Gretsiia v epocku mirovoi voiny po sekretnym materialam b. ministerstva inostrannykh del s prilozheniem kopii diplomaticheskich dokumentov* [The European Major Powers and Greece in the Era of the World Wars According to Secret Materials of the Former Foreign Ministry with Copies of Diplomatic Documents], Moscow 1922; *Evropeiskie derzhavy i Turtsiia vo vremia mirovoi voiny. Po sekretnym materialam b. ministerstva inostrannykh del* [The European Major Powers and Turkey during the World Wars According to Secret Documents of the Former Foreign Ministry] Moscow 1925–1926; *Padenie tsarskogo rezhima. Stenograficheskie otchety doprosov i pokazanii, dannykh v 1917g. v Chrezvychainoi sledstvennoi kommissii Vremennogo pravitel'stva* [The Collapse of the Czarist Government: Stenographical Reports of Hearings and Statements before the Special Investigation Commission of the Provisional Government, 1917], vols. 1–7, Leningrad 1924–1927; *Mezhdunarodnye otnosheniia v epocku imperializma. Documenty iz arckivov tsarskogo i Vremennogo privatel'stv 1878–1917 gg.* [International Relations in the Era of Imperialism. Documents from the Archives of the Czarist and the Provisional Government, 1878–1917], series 1–3, Moscow 1931–1938.

4. M. D. Bonch-Bruevich, *Vsia vlast' Sovetam* [All Power to the Soviets] Moscow 1964; A. Brusilov, *Moi vospominaniia* [My Memoirs], Moscow 1963; *Na trudnom perevale* [On a Difficult Change of Direction], Moscow 1959; M. N. Gerasimov, *Probuzhdenie* [The Awakening], Moscow 1965; A. M. Zaionchkovskii, *Mirovaia voina 1914–1918 gg.* [The World War, 1914–1918], vols. 1–3, Moscow 1938–1939; A. A. Ignat'ev, *Piatdesiat' let v stroiu* [Fifty Years on Duty], vols. 1–2, Moscow 1959; R. Ja Malinovskij, *Soldaty Rossii* [Russia's Soldiers], Moscow 1969; M. Paleolog, *Tsarskaia Rossiia nakanune revoliutsii* [Czarist Russia on the Eve of the Revolution], Moscow, Petrograd 1923; A. A. Polivanov, *Iz dnevnikov i vospominanii po dolzhnosti voennogo ministra i ego pomoshchnika, 1907–1916 gg.* [From the Journals and Memoirs in the Office of the Minister of War and His Deputies, 1907–1916], Moscow 1924; A. A. Samojlo, *Dve zhizni* [Two Lives], Leningrad 1926; *Vospominaniia Sukhomlinova* (Sukhomlinov's Memoirs] Moscow, Leningrad 1926; B. M. Shaposhnikov, *Vospominaniia. Voenno-nauchnye trudy* [Recollections: Articles on Military Science], Moscow 1974.

5. *Pervaia mirovaia voina. Diskussionnye problemy istorii* [The First World War: Historical Discussion Problems], Moscow 1994; *Pervaia mirovaia voina. Praviteli i voennonachal'niki. Biograficheskii entsiklopedicheskii slovar'* [The First World War: Biographical Encyclopedic Dictionary], Moscow 2000; *Vsemirnaia istoriia. Pervaia mirovaia voina. Obrazovanie SSSR* [World History: First World War; Education in the USSR], Moscow 2001; A. I. Utkin, *Pervaia mirovaia voina.* [First World War], Moscow 2002; *Mirovye voiny XX veka, kn 1:Pervaia mirovaia voina. Istoricheskii ocherk* [The World Wars of the 20th Century, Book 1. The First World War. Historical Survey] Moscow 2002. Mirovye voiny XX veka, kn 2; *Pervaia mirovaia voina. Dokumenty i materialy* [The World Wars of the 20th Century, Book 2: The First World War: Documents and Materials], Moscow 2002. V. K. Shatsillo, *Pervaia mirovaia voina 1914–1918. Fakty. Dokumenty* [First World War, 1914–1918: Facts, Documents], Moscow 2003.

6. Russia's material reserves, as it turned out, were much too low. As early as November 1914, the earliest inventory of weapons lagged behind the target amount by 870,000 pieces, and they had planned to produce only 60,000 pieces per month.

7. In this essay, the first date given refers to the Julian date from the "old-style" calendar that was used in Russia up to 1918; the second (in parenthesis) refers to the normal European Gregorian calendar, or "new style."

8. From 23 August 1915 (when Grand Duke Nikolai Nikolaevich resigned), Czar Nicholas II himself became the supreme commander until 2 March 1917 (time of abdication), while the post of chief of general staff was occupied by General M. V. Alekseyev.

9. In this essay the Russian-German front will be called the "eastern front," as is usually done in German historiography. In Russian historical writing, however, the front that advanced against Germany (since August 1915 this meant the northwest front, in accordance with the manner in which the front was divided into the northern and the western fronts) is of course referred to as the "German front."

10. Despite their failure, the East Prussia offensive operation by the Russian troops enabled the armies of the Entente to achieve important strategic results in the western European theater of war: the Russians' East Prussia Operation was one of the causes of the defeat of the German Army in the battle of the Marne in early September 1914. Lloyd George (British prime minister from 1916 to 1922) recalled this fact in a speech shortly before the beginning of the Second World War. "Without Russia's sacrifice of 1914, the German troops would not only have occupied Paris, but would still hold their garrisons in Belgium and France today." Quoted in N. N. Iakovlev, *Posledniaia voina staroi Rossii* [The Last War of Old Russia], Moscow 1994, 66.

11. Ibid., 82.

12. Ibid.

13. G. Korol'kov, *Srazhenie pod Shavli* [The Battle at Shavli], Moscow, Leningrad 1926, 53.

14. E. Fal'kengein, *Verkhovnoe komandovanie 1914–1966 gg. v ego vazhneishikh resheniakh* [The Army Leaders, 1914–1916, in Their Most Important Decisions], Moscow 1923, 53.

15. P. Hindenburg, *Vospominaniia* [Hindenburg, *Memoirs*], Petrograd (Petersburg) 1922, 65.

16. On the German deployment of gas on the eastern front in January 1915 see Utkin, *Pervaia mirovaia voina*. See also *Rossiia i SSSR v voinakh XX veka. Poteri vooruzhennykh sil, Statisticheskoe issledovanie* [Russia and the USSR in the Wars of the 20th Century: Military Casualties, Statistical Studies, chapter 2: "Pervaia mirovaia voina (1914–1918 ff) Kampaniia 1915g." [The First World War, 1914–1918: The Campaign of 1915].

17. In comparison with the armies of the other members of the war coalition, Russia suffered the most losses in the First World War; these losses comprised over 60 percent of the total numerical strength of the military (i.e., more than in the defeated countries Germany and Austria-Hungary). At the beginning of 1916 almost the total pre-mobilization standing army (1.4 million men) and the draftees of the first and second wave (5.6 million men) were killed. After three years of war, the Russian Army experienced a catastrophic decline of combat effectiveness ending in its actual disintegration between the close of 1917 and the beginning of 1918.

5

Of Bastards and Brothers in Arms

Practical Constraints and Resentments among the Central Powers in 1914–1915

Günther Kronenbitter

War coalitions are rarely harmonious, even during times of victory. This is true of the Austro-Hungarian and German coalition in the First World War. In terms of strategy, these two Central Powers were inferior to their enemy, an imbalance that could have been resolved only through extensive and well-planned cooperation, if at all.

In modern scholarly research on that era, the subject of military cooperation between these two allies has therefore received particular attention.[1] In retrospect it seems that the missed opportunities for victory and the challenges of coalition war leadership can be traced back to the top leadership of both empires. Further, it seems that the military agreements that had been concluded within the context of the Dual and Triple Alliances prior to 1914 created misunderstandings and encouraged delusional thinking. It also appears that the alliance between Austria-Hungary and Germany formed during peacetime became ineffective when faced with the demands of the war.[2] However plausible retrospective criticism may seem, it is often based in the military alliances of the Cold War and therefore hardly does justice to the circumstances in relation to security and politics of the decades between 1879 and 1914.

Prior to 1914, the cooperation between the armies of the Habsburg Monarchy and the German Empire in the context of the defense alliance had been formulated only in broad outlines. In addition to the chiefs of General Staff in

Berlin and Vienna, who had been making frequent agreements since 1882 concerning the conduct of war against Russia, the military intelligence offices cooperated regularly and relatively closely. As one would expect among allies, there was an exchange of information concerning the war preparations of potential enemies and suggestions concerning counterintelligence. Specific preparations deemed necessary to defense issues under the Triple Alliance were discussed at the expert level, but these were primarily issues having to do with the transport of Italian troops through Austria to the German western front.

Concerning the war against Russia, neither country demanded detailed agreements from the other, since they had already agreed in 1895 that the German East Army would deploy in East Prussia for the most part. Direct contact between German and Austro-Hungarian troops would be confined to the border area between Silesia and Galicia or the peripheral area of Congress Poland. The first victories were supposed to occur further to the east, and it was therefore considered superfluous to institute large-scale combined operations.[3] What did exist in terms of information exchange dealt with the anticipated outbreak of war and related issues of sovereignty. The Habsburg Monarchy, unarguably the weaker partner militarily, now made all the more effort to minimize its unavoidable security and political dependence on the Germans. Combined maneuvers were not among the military requirements—this had been an assumption in Vienna and Berlin prior to 1914—nor was there any agreement to establish a combined high command for the eastern front.[4]

The annexation crisis in 1909 provoked a new round of agreements between the chiefs of General Staff in Berlin and Vienna. The series of crises in the following years initiated a vigorous military diplomacy, but there was never any planning for close military cooperation during an initial offensive of a war with Russia. Any agreements, even in comparison to those of the Entente, remained vague.

The pessimistic assessment of the strategic situation of the two allies in the early summer of 1914, which was shared by both of the chiefs of the General Staffs, did not prompt a critical analysis of the war plans or an assessment of one another's capabilities. Instead, the Austro-Hungarian chief of General Staff, Franz Conrad von Hötzendorf, operated on the assumption that Germany would be able to defeat France's army decisively within a few weeks. His counterpart in Berlin, Hellmuth Graf von Moltke the Younger, didn't question the Austro-Hungarian Army's ability to contain a Russian attack. Genuine cooperation between the allied armies did not develop quickly, even after the "blank check" of July 1914. When threatened with a possible intervention by Russia, for instance, which would have prompted combined action, Conrad did not immediately break off the deployment of the B-Staffel (B-Group) in Serbia. With this, Moltke finally became more attentive. Such were the divergent strategic priorities that presented themselves on the eve of the outbreak of the war.[5]

The first to intensify their cooperation during the July Crisis were the intelligence offices. Soon after, delegates were sent to the army headquarters of each respective ally, and were supposed to receive support from their own military attachés. The delegate from the German High Command (OHL), General Hugo Freiherr von Freytag-Loringhoven, arrived at the headquarters of the Austro-Hungarian Army at the beginning of the war. At the Austro-Hungarian High Command (AOK) he worked with the German military attaché Karl M. V. Graf von Kageneck. Later, when Freytag-Loringhoven was appointed quartermaster general of the German Army, he was succeeded as delegate by General August von Cramon.

Cramon had run the Austrian section of the German General Staff for a time, and had sufficient rank and experience to be able to represent the German High Command in the Austro-Hungarian High Command. Together with his closest colleague, intelligence officer Paul Fleck, Cramon took a firm hand in coordinating the coalition, more so than his predecessor or even the military attaché.[6]

The delegate from Austria-Hungary to the German headquarters was Josef Graf Stürgkh, who had previously been the military attaché in Berlin for several years at the turn of the century. He was to receive support from the Austro-Hungarian military attaché in Berlin, Karl Freiherr von Bienerth.[7] Stürgkh, however, usually remained cut off from important military information. When Conrad lost confidence in him, Stürgkh was relieved of his post and was replaced in May 1915 by Alois Klepsch-Kloth von Roden.[8] The delegate from the Austro-Hungarian Army to the Eastern High Command (Oberkommando Ost, or Ober Ost) was Moritz Fleischmann von Theissruck, the Viennese General Staff's expert on Germany.

Due in part to the nature of their positions, the men in this circle were faced with the task of preventing friction within the war coalition. It soon proved a tedious undertaking. After a turbulent time at the end of July and in early August, the interaction between the leadership levels of the allied armies began to evolve quite well. At the outbreak of war, the Austro-Hungarian High Command instructed the commanders in I Corps to make contact with the neighboring Prussian troops and to coordinate the combined offensive with the Woyrsch Corps.[9] The Austro-Hungarians expected, among other things, the German army to be reinforced by five reserve divisions after 12 August, tactical cooperation with the allies in southwest Poland, and a German attempt to engage the northern and western Russian army groups. "If the German Army is not hampered by a premature Russian offensive, it will be expected to proceed to Russia in the direction of Siedlce."[10]

At this point the problems between the "comrades in arms" were limited to each side pressuring the other to undertake a vigorous attack on the Russians. This changed as soon as it became clear that Moltke and Conrad's plans for the opening operations of the war could not be implemented. Because the Austrians suffered setbacks at the beginning of the war from which they could no longer recover under their own strength, an ever closer cooperation along the eastern front became necessary in the ensuing months and years of the war. While a massive reinforcement of German troops would soon be unavoidable, it was still uncertain as to how many were to be drafted, when, on which sectors of the eastern front they would be deployed, and to whose command they would be assigned.

By the beginning of September, confidence in victory was fading. At the same time, however, the military victories of the 8th Army in East Prussia appeared to open the way for a German offensive that could relieve the Austro-Hungarian Army quickly and effectively. This was why, after the victory of Tannenberg, Conrad vehemently demanded the "push to Siedlce," while the leaders of the 8th Army under Paul von Hindenburg and his chief of General Staff Erich Ludendorff were bent on first defeating the Russian Neman Army.

By the time the Neman Army had been defeated and there was a possibility of new offensive operations by the 8th Army, Conrad assumed it was already too late for a pincer attack on Congress Poland. Thus, after the defeat at Lwów (Lemberg), instead of a pincer attack the AOK pressed for the deployment of four German army corps and one cavalry division in direct affiliation with the Austro-Hungarian Army in Galicia. By this time the battle of the Marne in the west had taken place. The German High Command saw itself forced onto the defensive in the west, but still decided to transfer two corps from East Prussia to Galicia, to which two further corps would be added later. The focus of the German operations, however, was to remain in the west. Neither Moltke nor his de facto successor Falkenhayn left any doubt about this.[11]

For Conrad, it was obvious that the war coalition had to reset its military priorities. It was becoming clear that the German attack in the west would not be a decisive victory. The German High Command left its ally in the dark about the collapse of the western offensive, just as it did the German public. Despite hints that the situation was "not rosy," an exact assessment of the circumstances was hard to come by.[12] One could not depend on the talents and powers of judgment of Austria-Hungary's representatives in German headquarters. It was not until the end of September that Stürgkh reported to the Austro-Hungarian High Command that at mid-month the Germans had been forced into a "retreat movement" and a withdrawal from the area between the Marne and Aisne. "So they were defeated!" Conrad noted, showing that he correctly understood the outcome of the battle of the Marne.

Stürgkh, on the other hand, saw no development that was especially dramatic, was bored by the "static warfare" that had developed in the meantime, and hoped for the "arrival of an event, if not a decisive one, then one that will expedite a decision, which still, however, must be awaited, and I therefore postponed submitting reports day after day." Stürgkh accepted the more euphemistic explanations from the German High Command; Conrad, in contrast, was quite aware of the ramifications of the event.[13] The Austro-Hungarian chief of General Staff saw the German defeat as proof that the conditions that had once formed the basis for the agreement for a coalition war had now changed fundamentally.

Conrad's personal position was made insecure by the reversals in Galicia. He wanted permission to marry his mistress who, prior to 1915, had been married to someone else. With the rise and fall of his reputation as field commander, his chances of receiving this permission also rose and fell.[14] Chief of General Staff Conrad was therefore highly motivated to defend his reputation as a military leader. He sought excuses for the failure of the Galicia offensive and for the Russian occupation of large parts of the crown land. From September 1914 onward his primary complaint concerned the absence—or inadequacy—of German support on the eastern front. In fact, as Germany's representatives in the Austro-Hungarian High Command stated, the German High Command had not informed Conrad about the deployment area of the promised reserve divisions.[15] Conrad never grew weary of representing the absent "push to Siedlce" as the basic cause of the Russian victory in Galicia. The Austro-Hungarian Army, he maintained, had paid all too high a price for the quick liberation of Wilhelm II's beloved "stud farm" in East Prussia. Using the same persistence with which he had evangelized for a preventive war prior to 1914, Conrad now spread his own interpretation of the situation. In late summer 1914, he said, the Germans had forsaken Austria-Hungary. Conrad's complaints about German infidelity, which he brought up after the first defeats in Galicia, never ceased.[16]

Conrad's insistence that the German High Command had broken the promise it made before the war actually flew in the face of reality. In the agreements made between 1909 and 1914, each side was trying to convince the other that it would commit to a vigorous offensive operation. Moltke promised an attack by the German East Army, and Conrad assured the Great General Staff that he would launch an offensive out of Galicia. Out of this came inflated expectations that were impossible to fulfill in August 1914. Misunderstandings were naturally inevitable, many of which were consciously encouraged, but the worst strain was put on the partnership by the failure of strategic planning. Because of the rapid escalation of the July Crisis, Austria-Hungary was forced to break off the major offensive against Serbia. The battle of the Marne dashed all hope for a quick victory in the west. Still, the German 8th Army fulfilled its commitment to tie down strong Russian forces in order to relieve the Austro-Hungarians. Conrad, although deeply disappointed by the situation of the early months of the war, may now have been genuinely convinced that it would have been possible to rescue Lwów (Lemberg) by means of a German push to Siedlce.[17]

After the newly formed German 9th Army attacked Warsaw in fall 1914 and failed, the Austrians also became scapegoats. Although initially successful, the allied offensive was not able to defeat the Russian troops decisively in the Vistula area as had been hoped. Now the German leaders sought face-saving excuses. Max Hoffmann of the general staff of the 9th Army grumbled in a letter to his wife that the Germans were forced to retreat because otherwise, the Austrians in the rear would have suffered defeat. "You cannot imagine a more pathetic bunch," he wrote of the Austrians. "It is my greatest concern that these fellows are useless and will make peace in the end!" Out of consideration for his former military brothers in arms, Hoffmann did not publish these harsh words in his 1923 *Aufzeichnungen* (Chronicles). But the "cursed gang of Austrians" continued to provide Hoffmann new causes for outbursts of rage. Setbacks on the eastern front continued to be a problem, and German officers assigned to Ober Ost or to mixed formations continued to blame their failures on the miserable fighting morale of the Austro-Hungarians. In the Carpathians in late winter 1915, the Austrians continued to lose ground, even against Russian units with inferior numbers. In late winter of 1916, in the early phases of the Brusilov offensive, the Austrians' failures were even more dramatic: "Those wretches, the Austrians, have gotten themselves trounced again by the Russians at Rovno . . . the (Schweinehunde) bastards simply bolt."[18]

Germans' rage against their ally was partly fed by arrogance, partly by despair over the fact that there was no way to prevent the collapse of the Austro-Hungarian Army, even at the price of considerable German casualties. In fall 1914, Ludendorff and his entourage in the 9th Army bluntly referred to the Austrians as *Scheisskerls* (sons of bitches), an expression of their deeply felt frustration. For the German officers whose main mission it was to maintain as smooth a relationship as possible between the allies, such deliberate and openly displayed disgust for the Austrians complicated their job. Therefore, Kageneck criticized Ludendorff harshly. Freytag-Loringhoven worried that the kind of views held by the 9th Army could possibly be adopted in Berlin and lead to a poisoning of their relationship with the Austrians. For this reason Freytag resisted attempts to lay the blame for the collapse of the Vistula operation of October 1914 on the doorstep of the Austrians. As he saw it, the Austro-Hungarian Army, which had less military capability, was given the more difficult mission, provided valuable logistic support to the Germans and was—in contrast to the 9th Army—always very cooperative when problems arose as a result of the integration of German and Austrian troops.[19]

As Freytag acknowledged in a letter to Hindenburg himself, the Austro-Hungarian Army was altogether too weak to be able to handle large missions. This was, in Freytag's opinion, not simply due to insufficient artillery. The Austro-Hungarian troops were, "due to their weak peacetime cadres, basically only a better trained militia, something to which we have not paid sufficient attention." On the other hand, while there was no lack of goodwill on the part of the troops or deficiencies in the abilities of the army leaders, "individual military leaders and whole units attacked too boldly, which resulted in fighting without cohesiveness and severe setbacks, and probably led to situations in which too much carefulness was exercised." This was intended not only as a plea for more patience for Austria-Hungary but also to garner appreciation for the position of German representatives in the Austro-Hungarian High Command. As Freytag wrote, despite whatever Hindenburg may have thought, "for me it is a matter of the effect on the leaders of the army of a country that is quite closely tied and friendly, but an independent one, and I, with the best of intentions, am not in the position to eliminate the inadequacy from this military system, which naturally inheres in its mix of ethnic peoples."[20]

For Kageneck or Freytag, whose mission it was to create as conflict-free a cooperation between the allies as possible, it was a matter of continually trying to calm the waves on both sides. The greater the extent of German involvement in the east and the closer the cooperation between the German and Austro-Hungarian formations, the more often there arose the need for mediation. There was no centralized control, and the areas of friction increased constantly. In their retrospective analysis of the coalition, Cramon and Fleck commented: "It is probably an inevitable part of a coalition war that agreements are judged from different points of view, as long as a single high authority does not curtail the possibilities for interpretation. And if, because of these experiences, it should come to the establishment of a unified single authority, then these experiences stand in the way of actually achieving the necessary unanimity."[21] It was no different with the Entente in the west.

The formation of the 9th Army under Hindenburg's command represented not only the first direct rendering of aid in grand style by the Germans to their allies; for the first time it also brought up a serious discussion concerning the kind of command structure that had to be created in the east to govern the cooperation between German and Austro-Hungarian units. At the beginning of the war, Conrad had very carefully inquired of Moltke whether a political safeguard in the form of a cabinet order would be necessary for the cooperation of the Landwehrkorps in Silesia and the Kummer Army Group. In response, Moltke had stipulated that an authentication of this kind was not necessary, and that the Landwehrkorps were to function with the allies according to the needs of the situation.

Now, with the sending of strong German forces into the Silesian-Polish territory, the situation had been reversed. Hindenburg, in any case, did not want to be subordinated to Conrad. For his part, he demanded both Austro-Hungarian support for the counter push into the bend of the Vistula River south of Warsaw, and that the Austro-Hungarian troops deployed there be subordinated to German command.[22] This time it was Conrad's turn to reject this subordination in the interest of the prestige of the Habsburg Monarchy. Kaiser Franz Joseph supported him in this position.[23]

From then on, the question of the chain of command structure for the coalition war remained pending. The Austro-Hungarian Army had a constant need of German troops to help stabilize the front or win sweeping victories, but for Austria-Hungary to subordinate itself to a German High Command on the eastern front in order to come up to the necessary strength ratios was out of the question. In fact, the more asymmetrical the ratio of forces was, the more stubbornly the Austro-Hungarian High Command struggled against such a subordinate role. It took the Brusilov offensive of June 1916, which was catastrophic for the Austro-Hungarian Army, to force it to give in. Further, as a result of the Sixtus Affair, an attempt by Austria to negotiate a separate peace, the government of the German Reich completely lost its inhibition against lashing out, so that the Habsburg Monarchy was now denied even the appearance of equal justice. Yet during the first two years of war the command structure basically remained under the old system, and therefore the two allies repeatedly relied on ad hoc solutions.

Commanders and chiefs of the Great General Staff were placed together, one for each army, for the purpose of working out compromises between the interests of each side. The leadership of the Austro-Hungarian Army placed great importance on preserving its prestige. This was naturally true for the Germans as well, but they also wanted to shield German troops from the consequences of the poor performance of the Austro-Hungarian leaders.

In the ensuing months on the eastern front, discussions between the allies concerning the command structure and mutual accusations of guilt and resentment were quite common, such as those that had arisen with the deployment of the 9th Army. There were also frequent conflicts between the leaders of the Austro-Hungarian High Command and the German East Army, which as of 1 November 1914 operated under the name Ober Ost. But with regard to the struggle for the distribution of forces between the eastern and western fronts, the two entities formed an alliance. Their common enemy in this was the German High Command. Under Falkenhayn's leadership, it initially maintained the primacy of the western front, despite protests from the Austro-Hungarian High Command.

At the end of October AOK once more requested that the German High Command move the focus of operations to the eastern front. The Austro-Hungarian High Command believed that east of the Vistula, there were 364 Austro-Hungarian battalions facing 424 Russian battalions. In the best-case scenario, these forces were sufficient to hold the enemy, but west of the Vistula around 650 Russian battalions faced 300 battalions of the Central Powers. Any pushing back of the Austro-Hungarian and German troops west of the Vistula and the mouth of the San would force a retreat in the east as well. This meant that considerable German forces would be needed to the left of the 9th Army in order to attack the right wing of the Russians in Poland. Conrad demanded another 30 German divisions. Falkenhayn initially insisted on trying a second attack on Ypres, although he began to realize that in the west there was not much to be won at the moment while in the east, on the other hand, there was much to lose. The embattled Austro-Hungarian Army could rely on the fact that Ober Ost had developed its own institutional interest in an active conduct of war on the Russian front and was not shy about confronting the German High Command.[24]

The attack initiated by Ober Ost in Poland actually led to the victorious battle at Lódź, but the offensive was followed by some severe setbacks. Now Ober Ost and the Austro-Hungarian High Command increased the pressure on Falkenhayn. This found support from the Reich chancellor, whom the chief of the German Army High Command only shortly earlier had confronted with a pessimistic opinion of the military situation and the desire for a separate peace with Russia. Two days after Falkenhayn, Ludendorff, and Bethmann-Hollweg had agreed to continue the attack on the central Vistula, Falkenhayn and Conrad met on 19 December 1914 in Opole. Conrad reintroduced his favorite idea, a pincer attack on the Russian troops in Poland, preferably with a German push through Siedlce. Falkenhayn could not be talked into such an extensive and extravagant operation. In addition, Russian counterattacks in Galicia were putting pressure on the Austro-Hungarian front.

In the meantime, the Austro-Hungarian High Command had learned that four new corps had been established in Germany. Conrad tried to convince Falkenhayn to deploy these troops in the east and brought in Hindenburg to lobby the German High Command in favor of his position. As leverage, Conrad insisted that in the absence of German troops he would have to pull back the 2nd Army, which was fighting in conjunction with the 9th Army in Poland in the area south of the Vistula. Freytag, who found himself once again in the thankless position of broker between the OHL and AOK, did in fact realize the necessity of further support. Still, he opposed Conrad's request for a quick dispatch of German troops, particularly because a few days earlier in Opole he had still supported very extensive operations. Freytag had therefore placed himself completely on Falkenhayn's side.[25] Still, the chief of the OHL now found himself in an increasingly difficult position with respect to criticism within his own ranks.

The conference between Falkenhayn, Conrad, and Ludendorff in Berlin on New Year's Day of 1915 proved once more how far apart their concepts were for the conduct of the war. Ludendorff and Conrad wanted to support an Austro-Hungarian offensive from the Carpathians with three to four divisions of the German 9th Army, but Falkenhayn, as chief of the OHL, withheld his approval. Falkenhayn proposed deploying the new corps on the eastern front, but he was still playing for time. He tried to persuade Conrad that the troops that had been made available from the 9th Army, along with further forces, should be used for a field campaign against Serbia. Conrad had little regard for these plans. Instead, the Austro-Hungarian High Command decided to begin the planned Carpathian offensive. This decision was influenced by the political impact of the war on the eastern front on Italy and Romania, by the Hungarian regime's fear of a Russian advance in the Danube basin, and the urgently needed relief for Przemyśl. The German High Command announced that it was prepared to hand over two and a half infantry divisions and one cavalry division for a composite South Army, which would be newly established under German command for deployment in the Carpathians.[26]

In January 1915 the Austro-Hungarian High Command could hope for a better understanding with the German High Command and a turn of the tide in the war on the eastern front. Ober Ost, in any case, represented an ally for the AOK, primarily in the war with the Russians but also in its quarrel with the OHL. Dissention between German and Austro-Hungarian military authorities in Poland compromised Ober Ost's readiness to cooperate only in the short term. Falkenhayn's partial accommodation here seemed quite surprising. Because of the urgent need to prevent the collapse of Habsburg Monarchy's military and because of an open power struggle within the German military leadership that involved even the Reich chancellor, Falkenhayn was forced to act. After the collapse in the west, Bethmann-Hollweg joined forces with some of the dissatisfied military leaders and together with Ober Ost agitated against Falkenhayn: "From a military-political standpoint, it appears to me that the moment in which victory in the east had to be sought was not recognized soon enough. Since it was possible to relocate troops to the east after the offensive failure at Ypres without jeopardizing our Belgian leverage power, it appears to me that this relocation also would have been possible *beforehand*. But once the struggle for a position in the west had begun, the first opportunity to free up our rear by means of a *decisive* strike in the east, and thereby possibly even bring Russia to a separate peace, *had* to be exploited under any and all circumstances."[27] Falkenhayn survived the intrigues of his enemies, but he did have to face up to the facts behind their criticism and devote more attention to the eastern front. A gratifying secondary effect was the chance to make Ludendorff chief of General Staff of the South Army, thereby separating him from Hindenburg.[28]

The victorious duo of Tannenberg protested this change, ultimately with success. Up until Falkenhayn's fall from grace in 1916, the relationship between the two central decision-making entities for German land warfare remained tense. The trench wars between OHL and Ober Ost were fought out tenaciously. The conflict was fed by rivalries and mutual aversion on a personal level and ignited over issues concerning areas of jurisdiction and differing strategic and operational concepts. On closer examination, material differences between the protagonists quite often functioned as camouflage for underlying resentments and competition for power. Nevertheless, the impact of this conflict on the course of the war should not be overstated, because within their respective areas of competence, the OHL and Ober Ost usually acted appropriately. Max Hoffmann, whose anger over the mistakes made by the OHL was exceeded only by his disgust for the allies, brought the relationship to a boil when he stated: "Today a rather long set of instructions came from the OHL again. Good Lord, what kind of war these people are waging! Naturally we are not going to do what they tell us, so in this respect the thing is harmless."[29]

In terms of the relationship between the allies themselves, the long-term conflict between the German High Command and Ober Ost had a rather favorable effect, for it allowed more room for the weaker coalition partner to maneuver. Still, compromises between the OHL and Ober Ost and the Austro-Hungarian High Command did not guarantee success. Despite German help, the Carpathian offensive, which had been the result of consultations at the turn of the year, ended in disaster for the AOK. Conrad had planned to give the 2nd Army the mission to relieve Przemyśl; this failed completely and he now even feared for the defensive strength of the army. After the fall of Przemyśl on 23 March 1915, the Russians intensified their offensive efforts in the Carpathians and pulled in additional troops from the Vistula area. The AOK saw this as a chance to penetrate the Russian lines in the front sector at Gorlice. This required more German help in order to have sufficient forces standing ready for the attack. As the best means of stopping the Russian offensive, Conrad proposed "a vigorous offensive against the rear lines of communication of the attack wing of the Russian 3rd Army from the Gorlice area in an east or northeast direction." For this, however, about four German divisions were needed for support, a contingent of forces that Cramon felt was unlikely to be received.[30] This concern proved to be unfounded, however, for Conrad ran with his proposals to the open doors of the OHL; Falkenhayn was now fully aware of the needs and opportunities arising out of the situation in the east.[31] With this, the foundation stone was set for the Central Powers' most successful offensive operation, the breakthrough in the battle of Gorlice-Tarnów.

German public relations efforts touted the victory as mostly the work of their own troops, especially the newly formed 11th Army. August von Mackensen, commander of the 11th Army, along with his chief of General Staff Hans von Seeckt, had led the High Command of the German and Austro-Hungarian troops in the offensive operation and was described as a hero. The participation of the Austro-Hungarian Army, on the other hand, was for the most part ignored. Understandably, this embittered the Austro-Hungarian ally. Long into the era between the world wars, the question of who deserved credit for the victory remained a source of controversy between the two former brothers in arms. Cramon was correct in concluding that Conrad was "the inventor of the breakthrough concept," while Falkenhayn deserves credit because "during the heavy defense battles in the west he still took on the responsibility for four of the best German corps in the east."[32] In 1915 German war propaganda was still a long way from interpreting this victory in such a balanced manner. As for the Austro-Hungarian chief of General Staff, the lack of appropriate appreciation for the accomplishments of the Austro-Hungarian High Command and its army deepened his already present antipathies. As Stürgkh noted, "Conrad's feelings towards our allies were, in my opinion, deeply hostile, and only the relentless pressure which he was under [and] the realization of how urgently he needed this very cantankerous ally were able to cause him to hide these feelings from sight."[33] The reason for this attitude, Stürgkh concluded, was that Conrad could not do otherwise than to interpret "each restriction to his command authority in our theater of war, no matter which form it took, as a constant assault on his pride and feelings of self-worth."[34]

The war situation forced cooperation, no matter how frustrating or degrading it seemed. The official propaganda of the Central Powers highlighting the cult of unity and inviolable loyalty contrasted sharply with the practical realities of the coalition war. Such circumstances provide a clearer view into the less pretty side of the brotherhood in arms. Indications of the aggravation that existed between the allies can be seen in the war journals of the German units on the eastern front and in the correspondence of the officers assigned there. The coalition war led to a situation in which some German officers were given a quick succession of assignments on the Austro-Hungarian eastern front. In the late winter of 1915, Wilhelm von Dommes, Moltke's former adjutant, was assigned as chief of General Staff under General Marschall, who was to command an Austro-Hungarian infantry division and an Austro-Hungarian cavalry division. The South Army leadership hoped in this way to exert its influence on the Austro-Hungarian Pflanzer Army Group. This displeased Karl Freiherr von Pflanzer-Baltin. Further, the German officers, who felt cut off from the army commander, asked to be placed under the South Army. Dommes's sharp criticism of Pflanzer's leadership style reveals both frustration with everyday matters and a deep-seated contempt:

> They were averse to each attack. If one decided on an attack, then the execution was overly hurried. The unit received the order at night to attack at daybreak. Then everything broke loose, usually with no artillery preparation and without careful instructions. The troops quickly took unbelievable casualties, turned around, and were completely shot up on their retreat. Then the leaders would say something in a peeved

> manner such as: Look here, this is unacceptable, there you have it. In the final weeks the army was said to have taken horrendous losses (fifty thousand, we are told), without having accomplished the smallest thing. I felt myself duty bound to report this untenable situation on a regular basis to the South Army and Cramon. The answer was, unfortunately, that Pflanzer was seated so firmly that no one could touch him.[35]

The AOK still supported Pflanzer-Baltin at that time, even though he clearly had no particular leadership talent, and it was not for nothing that he was given the nickname Pflanzer "Bald her, bald hin" (Back and Forth Pflanzer).[36]

The South Army, under General Alexander von Linsingen and his chief of staff Stoltzmann, once more gave the duo of Marschall and Dommes command over an army group consisting of a mixture of one Austro-Hungarian corps and a Prussian cavalry division. In summer 1915, Felix Graf von Bothmer, much to the relief of the Austro-Hungarian officers, dismissed Linsingen as commander of the South Army.[37] Marschall was now given a corps that was created from parts of the 3rd Guards Division and two Austro-Hungarian divisions. For Dommes, there was no cause for joy. "It is an evil matter to have to fight here between the Austrians. I do not wish to descend into the wild ravings against the allies that have become the norm here. I have met very decent people, brave men, whose hearts are in the right place. The Austrian soldiers I consider to be good, aside from the soldiers of Romanian and Serbian origins, who jump at the first chance to run off or defect—what is missing is the higher leadership. The technique of battle leadership is missing. In the same proportion, the battle casualties of the Austrians are higher than ours. Also the earnestness of their opinion is missing, and so is the understanding of our large goals."[38]

The conviction that the generals and the AOK of the Austro-Hungarian Army committed disastrous mistakes on a continual basis was shared by many of the German officers who came in close contact with the allies on the eastern front. This was primarily true of the 9th Army, whose staff under Erich Ludendorff harbored great plans for a decisive offensive against the Russians but then had to break off the invasion of Poland. In the German Army South as well, which was formed in winter 1914–1915 in order to stabilize the Carpathian front, resentment against the allies quickly increased. As is seen in the letters of German officers, the Austro-Hungarians became the subject of constant criticism. This was true both for the officers, who tried to maintain their accustomed comfortable lives in the AOK as well as on the front, and for the soldiers, who were little enthused about being deployed or sacrificing themselves. This could be a burden on the relationship, Cramon noted: "The Austro-Hungarian Army, including the officer corps, was quite weak, while the Germans were still as hard as steel. The Germans often pointed this out in public, which sparked displeasure and bitterness among our allies."[39]

The top representatives of the Austro-Hungarian Army were judged with much more discernment. Archduke Friedrich, the high commander of the Austro-Hungarian Army, met with little respect among the Germans. Hoffmann found him to be "a complete fool with the aura of the grand feudal lord."[40] Opinions about Conrad were usually kinder, but not without critical barbs. Representative of the German side is the opinion of Max Bauer, who wrote that Conrad "was a smart, clear-thinking man with a decisively military character. His operational ideas always had something noble about them; unfortunately he overlooked the fact that the Austrian troops were not in any state to implement his ideas. He was absolutely loyal to us and did his utmost."[41]

Conrad, on the other hand, along with his closest entourage, harbored anti-German sentiments. These were by no means shared by all high-ranking Austro-Hungarian officers. Falkenhayn and the OHL were viewed sympathetically, and not just in retrospect. Even in the AOK, officers distanced themselves from the recriminations and the sensitivities that marked the Austro-Hungarians' relationship to their German allies.[42] Among the officers of the Austro-Hungarian Army, even before the outbreak of the war, there was widespread admiration for the victors of Sedan and Königrätz. The experiences of the war confirmed many of their expectations of the German military and many of their fears about their own military forces, although confidence in German invincibility soon faded. Criticism from the Germans was partly enlightening, and in that regard it was acceptable. An analysis by August von Cramon in 1915, although it attempted to be more discerning than others, nevertheless contained some polemic barbs. "One often hears among the German troops: 'The Austrians do not attack.' This is rather true, but not always relevant. They do attack, but the problem is the way they attack. If, at a long distance, due to insufficient use of the terrain, a huge number of casualties occur, the push forward very soon stalls out, and more so if there is weak leadership; it is often noted that Austrian troops cope well in conjunction with Germans because they allow the latter to do the main work and then follow up if necessary."[43] Further, they had never learned to march and did not move energetically: "They limp forward and slowly sit down on the ground." The officer corps, he noted, lacked self-confidence, but absolutely did not lack the desire to cling to everyday amenities. This had a disastrous effect on the soldiers in terms of setting an example, for "as the master, so the servant . . . one can in this respect have the most amazing experience and hardly believe at the same time that one is seeing a soldier, . . . in fact the whole manner of saluting with the hand, even with the left hand when the expectation of strict bearing is the only possibility, carries in it the seeds of lack of discipline."[44]

To German observers, providing an analysis of the weaknesses of the Austro-Hungarian Army was the obvious way to build a more powerful ally for the future. It was precisely for this reason that Cramon prepared his memorandum—to address the necessary goals for a close cooperation in all aspects of war preparation. In the context of a military accord, and ultimately according to the German example, the ramshackle Austro-Hungarian Army had to become stronger. Cramon explicitly drew from Friedrich Naumann's vision for central Europe. In it lay the explosive power of the lessons that the Germans took from the experiences of the coalition war. The sought-after military accord was part of a very extensive plan for the long-term integration of the Habsburg Monarchy into a German power bloc. Like other elements of Naumann's visions for central Europe, Cramon's plans met with little reciprocal favor. Unlike the economic and political components of the concept, which found favor with the government of the German Reich, the military accord would become a reality in May 1918 in the form of a contractually stipulated "military alliance" on paper, as part of the price that the Habsburg Monarchy had to pay for the Sixtus Affair.[45]

At the end of 1915, the Danube Monarchy, despite the heavy retreats during the offensive against Rovno (internally aptly nicknamed *Herbststau*), was still able to prevent massive incursions into its own sovereignty. The monarchy was aided by its desire for self-assertion, the tenaciousness of the top political and military levels vis-à-vis its allies, and a military strength that was still sufficient to keep it from becoming a *quantité negligible* in the event of war. But above all, it was the obvious instability of the army and of the political order that worked in the monarchy's favor. Except in the case of a separate peace with Russia, the German Reich could not risk the loss of its ally who, although it was important strategically, was in need of long-term support and was pushing for equal status.

At the same time, the Habsburg Monarchy was also dependent on German help, even though a separate peace with the Czarist Empire would free up the rear of the Austro-Hungarian Army so that it could be done with Serbia and Italy. In this constellation of affairs, it was inevitable that during the first year of the war the various political priorities of the allies exerted their influence on the coalition. The cooperation between the two army headquarters was always influenced by politics.

In a memorandum on the strategic situation in fall of 1914, the strongman of the Habsburg Monarchy (if there was one at all), Hungarian prime minister Tisza, wrote of the implications that accompanied the collapse of all early offensives: "The whole war from the standpoint of Germany and Austria-Hungary can be regarded only as an organic whole. This is a natural consequence of the circumstance that we are not only fighting in conjunction with Germany in the Russian theater of war, but our efforts against Russia constitute the absolutely necessary precondition for the German victories in the west, and along with this we constitute an integral role in the German victory. From this it follows that we have to agree in large general lines about the goals of the war and share victories or burdens of these in a ratio that conforms by and large with the development of our forces." As important as it was to accomplish this, it was impossible. The Habsburg Empire would acquire its desired room for political maneuvering only if the attack on Serbia were successful, if the Italians could be deterred from entering the war on the side of the Entente, and if a strategically effective strike were carried out with massive German support. A German victory in the west would have all the more ensured that the Austro-Hungarians were pushed into the role of the junior partner. There was nothing that could be done against this, except perhaps a separate peace. This, however, would not only be risky and underhanded but also very difficult to come by. England and France had nothing to offer Austria-Hungary, and Russia did not stand to gain much if the eastern front were to be shortened for the German troops.

The war goals of the Habsburg Monarchy at the beginning of the hostilities were still quite imprecise, but less a matter of clearly defined aims in terms of territory acquisitions than of securing influence and major power status. In a memorandum from the end of August 1914, the diplomat Leopold von Andrian-Werburg stated that after the war, Austria-Hungary absolutely had to become a major power of the first rank, together with Germany, Great Britain, and Russia—not a second-ranking one. In order for this to happen, it would be necessary to include the largest portion of Poland in some form or another in the power sphere of its monarchy, while the Ukraine should remain with Russia. Portions of Podolia and Volhynia, however, should be annexed, which would reinforce the united Ruthenians and form a counterbalance against the Poles.

The so-called Austro-Polish solution was the attempt to accommodate the complicated ethno-political structure of the Habsburg Monarchy and remain within the rules of the game of international power politics.[46] The ambivalence of the Austro-Hungarian war goals with respect to Poland was not unlike that of the Germans. From the perspective of domestic policy, Poland represented a possibly unattractive expansion area, and beyond generously customized border adjustments, annexation found few advocates. As long as a separate peace with the Czarist Empire still did not appear to be out of the question as an exit from Germany's dilemma, Congress Poland represented a bargaining chip.[47] In case no gains were made in the west, then a prize had to be captured nevertheless. Thus, Poland was primarily an instrument rather than a central goal of the political and military strategy in general. The Polish issue also functioned as a tool in the structuring of Germany's ties with the Habsburg Monarchy.

Here it became a matter of presenting Austria-Hungary with a goal that would strengthen its will to persevere. If the Habsburg Monarchy went along with the plan, it would be expanded to include Poland. On the other hand, it would be controlled by means of a central European customs union dominated by Germany. In this, Berlin saw an opportunity to increase its power, even though a rapprochement between Vienna and Petrograd would then have been rendered impossible for the unforeseeable future. With this in mind, in the summer of 1915 Bethmann-Hollweg supported an Austro-Polish solution because he did not want to further pursue the thought of reconciliation with Russia at the cost of the Habsburg Monarchy. When it became clear, however, that Austria-Hungary did not accept the "central European" agenda of the German Reich leaders, Bethmann-Hollweg balked at the incorporation of Congress Poland by the Austro-Hungarian Monarchy.[48]

The Polish question was essentially about the distribution of war booty. But the issue that greatly strained the relationship between the allies was the lack of consensus on how to handle two neutral states, Italy and Romania. These two countries had been bound to Germany and Austria through alliance treaties, although due to the defensive character of these treaties they were not part of the coalition. Even as early as the July Crisis, the German government had pledged to encourage Bucharest's loyalty to the alliance, while it also urged Vienna to actively try to engage Italy in the same way. After Italy declared itself neutral by invoking the literal wording of the Triple Alliance, and Romania adopted the same stance, the problem became a priority issue for the coalition members. Until these two neutral kingdoms entered the war on the side of the Entente, the basic model remained somewhat constant. The Germans, for strategic reasons, wanted extensive concessions by the Habsburg Monarchy, and those responsible in Austria-Hungary delayed concessions. They always remained conscious of the fact that the war had ultimately been started for the sake of the safeguarding territorial integrity, and they were counting on positive aftereffects from the victories of the Central Powers on the eastern front. Thus conflict was inevitable. On the issue of concessions, the Germans thought its allies were, in the words of cabinet advisor Kurt Riezler, "arrogantly obstinate and narrow, as if struck by God."[49]

The issues surrounding Italy and Romania were not only very similar, they were also closely intertwined. It was generally expected that Romania would ultimately orient itself along the lines of the Italian example and enter the war on the side of the Entente. Concessions to Rome and Bucharest appeared as two sides of a coin. Therefore it was no surprise that Tisza, along with Istvan Burian, successor to Berchtold as foreign minister, attempted to delay concessions to Italy. Tisza and Burián could rely on their king in this matter but not always on the AOK, which viewed the chances of victory in a multiple-front war in spring of 1915 with pessimism. Conrad allowed himself to be roped in by Falkenhayn as mediator in the conflict over German and Austro-Hungarian foreign policy. It was a pragmatic decision, for there could be no doubt as to the deep aversion that the leaders of the Austro-Hungarian High Command had for the Italians. As the Italians raised the ante and demanded further territories on the Adriatic coast in addition to Trentino, Conrad attempted to turn the tables on them. He revealed to the German government, via the German High Command, the limits of readiness to compromise. "One would never allow the vital nerve to the sea to be cut off, in which case, one would prefer—obviously in agreement with Germany—to begin negotiations with Russia and sacrifice Galicia to them. From the perspective of Austria, this solution to the question has much to recommend it; it is only a question of whether Germany can agree to it, on one hand, and on the other, whether Russia would approve."[50] Neither the OHL nor the AOK allowed itself to be deterred in its decision to undertake an offensive in Poland at the end of April, even though Austria-Hungary was making military preparations for a war against Italy.[51]

When Italy entered the war, it relieved a sore point between the two allies. Early on, Austria-Hungary saw that Germany had been keeping itself out of the war between its two former partners in the Triple Alliance for as long as possible.[52] Italy's entry into the war also affected another pressure point related to cooperation within the Central Powers—the war in the Balkans. Crucial here was the interconnection of the Ottoman Empire's participation in the war alongside Germany and Austria-Hungary, the strategic role of Serbia, and the relationship of Vienna and Berlin to Sofia. In November 1914, Germany pleaded for a quick capture of the northeastern part of Serbia in order to enable munitions deliveries for the Ottoman Empire, thereby propping up the German strategy in the Orient.[53] It was in this context that the German government developed an interest in an alliance with Bulgaria. Although prior to July 1914 the greatest efforts were needed by Austro-Hungarian diplomats to counteract Wilhelm II's enthusiasm for his Romanian family connection and his distaste for Bulgaria and its rulers, the wind changed course very quickly. In 1914 the Austro-Hungarian prescription of handing over to the Bulgarians as much as possible of the unpleasant work of an attack on Serbia failed. After the collapse of the second offensive against Serbia in December, priorities shifted for the Habsburg Monarchy. As long as the Austro-Hungarian Army was tied down in the battle of the Carpathians and the Habsburg Monarchy evidently could no longer survive without German help, a campaign against Serbia, and therefore even an offensive with cooperation from Bulgaria, appeared less urgent.

The OHL saw it differently. For Falkenhayn, the rescue of the Ottoman Empire stood very high on the list of priorities, and supporting Turkey with weapons and munitions could be achieved only if Serbia were neutralized.[54] For this, Sofia was necessary. The negotiations for the sealing of a military agreement between Germany and Bulgaria bore signs of the evolving overall military situation at the time. The German defeat on the Marne and the Austro-Hungarian defeats in Galicia and in Serbia put the brakes on the negotiations, and even the situation in the Carpathians threatened to bring them to collapse. Only the victory by the allies in Congress Poland smoothed the way to a military agreement.[55] The Entente's offensive on the western front at the end of September 1915 placed Germany in a moment of decision that was similar, although less dramatic, to that of the Habsburg Empire a few weeks before the entry of Italy into the war. Like the leaders of the Habsburg Monarchy, now the German government also committed itself to the campaign prepared against Serbia.[56]

The combined attack on Serbia became a new triumph for the Central Powers. The Serbian Army was, in fact, able to escape destruction and was evacuated to Corfu. But Serbia was conquered, the connecting roads to Constantinople were open, Austria-Hungary's southeastern border was secured, and Bulgaria was firmly established in the alliance. On the German side, satisfaction reigned supreme during the campaign: "At long last, a decent ally."[57] After the victory the Germans were also quite ready to accommodate the new ally during the division of the spoils.

In Vienna and in the Austro-Hungarian High Command, on the other hand, the Bulgarian desires for expansion were seen in a different light. There was no question that Sofia was owed territorial gains at Serbia's expense, but Austria-Hungary's political leaders wanted to limit Bulgaria's expansion. As the quarrels between the Bulgarian and Austro-Hungarian occupation troops escalated, Mackensen stood on the side of the Bulgarians. Differences were intensified by the decision of the AOK to proceed on its own with the defeat of Montenegro, against the express desire of the OHL, in order to secure its own sphere of influence in the western Balkans. In the winter of 1915–1916, the relationship between Conrad and Falkenhayn was so tense that the chiefs of the two general staffs broke off direct contact with one another.[58] "The War between Falkenhayn and Conrad" lasted only until the end of January 1916, however, for the allies needed each other further, primarily as a backup for their respective "private wars" in the west and against Italy.[59]

Austria-Hungary's representatives struggled to keep its status as a major European power from shrinking, but the imbalance in military capability was growing more obvious as the war went on. Austria-Hungary had picked this quarrel in the first place in an attempt to defend its status as a major power, yet this goal itself bred conflict. The two allies had different strategic priorities, and their goals often diverged from one another's. Each side, as is normal in alliances, tried to impose as much of the costs of its own security onto the other. Even so, the resulting aggravations were held in check. Although tempers flared between members of the alliance, the same thing occurred among the military leaders of the Entente.[60] Even Falkenhayn and Conrad put their personal sensitivities aside when the situation demanded it. During the first year of the war, the practical constraints of the situation transcended resentments. After 1915, when the war coalition had fully passed its performance test, the OHL and AOK concentrated on their respective "special wars." In this, they followed their own respective political and strategic priorities. In this respect, the escalating conflict between the general staff chiefs of the two militaries in the winter of 1915–1916 was less an expression of personal animosity than a logical consequence of the military victories in summer and fall.

Even Conrad's aversion for the allies (Austria-Hungary's "secret enemies," as he supposedly called them) had its limits, as is shown by the appreciation that he bestowed on his counterpart.[61] When, at the beginning of September 1916, Klepsch-Kloth reported on Falkenhayn's downfall and blamed the fired OHL chief for worsening the war situation by his lack of success as military leader, Conrad came to Falkenhayn's defense. He may have been thinking of his own position and his own place in history when he responded to Klepsch-Kloth's conclusions, stating that any problems were the "result of the mishandling of forces between us and our enemies. That's all!" Any deficiencies in the art of leadership among either of the allies as well as any misunderstandings, rivalries, and resentment weighed little in comparison to the strategic structural conditions of the coalition war.

Notes

1. For a discussion of the coalition war prior to 1916, see Heinz Kraft, *Staatsräson und Kriegführung im Kaiserlichen Deutschland 1914–1916. Der Gegensatz zwischen dem Generalstabschef von Falkenhayn und dem Oberbefehlshaber Ost im Rahmen des Bündniskrieges der Mittelmächte,* Göttingen 1980; Gary W. Shanafelt, *The Secret Enemy: Austria-Hungary and the German Alliance, 1914–1918,* New York 1985; Wolfgang J. Mommsen, "Das Deutsche Reich und Österreich-Ungarn im Ersten Weltkrieg. Die Herabdrückung Österreich-Ungarns zum Vasallen der deutschen Politik." In: *Der "Zweibund" 1879. Das deutsch-österreichisch-ungarische Bündnis und die europäische Diplomatie,* edited by Helmut Rumpler and Jan Paul Niederkorn, Vienna 1996, 383–407; Gordon A. Craig, "Die militärische Kohäsion des österreichisch-deutschen Bündnisses 1914–1918." In: *Krieg, Politik und Diplomatie,* edited by Gordon A. Craig, Vienna 1968, 66–80; Rudolf Kiszling, "Bündniskrieg und Koalitionskriegführung am Beispiel der Mittelmächte im Ersten Weltkrieg." In: *Wehrwissenschaftliche Rundschau,* 10 (1960), issue 12, 633–41; Holger Afflerbach, *Falkenhayn. Politisches Denken und Handeln im Kaiserreich,* Munich 1994 (= *Beiträge zur Militärgeschichte,* 42); Rudolf Jeřábek, *Die Brussilowoffensive 1916. Ein Wendepunkt der Koalitionskriegführung der Mittelmächte,* Vienna 1982; Holger H. Herwig, *The First World War: Germany and Austria-Hungary, 1914–1918,* London 1997; Manfried Rauchensteiner, *Der Tod des Doppeladlers. Österreich-Ungarn und der Erste Weltkrieg,* Graz 1993; Norman Stone, *The Eastern Front, 1914–1917,* London 1998 (original edition 1975).

2. Günther Kronenbitter, "Waffenbrüder. Der Koalitionskrieg der Mittelmächte 1914–1918 und das Selbstbild zweier Militäreliten." In: *Mythen und Legenden in der Geschichte,* edited by Volker Dotterweich, Munich 2004, 157–86.

3. *Der Weltkrieg 1914 bis 1918. Die militärischen Operationen zu Lande,* edited at the Reichsarchiv, vol. 2, *Die Befreiung Ostpreussens,* Berlin 1925, 12: "These agreements

were worked out for the first weeks of a war in which the close interaction of the two allies—outside of the attack from Silesia—had not yet become an issue."

4. Günther Kronenbitter, *"Krieg im Frieden." Die Führung der k.u.k. Armee und die Grossmachtpolitik Österreich-Ungarns 1906–1914,* Munich 2003, 277–314.

5. Ibid., 452–54, 499–515.

6. A[ugust] v[on] Cramon, *Unser Österreichisch-Ungarischer Bundesgenosse im Weltkriege. Erinnerungen aus meiner vierjährigen Tätigkeit als bevollmächtigter General beim k.u.k. Armeeoberkommando,* Berlin 1920, 1–4.

7. Josef Graf Stürgkh, *Im Deutschen Grossen Hauptquartier,* Leipzig 1921, 11f.

8. Ibid., 129f, 135–38, 147–49. Among the chiefs of General Staff of the Triple Alliance powers agreement was made to send one general and one military attaché as delegates to the ally's headquarters. Originally, Stürgkh was not slated for Germany because he was not considered to be assertive enough. See Kriegsarchiv, Vienna (hereafter KA), MKFF 1913, 42–48. On Stürgkh's weak position and his successor, see also Peter Broucek, "Chef des Generalstabes und Oberster Kriegsherr. Aus den Erinnerungen des Feldmarschalleutnants Alois Klepsch-Kloth von Roden, k.u.k. Delegierten im Deutschen Grossen Hauptquartier, 1915/18." In: *Mitteilungen des österreichischen Staatsarchivs,* 27 (1974), 387–401, here 386–88.

9. KA, AOK OpAbt. 478, nos. 176 and 196.

10. KA, AOK OpAbt. 478, no. 351 (AOK to Kummer, 7/8/1914). See also the German deployment instructions in the Bundesarchiv-Militärarchiv, Freiburg i.Br.(hereafter BA-MA), RH 61/v.96.

11. KA, AOK OpAbt. 479; KA, B/16:2, *Marterer-Tagebuch,* "Reise ins deutsche Hauptquarter 16–21/9/1914"; Stürgkh, *Im Grossen Hauptquartier,* 40–47.

12. KA, B/16:2, *Marterer-Tagebuch,* 9/9/1914. See also Stürgkh, *Im Grossen Hauptquartier,* 41f., 45–47.

13. KA, AOK OpAbt. 555a, Stürgkh to AOK, 30/9/1914 (read and signed by Conrad on 8/10/1914). According to Stürgkh (*Im Grossen Hauptquartier*), "The only reason the German offensive on the Marne failed was probably, on one hand, the exhaustion of the troops and their significant recombining due to heavy casualties; and on the other, that just at this time, the French High Command was continually undertaking large troop shifts behind their own front from the right wing toward the left, with a very skilled use of the rail system, and in this way were able to engage the German flanks with forces that were in some areas often [!] considerably superior. The German Headquarters has come to the conclusion that a further offensive will not be possible without a pause for recuperation of the troops and the arrival of urgently needed personnel replacements, and that carefulness and practicality demand the troops be pulled back to an area further to the rear to coordinate with the forced rearward movement of the extreme right wing." In his memoirs, Stürgkh conceals his own failure as observer. See Stürgkh, *Im Grossen Hauptquartier* 41. See also (Feldmarschall) [Franz] Conrad [von Hötzendorf], *Aus meiner Dienstzeit 1906–1918,* 5 vols. Vienna 1921–1925, here vol. 4, 704.

14. Tisza to Burian, 14/11/1914, in *Count Stephen Tisza, Prime Minister of Hungary, Letters 1914–1916,* New York, 1991, 75–77. See Lawrence Sondhaus, *Franz Conrad von Hötzendorf. Architekt der Apokalypse,* Vienna 2003, 183–94.

15. BA-MA, PH 3/3328, Freytag-Loringhoven, "Kurzer Bericht über meine Tätig-

keit beim Oberkommando des k.u.k. österreichisch-ungarischen Heeres"; Kronenbitter, *Waffenbrüder,* 163f.

16. Joseph Redlich, *Schicksalsjahre Österreichs 1908–1919. Das Politische Tagebuch Josef Redlichs,* vol. 2, *1908–1914,* Graz 1953, 264 (entry of 2/9/1914); August von Cramon and Paul Fleck, *Deutschlands Schicksalsbund mit Österreich-Ungarn. Von Conrad von Hötzendorf zu Kaiser Karl,* Berlin 1932, 30–36; Kronenbitter, *Waffenbrüder,* 167f.

17. See Lothar Höbelt, "'So wie wir haben nicht einmal die Japaner angegriffen.' Österreich-Ungarns Nordfront 1914/15." In: *Die vergessene Front. Der Osten 1914/15,* edited by Gerhard P. Gross, Paderborn 2006, 87–119.

18. BA-MA, N 37/2, Hoffmann to his wife, 29/10/1914, 1/11/1914, and 6/6/1916, copies. See also Max Hoffmann, *Die Aufzeichnungen des Generalmajors Max Hoffmann,* edited by Karl Friedrich Nowak, 2 vols., Berlin 1929, here vol. 1, 59, 121.

19. BA-MA, PH 3/328, Freytag-Loringhoven to Hindenburg, 21/10/1914, draft, copy. See also BA-MA, PH 5 II/279, KTB 9th Army 1914, entries 26–31/10/1914; Hoffmann, *Die Aufzeichnungen,* vol. 2, 61f. See also Theo Schwarzmüller, *Zwischen Kaiser und "Führer." Generalfeldmarschall August von Mackensen,* Paderborn 1995, 97f.

20. BA-MA, PH 3/328 Freytag-Loringhoven to Hindenburg, 21/10/1914, draft, copy.

21. Cramon/Fleck, *Deutschlands Schicksalsbund,* 36.

22. Ibid., 57–63.

23. BA-MA, PH 3/328, Freytag-Loringhoven to Moltke, 21/10/1914, draft, copy.

24. BA-MA, N 56/3 from Haeften to Tappen, 20/10/1925 and 27/4/1926; Afflerbach, *Falkenhayn,* 196f.

25. BA-MA, PH 3/328, Freytag-Loringhoven to Falkenhayn, 28/12/1914, draft, copy; Conrad, *Aus meiner Dienstzeit,* vol. 5, 452–56, 649–60, 817–24; Hoffmann, *Die Aufzeichnungen,* vol. 2, 80–85; Afflerbach, *Falkenhayn,* 204–7; Sondhaus, *Franz Conrad von Hötzendorf,* 170–78.

26. Reformatus Egyház Zsinati Levéltára, Budapest (hereafter REZL), Burián iratok, B8 32, Thurn to Burián, 25/1–9/2/1915; *Österreich-Ungarns letzter Krieg 1914–1918,* edited by the Osterreichisches Bundesministerium für Heerwesen und dem Kriegsarchiv, vol. 2, *Das Kriegsjahr 1915,* part 1, Vienna 1931, 53–57, 91–98.

27. BA-MA, N 78/1, Bethmann-Hollweg to Moltke, 5/1/1915, copy; Afflerbach, *Falkenhayn,* 207–32; Heinz Kraft, *Staatsräson und Kriegführung im kaiserlichen Deutschland 1914–1916. Der Gegensatz zwischen dem Generalstabschef von Falkenhayn und dem Oberbefehlshaber Ost im Rahmen des Bündniskrieges der Mittelmächte,* Göttingen 1980.

28. Jeřábek, *Die Brussilowoffensive,* 99–102.

29. Hoffmann, *Die Aufzeichnungen,* vol. 1, 84 (entry of 28/8/1915).

30. BA-MA, N 266/60, Cramon to Falkenhayn, 2/4/1915, carbon copy; Cramon/Fleck, *Deutschlands Schicksalsbund,* 99–102.

31. KA, AOK OpAbt. 559, Cramon to Falkenhayn, 6/4/1915, copy; Cramon, *Unser Österreichisch-Ungarisch Bundesgenosse,* 11–13.

32. BA-MA, N 266/72, Cramon, *Rückblick,* draft; [Franz] Conrad von Hötzendorf, *Private Aufzeichnungen. Erste Veröffentlichungen aus den Papieren des k.u.k. Generalstabs-Chefs.* Edited by Kurt Peball, Munich 1977, 103–5; Kronenbitter, *Waffenbrüder,* 168f.

33. Stürgkh, *Im Deutschen Grossen Hauptquartier,* 133.

34. Ibid., 135.

35. BA-MA, N 78/2, Dommes to Moltke, 21/7/1915.

36. *Ein General im Zwielicht. Die Erinnerungen Edmund Glaises von Horstenau*, vol.1, *K.u.k. Generalstabsoffizier und Historiker*, edited by Peter Broucek, Vienna 1980, 317. See also KA, B/509:2, *Schneller-Tagebuch*, entry of 12/9/1915.

37. KA, MKSM, SR 93, Ottrubay, "Reise zur deutschen Südarmee 19/–27/7/1915."

38. BA-MA, N78/2, Dommes to Moltke, 21/7/1915.

39. BA-MA, N266/72, Cramon, *Rückblick*, draft.

40. BA-MA, N37/2, Hoffmann to his wife, 10/9/1916, copy.

41. (Oberst) [Max] Bauer, *Der grosse Krieg in Feld und Heimat. Erinnerungen und Betrachtungen*, 3rd ed., Tübingen 1922, 79. See also [Hugo] Freytag von Loringhoven, *Menschen und Dinge wie ich sie in meinem Leben sah*, Berlin 1923, 210–12; Wilhelm Groener, *Lebenserinnerungen. Jugend, Generalstab, Weltkrieg*, edited by Friedrich Frher. Hiller von Gaertringen, Göttingen 1957 (= *Deutsche Geschichtsquellen des 19. und 20. Jahrhunderts*, 530), entry of 26/1/1915; Hoffmann, *Die Aufzeichnungen*, vol. 2, 121; Erich Ludendorff, *Meine Kriegserinnerungen 1914–1918*, Berlin 1919, 58. For a much clearer criticism of Conrad's poor sense of the reality of modern war, see Cramon, *Unser Österreichisch-Ungarischer Bundesgenosse*, 101f.

42. KA, B/509:2, *Schneller-Tagebuch;* KA, B/16:2, *Marterer-Tagebuch; Ein General im Zwielicht*, vol. 1; Stürgkh, *Im Deutschen Grossen Hauptquartier*, 135.

43. Cramon, "Gedanken über eine Militärkonvention zwischen Deutschland und Ö. U. nach dem Kriege," draft, PA-AA Embassy, Vienna 188 (PA-AA = Politisches Archiv des Auswärtigen Amtes Berlin).

44. Ibid. Cramon was not alone in his distaste for the "louts with their . . . salute," (BA-MA, N 266/58, from Martiz to Cramon, 7/5/1915), but offered more detail: "I have seen . . . how Unteroffiziere [noncommissioned officers], both sergeants and ensigns, salute with the left hand in an extremely sloppy manner, while they keep their right hand in their coat pocket just for the sake of comfort. And that does not happen only with respect to German officers. I remember once when I met up with a private with his girlfriend at his right arm. As he passed by me, not only did he not let go of his companion's arm, but saluted me with the left hand in a manner we would hardly use for a beggar. When I watched after this tough warrior, inwardly angry, I saw to my not insignificant astonishment, that he gave the salute in exactly the same sloppy manner to a k.u.k. staff officer, even one who was following Chief of General Staff Generaloberst v. Conrad at a short distance, and without the slightest reproof."

Cramon, "Gedanken über eine Military Konvention zwischen Deutschland und Ö. U. nach dem Kriege," 10/11/1915, draft.

45. See Peter Broucek,"Die deutschen Bemühungen um eine Militärkonvention mit Österreich-Ungarn (1915–1918)." In: *Mitteilungen des Instituts für Österreichische Geschichtsforschung*, 37 (1979), 440–70.

46. REZL Burian iratok B 10 43, memorandum [Andrian], "Die Frage österreichischen Gebietserwerbes im Nordosten im Falle eines glücklichen Krieges der Zentralmächte gegen Russland," Vienna, end of August 1914; Tisza to Burian, 11/8/1914. In: *Tisza, Letters*, 8–22. See John Duncan Leslie, *Austria-Hungary's Eastern Policy in the First World War, August 1914 to August 1915*, Peterhouse, Cambridge 1975, 27–42. See also the chapter by Piotr Szlanta in the present volume.

47. L[ancelot] L. Farrar Jr., "Carrot and Stick: German Efforts to Conclude a Sepa-

rate Peace with Russia, November 1914–December 1915." In: *East European Quarterly,* 10 (1976), vol. 2, 153–79.

48. Heinz Lemke, *Allianz und Rivalität. Die Mittelmächte und Polen im Ersten Weltkreig,* Vienna 1977, 1–252; Volker Ullrich, "Die polnische Frage und die deutschen Mitteleuropapläne im Herbst 1914." In: *Historisches Jahrbuch,* 104 (1984), 348–71.

49. Kurt Riezler, *Tagebücher, Aufsätze, Dokumente,* edited by Karl Dietrich Erdmann, Göttingen 1972, 208 (entry of 20/9/1914).

50. BA-MA, N 266/60, Cramon to Falkenhayn, 2/4/1915, carbon copy. At the beginning of March, when it came to the question of German compensations for territory concessions by Austria-Hungary (the "Silesian offer," meaning the offer of the coal region of Sosnowiec), Conrad made similar comments. KA, B/15:2, *Kundmann-Tagebuch,* Conrad to Bolfas, 5/3/1915, copy: "Now only one thing remains . . . to continue to fight against Russia, to remain ready to defend against Serbia and not to enter into any premature obligations, thus not to bluff and not to allow ourselves to be urged on by Germany, all the more so because this unscrupulous, brutal egoism has been unmasked. If the latter goes too far, then one still has the threat of a separate peace with Russia as a countermeasure, without my wanting to put forth the case for such an agreement. This threat could become significant if it becomes a matter of our demanding compensation from Germany should we be forced to agree to territorial concessions for the sake of preserving the existence of both sides."

51. See Hans-Jürgen Pantenius, *Der Angriffsgedanke gegen Italien bei Conrad von Hötzendorf. Ein Beitrag zur Koalitionskriegsführung im Ersten Weltkrieg,* Cologne 1984, 524–90.

52. See Falkenhayn's barbed comments justifying the instructions to the Alpine Corps not to take part in an offensive against Italy in KA, B/1450:121, Falkenhayn to Conrad, 11/6/1915: "The Tyroleans have every reason to be thankful for being able to make comments about the 'Bavarians,' who, for the most part, do not belong to the Bavarian stock but to the other German stock. Obviously the instructions temporarily preclude the use of German troops for major offensive operations into Italy. That is completely consistent with my military convictions, which make me the absolute enemy of offensives with insufficient forces."

53. KA, B/1450:112, *Kundmann-Tagebuch,* entries of 18/9 and 19/9/1914; Conrad, *Aus meiner Dienstzeit,* vol. 5, 552f.

54. KA, B/15:2, *Kundmann-Tagebuch,* entry of 23/3/1915.

55. BA-MA, W 10/50310, Goltz to IIIb, 13/8/1914, Goltz, Militärattachébericht, 2/9/1914, Tschichowitz to Freytag-Loringhoven, 21/11/1915, copies.

56. Volker Ullrich, "Entscheidung im Osten oder Sicherung der Dardanellen. Das Ringen um den Serbienfeldzug 1915." In: *Militärgeschichtliche Mitteilungen,* 32 (1982), 45–63.

57. BA-MA, N 37/1, Hoffmann to his wife, 16/10/1915, draft.

58. Jeřábek, *Die Brussilowoffensive,* 111–27; Rauchensteiner, *Der Tod des Doppeladlers,* 303–10, 321–23.

59. *Ein General im Zwielicht,* vol. 1, 354.

60. See Kronenbitter, *Waffenbrüder,* concerning the culturally based differences that persisted and their impact during the interim between the wars.

61. Stürgkh, *Im Deutschen Grossen Hauptquartier,* 116.

Part 2

The Battlefields of Concepts / Concepts of the Battlefields

The Eastern Front of the First World War and Perceptions of the Enemy

6

Introductory Remarks

Jörg Baberowski

Wars do more than simply put soldiers into battle; they also change the way nations perceive one another. At the outset of the First World War, most German soldiers had no comprehension of the distant land of Russia. For them the Czarist Empire had been a terra incognita. As Norbert Elias said of perceptions in the years leading up to the outbreak of the war, "The czar and the Cossacks—barbarians, one and all. The barbaric east—it exceeded our imaginative powers."[1]

Many a soldier found his previous beliefs about the multicultural empire of the czar to have been justified. "If someone had told me I was in Africa, in a native village, I would probably not have been surprised," wrote a soldier recalling his war experiences. The villages were a collection of "pathetic huts," and even the smaller cities left "an impression of complete desolation."[2] As to the populace, the soldiers often had nothing more to say than that they were "dull" and "sluggish." Russians, the report went, tended toward "habitual drunkenness and cruelty"; they had "little resistance to temptations of any kind, from bribery, mendacity, and destructiveness, and showed indifference to the more noble goals. They were even indifferent to illness, hunger, and death."[3] But because, unlike the German Empire, Russia was a multiethnic empire, there were more than just "dull" and "cruel" Russians. Russia was comprised of many people whose languages, customs, and habits were unknown to the invaders. The German soldier had to try to assemble the pieces of this puzzle of diversity for himself.

Prior to the outbreak of the war, the officers in the German General Staff had made positive references to the combat power of the Czarist Army. After Russian troops' entry into East Prussia, however, the Germans began referring to them in old clichés. The enemy soldiers became "Asians," barbarians who ignored the rules even during hostile conflicts, abused their own civilian populations during retreats, burned villages, and abducted peasants. Where the foreigners lived, there were illnesses and epidemics that did not exist in the Germans' own country. This experience led many soldiers to conclude that illness could be ascribed to ethnic groups. Dirty streets, miserable living conditions, and epidemics became associated with what they called "grimy Kaftan Jews." Ultimately, the Jews, Russian peasants, refugees, soldiers, and prisoners of war were all seen as bearers of lice and illnesses.[4]

Under these circumstances, the conquerors could only perceive the populace in the occupied territories as a threat, as people who lived in a foreign environment that they did not understand, and whose diseases were to be feared. The clear concept of the autocratic Czarist Empire, in which powerful rulers reigned over Russian peasants, gave way when soldiers were confronted with the multiethnic periphery of the empire. But now they began to perceive their own world differently. To be a German now meant living in a nation-state and in prosperity, to be free of disease and safe from epidemics.

The conquerors could have approached their insecurity in two ways. As Vejas Gabriel Liulevicius points out in this volume, they could have chosen either to "civilize" the subjugated population or drive them out. The National Socialists chose the approach of either displacing or exterminating them. But during the First World War, the Imperial Military Government of Ober Ost saw itself in the role of the *Kulturträger* (bearers of culture). The Germans had now become crusaders for the spread of the civilization of the West. From this perspective, Germany's colonial ambitions of transforming uncivilized peoples into cultivated Europeans were realized on the eastern front. German physicians decreed mandatory inoculations and disinfections; military professionals flooded the conquered territory with new administrative boundaries and gave out passports, all intended to accustom the population to living within the regulations of the German ruler.[5]

The strategies and crimes that took place during the Second World War did exist during the First World War, but the German soldier of the First World War was not a racist. The ambivalent experiences of German soldiers and officers on the eastern front argue against this kind of continuity. This is made evident in the essays in this volume by Hans-Erich Volkmann and Peter Hoeres. After the battle of Tannenberg, Paul von Hindenburg spoke with appreciation of the military achievements of the Russian armies, Russian prisoners of war were treated humanely, and no more than 5 percent of all prisoners died in German custody, compared to more than 20 percent of the Central Powers' soldiers captured by the Czarist Army who died in Russian camps. Further, among the German soldiers there was never a general consensus in their perceptions of the land and its people. Particularly in the Baltic areas, Catholics and Protestants alike saw the same kinds of market squares as at home, houses built in the architectural style of their own home regions, and churches with familiar silhouettes. The anti-Semitism of many of the higher-ranking officers was far removed from the attitude of most soldiers. Jews, after all, spoke a language that was understood, and they treated the occupiers with friendliness and openness. In some areas, Jews served the German occupation government as mediators and translators. There is no convincing connection between the National Socialist policy of extermination and the soldiers' experiences of the First World War.[6]

In Russia, the First World War was perceived as a historical turning point by state officials and officers as well as by soldiers, civilians, and refugees. The war experience had affected the whole territory of this multiethnic empire, therefore affecting the life circumstances of everyone. As Birgit Menzel and Hubertus F. Jahn show in their case studies, in the first year of the war the bureaucratic and intellectual elites of the Czarist Empire were still focused only on the danger from Germany. Anything positive that might have been said about the Germans before the war now had to remain unsaid. The Germans were now a symbol for the abyss of modernity, rationalism, and cold materialism of modern Western society. Only a society that cleansed itself of its "Germanization" and banned everything German from its life could be a national Russian socicty. In this, however, the Russian elites proved to be eager students of German intellectuals, who themselves rationalized their war as a struggle of the German spirit against materialism and the decadence of Western modernism.[7]

For Russians, however, the war did not merely expose the deviousness and depravity of the enemy. It also revealed his superiority. For the czarist elites, there was no doubt that the reason the multiethnic empires lost wars was because they were underdeveloped. The Germans, in contrast, won because they lived in a nation-state, served in a national army, and could exploit the ethnic tensions in the territory of the Russian Empire for their own purposes. The Czarist Empire, therefore, would have to stop being a multiethnic empire. Generals Kuropatkin and Januskevic saw the multiplicity of languages and religions in the border regions of the Czarist Empire as a danger to the stability of the empire. They charged the national or ethnic groups living in their territory, such as Germans, Jews, Poles, and Gypsies, with being in an alliance with the enemy and set to work to destroy the multiethnicity of the empire. The Austrians, as Piotr Szlanta shows in his essay here, were of the same mind, and punished the Ukrainian and Polish peasants for collaborating with the occupiers in Lwów (Lemberg).[8]

During the year of 1915, in the larger cities of the Czarist Empire there were occurrences of pogroms and brutality committed against Germans, and in the Baltic provinces there were systematic expulsions. In the Ukrainian border regions, Jews and Germans were registered, chased out, or deported. On the Caucasian front, the nationalist cleansing by the Russian generals targeted Turks and Muslims, whom they cleared from the border areas.[9]

This sort of national stigmatization carried over into the prisoner of war camps of the Russian military. Czechs, Serbs, and Italians could count on privileged treatment. Czech war prisoners were allowed to move freely and even take on supervisory roles. German and Hungarians, in contrast, were placed in work camps in Siberia and central Asia, where more than 20 percent of them died, as discussed further in the chapter by Peter Hoeres.[10]

During the First World War not only enemies but also friends were ranked according to national categories. There were now Ukrainian, Polish, Czechoslovakian, and Serbian brigades in the Czarist Army fighting on the side of Russian units against the multiethnic army of the Habsburg Monarchy. They fought so successfully that on many sectors of the front, Slav soldiers deserted from the Austrian Army and defected to the enemy.[11]

But the government in Petrograd overlooked the fact that ultimately the nationalizing of all aspects of society undermined the stability of its own empire. Because both conquerors and defenders insisted on assigning friends and enemies to ethnic groups, social communications revolved around ethnicities. Among the country's own subjects, fellow citizens had become foreigners. The question of which rights were due to them and what kind of treatment they would receive depended on their place in the ethnic hierarchy.

No other war in Russia had ever stirred so many people into action. Several million peasant soldiers experienced life beyond their own villages and gained a concept of the size and multiplicity of the empire whose subjects they were. But this multiplicity was not perceived as an asset; instead, it was seen as a threat: the state of multiethnicity was also the state of defeat. For the generals as well as for many soldiers it appeared as though the populations in the border regions were conspiring against them. In Poland, in the Baltic states, in the Caucasus, and in many regions of the Ukraine, the armies of the czar were operating on foreign territory—at least in the perception of the soldiers deployed to the western front. As Igor Narskij demonstrates in his chapter, their experiences of isolation contributed to the xenophobia and paranoia of the Bolsheviks. For the young soldiers and *Unteroffiziere* (secondary level or noncommissioned officers) who later joined the Bolsheviks, the war was not won only at the front but also in the rear, or on the home front. In the army, the young soldiers had learned the kind of discipline and subordination that was lacking in the society of the empire. Yet this military discipline was constantly challenged on the homeland front. Many resisted the rules of war and committed treason against the troops who fought in enemy territory; they were treated as traitors and saboteurs who had to be punished. After the war, soldiers brought the principles of military organization into civilian life. A further element possibly influenced by the experience of the First World War was the Stalinist *idée fixe* of an enemy that was working to destroy the empire.[12]

During the war several million men lost their homeland, either because they were displaced or had left their villages out of fear of the Central Powers. They were mostly Germans, Jews, Ukrainians, Turks, and Armenians. Many cities doubled their number of inhabitants with the flood of refugees; within only a few months the cities of Ekaterinoslav, Kiev, and Poltava saw a change in their ethnic composition. Along with the refugees, diseases, epidemics, and crime entered the cities. Refugees represented disorder and illness, and their arrival threatened to disrupt the accustomed systems of regulation.[13] The German soldiers could turn their back on the chaos and return home, but in Russia at the end of the war, there was no area of retreat nor any place that had been unchanged by the war. It also became apparent that the new concepts of order were sharply at odds with the real lives of those who returned from battle; the insistence on the part of the elites to put these modern concepts into effect had devastating effects.

The events on the eastern front of the First World War are not well embedded in the collective memory of Germans and Russians. Because the war has been overshadowed by the extermination campaigns of the Second World War, it is little known. In the Soviet Union the First World War was considered to have been conducted by an illegitimate government for illegitimate reasons; therefore, no public remembrance was allowed. From the perspective of the Bolsheviks, the First World War was nothing but the prologue to their revolution. Their heroes were created not during their struggle against the Germans but during their Civil War.

Even at the end of the Soviet regime, mythical tales of the Civil War and the Great War of the Fatherland of 1941 to 1945 were the dominating themes in the collective memory of the Soviet population.[14] It is unlikely that this will change much in the future. But while people within a society may consider such myths to be indispensable, it is nevertheless the task of the historian not to justify such myths but to shed light on them. In focusing attention on the history of the First World War on the eastern front, we learn how people interpreted and changed their world amid conditions of war. Further, we gain a better understanding of what this meant for the societies of Germany and the Czarist Empire. And lastly, such inquiry also compels us to consider the history of Germany and the Soviet Union in the twentieth century in a new way.

Notes

1. Arend-Jan Heerma van Voss and Abram van Stolk, "Biographisches Interview mit Norbert Elias." In: *Norbert Elias über sich Selbst*, Frankfurt 1990, 7–105, here 28.

2. *Wie Helden sterben. Erlebnisse an der Ostfront August/September 1915 von Frau C.L.*, edited by Friedrich von Bernhardi, Leipzig 1917, 89f.

3. Jon Alfred Mjöen, *Germanen oder Slaven? Die Mongolisierung Europas. Eindrücke eines Neutralen von einer Reise an die Ostfront und zu Hindenburg*, Berlin 1917, 86f.

4. *Ludwig Weichert, Kriegsfahrten eines Friedensboten an die Ostfront*, Hamburg 1916, 48f.

5. See also the collection of field mail in *Von Flandern bis Polen. Feldpostbriefe der Täglichen Rundschau aus dem Weltkriege*, Berlin 1915; Paul G. Plenz, *Kriegsbriefe eines Feldarztes der Armee Hindenburg*, Gotha 1916; Vejas Gabriel Liulevicius, *Kriegsland im Osten. Eroberung, Kolonisierung und Militärherrschaft im Ersten Weltkrieg*, Hamburg 2002; and Anne Lipp, *Meinungslenkung im Krieg. Kriegserfahrungen deutscher Soldaten und ihre Deutung 1914–1918*, Göttingen 2003.

6. On the theme of continuities, see Hans-Heinrich Wilhelm, "Personelle Kontinuitäten in baltischen Angelegenheiten auf deutscher Seite von 1917/19 bis zum Zweiten Weltkrieg." In: *The Baltic in International Relations between the World Wars*, edited by John Hiden and Aleksander Loit, Stockholm 1988 (= *Acta Universitatis Stockholmiensis. Studia baltica Stockholmgiensia*, 3), 157–70. For an opposing view, see Bernhard Chiari, "Geschichte als Gewalttat. Weissrussland als Kind zweier Weltkriege." In: *Erster Weltkrieg –Zweiter Weltkrieg. Ein Vergleich. Krieg, Kriegserlebnis, Kriegserfahrung in Deutschland*, edited by Bruno Thoss and Hans-Erich Volkmann, Paderborn 2002, 615–31.

7. Kurt Flasch, *Die geistige Mobilmachung. Die deutschen Intellektuellen und der Erste Weltkrieg. Ein Versuch*, Berlin 2000, 55–61. For Russia, see above all N. Plotnikov and M. Kolerov, "'Den inneren Deutschen besiegen.' Nationalliberale Kriegsphilosphie in Russland 1914–1917." In: *Traum und Trauma. Russen und Deutsche im 20. Jahrhundert*, edited by Dagmar Herrmann and Astrid Volpert, Munich 2003 (= *West-östliche Spiegelungen*, 2), 15–59.

8. See also Peter Holquist, "To Count, to Extract and to Exterminate: Population Statistics and Population Politics in Late Imperial and Soviet Russia." In: *A State of Nations: Empire and Nation-Making in the Age of Lenin and Stalin*, edited by Ronald Grigor Suny and Terry Martin, Oxford 2001, 111–14.

9. Eric Lohr, *Nationalizing the Russian Empire: The Campaign against Enemy Aliens during World War I*, Cambridge, MA 2003, 31–54, 121–65; Victor Dönninghaus, *Die Deutschen in der Moskauer Gesellschaft. Symbiose und Konflikte 1494–1941*, Munich 2002, 367–516; Melissa K. Stockdale, "'My Death for the Motherland Is Happiness'; Women, Patriotism and Soldiering in Russia's Great War, 1914–1917." In: *American Historical Review*, 109 (2004), 79–116; Jörg Baberowski, *Der Feind ist überall. Stalinismus im Kausasus*, Munich 2003.

10. See also Rüdiger Overmans, "'Hunnen' and 'Untermenschen'—deutsche und russisch/sowjetische Kriegsgefangenerfahrungen im Zeitalter der Weltkriege." In: *Erster Weltkrieg-Zweiter Weltkrieg*, 335–65.

11. Mark L. von Hagen, "States, Nations, and Identities: The Russian-Ukrainian Encounter in the First Half of the Twentieth Century." In: *Culture, Nation, and Identity. The Ukrainian-Russian Encounter, 1600–1945*, edited by Andreas Kappeler et al., Edmonton 2003, 360–74; Manfried Rauchensteiner, *Der Tod des Doppeladlers. Österreich-Ungarn und der Erste Weltkrieg*, Graz 1993, 480–85.

12. Dietrich Beyrau, "Der Erste Weltkrieg als Bewährungsprobe. Bolschewistische Lernprozesse aus dem 'imperialistischen' Krieg." In: *Journal of Modern European History,* 1 (2003), 96–123; A. B. Astasov, "Russkii krest'ianin na frontakh pervoi mirovoi voiny." In: *Otechestvennaia istoriia,* 2003, 3, 74–86.

13. Peter Gatrell, *A Whole Empire Walking: Refugees in Russia during World War I,* Bloomington 1999.

14. Lev Gudkov, "Die Fesseln des Sieges. Russlands Identität aus der Erinnerung an den Krieg." In: *Osteuropa,* 55 (2005), 4–6, 56–73; Harald Welzer, "Die Gegenwart der Vergangenheit. Geschichte als Arena der Politik." In: ibid., 9–18.

7

The Creation of an Identity for the Modern Polish Nation in the First World War, 1914–1915

Piotr Szlanta

At the beginning of the First World War, Poland was already an established nation whose political system had existed for nine hundred years. Since the division of their country at the end of the eighteenth century, the Polish had repeatedly demonstrated their commitment to the idea of independence and their preparedness to sacrifice themselves for it. They had taken part in the Napoleonic Wars and organized three rebellions against the Russian partitioning power.

The Polish elites were aware of the fact that the only chance of reestablishing their independence was a general European war. In the middle of the nineteenth century, the great Polish writer Adam Mickiewicz, who was very active politically, wrote in one of his poems, "We implore of you, dear God, for a general war in the name of ethnic freedom."[1] But since the unification of Germany, from the Polish point of view, the political situation did not favor this. France's position in Europe had weakened; the country had been reduced to a second-rank power. In addition, the three partitioning powers had formed the Alliance of the Three Emperors. This situation began to change in 1879 after the emergence of the Dual Alliance and the Triple Entente. By the beginning of the twentieth century the international situation began to deteriorate. Due to the rivalry of the major European powers, a general war appeared to be increasingly likely.[2]

The Options

During the years shortly before the outbreak of war, two political camps developed in Poland: one pro-Austrian and one pro-Russian. In Cracow, just prior to the Bosnian annexation crisis, the Związek Walki Czynnej (Alliance of Active Struggle) was brought into existence by the PPS (the Polish Socialist Party under the leadership of Józef Piłsudski), which planned to set off an anti-Russian rebellion in case of an Austro-Russian war. Four years later, after the start of the First Balkan War, a European war appeared inevitable. Polish parties in Galicia that hoped for a resurrection of Poland through an alliance with Austria-Hungary banded together in a political umbrella organization under the name Tymczasowa Komisja Skonfederowanych Stronnictw Niepodległościowych (Temporary Commission of the Parties Struggling for Independence). The question of why many Poles placed their hopes on Austria-Hungary in particular is easy to answer: Poland was one of the nations of the Danube Monarchy that enjoyed many rights and had extensive political and cultural autonomy dating back to the early 1860s. Polish political parties played an important role in the State Council in Vienna. Politicians from Galicia, such as Agenor Gołuchowski and Kazimierz Badeni, who had both been minister presidents, occupied the highest offices. The junior Agenor Gołuchowski was foreign minister, and Leon Bilinski was finance minister. Political refugees from Russia found asylum in Galicia, where there was a free Polish press and a Polish school system had been developed. With these advantages of Austro-Hungarian rule in mind, shortly after the beginning of the war Galician conservatives even considered a tripartite solution that would restructure Austria-Hungary into Austria-Hungary-Poland. This last portion of the new Habsburg Empire was to result from the unification of Galicia and the Polish territories which, in case of a victory, would be liberated from the Russians.

As early as 1910, quasi-military rifle leagues had come into being with the goal of preparing Polish youth for military service. These efforts were not only tolerated by the Austrian authorities but even supported. They lent weapons from the military warehouses to the leagues and granted them entry to military firing ranges. Despite the diplomatic pressure that Russia exerted on the Danube Monarchy, these organizations were not disbanded.[3]

On the other end of the political spectrum stood the nationalistic party Narodowa Demokracja (National Democracy) under the leadership of Roman Dmowski. As Dmowski emphasized in his 1908 treatise, *Niemcy, Rosja a sprawa Polska* (Germany, Russia, and the Polish Issue), he had no faith that the reestablishment of an independent Poland would result from a war between the partitioning powers. Instead, he set his sights on the unification of all Polish territories under Russian rule with the hope of autonomy in the future. The Poles were to support the czarist government unconditionally for the sake of solidarity among the Slavs, in the hope that soon after, the Russian elites would finally realize their mistaken policy with respect to Poland and make concessions. Long term, Dmowski believed this course would bring independence. But the policy of the Russian authorities in the final years before the war made it difficult for him to gain support for his ideas from his fellow countrymen. As of 1909, the Russian government was already revoking earlier concessions. It limited the number of the Polish delegates in the Duma and dissolved Polish cultural associations and educational organizations. In 1912, the Chelm government, whose population was two-thirds Catholic, was severed from Congress Poland and subjected to a ruthless process of Russianization. Despite this, Dmowski stood firmly on the side of Russia and posited the Germans as the primary danger to the survival of the Polish nation. Prior to the outbreak of the war, a split occurred in the ranks of his adherents, and most of those in Galicia came out in favor of the pro-Austria option. On the other hand, in the German Empire, because of the uncompromising Germanization policy with respect to the Poles, there was no corresponding pro-German option.[4]

It must be emphasized that the boundaries between the pro-Austrian and pro-Russian options were flexible, and their adherents worked together in both directions in order to make the everyday life of the Poles more bearable. Russia's Western allies, on the other hand, viewed the Polish issue as a Russian domestic affair.

The Outbreak of War

With the outbreak of war, the level of priority of the Polish issue in international relations changed radically and inescapably. The partitioning powers were at war with one another and their solidarity had broken down, something the Poles viewed as long overdue. But the disadvantage for the Poles was that this war was to take on the character of a civil war. An estimated 1.5 million or more soldiers of Polish origin served in the armies of the Polish partitioning powers, and 400,000 of them died during the war.[5] The story of a Cracow book dealer, Filipowski, for instance, illustrates what the service of young Poles could mean for a Polish family. Filipowski had twelve nephews: one served in the Prussian Army, eight in the Austro-Hungarian Army, two with the Russian troops, and one on the American side. At one point during the Christmas holidays in 1914, at Łowczówek near Tarnów, the soldiers of the Piłsudski Legion and the Siberian divisions of the Russian Army on both sides of the front began singing Polish Christmas songs.[6]

From the outset, because the eastern front ran primarily through Polish territories, the warring parties attempted to gain the sympathy of the Poles. This meant they had to at least partially recognize Polish political aspirations, especially because it looked like the war would last a long time. This led, for instance, to the proclamation of the Russian high commander Grand Duke Nikolai on 14 August 1914 announcing the reestablishment of Poland's "independence and freedom of religion and speech," at which time he made specific reference to the battle of Grunwald (Tannenberg) of 1410. In addition he promised the unification of all Polish territories under the scepter of the Romanovs. He made no reference, however, to the precise borders of this territory.[7] The significance of this announcement was huge, as it ended the deadly silence concerning the Polish issue and at the same time meant a step in the direction of its internationalization.[8] Now the two other partitioning powers also felt pressured to make at least a gesture that was pro-Polish. The Polish subjects of the czar responded to the proclamation with optimism.[9]

In the first days of the war, the German and Austro-Hungarian troops pushed into the Russian sector of Poland. At the beginning of the war, the German military published an appeal for a combined war effort between the Germans and Poles against the "Asiatic hordes." The publication invoked the persecutions against the Catholic Church and the United or Eastern Catholic churches as well as the massacre of the inhabitants of Praga (a sector of Warsaw) by the Russians in 1794. The Poles, however, did not buy the German assurances that "we will bring you freedom and independence."[10] These words from the mouths of the Germans, who had carried on an unscrupulous policy of Germanization in their sector of Poland, must have sounded dubious and paradoxical. People remembered very well the anti-Polish legislation and the use of brutality against the Poles within the German Empire. In the first days of the war, the Germans hung placards showing the Madonna of Czestochowa (the most important pilgrimage site for Catholic Poles) alongside Wilhelm II and the pope, and the position of the bishop of Poznań and Gniezno, which had been vacant for many years, was now filled by a Pole, Edmund Likowski. Nonetheless, the anti-Polish legislation in the Prussian sector of Poland was never rescinded.

After the outbreak of the war, no celebrations took place in the streets of Polish cities in either Germany or Russia. In Warsaw, for instance, on 30 August 1914, only one group of Russian students demonstrated their solidarity with Serbia; the Polish population did not take part in this demonstration.[11] Only in Galicia was there any sign of enthusiasm.[12] But most Polish subjects remained loyal to their respective nations. The mobilization in all three Polish sectors took place without great problems. In her memoirs, Princess Maria Lubomirska wrote on 2 August 1914: "In front of the Krasiński Palace there is a large mass of people. Conscriptions continue. Volunteers go gladly—only their wives mourn, and Jewesses wail like in the Bible. Great loyalty is displayed here because the Germans are very much hated." Two days later she noted: "Evenings the troops marched past under our window in long columns. They were accompanied by a mass of people shouting their hurrahs. Hurrah for the military!!! The whole street swayed with excitement."[13] After the first victories by the Russian troops in East Prussia and Galicia, thanksgiving masses were held in Warsaw churches.[14]

The Activity of the Pro-Austrian Camp

In Galicia Józef Piłsudski organized Polish volunteer units for the fight against Russia. On 6 August 1914, a two-hundred-man cadre company moved from Cracow toward Kielce with the intention of releasing a massive revolt in Congress Poland against Russia, but the spontaneous enthusiasm of the "liberated brother" contained itself. The inhabitants of the Russian sector of Poland initially kept their distance from the idea of a new revolt against Russian rule. In Kielce, the priests referred to the legionnaires as "Red Danger," as Piłsudski was a member of the Socialist Party. There was great disappointment among the Polish soldiers.[15] At the same time, on 16 August, the Naczelny Komitet Narodowy (National Main Committee) was formed under the leadership of the democrats and the mayor of Cracow, Juliusz Leo. It was to become the main organ of the united Polish political forces in Galicia and the highest political representative of the Poles.[16]

After the fiasco brought on by the idea of revolution, the Austro-Hungarian High Command (AOK) considered dissolving Piłsudski's volunteer units, but thanks to the intervention of Galician politicians they were absorbed into the Austrian Landsturm. They were allowed to expand to the strength of a regiment. Their pay and modern weapons were provided by the Austro-Hungarian Army. In their ranks were members of the intelligentsia along with skilled workers and laborers but, at least initially, very few peasants. These units fostered the democratic and middle-class traditions of the Dąbrowski Legion from the era of the Napoleonic Wars. They were highly motivated and willing to make sacrifices based on their commitment to the struggle for a free Poland. The number of volunteers was so great that in December 1914 the regiment was re-formed into the so-called First Brigade of the Legions. The second was established in the spring and the third in the summer of 1915.[17]

The Activity of the Pro-Russian Camp

The adherents of the pro-Russian option were also active from the beginning of the war. Despite many challenges, the Poles tried to organize themselves. During the war, many citizens committees were founded, such as the Central Citizens' Committee under the leadership of Władysław Grabski in Warsaw, which undertook primarily charitable tasks. In June 1915 a committee made up of Poles and Russians living in Russia was established for the purpose of submitting suggestions for the realization of the manifesto of Grand Duke Nikolai; its ideas were recorded and published.[18] There were also efforts to organize a Polish voluntary military unit on the Russian side, the so-called Puławski Legion, which numbered only one thousand soldiers. Altogether, about twenty-five hundred soldiers eventually served in the ranks of this legion. The Russians viewed the legion with distrust and blocked its efforts to recruit soldiers. In January 1915, it was absorbed into a brigade of the Russian Army, and after taking heavy losses in the fall of 1915, it was dissolved.[19]

In November 1914 the Komitet Narodowy Polski (Polish National Committee) was organized; its sphere of action placed limits on the Russians. Its top leaders were the conservative Graf Zygmunt Wielopolski and the nationalist Roman Dmowski. They made it clear in a public appeal that "any voluntary help from the Polish side to the Germans and their allies would be considered a punishable act against Poland." After the conquest of Congress Poland by the Central Powers, the committee moved to Petrograd.[20] At this point, in November 1915, Dmowski left Petrograd and went to Paris in order to drum up support for the Polish issue. There, however, he encountered only indifference. France and Great Britain had their hands tied as they had already stated in a declaration that the Polish issue was a Russian internal affair, and Russia would have to come to its own decision concerning its western boundaries.

The Russian Occupation of Galicia

The Polish inhabitants of Galicia feared the approaching Russian Army. During the Russian offensive of 1914, people bought massive numbers of pictures of the Holy Virgin in order to be able to prove that they were neither Jews nor German Protestants. There were incidents of Russian soldiers breaking into the homes of private citizens, stealing possessions, and raping women. Although these cases were rare, many Poles had the impression they were common.[21] One victim was Karolina Kózka, a sixteen-year-old farmer's daughter from the Tarnów area who was killed by a Russian soldier during an attempted rape in November 1914.[22]

Georgij Bobrinskij, who was appointed by the czar as general governor of Galicia, pursued a policy that was catastrophic to the Polish issue. On 13 November 1914 he let it be known that the eastern part of Galicia, the Bukovina area, and the Ukrainian areas in the Carpathians that extended as far as Nowy Sącz were to be considered original Russian territories and they would therefore be incorporated into Russia. In a declaration published at the beginning of the war, the Russian side even spoke of the liberation of "Halic Russia" and of releasing the Russian inhabitants in the area around Halic from a six-hundred-year bondage. As one of the most important goals of his policy, Bobrinskij proposed the conversion from Eastern Catholicism to Orthodoxy. In February 1915 the seat of the Orthodox archbishop of Wohlynien was relocated from

Żytomierz (now Zitomier, Ukraine) to Lwów (Lemberg; now L'viv, Ukraine). Archbishop Elogiusch began a campaign to convince the Eastern Catholics to convert to the Orthodox denomination; about 10 percent of the Eastern Catholics gave in to this pressure. Along with this, Bobrinskij announced the introduction of the Russian language and Russian law. The University of Lwów (Lemberg), the Technical University, more than one hundred middle schools, and about two thousand elementary schools were closed by the Russian authorities. Even meetings of the state parliaments and the self-governing bodies were forbidden.[23] And Czar Nicholas II himself said in a balcony speech during his visit in Lwów (Lemberg) on 22 April 1915: "There is no Galicia, only a Great Russia as far as the Carpathians."[24]

Such steps had to be perceived by the Poles in Galicia with great concern, as these sorts of policies meant the end of the existing autonomy of the Polish populace in Galicia. The Galician Poles would have to expect the same fate as their brothers in the Russian sector.[25]

The German and Austro-Hungarian Occupation of Russian Poland

As the Germans pushed further on and the Russian Army pulled back from Congress Poland, the wounded and Russian soldiers who had been left behind were not subject to revenge by the Polish population but instead were often bid a sorrowful farewell. The people observed the retreating czarist troops in silence, often giving them cigarettes and food, as many Poles considered them to be their "own" people.[26] But in late summer 1915 it became clear that the Russians were carrying out a massive scorched-earth policy, destroying crops, orchards, roads, railroad tracks, and railway stations, and forcing farmers (mainly those from the eastern government areas) to move with the troops into the interior of Russia and ultimately dismantle factories and transport them away together with their workforce. According to research by Cracow historian Andrzej Chwalba, the Russian commanders would refuse to carry out their barbaric orders if they were offered suitable bribes.[27] Only under these conditions did pro-Russian sympathies and nostalgic ties diminish, especially in light of news of Bobrinskij's policy in occupied Galicia.[28]

The surprising success of the attack of Gorlice-Tarnów changed the situation of the Polish nation profoundly. All of Congress Poland fell into the hands of the German and Austro-Hungarian troops, including a portion of Russia's western government. Because in territories such as Vilna the Polish nobility predominated, and because these areas were centers of Polish culture, this portion of Congress Poland had always been viewed by the Poles as "stolen ground." But rather than viewing the Germans as liberators from the Russian yoke, the Poles greeted them with a mixture of fear and enmity. After the occupation of Warsaw by German troops on 5 August 1915, the Poles regarded German policy with great caution.

There are several reasons for this. No one had forgotten the German bombardment and destruction of Kalisz, a town on the German-Russian border, during the first days of the war (4–7 August 1914). This act of barbarism, allegedly prompted by shots from the city into the rear of the German troops, resulted in the burning and destruction of almost 95 percent of the old city, or historic quarter.[29] The news of this event spread quickly and angered many inhabitants of Poland's Russian sector.[30] After the German occupation began, people held their breath in expectation. Both politicians and populace doubted the occupiers' words and anticipated their next moves with trepidation. The mood among the general public worsened, as did the economic situation—the occupied territories had been integrated into the German war economy and were being squeezed dry. Along with this came deforestation, the dismantling of machinery in factories, and the requisitioning of items such as food and coal as well as brass items such as bells and metal blades. The high unemployment rate also contributed to the sinking standard of living; inflation climbed and with it came black marketeering and speculation.

General Hans von Beseler, the governor of Warsaw, attempted to gain the sympathy of the Poles with his policies. After long negotiations in November 1915 in Warsaw, the university and the technical high school, now Polish once more, resumed their work.[31] Von Beseler also allowed Polish society a limited degree of self-organization. Then charitable councils were founded, such as the Rada Główna Opiekuncza (Central Main Council for Charity). Its advisors included Polish elite such as bishops, nobility, and landowners. Very quickly the school system was also re-formed in the Polish manner and spirit.[32]

It was obvious to the Central Powers that Poland needed to be sparked into military action. Piłsudski, however, did not want to increase the strength of the legions without a concrete assurance with respect to the postwar borders and the safeguarding of Poland's future political system. At the end of 1915, the three Polish brigades that were fighting on the side of Austria-Hungary against the Russians had twenty thousand soldiers.

This was another reason for the disagreement between Piłsudski and Władysław Sikorski. Piłsudski wanted to make the further development of the legions dependent on a clear political declaration from the Central Powers as to the future resurrection of Poland. His colleague Sikorski argued against this, saying the Poles could increase their chances and their position in the negotiations with the Central Powers if they had more soldiers deployed. The number of potential soldiers was considerable, since the Russian authorities in Congress Poland had an estimated eight hundred thousand men able to bear arms who had not yet been drafted.[33]

In Congress Poland, Polish society was split into the so-called Aktywiści

(Activists) and the Pasywiści (Passives). The first were ready to work in cooperation with the occupiers under certain conditions. In order to strengthen his position with respect to the occupying powers, in December 1915 Piłsudski decided to institute political representation of the Polish kingdom by setting up the Centralny Komitet Narodowy (Central National Committee). Only a few, mainly left-leaning, parties sent their representatives to this organization: the PPS, the PSL "Wyzwolenie" (Polish Peasant "Liberation" Party), and the Narodowy Zwiazek Robotnikow (National Alliance of Workers).[34] In contrast, the Conservatives and Nationalists held their breath in expectation and observed the further development of the war. In October 1915 they convened the Międzypartyjne Koło Polityczne (Political Circle of Combined Parties).[35]

The Activity of the Austro-Hungarian Army in Reconquered Galicia

For the Polish inhabitants of Galicia, liberation from Russian occupation went hand in hand with brutal Austrian retaliatory measures. In the liberated areas, notices were posted offering 250 crowns for information on traitors and collaborators with the Russians. Many Polish peasants fell victim to the field tribunals. In December 1917 Władysław Długosz, the Polish delegate to the National Council, estimated the numbers of the victims of these tribunals in Galicia to be as many as sixty thousand.[36] Biliński wrote in his memoirs about the activity of the Austrian authorities: "Archduke Joseph Ferdinand had Polish peasants hanged indiscriminately in front of the church in every village in western Galicia."[37] The responsibility for this act of terror was placed on the shoulders of Joseph Ferdinand because he, as a "desk criminal," as it were, had allowed it to occur. The peasants themselves complained: "The Muscovites are bad, the Germans are also bad, but the worst beasts are the Honveds [Royal Hungarian Landwehr]." The Austrian form of "justice" in this instance carried the mark of blind vengeance and the desire to find scapegoats to blame for their military defeats. After the liberation of Tarnów, for example, a mathematics teacher by the name of Łazarski was executed because at the same time that Russian troops had been present in the city, he received a visit in his home from his son-in-law, who was a Pole and Russian officer.[38] Even the Polish nobility and civil servants were accused of high treason. In 1915 the last Polish governor of Galicia, Witold Korytowski, was dismissed and replaced by General Hermann von Colard.

The Aftermath

Disputes concerning political alignments that existed during the First World War carried over significantly into the world of Polish politics during the later period between the wars. This was manifested to a large extent in the political rivalry between Dmowski's nationalistic National Democratic Party and Piłsudski and his adherents. Veterans of the Piłsudski Legions, the self-styled Sanacja ("Sanation Regime") that seized power in the country in May 1926 by military coup, governed Poland until the end of the Second Republic in September 1939. Dmowski remained Piłsudski's bitter enemy to the end.

The tradition of the legion played a major role both in the political life of Poland and in the expansion of political patriotism in this multiethnic society. It should be pointed out here that during the period between the wars ethnic Poles comprised only 60 percent of the Polish citizenry. The exaggerated emphasis on the merits of the Piłsudski camp and the simultaneous silence about the accomplishments of the other political entities was part of the daily agenda of national propaganda. This became most noticeable in the context of national holidays, educational systems, and elections to the Sejm, or lower house of Parliament. The popular song of the legions, "We Are the First Brigade," was given the rank of a second, unofficial national anthem.

This had consequences even in 1945. The new Communist rulers sought to completely erase the tradition of the legions from the public consciousness. "We Are the First Brigade" was banned, and the entire tradition was systematically discredited. This policy, however, also affected the tradition of Dmowski. Paradoxically, in patriotic and oppositional circles, efforts were made to maintain both lines of tradition. In Cracow beginning in the 1980s, demonstrations were organized on every anniversary of the deployment of the earliest cadre company in August 1914. More recently, the leader of the democratic opposition and Solidarity Union, Lech Wałęsa, wore a beard fashioned in the style of Piłsudski and had a sculptural bust of Piłsudski placed in his office. Both were very charismatic leaders.[39] Since the fall of Communism and the reestablishment of complete independence, there has been an official return to this tradition.[40] Thus, it can be argued that the First World War, especially its first two years, made an essential contribution to the emergence of a modern political culture and tradition.

Notes

1. Adam Mickiewicz, *Księgi Narodu i Pielgrzymstwa Polskiego, wydanie drugie w Awinjonie,* Avignon 1833, 69.

2. Roman Dmowski, *Polityka Polska i odbudowanie państwa polskiego,* vol. 1, Warsaw 1988, 171.

3. Marian Zgórniak, *1914–1918. Studia i szkice z dziejów I wojny światowej,* Cracow 187, 102–15; Piotr Szlanta, "Die Polen—ein Volk ohne Pazifisten? Das Verhältnis der Polen zum Krieg vor 1914." In: *Der Grosse Krieg beginnt: Sommer und Herbst 1914* [*The Great War Begins: Summer and Autumn 1914*], edited by Joachim Tauber, Lüneburg 2016, 11–26.

4. Janusz Krawat, *Od idei do czynu: Myśl i organizacjc niepodległościowe w Poznańskiem w latach 1887–1919,* Poznań 2002, 288–91.

5. Stefan Kieniewicz, *Historia Polski 1795–1918*, Warsaw 1996, 491f.

6. Wacław Sobieski, *Dzieje Polski*, Warsaw 1938, vol. 3, 139; Marian Kukiel, *Dzieje Polski porozbiorowe (1794–1921)*, London 1993, 561.

7. *Zbiór dokumentów dotyczących sprawy polskiej. Sierpień 1914 r -styczeń 1915 r*, Szwajcarya 1915, 12f.

8. Aleksander Achmatowicz, *Polityka Rosji w kwestii polskiej w pierwszym roku Wielkiej Wojny 1914–1915*, Warsaw 2003, 243–304; Wiesława Toporowicz, *Sprawa polska w polityce rosyjskiej 1914–1917*, Warsaw 1973, 89–92.

9. Jan Gebethner, *Młodość wydawcy*, Warsaw 1989, 176; Władysław Leopold Jaworski, *Diariusz 1914–1918*, Warsaw 1997, 70; Hipolit Korwin-Milewski, *Siedemdziesiąt lat wspomnień (1855–1925)*, Warsaw 1993, 265f.; Aleksander Kakowski, *Z niewoli do niepodległości. Pamiętniki*, Cracow 2000, 123f.

10. Janusz Pajewski, *Odbudowa państwa polskiego 1914–1918*, Warsaw 1928, 51–54; Kazimierz W. Kumaniecki, *Odbudowa państwowości polskiej*, Warsaw, Cracow 1924, 25; *Zbiór dokumentów dotyczących sprawy polskiej*, 44–45, 61.

11. Krzysztof Dunin Wąsowicz, *Warszawa w latach 1914–1918*, Warsaw 1989, 5.

12. Michał Baczkowski, *Pod czarno-żółtymi sztandarami. Galicja i jej mieszkańcy wobec austro-wegierskich struktur militarnych*, Cracow 2003, 382f.; Kakowski, *Z niewoli do niepodległości*, 120f.; Wincenty Witos, *Moje wspomnienia*, Paris 1964, vol. 2, 9; Jerzy Holzer and Jan Molenda, *Polska w pierwszej wojnie światowej*, Warsaw 1973, 138.

13. *Pamiętnik księżnej Marii Zdzisławy Lubomirskiej 1914–1918*, Poznań 1997, 13, 15.

14. Piotr Szlanta, "Der Glaube an das bekannte Heute, der Glaube an das unsichere Morgen. Die Polen und der Beginn des Ersten Weltkriegs." In: *Jahrbücher für Geschichte Osteuropas*, Vol. 61 Issue 3 (2013), 411–32.

15. Roman Starzyński, *Cztery lata w służbie Komendanta*, Warsaw 1937, 50f.

16. Andrzej Garlicki, *U źródeł obozu belwederskiego*, Warsaw 1981, 240–63.

17. Mieczysław Wrzosek, "Udział Legionów Polskich w austro-węgierskim wysiłku wojennym." In: *Między Wiedniem a Lwowem. Referaty polsko-austriackiej sesji poświęcone 80 rocznicy wybuchu pierwszej woijny światowej*, edited by Andrzej Rzepniewski, Warsaw, 17 November 1994, 53–58; see also Wacława Milewska, Janusz Tadeusz Nowak, and Maria Zientara, *Legiony Polskie 1914–1918. Zarys historii militarnej i politycznej*, Cracow 1998; Mieczysław Wrzosek, *Polski czyn zbrojny podczas I wojny światowej 1914–1918*, Warsaw 1990.

18. Holzer/Molenda, *Polska*, 120–23.

19. Toporowicz, *Sprawa polska*, 129–48. Henryk Bagiński, *Wojsko polskie na Wschodzie*, Warsaw 1921, 9–22.

20. Kakowski, *Z niewoli do niepodległości*, 231–38; *Zbiór dokumentów*, 34–38.

21. Bronisław Świeykowski, *Z dni grozy w Gorlicach—od 25/IX/1914 do 2/V/1915*, www.cmentarze.gorlice.net.pl.

22. In 1987 she was beatified by Pope John Paul II.

23. Kukiel, *Dzieje Polski*, 557.

24. Władysław Konopczyński, *Historia Polityczna Polski 1914–1939*, Warsaw 1995, 20.

25. Achmatowicz, *Polityka Rosji*, 348–91.

26. Andrzej Chwalba, *Polacy w służbie Moskali*, Warsaw, Cracow 1999, 241–43.

27. Next to cash, wristwatches were said to be a favorite gift. Andrzej Chwalba, *Historia Polski 1795–1918,* Cracow 2000, 576. For an in-depth treatment, see Andrzej Chwalba, *Imperium korupcji w Rosji i w Królestwie Polskim w latach 1861–1917,* Cracow 1995.

28. Dmowski, *Polityka Polska,* 204f.

29. Details in Mieczyław Arkadiusz Woźniak, *Kalisz 1914: Pogrom miasta,* Kalisz 1995; Laura Engelstein, "A Belgium of Our Own. The Sack of Russian Kalisz, August 1914." In: *Kritika. Explorations in Russian and Euroasian History,* Vol. 10 Issue 3 (2009), 441–73.

30. Gebethner, *Młodość wydawcy,* 176.

31. *Dzieje Uniwersytetu Warszawskiego 1915–1939,* edited by Andrzej Chojnowski, Warsaw 1982, 13–23.

32. Bolesław Wieniawa-Długoszowski, *Wymarsz i inne wspomnienia,* Warsaw 1992, 91–107.

33. Ryszard Świątek, *Lodowa Ściana. Sekrety polityki Józefa Piłsudskiego 1904–1918,* Cracow 1998, 815f.

34. Jerzy Z. Pająk, *O rząd i armie. Centralny Komitet Narodowy (1915–1917),* Kielce 2003, 68–83.

35. Dmowski, *Polityka polska,* 229f.

36. Sobieski, *Dzieje Polski,* 140.

37. Leon Biliński, *Wspomnienia,* Warsaw 1924, vol. 1, 285.

38. Sobieski, *Dzieje Polski,* 148.

39. Tadeusz Biernat, *Józef Piłsudski-Lech Wałęsa: paradoks charyzmatycznego przywództwa,* Toruń 2000.

40. Heidi Hein, *Der Piłsudski-Kult und seine Bedeutung für den polnischen Staat 1926–1939,* Marburg 2002, 365.

8

The Germans

Russian Perceptions of the Enemy

Hubertus F. Jahn

While Germany and Russia have historical connections that reach many centuries into the past, as Günther Stökl points out, the relationship exhibits a "troubling instability."[1] This instability, entwined as it is with political rivalries, areas of cooperation, broad cultural exchanges, wars, economic relationships and, of course, personal contacts, has led to a situation in which each side holds highly diverse perceptions of the other. These perceptions are as numerous as the individuals who hold them.

Georg von Rauch, in his 1964 article on Russian perceptions of Germany, poetically describes the situation as resembling the movement of the beam of a searchlight across the dark sky.[2] Perceptions and ideas are similar to this roaming beam of light in that from a historical perspective they are fleeting notions that cannot be pinned down in a consistent, scientific manner. Perceptions lack statistical components, continue to change and evolve, and are constantly reviewed and revised.[3] Moreover, they are dependent on the individual perceiver and are therefore impossible to comprehend in their totality. A study of the Russian perception of its military enemy during the First World War can therefore be treated only in very general terms. My purpose is not to examine the perception of Germany held by all Russians, but to look at those of selected individuals, interest groups, and mass media. Source material includes written statements and recorded images, materials that had undeniably been subject to ideological influences and had served purely propagandistic goals.

The issue of the *Feindbild*, the "enemy-concept," and the real "enemy" that lies behind it is not only about the actual enemy one would encounter at the front. It is also about personal, social, and national identities, and it calls for formal distinctions to be made between "the Other" and "the Self": "The 'enemy' as a conceptual object is thus a question of internal as well as external social classification, a question of 'objectivized' definition through the badges and categories of official documentation as well as a subjective understanding of one's actual place and role in broader communities."[4]

Selbstbild (self-concept) and enemy-concept are thus very closely entwined with one another. Numerous sources are available for researching these concepts, although they have their limitations in terms of power of expression. Definitions of the Other and the Self are most readily found in official propaganda and written eyewitness accounts by the political and artistic elite. This material is published, easily accessible, and has often been used by historians in other contexts. A monographic overview of official Russian propaganda in the First World War is, of course, still lacking. Any propaganda that was guided by the state appeared in a much less developed form and will therefore be discounted here. It will also be more difficult to grasp the self-concept and enemy-concept among the broader, mostly illiterate sectors of the population. Joshua Sanborn, Eric Lohr, and Melissa Stockdale have recently analyzed specific conduct and social practices in contrast to states of consciousness. Their research focused on national identity and concepts of citizenship among Russian peasants, the underclasses in cities, and members of women's battalions. Their work investigated behavior during mobilization and anti-foreigner outbursts during the war. On the subject of inner motivations, enemy-concept and/or self-concept, they were able to make only speculative statements.[5] Finally, Peter Gatrell, in his study of the refugees of the eastern front, argues convincingly that the experiences of expulsion and the physical placing together of ethnic groups at least encouraged national self-understanding and brought balance to their perception of the enemy. This applied primarily to national minorities in the Russian Empire.[6]

Because of the available resources in this area, a good starting point for research is the Russians' perception of their enemy in the area of politics. Although it is hardly possible to trace specific political strategies and decisions directly to personal attitudes, it can be presumed that policies did not evolve without the presence of such attitudes. Russia's political scene changed fundamentally after the Revolution of 1905. Through the establishment of a parliament, the Duma, and the lifting of press censorship, public (and publicized) opinions had a greater importance than previously. With respect to Germany (and Austria-Hungary as well, at least since the Bosnian annexation crisis), public opinion fell into two camps, something that also occurred in the area of politics. For instance, on one hand, there were the proponents of an alliance with Great Britain and France, found primarily in liberal circles within the Duma, in business circles, and among moderate members of the government. On the other hand, there were some who supported a pro-German course of action, primarily in the sphere of the radical Right, conservative circles, and the Ministry of the Interior.[7] But the anti-German politicians were by far in the majority. Their negative sentiments had evolved over a long period and were driven by a multitude of different factors. In order to understand the perception of Germany held by most Russian politicians during the First World War, it is helpful to at least outline the most important key events that preceded the war.

The "official" Russian perception of Germany had been deteriorating at least since 1890, with the German refusal to extend the Reinsurance Treaty. This event in particular, in concert with pervasive concerns about the German economic and military expansion that had taken place since the founding of the German Empire in 1871, prompted Russia to enter an alliance with France. This led to their close cooperation, primarily in military and financial spheres. Beginning in 1906, financial considerations also led to a Russian rapprochement with Great Britain. Despite this alliance, Russia transacted almost half of its foreign trade with Germany, which contributed to the widespread sense of Russia being a kind of German colony.[8] This was underscored all the more by the strong presence of German firms and businessmen in Russia as well as by the large number of bureaucrats of German origin in public administration. Since the time of Peter the Great, Russia had continually recruited skilled workers from other countries, and since the incorporation of the Baltic states into the Russian Empire, German-Baltic nobility comprised a strong contingent among national officials. Although the greatest number of these "Baltic barons" had long since become Russianized, having few ties in the Baltic and none at all in the German Empire, they still represented a bastion of German interests and reactionary attitudes.[9] German-Russian relations had suffered particularly long-term damage due to events in the Balkans. Germany's support of Austria in the Bosnian annexation crisis and its stance on the question of war reparations after the First Balkan War were most humiliating to Russia. Liman von Sanders's mission to Constantinople in 1913 was ultimately viewed as a direct threat to Russia's vital interests in the Straits.

It is hardly surprising, then, that in 1914, with few exceptions, Russian public opinion had an anti-German orientation. Influenced by liberals and radical ideas, Russians celebrated their rapprochement with France and Great Britain and hoped that in consequence Russia would develop into a liberal constitutional state.[10] Germany, in contrast, was represented as the epitome of militarism and authoritarian rule. Under the influence of pan-Slavic ideas, that is, the idea of a union of Slavic nations in opposition to the Germanic cultural sphere, the catchphrase "Drang nach Osten" (Push to the East) made the rounds. On the basis of this general concept of German expansionism, which had little basis in reality, a threat situation was easily construed, one that was alleged to have roots in the distant historical past.[11] Essential factors in this climate of fear were the German arms buildup, German economic power, Volga German colonists, anti-Russian attacks by Baltic German activists, the goals of the Pan-German League, and political events in the Balkans.[12] The slogan "Drang nach Osten" was such an essential component of the Russians' concept of their enemy, and so widely used before and after 1914, that it even found its way into diplomatic correspondence and appeared in the memoirs of Foreign Minister Sergei Sazonov after the war.[13]

The few proponents of a closer alliance with Germany had little with which to counter the widespread anti-German mood among Russian politicians. Almost without exception they stood on the right margins of the political spectrum, supported by papers such as *Grazhdanin* (the Citizen) and *Moskovskie Vedomosti* (Moscow News), which had very limited readership. They touted monarchical principles and posited Imperial Germany as a natural ally of autocracy and a bulwark against liberalism and revolutionary dangers. Dubronin, the leader of the notorious Black Hundredists, went so far during the war as to assert that a victory by the Hohenzollerns would be a lesser evil than a victory of democracy in Russia.[14] A war with Germany, according to the views of many conservative politicians, would certainly lead to a socialist revolution and the subsequent collapse of the Czarist Empire.[15] This point was emphasized with particular force in a memorandum addressed to the czar in February 1914 by the former minister of the interior and mastermind of the pro-German camp, Petr Durnovo.[16] In it, he described with almost prophetic foresight the economic and military problems that would confront Russia in a war with Germany and very accurately predicted the social upheaval that would result. The weakness of the pro-German camp obviously lay in the fact that many of its adherents were positioned close to—but not directly in—seats of power. Some of them served in the administration of the court, others were placed in diplomatic positions abroad or had retired prior to 1914. Durnovo and Sergei Vitte, the former prime ministers, enjoyed great prestige as elder statesmen but were no longer given any say in political decisions. Such decisions lay to a large extent in the hands of men for whom strategic and diplomatic considerations, such as those relating to the alliance with France and Great Britain, were more important than issues in the domestic sphere, where there was a pronounced antipathy toward Germany and problems that were difficult to anticipate.[17]

As tempting as it may be to speculate about the sympathies and antipathies of politicians on the basis of their decisions and official statements, such an approach obviously overlooks the fact that politicians are usually engaged in realpolitik. The political process is also affected by a great many other factors and interests. Furthermore, a specific self-concept, be it Russia as a liberal constitutional state or Russia as a monarchy, does not automatically reflect anything specific in terms of an enemy stereotype. Durnovo's memorandum, for instance, shows more about his sense of reality and sound knowledge of the Russian situation than it does about his pro-German enthusiasm. In order to more precisely examine personal attitudes toward Germany among Russian politicians, it is better to turn to primary sources. In private correspondence, memoirs, and autobiographies, as sugarcoated and controlled as they might have been, one nevertheless finds more authentic voices between their lines than in many official announcements.[18]

Of particular interest in this regard is the Russian Foreign Service, where both anti-Germans and pro-Germans were active, and which is therefore more representative of the political sphere in Russia as a whole. These political figures provide a relatively large body of primary sources. The anti-German stance of foreign ministers Aleksandr Izvol'skii (1906–1910) and Sergei Sazonov (1910–1916) is generally well known. As one would expect, their personal archival material reflects this bias. Izvol'skii was fond of vacationing on the Tegernsee, a lake in Bavaria, and in a personal letter to Sazonov in 1912 he lamented that he "quite unjustly had the reputation as a Germanophobe." Nevertheless, he held some strikingly negative ideas about Germany, in particular about the German national character.[19] In his memoirs, he described what, in his opinion, was the classical stereotype of the German bureaucrat. His example was the chairman of the Court of Auditors, Imperial Controller Peter Schwanenbach, "who represents the most accomplished of the functionaries of German origin, most of whom come from a very humble milieu, often very hard working, but who have primarily succeeded in acquiring rank within the Russian hierarchy through intrigue and perfidy."[20]

Because the ascendant German bureaucrats supposedly used intrigue and baseness to acquire positions in the Russian state government, it was only logical to Izvol'skii that he should try to foster the active advancement of young Russian talent. When he was looking for ministry assistants in 1908, he chose Nikolai Charykov—not just because he was an old school friend who was well versed in the Eastern Question but also because, as he wrote, he saw in Charykov a man with roots in the traditional circles of the Russian landowning nobility that dominated in the country's representational bodies.[21] On the other hand, he was not particularly pleased when, during his time as ambassador in Paris, a Baron Uexküll was recommended to him as attaché. Uexküll made a "very unfavorable impression," he complained to Sazonov, adding: "Can we really not find a young man with a university education and a proper Russian family name?"[22] Izvol'skii's colleague Aleksandr Savinskii who was later the chief of the Russian mission in Bulgaria, also found the strong presence of the Baltic Germans among his colleagues a thorn in his side. "Although Russian subjects, most of them remained German in soul and sentiment, and faithful servants of the German cause," he wrote in his memoirs.[23] Unlike Izvol'skii, who was more biased against specific German character traits, Savinskii was seriously convinced that the "Teutons," ever since the founding of the Teutonic

Order in the late twelfth century, were trying to advance against the eastern Slavs, and that they had been systematically colonizing Russia since the time of Fredrick the Great.

Sergei Sazonov's opinion was less coarse and less influenced by such one-sided propaganda. He had long been regarded as pro-German, and even after the Balkan Wars was accused of anti-Slav attitudes in pan-Slavic circles. It seems that he most likely did not completely shift to the anti-German camp until 1913, during the Liman von Sanders crisis.[24] His memoirs, written during the First World War, also reflect his ambivalent relationship with Germany. He makes reference to the Push to the East, blames German politics and diplomacy for "mendacity and duplicity," writes of "warlike Germanism," predicts the inevitable clash between Germanism and Slavism, and points to the "unbelievable tendency towards self-intoxication that is particular to the German people." But he also professes that he "never suffered from Germanophobia." On the contrary, he displays high respect for the Germans, acknowledging that their science and culture have enriched "the intellectual domain of all thinking mankind." He sincerely admired German art, above all the music and written word of older eras. After the founding of the empire "under the banner of 'blood and iron,'" however, he believed German art and science had taken on the distinctive feel of barracks and factories. Continuing in the same metaphoric style, he writes: "The tree of the German national and economic power grew and threw a giant shadow on all parts of the world, but the fount of the intellectual and moral powers of the German people gradually began to run dry. The beneficent cultural influence of Germany on the European people began to disappear and ultimately gave way to a sense of antipathy."[25]

Not surprisingly, some of Sazonov's pro-German colleagues also expressed enthusiasm for German art and culture, although without the reservations expressed by Sazonov. When Petr Botkin, the longtime envoy to Portugal, visited the building of the Foreign Ministry in Petrograd for the first time, he found its grim stairwells reminded him of the final words of Johann Wolfgang von Goethe—"Mehr Licht" (more light). He too was touched by the music of Richard Wagner, whom he mentions quite often in his memoirs.[26] Iurii Solov'ev, a career diplomat posted in Stuttgart from 1909 to 1911, was pleasantly surprised on his arrival in the city. Based on what his superiors had told him, he expected to find that the Germans harbored a malicious attitude toward Russia. During his stay there, he attended the Bayreuth Festival several times and was otherwise impressed by the cleanliness of Wurttemburg villages and the good condition of German roads.[27]

The Russian concept of Germany obviously evolved from many different impressions and experiences. These were not always related to high politics, diplomatic power plays, notions of social Darwinism, or apocalyptic myths. Even politicians were only human, with personal experiences, prejudices, and varying abilities to perceive reality. Their attitudes toward Germany fluctuated and changed over the course of time, ranging from enthusiasm to the deepest condemnation and hatred. True to the atmosphere of the times, it was difficult to distinguish more subtle stages or gray areas on this scale. While the Russian perception of the enemy was subject to changes, gaps, and contradictions, such as in Sazonov's case, it was also difficult to establish only half of an enemy-concept. But perhaps it is also simply that the term *enemy-concept* is too restrictive and has too many military connotations to permit the mutual perceptions of two countries to be drawn in precise lines. Under the conditions of war, at least, it was only a matter of choosing sides and giving the enemy a name. Pro-German voices fell quiet after 1914, and anti-German clichés defined everyday life in Russia.

Sazonov's disappointment in Germany, incidentally, was shared by many Russian intellectuals and artists. For them, the war meant a reevaluation of their relationship to Germany as well as to their own country. Germany had traditionally been the country from which Russian intellectuals drew their ideas.[28] Many artists as well took inspiration from Germany. Russian music, painting, and literature from the romantic to the modern and avant-garde periods would have been unimaginable without the close interrelationship with Germany. During the war, many of these relationships broke down, at least temporarily. German musical compositions, for instance, if they could not be specifically categorized as classical or earlier in origin, were either removed from programs or attributed to composers whose names were Russian, or at least Russianized. Thus, at one event in Rostov on Don, composer Franz von Suppé was given the very politically correct name "Zupeiskii." The operas of Richard Wagner had dominated the music offerings in the main cities and even the provinces prior to 1914: eight new performances of his works were staged during the 1913–1914 season alone. Now his works were completely shunned and their contents reinterpreted as purely chauvinistic. The struggle over the treasure of the Nibelung, for instance, was now understood as symbolic of German imperialistic intentions. Wagner's bombastic style was now associated with the boastfulness of Wilhelm II, whose car horn supposedly played the tune of the "Ride of the Valkyries." The only place Wagner still found a home was the cabaret. In 1914–1915, Petrograd's Troitskii Theater featured a performance of *Hoch Patrioten: Götterdämmerung* (Hail the Patriots: The Twilight of the Gods). Advertised as a "German patriotic opera," it showcased many heroes from Wagner's operas, but they were depicted in a comical exaggerated manner, allegorical figures representing German high-handedness and pomposity.[29] On the stages of the Petrograd Mariinskii Theater as well as in the Moscow Bolshoi Theater during this time, Michail Glinka's "A Life for the Tsar" was performed together with a "Ring" of quickly cobbled together operas by Nikolai Rimskii-Korsakov, which, however, did not even come close to Wagner's Ring Cycle. Further, it became customary to play the national anthem before opera performances, sometimes supplemented by those of Russia's allies.

The arts and culture reacted to the war in very different ways. They presented the enemy and their own heroes in a variety of versions and in doing so created a rich stock of stereotypes of both enemy and self in literary, visual, and representational genres. This supplied the Russian general public with a concept of Germany and its allies as well as a concept of Russia and its allies. This collection of stereotypes included first and foremost the German kaiser, followed by his Austro-Hungarian colleague and the Turkish sultan. One-third of all satirical postcards in Russia during the war were devoted to Wilhelm II.[30] Primarily at the beginning of the war, German atrocities also figured quite prominently, such as the shooting of civilians in Kalisz or the destruction of Reims Cathedral.

The Russian self-image consisted mainly of prominent heroes, such as the daring Cossacks, or figures from Russian history, for instance, famous field commanders and medieval knights. (A revival of representations of this sort of historical hero also took place during the Second World War.) On a more abstract, philosophical level, the Russian self-concept was defined by a flowering of Slavophile ideas that interpreted the war as a contest of basic principles and as a struggle of Germanic versus Slavic cultural forces.[31] In this struggle, Russia fought for a spiritual and religious rebirth against the powers of Western materialism.

For an overview of the most important components of the Russian self-concept and its enemy-concept in art and culture in general, one might, for instance, glance through a volume of Russian poetry about the war published in 1915.[32] It begins with several poems about the Slavs. In the typical pan-Slavic tradition there are exhortations to other Slavic peoples, Serbian songs, and Slavic prayers. Other selections are dedicated to Galicia and Poland. Poems describe Poland as the little sister of Russia or designate the Poles as the brothers of the Russians. Obviously, here was an effort to emphasize close connections with a Slavic nation—which in other contexts was the least trusted of all due to its constant strivings for independence. The largest portion of the volume, composed of just over thirty poems, is titled simply "Voina" (War). This contains poems about actual experiences of the war that had just begun, such as one by Sergei Gorodetskii about the patriotic demonstrations at the outbreak of war, and one by a leading symbolist and war reporter of the time, Valerii Bryusov, concerning the position of Russia between East and West.[33]

Hero cults and the memorializing of outstanding warriors have always been important components of a nation's self-concept. Consequently, two parts of the poetry volume are devoted to this theme: one on heroes in general and one specifically about the Cossacks. In the Russian imagination, these elite troops embodied all possible personal characteristics worth striving for. They were swift and skilled, persevering and daring, brave and loyal. Furthermore, they had their share of peasants' cunning and thus were ideal identification figures for a broad spectrum of the population. Cossacks were at their most popular during the war. One in particular, Kuzma Kriuchkov, who allegedly speared eleven German soldiers with his lance, was depicted in all genres of mass culture. To him were devoted countless *lubki* (traditional popular prints). His heroic deeds were celebrated in genres from film to circus performances, where horseback acrobatics by Cossacks had always been a great attraction.[34]

If Cossacks were the most prominent male heroes, mothers and nurses were their feminine counterparts. Both had a section of poetry dedicated to them. Research on the experiences of Russian women during the First World War is still in its early stages.[35] Their role as identification figures is apparent in the fact that "Little Mother Russia" appears in many *lubki* and in many allegorical representations, sometimes even taking up the sword against German soldiers.[36] Much closer to the reality of war, however, were the nurses. On countless postcards and prints in popular periodicals, they embodied practical patriotic virtues and disseminated the notions of feminine sentimental devotion and women's readiness to make sacrifices, corresponding to paternalistic images of women in the era. On the other hand, the activity of a nurse obviously could also signal feminine independence and civil courage in the best sense of the term, and in this way such depictions could have a politically subversive effect, symbolizing engagement in social causes and declarations of equal status.[37]

Moreover, personal images can sometimes be misleading. As is true of pictures in general, their interpretation is ultimately beyond the artist's control. Even Leonid Pasternak discovered this. The father of the famous author created a poster in 1914 that called for supporting victims of the war. It depicted a wounded soldier bleeding from a head wound. (The depiction of the blood of one's own soldiers, incidentally, was a taboo even then.) Czar Nikolai disliked this picture because it supposedly showed a weakened Russian soldier instead of a brave one. Public response to the poster, however, was enthusiastic. A great many people gathered in front of the picture in the streets of Moscow and contributed money to the cause; pirated copies appeared on packages of chocolate; and the Bolsheviks even used the poster in 1917 for their antiwar propaganda.[38]

Three sections of this collection of poems were dedicated to the Russian allies. Belgium was especially prominently represented.[39] Having been overrun by the Germans, Belgium had taken on an exceptional status. Russians identified with the country on an emotional level, as was evident in other artistic genres as well. A popular *lubok* carried the title *Rossiia—Za pravdu* (Russia Stands for Truth).[40] This, too, was an expression of the intent to rush to the aid of those who, like Belgium, had been unjustly treated. Thus, self-concept and enemy-concept were brought together and utilized in a rather brilliant fashion.

The issue of atrocities committed by the German invaders also resonated. This subject received particular attention in 1915 in one of the first Russian animated films, *Liliia Belgii* (The Lily of Belgium) by Władisław Starewicz. The film shows a proud and freedom-loving Belgium, symbolized by a lily, blooming white, bathed in sunlight, and surrounded by butterflies. The lily is violently struck down by stag beetles that come from dank holes in the ground, led by one particular beetle with an especially large, threatening pair of horns reminiscent of a Viking helmet. At first they are shown brandishing beer tankards; then, carrying guidons, they cut down the lily with halberds because it is blocking their path. But then the beetles sink into a flooded polder. This prompts a victory celebration among the other small animals and plants, which symbolize the Belgian population and the allies, complete with a Cossack dance performed by pinecones, one of which is playing an accordion.[41]

The stag beetle with the especially large horns obviously stood for Wilhelm II. Several poems are devoted to him in a section whose very title, "Enemies," signals that the material deals with the creation of the ultimate enemy stereotype. It starts with a work by the symbolist Fedor Sologub entitled *Vil'gel'm Vtoroi* (Wilhelm the Second). The author alludes to the Push to the East and accuses the kaiser, who has been "intoxicated by blood," of conducting the war only to create markets for the Prussian Junkers' agriculture and German manufacturers.[42]

A widespread motif in Russia was the kaiser as a bloodthirsty beast. In better circles during the winter of 1914–1915, one might dance to the melody of "Krovavoe tango Vil'gel'ma" (Wilhelm's Bloody Tango), while in Petrograd's Circus Modern, the kaiser and his bloody warriors were chased through the arena.[43] Wilhelm was sometimes compared with a rabid dog, but was even more often associated with the Antichrist. In this guise he had allegedly, as some peasants firmly believed, haunted the province of Kostroma, where he was said to have drunk human blood.[44]

But the kaiser was not depicted only as a murderous spawn of hell. As in the other warring countries, there were countless caricatures of him in films, plays, and cabaret performances in which he appeared as a laughingstock. His grandiloquent behavior and mustache were particularly good material for laughs and could be made ridiculous with little effort. In comparison with Wilhelm II, other potential enemy stereotypes paled. Austrian kaiser Franz Joseph and the Turkish sultan usually entered the picture only in association with the German kaiser, and only rarely were German soldiers and generals or figures from German history depicted.

At the end of the volume of poetry we've been describing, examples from the vernacular were quoted. These reveal a popular concept of the Germans held by a broad spectrum of the Russian population. It is naturally difficult, however, to differentiate between the authentic voices of the population and those of, say, ethnographers and folk song writers. In the *chastushki* (Russian satirical poems or songs similar to limericks) contained in the book are found classical clichés of the German national character, although they have little direct connection with the war. That the Germans tend to enjoy drinking beer is generally known. And in Russia, they have long been known as *kolbasniki,* meaning producers and consumers of sausage. In the Russian puppet theater, that is, in the Russian version of Punch and Judy, it was usually the German figures who caught trouble from the Punch figure, Petrushka. And thanks to the fact that the Russian term for cockroach, *prusak,* is only one letter away from the Russian word for Prussian, *Prussak,* the floodgates were opened. The Germans, on the other hand, characterize these creatures as Russian. Such national stereotypes developed over hundreds of years amid close interaction between Russians and Germans, large numbers of whom lived in Russia as colonists, laborers, and merchants. To say that what was being created here was an "enemy-concept" may be overstating the case; instead, it appears more a matter of creating mutual cultural boundaries.[45]

The Russian perception of the Germans had many facets. Because it is difficult, if not impossible, to get to the root of individual perceptions of the enemy or of a nation's self-perception, one must extensively turn to the enemy stereotypes and self-concepts that appear in published form, meaning those that are manufactured, produced, and constructed for the public. Along with relatively vague ideological pan-Slavic concepts, the Push to the East idea, and other such concepts that had been growing for decades, a look at the cultural life of Russia during the war shows that the enemy was epitomized by its ruling figures, in particular Wilhelm II. On the other hand, to turn this argument around and conclude that the czar was the most important identification figure for the Russian self-concept would be misleading. He hardly appeared at all in allegorical materials and never onstage or in film. In the volume of poetry that was cited here, it is revealing that no distinct section was devoted to him, and only rarely did a poem even make reference to him. In the absence of a clear, universally accepted national symbol in mass culture, Russians turned to their own history, to the adventures of individual Cossacks, or to the traditions of the Russian village. For most Russian soldiers, this would likely have had more of a motivating effect than an unapproachable czar on a postcard or printed illustrations of an arrogant, pompous kaiser.

Notes

1. Günther Stökl, *Osteuropa und die Deutschen. Geschichte und Gegenwart einer spannungsreichen Nachbarschaft,* Munich 1970, 96.

2. Georg von Rauch, "Streiflichter zum russischen Deutschlandbilde des 19. Jahrhunderts." In: *Jahrbücher für Geschichte Osteuropas* (*JbGO*), 12 (1964), 5–47.

3. On the historical relativity and evolution of beliefs, see Günther Stökl, "Die historischen Grundlagen des russischen Deutschlandbildes." In: *Deutsche im europäischen Osten: Verständnis und Missverständnis,* edited by Friedhelm Berthold Kaiser and Bernhard Stasiewski, Cologne, Vienna 1976, 18–34, here 18f.

4. William Rosenberg, "Introduction." In: *Rossiia i pervaia mirovaia voina* (*Materialy mezhdunarodnogo nauchnogo kollokviuma*). Edited by Nikolai N. Smirnov, St. Petersburg 1999, 9–13, here 10.

5. Joshua A. Sanborn, *Drafting the Russian Nation: Military Conscription, Total War, and Mass Politics, 1905–1925,* DeKalb, IL 2003; Eric Lohr, *Nationalizing the Russian Empire: The Campaign against Enemy Aliens during World War I,* Cambridge MA 2003; Melissa K. Stockdale, "'My Death for the Motherland Is Happiness:' Women, Patriotism, and Soldiering in Russia's Great War, 1914–1917," In: *American Historical Review,* 109 (2004), 78–116.

6. Peter Gatrell, *A Whole Empire Walking: Refugees in Russia during World War I,* Bloomington IN 1999, 144–70.

7. Horst Jablonowski, "Die Stellungnahme der russischen Parteien zur Aussenpolitik der Regierung von der russisch-englischen Verständigung biz zum ersten Weltkriege." In: *Forschungen zur Osteuropäischen Geschichte,* 5 (1957), 60–92.

8. Bernd Bonwetsch, "Handelspolitik und Industrialisierung. Zur aussenwirtschaftlichen Abhängigkeit Russlands 1890–1914." In: *Wirtschaft und Gesellschaft im vorrevolutionären Russland,* edited by Dietrich Geyer, Cologne 1975, 277–99, here 282, 289–94.

9. Dominic Lieven, "The Russian Civil Service under Nicholas II: Some Variations on the Bureaucratic Theme." In: JbGO, 29 (1981), 366–403; Dominic Lieven, "Pro-Germans and Russian Foreign Policy, 1890–1914." In: *International History Review,* 2 (1980), 34–54, here 41.

10. See Uwe Liszkowski, *Zwischen Liberalismus und Imperialismus. Die zaristische Aussenpolitik vor dem Ersten Weltkrieg im Urteil Miljukovs und der Kadettenpartei.* Stuttgart 1974, 94–96; and Igor' V. Bestuzhev, *Bor'ba v Rossii po voprosam vneshnei politiki 1906–1910,* Moscow 1961, 129.

11. On the problematic nature and history of the term, see Hans Lemberg, "Der 'Drang nach Osten.' Schlagwort und Wirklichkeit." In: *Deutsche im europäischen Osten,* 1–17.

12. Walter Laqueur, *Russia and Germany: A Century of Conflict,* Boston 1965, 30–37.

13. Sergei D. Sazonov, *Sechs schwere Jahre,* Berlin 1927, 60.

14. Laqueur, *Russia and Germany,* 15.

15. Lieven, *Pro-Germans,* 43.

16. Petr Durnovo, *Zapiska,* Paris [ca. 1923], 6–31.

17. Lieven, *Pro-Germans,* 44f., 53.

18. On the relative importance of these sources, see Stökl, *Die historischen Grundlagen,* 16.

19. Friedrich Stieve, *Der diplomatische Schriftwechsel Iswolskis 1911–1914,* 4 vols., Berlin 1924, here vol. 2, 67.

20. *Memoires de Alexandre Iswolsky. Ancien ambassadeur de Russie á Paris* (*1906–1910*), Paris 1923, 131.

21. Nikolai V. Charykov, *Glimpses of High Politics: Through War & Peace, 1855–1929,* London 1931, 22, 268.

22. Stieve, *Der diplomatische Schriftwechsel,* vol. 1,24.

23. Aleksandr A. Savinskii, *Recollections of a Russian Diplomat,* London 1927, 144.

24. Stieve, *Der diplomatische Scriftwechsel,* vol. 2, 67, 289–302; Vladimir N. Kokovtsov, *Out of My Past: The Memoirs of Count Kokovtsov, Russian Minister of Finance, 1904–1914,* Stanford, CA 1935, 360.

25. Sazonov, *Sechs schwere Jahre,* 36, 44–46, 60–62, 265.

26. Petr S. Botkin, *Kartinki diplomaticheskoi zhizni,* Paris 1930, 23, 38–40, 66f. Botkin was only one of the countless Wagnerians in Russia. On the great popularity of the composer in Russia, see Bernice Glatzer Rosenthal, "Wagner and Wagnerian Ideas in Russia." In: *Wagnerism in European Culture and Politics,* edited by David C. Large and William Weber, Ithaca, NY 1984, 198–245.

27. Iurii Ia. Solov'ev, *Vospominaniia diplomata. 1893–1922,* Moscow 1959, 206–18, 226f., 235.

28. Laqueur, *Russia and Germany,* 19.

29. Hubertus F. Jahn, *Patriotic Culture in Russia during World War I,* Ithaca, NY, London 1995, 108, 142, 145.

30. Ibid., 48–50.

31. Ben Hellman, "Kogda vremia slavianofil'stvovalo. Russkie filosofy i pervaia mirovaia voina." In: *Problem istorii russkoi literatury nachala XX veka,* edited by Liisa Byckling and Pekka Pesonen, Helsinki 1989 (= *Studia Russica Helsingiensia et Tartuensia*), 211–39.

32. *Sovremennaia voina v russkoi poezii,* edited by Boris B. Glinskii, Petrograd 1915.

33. Ibid., 78f., 89. On the relationship of Briusov and other Russian symbolists to the World War, see Ben Hellman, *Poets of Hope and Despair: The Russian Symbolists in War and Revolution (1914–1918),* Helsinki 1995.

34. Jahn, *Patriotic Culture,* 23f., 87, 158.

35. Stockdale, "'My Death for the Motherland Is Happiness,'" 78–82.

36. Joanna Hubbs, *Mother Russia: The Feminine Myth in Russian Culture,* Bloomington, IN 1988, 153–60; Jahn, *Patriotic Culture,* 24–26.

37. Ibid., 42–47.

38. Ibid., 68f.; *Russische Graphik, 1880–1917,* edited by Mikhail Anikst, Munich 1991, 138f.

39. According to Ben Hellman, the Belgian theme dominated Russian literature in the first months of the war; see Hellman, *Poets of Hope and Despair,* 63–67.

40. *Rossiia–za pravdu,* Moscow 1914, reproduced in Jahn, *Patriotic Culture,* 27.

41. *Early Russian Cinema: A Unique Video Anthology in 10 Volumes,* produced by Erich Sargeant, London 1992, here cassette 3: "Starewicz's Fantasies."

42. *Sovremennaia voina,* 190; Hellman, *Poets of Hope and Despair,* 93f.

43. S. Frederick Starr, *Red and Hot: The Fate of Jazz in the Soviet Union, 1917–1980,* New York 1985, 20–34; Tsirk 'Modern'; Otzyvy sovremennoi pechati s 1908–1915 g. (Typoskript, Gosudarstvennyi muzei tsirkovogo iskusstva, Sankt Peterburg).

44. "Antikhrist." In: *Sine-Fono,* 13 (1915), 48, 90.

45. Svetlana V. Obolenskaia, "Obraz nemtsa v russkoi narodnoi kul'ture XVIII–XIX vv." In: *Odissei. Chelovek v Istorii,* Moscow 1991, 160–85, here 182.

9

The Slavic Peoples

The Central Powers' Self-Concept and Concept of the Enemy

Peter Hoeres

The eastern theater of war of the First World War is generally viewed by Western scholars, particularly in Germany, as a "secondary front" (Wilhelm Deist), and as such, has been neglected in scholarly research.[1] In the region ruled by the Austro-Hungarian Monarchy of that era, especially in the southeast and central European countries, the perspective has naturally evolved quite differently.

The same holds true for the eastern front during the Second World War, which is treated in historiography as a "war of extermination," with the First World War as its possible historical prologue.[2] This marginalizing approach to the war in the east of the Great War of 1914 to 1918 in Western and German research, however, is also an outcome of German strategic planning within the context of the Schlieffen Plan.[3] The plan had been to first concentrate on the western front, making a detour through Belgium in order to ensure a speedier victory against France. The troops that were expected to become available as a result of this victory would be relocated to the eastern front, which was still only weakly defended, thus ensuring a decisive victory against the Russians. Considering the vastness of the Russian territory, the clumsiness of the czarist military bureaucracy, and the inadequate rail network in the east, the Germans expected the Russian Army to take a long time mobilizing. They therefore moved seven German armies to the west and only one to the east. This mistaken strategy came back to haunt them in August 1914, when Russian units entered East Prussia. The Russian *Dampfwalze,* or steamroller (a widespread stereotype that had been operative for two decades), moved into the defenseless east, leaving a deep impression in the collective German mentality. This event placed the reactionary General Paul von Beneckendorff und von Hindenburg and his chief of staff Generalmajor Erich Ludendorff in the seemingly predestined role of liberators of East Prussia, even the guardians of the entire German Empire.

Hindenburg and Ludendorff had triumphed over the Narev Army of General Samsonov in the encirclement battle of Tannenberg. The battle, which raged from 21 to 23 August, actually did not take place directly at Tannenberg; the name was used in remembrance of the defeat there of the German Teutonic Order in 1410 in a battle against a Polish Lithuanian army that signaled the end of German eastern expansion.[4] The subsequent victory against the isolated Neman Army of General Rennenkampf on 7 September made for a perfect victory for the Germans in East Prussia.

But for the Austro-Hungarian Army under the chief of the General Staff Franz Freiherr Conrad von Hötzendorf, matters took a different turn. Despite having a population of similar size as Germany, Austria-Hungary (the "k.u.k. Monarchie," or, as author Robert Musil parodied it, "Kakania," alluding to cockroach infestation), could provide an army of only half the strength of the German Army. The Austro-Hungarian offensive ended with the temporary loss of Galicia and the retreat behind the Carpathians. Even the campaign against Serbia was unsuccessful. Although George Kennan was referring to the First World War as a whole when he came up with the phrase "the great seminal catastrophe," it could also be applied to this multinational army.[5] With the defeats suffered by the Austro-Hungarian Army, the coordination problems between the Germans and the Austrian military were magnified. The irritations between the military leaders that had been visible as early as the July Crisis expanded into serious friction between the countries of the Central Powers. The German Army repeatedly had to bail out the Austrians. After the capitulation of the Galician fortress Przemyśl on 22 March 1915, for instance, disaster was averted only by bringing in German troops from the north, which meant that on 3 June the Bavarians pulled into the fortress ahead of their comrades of the Austro-Hungarian Army. This reinforced the German claim of supremacy in questions of strategy, tactics, and leadership, and led to a substantial argument between the chiefs of the two general staffs, Erich von Falkenhayn and Conrad von Hötzendorf.

Falkenhayn, contrary to his original intentions, tried to improve the Austro-Hungarian situation through a strengthened commitment in eastern and southeastern Europe. The newly formed army group under Generaloberst August von Mackensen and his chief of staff Hans von Seeckt succeeded in a breakthrough between Tarnów and Gorlice. The Russian troops were subsequently forced further and further back. The Austro-Hungarian Army suffered setbacks as a result of the Brusilov offensive in the summer of 1916, the Kerensky offensive in the summer of 1917, and the counterattack that took place immediately afterward, which lasted until the conquest of Riga on 3 September 1917. It was not until after the October Revolution that the Central Powers won their longed-for separate peace in the east.

The armistice took place in December 1917, and Lenin signed the peace treaty of Brest-Litovsk on 3 March 1918 (a treaty that came into being without the participation of the Czechs, which caused the Austrian minister president Seidler to cast a no-confidence vote in the Reichsrat [Imperial Assembly]). With this, Germany was finally free from its nightmare of the two-front war or, as Bismarck called it, its "nightmare of coalitions." Despite this, there were still over 1 million German soldiers, a good many fewer than before, of course, who were still either standing or marching in the east. They undertook forays along the Black Sea toward Odessa, into Crimea, along the Don, and into the Ukraine, an important area due to its immense potential for grain.[6]

The temperament, patterns of perception, and conduct of the Central Powers during these profound events had an impact on the soldiers and populace of the east that has been given little scholarly attention. During the war, the soldiers, officers, journalists, scientists, and politicians of the Central Powers—at least on the side of Imperial Germany—came to refine their rather vague preconceived notions of the Slavs. The first steps toward researching this dense, multilayered process must begin with the understanding that the construct and knowledge of the Other also requires the construct and knowledge of the Self. Heterostereotypes and autostereotypes, one's own self-conception and the concept of the stranger or enemy, belong together.[7] In research on prejudice, the emphasis is on self-conception and self-image. In research on stereotypes, however, the emphasis is on the image of the Other. In other words, stereotype research focuses on the manner in which the Other is perceived. Approaching the process from this perspective, one cannot view the stereotype as something completely divorced from reality, nor as a copy of reality. In the particular area between the German- and the Russian-language border, where fifteen nationalities intermingled, the formation of national stereotypes served to clarify and promote understanding in a mixed zone that would otherwise have been difficult to grasp.

Before the process matured to the point of national inner-differentiations, there existed the same basic differences that had always existed between the Occident and Orient, the West and the East, Europe and Russia, or the Germanic as opposed to the Latin or Slavic. The term *Slavic* had been the umbrella term and a mostly negative designation for the peoples of eastern Europe. The chain of stereotypes replicated itself along an axis between West and East. The French saw themselves as civilized, and the Stranger, or the Other, was barbaric. The opposing perspective saw the West as decadent and the East as wholesome. At the same time, however, the Other could also be idealized and the Self could be devalued using the same criteria (such as decadence, artificiality, and so on).[8]

Dispositions and Political Planning

The Central Powers had other subjects besides Slavs. Since the last division of Poland, both Prussia and Austria-Hungary had shared a border with Russia for over a hundred years.[9] This border area was naturally mostly populated by Poles, so that direct contact with Russia seldom occurred. While in the nineteenth century, the conservatives were considered to be traditional Russophiles and the liberals and leftists as Russophobes, this changed with the turn of the century. Now the Russian revolutionaries found sympathy from the Left. Along with this, among the middle class and intellectuals, there was still a fascination with Russia, primarily with Russian literary figures. The German image of Russia was influenced by the east European historian Otto Hoetzsch (1876–1946) and the philosopher and politician Tomáš G. Masaryk (1850–1937).[10]

Perception of the Slavs in the German Empire prior to the First World War was defined by cultural affinities; in the Austro-Hungarian Monarchy, such affinities were displaced by the ghost of pan-Slavism and the Russo-Serbian connection.[11] Austria-Hungary was populated by eleven nationalities—German, Magyar, Czech, Polish, Ukrainian, Romanian, Croatian, Serbian, Slovakian, Slovenian, and Italian, not to mention the Jewish and Muslim religious minorities. Although in Austria the nationalities basically had equality under the law and the Poles had a strong position at court, this did not hold true for the Romanians, Slovakians, Germans, Croatians, and Serbians in Hungary.[12] A considerable problem area also arose in Austro-Hungarian society in 1848 with the ascendancy of Czech nationalism. In the nationality conflict between German Bohemians and the Czechs—the "Bohemian question"—the Czechs hoped that the German Empire would play a mediating role. However, prior to 1914, the public sector of the German Empire wavered between indifference and taking the side of the German Bohemians, which was the case mostly among the middle class. Among Austrian Germans, especially the middle class and the military, the tensions between the Austrians and Serbians before 1914 not only intensified the sense of a threatening war but also the underscored the need to reinforce the German element in proportion to that of the Slavs within the Danube Monarchy in order to secure its superior position.

Initially, once the war started, both Germany and the Austro-Hungarian Dual Monarchy were impressed with the unity of the multiethnic state and the demonstration of loyalty by the people of Austria-Hungary; their united front against czarism and the east was attributed to German superiority and to the desire of the Slavic peoples in multiethnic Austria to participate in this superiority. The brisk debate over the German-Czech relationship was, however, carried on by the Austrian Germans and to a great extent in the press in the German Empire. The Czechs enjoyed the highest esteem from the Slavs and even among the German Bohemians.[13] The policy of the German Empire with respect to the Czech national movement was, however, considerably more hard-line than that of the Dual Monarchy. They "considered any sort of manifestation of Czech loyalty as a synonym for treason, pan-Slavism, and sympathy for the Entente, all the way up to the summer of 1918."[14]

Directly after the outbreak of war, Czech politicians began to make a connection between the Czech and Slovakian issues.[15] After the Czech Imperial Assembly delegate Masaryk had to go into exile because of secret activities against Austria-Hungary, an overseas initiative was organized in 1915, financed by the American Bohemian National Alliance and the Slovak League, which sought a new order in eastern central Europe with a Czechoslovakian nation. Masaryk and Edvard Beneš (1884–1948) had worked for a long time on the dissolution of the Dual Monarchy and in Paris in 1916 they founded the Czechoslovakian National Assembly. The domestic situation in Austria became precarious because of desertions by Slavic soldiers, whose numbers were expected to reach several hundred thousand by 1918. Most of the blame for the failure of the 4th Army during the Brusilov offensive was placed on the shoulders of the Slavic deserters, as a large part of the Moravian Infantry Regiment 8 had defected to the enemy.[16]

During the Kerensky offensive in 1917, near the village of Zborov, dramatic scenes played out as Czechs from the Austrian 35th and 75th Infantry Regiments noticed that they were on the opposite side of the Czechoslovakian Rifle Brigade, which had been deployed in Russia; now 3,000 of the Czechs fighting with the Austro-Hungarian division deserted. This episode involved Czech battle units that had been fighting on the side of the Central Powers' allies since 1914. In all, 11,000 Czech soldiers fought with France, 23,500 with Italy, and 76,832 in Czechoslovakian Legions on the Russian side.[17]

The relationship between Austrian Germans and Czechs deteriorated still further when, on 30 May 1917 in the reopened National Assembly, a demand was made to restructure the Danube Monarchy into a national federation with Czechoslovakia as one nation. In an inquiry in the Austrian House of Representatives on 5 December 1917, a group of German-Austrian delegates presented four hundred pages of documented evidence, also published as a book, concerning the disloyalty of the Czechs during the war and demanded action from the government: "One cannot insist that the Austrian government has remained unwarned and uninformed of the dangerousness of the Czech-Russophile movement, or that it can be surprised by the events that took place soon after the outbreak of the war among the Czech troops and in the rear areas, which caused very serious damage to the country's military, something that appears to be officially confirmed." And further, in addressing the Czechs, "We also appeal to the consciences of those Czechs who still harbor a sense of fairness and justice, [asking] whether that time has not finally come, through open commitment to the Austrian Fatherland and through victorious battles . . . , to make up at least to some extent for the terrible misery that their inimical co-nationals have summoned upon the monarchy."[18]

The Czech argument for autonomy was naturally reinforced by the Declaration of the Three Kings on 6 January 1918; it also received a powerful boost when, in spring 1918, the Western powers called for the dissolution of the Dual Monarchy. Masaryk and Benes then sought complete independence with the inclusion of the territories of Bohemia and Moravia that had been settled by Germans. The majority of the German-Austrian parties, which were brought together in the Federation of German Nationals, turned against this. The Germans, even the Social Democrats, emphatically rejected a Czech or a Czechoslovakian nation-state or, in other words, a Czechoslovakia in the federated style of the Dual Monarchy.[19] The German Bohemians now demanded their own province, and the German side considered the ideal solution to be a national separation between the Czechs and the Germans.

In fulfillment of the occupation policy of the Central Powers, the Imperial German General Government in Warsaw (Kaiserlich-Deutsche Generalgouvernement Warschau) was established in Russian Poland under General Hans H. von Beseler, who reported directly to the kaiser. It included the stable zone of occupied Congress Poland, which by 1915 was expanding, the Baltic states, and the White Russian territory (today Belarus). The Austro-Hungarian Military General Government was set up in Kielce, then in Lublin. In 1916 the Danube Monarchy set up two more general governments in Serbia and Montenegro. Like Romania, the area east of the general government, which initially included Courland, Lithuania, and the White Russian territory and later included Livonia and Estonia, remained under the control of sovereign military occupation forces. This territory, which had developed into a military state, was called Ober Ost, an abbreviation of Oberbefehlshaber der gesamten deutschen Streitkräfte im Osten (High Command of All German Forces in the East), or simply Ob. Ost., in conformity with the military fetish for abbreviations.

Before he took over the leadership of the German High Army Command (OHL), Paul von Hindenburg, who had meanwhile been promoted to field marshal, had stood at the head of Ober Ost, along with his chief of staff, General of Infantry Erich Ludendorff. On 29 August 1916, they were replaced by Field Marshal Prince Leopold von Bayern and Colonel Max Hoffmann. This 110,000-square-kilometer territory in the Baltic and White Russian territory would later include Latvia and Estonia. The population of the area totaled approximately 3 million and consisted of the Baltic peoples (excluding Slavs), Poles, (White) Russians, Ukrainians, Baltic Germans, and Yiddish-speaking Jews. Hindenburg, Ludendorff, and later Prince Leopold von Bayern commanded a harsh occupation regime. To a large extent, the commander and chief of staff were able to govern this military nation of Ober Ost autonomously.

In terms of the future of the occupied territories in the east, there were no clear and coherent ideas. Russian Poland (Congress Poland), the largest of the three sections into which Poland had been divided, having been conquered in summer 1915, became a bone of contention between the Central Powers. Vienna favored the Austro-Polish solution, initially in the form of a tripartite system, but after objections from Hungary it supported a sub-dualistic solution with a system that allowed self-government by the Poles. Berlin feared the Austro-Polish solution first because of the possible influence of Posen and West Prussia on the Poles and second because the Germans wanted to avoid building predetermined conditions into the Polish issue that could impact the separate peace with Russia they were striving for. Thus, Russia was once again the main enemy of the Dual Monarchy.

Despite the temporary German consent to an Austro-Polish solution, which never solidified in the German General Government, the Austrophiles' aspirations were contested. The respective administrations of the Central Powers sometimes devoted themselves more to the Polish groups that cooperated with partners of the alliance than to the Russophiles. In addition, there were rivalries and differences between the military and the political spheres.

Instead of an Austro-Polish solution, which obviously was never completely shelved in Vienna, the two general governments of the Central Powers in Congress Poland were ultimately supposed to be replaced step by step by the kingdom of Poland. This had been decreed by the general governments on 5 November 1916, but it took place de facto only in the most rudimentary way because of objections from Ludendorff. In addition, at one time there had been a plan to transfer a Polish border strip to the German Empire but, as in all annexation issues in the German Empire, there was no consensus. Still, the notion of a strip of border as a "protective wall against the Slavs" was popular, and the kaiser and von Beseler initially supported the idea as well because they viewed it as an element in their plan to compensate Poland with White Russian territories.

The Reich leaders therefore sought opinions on the subject of annexation and the resettling of the Poles who lived there. They queried administration chiefs, such as the governor of the province of East Prussia, the district president in Frankfurt/Oder, and the undersecretary of state Wahnschaffe of the Reich Chancellery, as well as Ober Ost. Opinions varied, but Wahnschaffe's view was very negative. No matter how the Reich government tried to hold all options open on this issue, the resettlement idea was not pursued further.[20] On 14 January 1917, a temporary Polish interim State Council was then formed, with the establishment of a Regency Council on 12 September 1917 whose legislation, administration, and justice system was to become autonomous.

Despite the tensions between the Poles and Russians, the Central Powers were never able to completely gain the sympathies of the Poles. This was due to the vague and poorly developed forecast projected by the Central Powers, which ultimately always considered the Polish as satellites. Further, Polish soldiers served only within the context of an auxiliary corps in the armies of the Central Powers. Therefore, the sub-dualistic plans of the Austro-Hungarian Monarchy and the efforts of the Minister President Stürgkh to establish a Ukrainian royal territory in Eastern Galicia after the war did not lend themselves to establishing Polish confidence in the Central Powers.[21] Even in economically underdeveloped Eastern Galicia, Vienna had to maneuver between the interests of the Poles and the Ukrainians who for their part were divided into Russophile and nationalistic Russophobes. Through the establishment of a Ukrainian province in Eastern Galicia, Vienna hoped to strengthen the anti-Russian bias of the Ukrainians. Among the Poles this option met with strong resistance and contributed significantly to Polish reservations about an Austro-Polish solution. In the Brest-Litovsk Peace Treaty, it was actually agreed to divide Galicia between Austria-Hungary and the Ukraine.[22]

With the defeat of the Central Powers, all plans for the east became obsolete. Before the German Freikorps could battle the "Reds" any further, the monarchy in Germany collapsed, and within the short period of 28 October to 3 November 1918, the Habsburg Monarchy fell.

Lessons Learned

At the beginning of the war, officers and soldiers had been unaware of the actual conditions in the east, and as a result they experienced genuine culture shock. On all fronts, they developed stereotypes through which they perceived their enemy. On the western front the stereotypes found expression in such terms as *Fritz, Hun, Boche, Tommy,* or *Franzmann.* This was also true of the eastern front, where the soldiers from the Central Powers used the term *Panje* (from the Polish word for pony or pony cart) or *Russki.* Both terms had pejorative connotations that only intensified with "Russian atrocities" during Russia's invasion of East Prussia in August 1914 and the devastation wrought by the Russians' scorched-earth policy during retreat, topics that have so far seen little research.

For insight into the world of perceptions of the soldiers on the eastern front at the beginning of the war, one valuable resource are letters from the field and pages of journals that were published in the daily periodical *Tägliche Rundschau* (Daily Review).[23] The usual source-critical considerations about military field mail, particularly in view of possible self-censorship (meant to avoid alarming relatives, for instance), must be broadened to also take into account the fact the material was selected for publication as an expression of national solidarity as well as an inner truce, or *Burgfrieden,* within the press as a whole and might have been subject to newspaper censorship.[24] Nevertheless, a wide range of perceptions can be seen in this collection, and it can be assumed that the publisher, not having any motivation to do so, did not censor or interfere with the material dealing with stereotypes. This collection of sources is significant in that it provides insight not only into the experiential world of the soldiers on the eastern front but also into their perceptions of the home front.

On 15 August 1914, the Russians invaded East Prussia. Beginning on 26 August when the Russians were driven back, German soldiers passed through the villages that had been liberated. The authors of field mail willingly conceded that the Russians behaved well: "In the villages that we now entered, they behaved with relative decency."[25] A civilian wrote something similar: "In the city, the Russians behaved correctly. In front of every grocery store, a guard came immediately, even offering to maintain order when the closed stores were opened under police orders."[26] One who had witnessed the enemy's cruelty, however, reacted much differently: "A dragoon had been bound arm and leg to four horses and ripped into pieces. Such and similar things also took place among the civilian population daily. You can imagine the terrible rage from all of us. . . . I have the strongest confidence that I will remain in good health, and have no trace of fear. Only the feeling of wanting revenge after I witnessed this horrific, howling atrocity. We must, as difficult as we may find it, treat our prisoners decently, a kick done secretly may well occur, but that is all, and we must still rail against it."[27]

Impressions of the land of the enemy certainly arise from experiences of loneliness, dirt, and disgust, primarily with respect to the landscape and the lodging: "Across the border immediately the genuine image of Russia! An avenue with deep red dust, without a tree or stone on its borders. Forests everywhere, birches and pine trees. Houses of wood, roofed with straw. Skinny cattle. Horses small and shaggy. The landscape not at all unattractive, only completely neglected."[28] The beds in particular came under fire, populated as they were by bedbugs and other creatures, along with the bad quality of the water. Soldiers longed for "German order and cleanliness."[29]

There was an essential sense of military superiority over the Russians: "The Cossack is a frightful coward—when the guns go off, he is gone."[30] There was also a sense of cultural superiority: "What we accomplished in three days: I say, more than the Russians in one hundred years. . . . And this culture! This is what the Russians want to spread to the West!"[31] The Jewish population however, was treated considerately, viewed by the Germans as "saviors" in a sense, and referred to in kinder terms.[32]

In his wartime letters, Paul Gerhard Plenz, a chief physician, described his experiences with Hindenburg's army from a privileged perspective.[33] As a field doctor, however, his knowledge of the army did not come from experience at the level of the military unit. What he learned or inferred about major movements and the magnitude of battles came through newspapers or by word of mouth, rather than from direct experience. Transferred often, Plenz gathered information from various barracks, wound treatment stations, during the marches and journeys to new garrisons, from the droning of the artillery battles, and through contact with the wounded of his own side and among the foreign prisoners of war. Plenz, who was not particularly squeamish, was nevertheless horrified by the Russian devastation and murder of the civilian population in East Prussia. The Cossacks had shot "innocent civilians" to death, "and even the attempts by individual Russian corps commanders to maintain discipline" were fruitless.[34] Plenz had better success than others in convincing his noncommissioned officers, who were eaten up with hatred for the Russians, that even Russian prisoners had to receive medical treatment. Plenz found it unsettling to witness the violations of the Geneva Conventions, not just through the new feature of this war, long-range artillery, but also through conscious defiance: "Here is what happened to a staff physician who was taken prisoner at a troop wound treatment station. He pointed to his Geneva insignia, and as a response, a Russian shot him in his upper arm and bandage. The wound was not essentially life-threatening, but a related blood poisoning ended his life. These are cultural signs, certainly permitted by a higher authority, but which bear witness to the low level of this illiterate folk. One fact speaks volumes, namely, that here in the east almost no physician wears the insignia of the Geneva Convention."[35]

Here again, Plenz expresses his sense of a hierarchy of moral values. His implication is that members of such a primitive population remain primitive even in uniform and will therefore commit acts of brutality by their own volition, and that their officers are incapable of stopping them. On the other hand, Plenz also concedes that the Russian soldiers had been exposed to anti-German atrocity propaganda and were forced to fight "actually under the lash."[36]

This sort of evenhanded commentary, however, was nowhere to be found in the writings of Königsberg professor Albert Brackmann.[37] Brackmann, whose work has received recent attention in the context of research on the eastern front of the Third Reich, was at that time director of the Provincial Commission for East Prussian Military History. In a report for the *Deutsche Kriegswochenschau* (German Weekly War Review), a war correspondence periodical founded in 1915 by the War Press Bureau, he railed against the Russian troops' "senseless destructive rage and the massacre and abduction of completely innocent people who were not involved in the war." Brackmann does not spare the Russian officers here. He describes Russian atrocities and gives places and dates (for instance, Ortelsburg on 27 August 1914 and Santoppen on 28 August). In summary, he notes: "Altogether in recent months, 34,000 buildings were destroyed, the contents of around 100,000 apartments destroyed, 873,332 cattle slaughtered, 1,620 people killed, 433 wounded."[38]

During the winter months of 1914–1915 the atrocities, now in the form of rapes, deportations, and abuse of prisoners of war, continued. The number of people killed has not been confirmed, either by official German research during the war or by later research on the larger complex of issues, which admittedly barely exists.[39] The report by the governor of the province of East Prussia, Adolf von Batocki-Friebe auf Bledau (1868–1944) to the minister of the interior on 20 March 1915 cites ten thousand buildings burned down during the first and second Russian invasions of East Prussia (that is, in August and September 1914 and from October 1914 to February 1915), eighty thousand plundered apartments during each invasion, and of thousands of civilians abducted or killed. The report, which has been reproduced in a collection published by the Foreign Office, additionally contains eighty-one statements made before military courts, some of them under oath, about individual instances of extremely savage abuse of civilians by the Russians.[40] The reports by private individuals about Russian conduct are ambivalent for the most part, as was clearly shown earlier. As historian Julius von Pflugk-Harttung (1848–1919) writes concerning the second Russian occupation, for instance, "Sometimes they carried on so horribly that they cut off the fingers of small boys, then they went back to humane behavior once more. . . . The advance on the Niemen in March appeared to be a purely raid-and-destroy operation and therefore brought German retaliatory disciplinary measures."[41] In any case, the reports and experiences of "Russian atrocities" made the image of the uncivilized and cruel barbarians from the east more concrete.

The popularization of the new experience in the east was coordinated by the Press Department of Ober Ost under Hauptmann (Captain) Friedrich Bertkau. The Press Section carried out a diligent propaganda program, engaged famous writers and painters, founded German local newspapers, published a soldiers' newspaper, *Korrespondenz B* (the Correspondence B), and newspapers in the Reich, held press conferences, and invited groups of German journalists to travel to Ober Ost, the territory under German military authority.[42] The journalists' impressions were then published in the newspapers.[43]

Carl Max Willy Strecker's book *Erlebnisse und Ergebnisse einer Studienfahrt in Ob. Ost.* (Experiences and Results of a Study Trip into Ob. Ost.) is primarily a reflection of its author's idealized concept of Germany.[44] His journalistic trip into this "ancient German cultural territory," which was sponsored by the military, made Ober Ost out to be another Germany, only better.[45] "Here were no endless consultations and deliberations out of the fear of violating of some interests somewhere. Here the civil servants were not made docile by pretentious pedantry, zigzag courses, and deliberate omissions; here no one knew 'confidential' warnings, no resentment, no partisanship, no anxious stolen glances at politicians and newspapers. Here each person obeyed readily and with pleasure, for he knew that Hindenburg and Ludendorff were surely fulfilling the law."[46]

In the east, according to Strecker, opportunities for the German spirit were not obstructed by bureaucracy, publicity, and politics. It must be kept in mind that at the time of the writing of this travel report, the Burgfrieden within the press organizations had already become fragile. The controversies about war goals and reforms of domestic policy, the economic need in the homeland, the *Steckrübenwinter* (winter of famine), and the continuing war put a strain on the domestic political climate. On the other hand, in the east, the author experienced a new rebuilding by Germans who, even in this primitive setting, set up scientific labs and conversed about Nietzsche, the arts, and theater. Strecker viewed the eastern area as a conquistador might have done, as a "new land" that had to be imbued with the "spirit of organization, of discipline and order," where previously there had been only a mix of peoples who lived in "filth, poverty and disorder." Now this land was to be "molded by the German intellect . . . , adapted into the German model, and embraced by the German economic life."[47] Another journalist emphasized the good deeds the Germans performed for Russian civilians. For him, these efforts helped to refute the allies' accusations of German barbarianism.[48]

In comparison to the manner in which the enemy to the west was viewed, the enemy in the east appeared as something foreign and unknown. At first there was an indifference to the mixture of peoples in the east, then came a cultural missionary attitude. Ultimately, however, linguistic and cultural factors led to an attitude by the German officers that sometimes favored Jews but was sometimes anti-Semitic, and that deliberately pitted the "White Ruthenians" against the Poles. While the Russians took shape as the main enemy on the eastern front, they also stood at the bottom of the civilization scale. Within this scale the Cossacks were once more differentiated as being particularly cowardly and cruel. Among the higher-ranking officers, enemy soldiers and officers were placed on a downward-sloping gradient in terms of morals and refinement. The strongest perception among the soldiers and journalists of the Central Powers on the eastern front was that of ethnic chaos, filth, and the endless expanse of the land. For officers and soldiers, there was a powerful growing sense of the foreignness and expanse of the eastern front, a place that was sparsely populated and economically and culturally idle, a situation that would have to be dealt with by means of a transportation and cultural policy.

Military and Political Ambitions

A further type of resource showing how the Germans viewed the east are the German field newspapers which, beginning in March 1916, were run by the newly established Feldpressestelle (Field Press Office) under the command of writer Walter Bloem. These publications championed the idea of East Prussia as a fortified area protecting the west from attacks from the east, along with the idea of settlements in Courland, Livonia, and Estonia, areas that were oriented toward the German Baltic nobility. Linked to this were ideas for the protection of the indigenous population, the formation of an eastern bulwark ("Plan Neuland 1916" [New Land Plan]) for "civilized Europe against the Russian Tatardom of Asia," and the zeal for a German cultural mission, all of which were eagerly promoted by the top military leaders in Ober Ost.[49]

The Kriegspresseamt (War Press Office), which distributed the *Deutsche Kriegswochenschau* newsreels, also furnished articles to the field newspapers, supplying information about the land and people of the newly occupied territories of the east and making material available for "instructions from the Fatherland" aimed toward disseminators of cultural improvement such as teachers and ministers of the church. Another such publication by the War Press Office was *Mitteilungen für den Vaterländischen Unterricht* (Materials for Instruction from the Fatherland).[50] This publication offered articles on German history in the east, such as the colonization in the east by the Teutonic Order during the Middle Ages, the German peasant settlements in Russia, the expulsion of the Germans by the Russians during the world war, and so on. These articles generally kept an informational tone, and current events were supposed to be placed in a historical context; nonetheless, however, they very often carried anti-Russian undertones.[51] Sometimes anti-Russian polemics were also present, as for instance in the case of the "Russian atrocity" of 1914 or the treatment of the Germans and other nationality groups in the Czarist Empire. At the same time, racial distinctions between Germans and Poles were rejected or relativized.[52]

An elaborately designed volume of articles entitled *Das Land Ober Ost* (The Land of Ober Ost) offers insight into the semiofficial image of the administration of this new country which, as the high command of the east, stood behind the two general governments and had the final say in everything that went on there.[53] This volume, produced by Ober Ost, contains articles by both officers and noncommissioned officers in the administration along with many illustrations, maps, and statistics. It provided information about the country, people, culture, and the activities of the occupying force in Ober Ost. Shortly before the publication of the volume, Riga was captured, and the newly won territory still remained part of the area of operations. Lithuania, Courland, and parts of White Russia, however, had been governed by Ober Ost since 1915. Naturally, then, the book makes reference to German efforts by the Hansa and the Teutonic Order in the Baltic, with particular attention given to the strong German connection to Courland. An attempt is made to grasp the wide variety of nationalities by giving an exact breakdown according to region, religion, and ethnicity. In general, the indigenous ethnicities, and even the eastern Jews, are treated here with understanding and sympathy, supplemented by a discussion of efforts to preserve self-government through the creation of governing councils for Courland and Lithuania.[54] The Poles were viewed more critically, especially because of their efforts to disseminate Polish culture among Lithuanians and White Russians. In this volume, the clearest enemy-concept is of the Russians, who were blamed for the suppression and Russifying of the autonomous population. The Russians were also to blame for the deterioration of the territory now occupied by the Germans. In the opinion of the authors, this was on account of the "idiosyncratic nature of the Russian ethnic soul" and the policies of "Great Russia."[55]

An analogous perspective, this time from the hindsight of 1928, is provided by the Austrian military administration on its occupied territories. This is a volume from the Carnegie Foundation for International Peace in which the Austrian military's leading representatives justify their activities. Regarding the Austro-Hungarian General Government in Russian Poland, Rudolf Mitzka, a major in the General Staff, emphasizes its cultural work and economic buildup as well as the establishment of an administrative apparatus to benefit the newly created Polish state. Mitzka, however, also reported on the failure to establish a Polish army and the increasing resistance among the population.[56] The chief of general staff of the General Government of Serbia, Hugo Kerchnawe, expressed himself even more enthusiastically about the restoration of the country, which was achieved despite the Serbian hatred for the occupying forces and the insufficient reserve of personnel. Kerchnawe referred in particular to the expansion of a communications network, hygiene programs and epidemic prevention, the improvement of the agrarian economy, and the reorganization of the school system.[57]

The Image of the Slav on the Home Front

In defining who their enemy was, the German Empire and Austria-Hungary had different priorities. For the German Empire, the enemy was Great Britain; for the Danube Monarchy, the main enemy was Russia. But the Germans and German-Austrians nevertheless held a shared hierarchical attitude. While they considered the French and British to be their equals, albeit degenerate, they viewed the Slavs as lazy, dull, disorganized, dirty, and downtrodden. An often-used symbol of this was the lash. This pejorative image of the Slav was disseminated in the media primarily on the home fronts, in newspapers, journals, and satirical publications.

What appeared particularly scandalous was the coalition of the Western Allies and the Russians, who were viewed as primitives. The accusation of barbarism during the invasion of Belgium and France and the accompanying "atrocities," mostly leveled against Germany by France, was passed on in the German media to the enemy in the east. The Social Democratic element in Russia had essentially been motivated to engage in war by animosity toward autocratic czarism. Accordingly, after the February Revolution of 1917, its support of the war eroded.

Along with the soldierly, military, administrative, and journalistic perception of the Slavs, there was also that of scientific experts. The doyen of Slavic and Polish studies, the literary historian Aleksander Brückner (1856–1939), who at the young age of twenty-two had become professor at the Friedrich Wilhelm University in Berlin, challenged the cliché-ridden image of the Slavs prevalent in Germany.[58] In an article published in 1916 on the Slavs and the world war, he said he believed that he could expose pan-Slavism as a fantasy.[59] Brückner labeled pan-Germanism and pan-Romanism as similar fallacies. Instead he emphasized sovereign nationalities, arguing that these were threatened by the egotistical brutal Russians. Brückner reserved the pejorative view of the Slavs exclusively for the Russians, White Russians ("the most passive, indolent Slavic people, without history and traditions"), and Ukrainians.[60] He himself, coming from a family that had become Polish citizens (although his last name is obviously German), definitely claimed to be loyal to Poland. Poland, which for Brückner was always a bulwark against the Russians, was a solid "wall against orthodoxy, Russianism, Byzantinism, despotism . . . behind this wall, Europe could follow its own development undisturbed, strive for external and internal human freedom, foster culture, establish ideals that have nothing in common with quietism, the congealed immovability, [or] the exclusivity of the Orient."[61] Thus, for Brückner, the dividing of Poland was extremely ill advised. Apart from this, his implicit criticism of Prussian policy, especially the policy of Germanizing Poland, must not be overlooked.

Brückner took on the ideas of race, proved the multileveled and nonhomogenous nationality of the Slavs, and reduced the distinguishing marks on which discrimination was based to "culture and religious denomination," precisely the features that divided such peoples as Poles and Russians.[62] The Russian culture was obviously very stable in Brückner's view; he considered the Central Powers' hope for a Russian revolution or a liberal regime a fantasy, and in any case a liberal Russia would be just as anti-German and expansionistic as the present reactionary one, and would be even better able to mobilize Russian reserves. The Revolution of 1905, Bruckner believed, changed nothing in Russia's internal situation, and neither "organizational talent, sense of responsibility, nor energetic initiative by the individual could be grafted onto the new pseudo-constitutionalism any more than it could be forced onto the old absolutism."[63]

Germany appeared to Brückner to be a disseminator of culture to the east. He cited as an example the opening of the new Polish Warsaw University after the withdrawal of the Russians on 5 August 1915. While Brückner's view of the east corresponded to the discourse of Slavic hegemony among the Central Powers, it was more discriminating and more restrained, and he wanted most of all to recognize and strengthen Poland's independent national existence. This brought with it a specific view of "Polish Jewry." Brückner sharply criticized the anti-Semitism of the Polish National Democrat Dmowski, just as he did that of the Russians, and called for the integration of Polish Jews into the Polish nation. He set aside the usual term "eastern Jews" and looked on Polish Jews as Polish citizens who had the distinctive feature of a religious denomination of their own.

In Brückner's writing, the usual image of the Slav was transferred to his representation of the Russians. The Russians were responsible for the war, their politics were imperialistic, their souls were Slavic and shiftless. Accordingly, Brückner saw food riots as local unrest, and even in 1916 he still considered revolution to be out of the question. Given the concept of a cultural construction of Russianism, which Brückner could not exclude, where would the impetus for the civilizing of Russia come from? He placed his hopes on the Russian prisoners of war who, upon their return to their homeland, could become the disseminators of Western civilization. On this convoluted path, he also saw the Central Powers as disseminators of culture.

In his detailed descriptions of Russia, Finland, the Baltic states, Poland, the Ukraine, the Caucasus, and Armenia, Max Friederichsen (1874–1941), professor of geography at the University of Greifswald, also portrays the Poles as being essentially different from the Russians. He sees them, as western Slavs, as belonging to a different ethnic group than the Russians. Primarily, however, it is their Catholicism that sets them apart from the Russians: "On this basis, and along with their generally higher general cultural level, they stand closer to western Europe than to the eastern Europe of Great Russia."[64] The national economist Max Sering (1857–1939), in his volume on west Russia and central Europe, suggested as "absolute security against the east" an independent Polish state, which would have to be united with the German Empire in the structure of "a lasting constitutional defense alliance."[65] Sering's main target was the "Anglo-American suppression syndicate." After the proclamation of 27 March 1917 by the Petrograd Soviets about a peace without annexations and assistance, he considered it an open question whether the Russians could free themselves from the "shackles of her bosses and exploiters," meaning the "Anglo-Saxon world domination bloc," and enter into a pact with central Europe under German leadership.[66]

Even among the German-Austrian experts on the east, the image of Russia was pejorative. The Serbian enemy was viewed only as instrument of the politics of Great Russia.[67] The historian and consultant for issues on eastern Europe in the Foreign Ministry, Hans Uebersberger (1877–1962), blamed the Russians for the outbreak of the war and accused them of conspiracy in the assassination of Franz Ferdinand. He accused Russian expansionism and imperialism not only on the leadership but the entire Russian people. Because Uebersberger had spent two years in Russia, he was familiar with the problems of the Czarist Empire, and hence his sharp criticism. Aside from his criticism of Russia, however, he based his ideas on the assumption that there would be a final battle between Slavs and Germans.[68] Uebersberger was certainly the sharpest critic among the anti-Slavic culture camp, but his aversion for the warring Russia and its despotism was nevertheless shared by broad sections of German-Austrian society, all the way to the Social Democrats. The German-Austrians as a whole believed themselves to be engaged in a defense war against Russia. And the solution to the southern Slavic issue in terms of a (partial) annexation of Serbia and Montenegro was also advocated at the War Aims Conference of the Council of Ministers in January 1916.[69]

German-Austrian military experts proposed a plan designed as an offensive move, a German-Austrian cultural mission in the east, an idea that tied in with the colonization of the east during the Middle Ages, something that had always been thought of as having been interrupted too early. It now it became a defensive concept for protection against a threatening Slavicizing of Austria, intended as bulwark, or border guard, against the east. Along with the institutional reinforcement of the German-Austrians within the context of the Dual Monarchy, the concept of a central Europe was adapted here, something they clung to through the end of the war. Later on the idea of a multiethnic state was abandoned in favor of the more popular idea of an annexation to the German Empire, which of course would also have taken care of the Slav problem.[70]

Like Brückner, the Catholic commentator Richard von Kralik (1852–1934) posited a normative differentiation of the Slavs. Culturally, according to the popular theory of a West-East culture gradient, he thought the Ruthenians were on a higher level than the Russians, with their imperialistic mind-set. Accordingly, he sided with the establishment on the subject of a Ukraine that would be autonomous from Russia, a view that agreed with the Army High Command of the Danube Monarchy.[71] Among the firmly committed Catholics such as von Kralik, obviously the distrust concerning a nationalistic policy of oppression was more pronounced. But even the liberals, such as journalist Richard Charmatz (1879–1965), criticized the anti-Slavic point of view and policy of the Austrian authorities, believing that they had intensified the pan-Slavism instigated by Russia.[72] The pacifistic pedagogue Friedrich Wilhelm Foerster (1869–1966), who until 1913–1914 had been guest professor in Vienna and now taught in Munich, went even further. He pleaded for a balance between the ethnic groups in the Austro-Hungarian Monarchy and proposed a Slavic-Germanic cultural community. The unusual aspect of his proposals, as well as those of the similarly minded expert in international law Heinrich Lammasch (1853–1920), was that they resonated with the new Kaiser Karl, who had spoken with Foerster and Lammasch and wanted to appoint them as ministers.[73] Both, however, were harshly rejected by the general public.[74] On the international propaganda front, the German-Austrians increasingly had to fight off allegations from their allies against the "multiethnic prison" of the reactionary monarchy. They could deal with anything else they were confronted with—central Europe, old Austria, federalism, nationality balance, annexation, the German mission—but in the face of the nationalism of the Slavic people and the principle of the right of the people to self-government, they always came up short.

Among the German populace, the image of the Slav as an enemy was somewhat mitigated by experiences of direct contact. This was also true of the prisoners of war, which included 1.4 million Russians. Their treatment by the Germans was extensively motivated by the new collective agreement on international war rights (the Geneva Conventions of 1864/1906 and The Hague Land Warfare Convention of 1899/1907), something German publicity never grew weary of pointing out.[75] In the homeland, there was mostly curiosity and sympathy for the prisoners of war. Authorities tried to discourage the population from having contact with and giving support to prisoners of war, and to encourage civilians to cooperate in the capture of escaped prisoners, but they met with little success.[76] The image of the enemy was further softened when the Russians were deployed in the war industry and on farms. For this reason, in the *Deutsche Kriegswochenschau* newsreels, German employers were cautioned about the dangers of blind confidence in Russian workers and warned of acts of sabotage by the prisoners of war.[77]

In contrast, the some 2.5 million soldiers of the Central Powers who were captured by the Russians, 170,000 of whom were Reich Germans, feared the worst. While the Slavic prisoners in the Russian prison camps were, in fact, privileged, the German and Hungarian prisoners were taken to Siberian camps where conditions were deplorable. Furthermore, in defiance of the peace agreement of Brest-Litovsk, they were not permitted to return home in March 1918 but instead were placed under the command of the Czechoslovakian Legion and the "White" Russians, who did not consider the war against the Central Powers to be over. Some 20 percent of German prisoners in Russian hands died, as opposed to the 5 percent of Russian prisoners who lost their lives. Considerable hostility arose between Slavic and non-Slavic prisoners in Russian camps. The desperation of the prisoners was known through letters, reports from refugees, and charitable organizations in the homeland. Even the governments assumed there were serious violations against international law. In the postwar era, the prisoner of war literature ensured that these experiences became widely known. In Edwin Erich Dwinger's successful novels, such as the 1929 *Armee hinter Stacheldraht* (Army behind Barbed Wire), written in response to Erich Maria Remarque, the horrors of the Russian camps were vividly described.[78]

Perspectives

To a great extent the perception of the Slavic soldier held by the Central Powers consisted of a discourse on hygiene. Tales of vermin and filth were relayed to the homeland, and in the context of social Darwinist theory, it was an obvious step to project this discourse onto both internal and external enemies. Nevertheless, the Central Powers were not the only ones to have this image of the Slavs during the era of the First World War. In other lands as well, such as England, there was a nervous "hygienic glance" toward the east.[79] Nevertheless, because of the war in the east, the perspective held by the Central Powers became based on practical experience as soldiers actually had to battle with the unfamiliar insects and epidemic plagues on the eastern front. Enemy soldiers were described as dull witted and dirty: "In total we had about 130 wounded to take care of, among them 40 Russians, some of them quite disgusting fellows."[80] Still, as Bernhard Chiari correctly wrote about the German occupation in White Russia, "pejorative adjectives such as 'dirty,' 'lousy,' 'greasy,' 'verminous' . . . in 1915 [were applied] mostly to objects, buildings, and villages."[81] For this reason as well, the German-Austrian perception of the Slavs and of the east from 1914–1915 until 1918 can hardly be compared to the situation during Operation Barbarossa. Therefore, in 1941 no one even inquired about experiences from the First World War. Along with the image of the cultureless east, which had prevailed for so a long time (the further east, the more cultureless), Bolshevism now played the central role, and along with this came radicalized anti-Semitism and the concept of the "Untermensch."

During the First World War, outside of the anti-Semitic camp, this perception and assessment of eastern Jews was founded for the most part on a mixture of somewhat traditional stereotyping, compassion, and fear of immigration (on the part of the Reich German Jews as well—the critical issues here being cultural differences and concern for a worsening of the relationship between Jewish Germans and the Christian majority populace). Additionally there were efforts to instrumentalize the "eastern Jews" against the Russians. The Russians were blamed for anti-Semitic pogroms and discrimination against the Jews, and this was seen as proof of their uncivilized conduct.[82] Even here it appears that what predominates are not "continuities" to the Second World War but "discontinuities."

Notes

1. For criticism and valuable suggestions on this essay, I thank Dr. Martin Moll, Graz.

2. On this not unproblematic interest in the eastern front of the First World War, see also Eberhard Demm, *Ostpolitik und Propaganda im Ersten Weltkrieg*, Frankfurt 2002; Vejas Gabriel Liulevicius, *Kriegsland im Osten. Eroberung, Kolonisierung und Militärherrschaft im Ersten Weltkrieg*, Hamburg 2002.

3. For a revisionist view of the Schlieffen Plan, see Terence Zuber's chapter in the German edition of this book as well as his book *Inventing the Schlieffen Plan: German War Planning, 1871–1914*, Oxford 2002.

4. On the battle of Tannenberg, see Markus Pöhlmann, "Tod in den Masuren. Tan-

nenberg, 23 to 31 August 1914." In: *Schlachten der Weltgeschichte. Von Salamis bis Sinai*, edited by Stig Förster, Markus Pöhlmann, and Dierk Walter, Munich 2001, 279–94.

5. The much-quoted phrase, "the great seminal catastrophy [*sic*] of this century," originates with George F. Kennan in *The Decline of Bismarck's European Order: Franco-Russian Relations, 1875–1890*, Princeton 1979, 3.

6. For a summary of the events on the eastern front, see Wilhelm Deist, "Die Kriegführung der Mittelmächte." In: *Enzyklopädie Erster Weltkrieg*, edited by Gerhard Hirschfeld, Gerd Krumeich, and Irina Renz, Paderborn 2003, 249–71; Holger H. Herwig, *The First World War: Germany and Austria-Hungary, 1914–1918*, 3rd ed., London 1998, 81–96, 230–44, 333–35, 365–73.

7. Just as stereotypes themselves tend to increase endlessly, so do the terminology and scholarly distinctions regarding them. Prominent offerings along with stereotypes are images, pictures, patterns of perception, and prejudices that evaluate and judge negatively. See the overview by Hans J. Kleinsteuber, "Stereotype, Images und Vorurteile. Die Bilder in den Köpfen der Menschen." In: *Die hässlichen Deutschen? Deutschland im Spiegel der westlichen und östlichen Nachbarn*, edited by Günther Trautmann, Darmstadt 1991, 60–68.

8. See Rudolf Jaworski, "Osteuropa als Gegenstand historischer Stereotypenforschung." In: *Geschichte und Gesellschaft*, 13 (1987), 63–76.

9. Previously the small borderland in Niemen Territory belonged to Lithuania, which also belonged to Russia.

10. Otto Hoetzsch, *Russland—eine Einführung auf Grund seiner Geschichte von 1904–1912*, Berlin 1913; Tomáš G. Masaryk, *Zur Russischen Geschichts-und Religionsphilosphie. Soziologische Skizzen*, 2 vols., Jena 1913.

11. See Hans Lemberg, "'Der Russe is genügsam.' Zur deutschen Wahrnehmung Russlands vom Ersten zum Zweiten Weltkrieg." In: *Das Bild "des Anderen." Politische Wahrnemung im 19. und 20. Jahrhundert*, edited by Birgit Aschmann and Michael Salewski, Stuttgart 2000, 121–31.

12. See Arnold Suppan, "Was kommt nach Österreich-Ungarn? Ein Österreichisches Memorandum und eine slowakische Antwort vom September 1918." In: *Nationalitäten und Identitäten in Ostmitteleuropa. Festschrift aus Anlass des 70. Geburtstages von Richard Georg Plaschka*, edited by Walter Kukan and Arnold Suppan. Vienna 1995, 55–83. On Austrian and Hungarian foreign policyconcepts, especially before the turn of the century, see Istvan Diószegi, "Einige Bemerkungen zur Frage der österreichisch-ungarischen Ostpolitik." In: *Österreich-Ungarn in der Weltpolitik 1900 bis 1918*, edited by the Deutsche Historiker-Gesellschaft, Arbeitsgemeinschaft für die Geschichte Österreichs und der deutsch-österreichischen Beziehung under the direction of Fritz Klein, East Berlin 1965, 230–49.

13. See Birgitt Morgenbrod, "Die 'böhmische Frage' in der reichsdeutschen Publizistik 1914–1918." In: *Der Erste Weltkrieg und die Beziehungen zwischen Tschechen, Slowaken und Deutschen*, published for the Deutsch-Tschechische und die Deutsch-Slowakische Historikerkommission, edited by Hans Mommsen, Dušan Kováč, and Jiří Malíř, Leipzig 2001, 221–40.

14. Jiří Kořalka, "Die Haltung des Deutschen Reiches zu den nationalstaatlichen Bestrebungen in Zisleithanien (April bis Oktober 1918)." In: *Die Auflösung des Habsburgerreiches. Zusammenbruch und Neuorientierung im Donauraum*, edited by Richard Georg Plaschka and Karlheinz Mack, Munich 1970, 209–18, here 211.

15. See Miroslav Bobrik, "Die Deutschen in der Slowakei und die slowakische Frage im und nach dem Ersten Weltkrieg (1916–1919)." In: *Der Erste Weltkrieg und die Beziehungen*, 131–39.

16. See Manfried Rauchensteiner, *Der Tod des Doppeladlers. Österreich-Ungarn und der Erste Weltkrieg*, Graz, Vienna, Cologne 1993, 348.

17. See Gerburg Thunig-Nittner, *Die Tschechoslowakische Legion in Russland. Ihre Geschichte und Bedeutung bei der Entstehung der 1. Tschechoslowakischen Republik*, Wiesbaden 1970; Rauchensteiner, *Der Tod*, 480–85; Frank Hadler, "Artikel Tschechoslowakei." In: *Enzyklopädie Erster Weltkrieg*, 929f.

18. *Das Verhalten der Tschechen im Weltkrieg. Die Anfrage der Abg. Dr. Scürff, Goll, Hartl, Knirsch, Dr. von Langenhan und K. H. Wolf im österreichischen Abgeordnetenhause.* Taken verbatim from stenographic records of the proceedings. pp. 4553–4828 of encl. II of the supporting documents for the forty-ninth meeting of the Austrian House of Representatives, 5 December 1917, no. 1749/I. Edited by the Deutschnationalen Geschäftstelle, Vienna 1918, 6, 408. On the public opinion of Czechs and Serbs in the Dual Monarchy, see Péter Hanák, "Die Volksmeinung während des letzten Kriegsjahres in Österreich-Ungarn." In: *Die Auflösung des Habsburgerreiches*, 58–66.

19. See Alojz Ivanisevic, "Die Idee des tschechischen Nationalstaates aus der Sicht deutsch-österreichischer Reichsratsabgeordneter 1917/18." In: *Nationalitäten und Identitäten*, 43–53.

20. See Wolfgang J. Mommsen, "Der 'polnische Grenzstreifen.' Anfange der 'völkischen Flurbereinigung' und der Umsiedlungspolitik." In: Wolfgang J. Mommsen, *Der Erste Weltkrieg. Anfang vom Ende des Bürgerlichen Zeitalters*, Frankfurt 2004, 118–36.

21. See Heinz Lemke, *Allianz und Rivalität. Die Mittelmächte und Polen im ersten Weltkrieg (bis zur Februarrevolution)*, East Berlin 1977; Hans Hecker, "Artikel Polen." In: *Enzyklopädie Erster Weltkrieg*, 777–79.

22. Heinz Lemke, "Die Regierung Stürgkh und die Pläne zur Teilung Galiziens." In: *Österreich-Ungarn in der Weltpolitik*, 266–83.

23. *Von Flandern bis Polen. Feldpostbriefe der Täglichen Rundschau aus dem Weltkriege*, Berlin 1915.

24. See Bernd Ulrich, *Die Augenzeugen. Deutsche Feldpostbriefe in Kriegs-und Nachkriegszeit 1914–1933*, Essen 1997; Bernd Ulrich, "Feldpostbriefe des Ersten Weltkriegs–Möglichkeiten und Grenzen einer alltagsgeschichtlichen Quelle." In: *Militärgeschichtliche Mitteilungen*, 53 (1994), 73–83.

25. "Aus den Kämpfen um Tilsit, Miekieten, 19. September 1914." In: *Von Flandern bis Polen*, 358–61, here 359.

26. "Die Russen in Allenstein." In: *Von Flandern bis Polen*, 324–28, here 326. See also "Die Besetzung des Postamts Endtkuhnen durch die Russen." In: ibid., 312–16.

27. "Furor teutonicus. Brief eines Hauptmanns. Wr., den 22.8.1914." In: *Von Flandern bis Polen*, 323; see also "Kosakengreuel. Brief eines Offiziersburschen." In: ibid., 338f.

28. "Aus der Stadt der schwarzen Madonna. Czenstochau, 14.8.1914." In: *Von Flandern bis Polen*, 318f, here 318.

29. "Zweimal dem Tode entronnen. Erlebnisse eines schlesischen Landwehrmannes." In: *Von Flandern bis Polen*, 389–99, here 399.

30. "Schulter an Schulter. Dienstag, 15.9.1914." In: *Von Flandern bis Polen,* 365–73, here 373. See also "Schlesische Landwehr schlägt die Russen. Sieben Bataillone gegen sechzehn." In: ibid., 405–9; "Wie zwei Mann 122 Russen gefangennahmen." In: ibid., 410f.

31. "Deutsche Ordnung. Anfang September 1914." In: *Von Flandern bis Polen,* 361–63, here 362f. The title of a 1917 article written by a captain is characteristic: Hauptmann Flegen, "Das deutsche Schwert als Kulturträger." In: *Deutsche Kriegswochenschau,* no. 63 of 17/2/1918, 954f.

32. See, e.g., "Cmielow, 10.10.1914." In: *Von Flandern bis Polen,* 382.

33. See Paul Gerhard Plenz, *Kriegsbriefe eines Feldarztes der Armee Hindenburg,* Gotha 1916.

34. Ibid., 16.

35. Ibid., 76.

36. Ibid., 26.

37. For a discussion of the opposing perspectives on the subject, see on the one hand Michael Fahlbusch, *Wissenschaft im Dienst der nationalsozialistischen Politik? Die "volksdeutschen Forschungsgemeinschaften" von 1931–1945,* Baden-Baden 1990; and Ingo Haar, *Historiker im Nationalsozialismus. Deutsche Geschichtswissenschaft und der "Volkstumskampf" im Osten,* Göttingen 2000; on the other hand, see the devastating criticism of these books: Christian Tilitzki, "Vordenker der Vernichtung? Neue Beiträge zur Kontroverse über 'Ostforschung' und Politik im Dritten Reich." In: *Jahrbuch für die Geschichte Mittel-und Ostdeutschlands,* 47 (2001), 301–18.

38. Albert Brackmann, "Die Russengreuel in Ostpreussen." In: *Deutsche Kriegswochenschau,* no. 37, 19/8/1917, 545–47, here 545f.

39. See John Horne and Alan Kramer, *Deutsche Kriegsgreuel 1914. Die umstrittene Wahrheit,* Hamburg 2004, 126–30.

40. See "Greueltaten russischer Truppen gegen deutsche Zivilpersonen und deutsche Kriegsgefangene, [Berlin 1915]. The report by Oberpräsident von Batocki-Bledau is listed as attachment 1, 9–11. The remaining reports, ibid., attachments 2–81, 11–127. In Horne/Kramer's *Kriegsgruel,* 127, these reports were trivialized and no convincing attempt was made to put them into perspective. In this respect the authors are in agreement with Imanuel Geiss, "Die Kosaken kommen! Ostpreussen im August 1914." In: *Imanuel Geiss. Das Deutsche Reich und der Erste Weltkrieg,* Munich, Vienna 1978, 58–66, here 62–64, which is based on two diplomatic reports and reports of a mayor and two district administrators. The collection at the Foreign Office is not mentioned by Geiss. See my review of the book by Horne and Kramer, which is problematic in other respects as well: "John Horne, Alan Kramer, *Deutsche Kriegsgreuel 1914. Die umstrittene Wahrheit.*" In: *sehepunkte 4* (2004), no. 7, http://www.sehepunkte.historicum. net/2004/07/6108.html.

41. See Julius von Pflugk-Harttung, *Die Weltgeschichte ist das Weltgericht. Ereignisse und Stimmungsbilder 1914 und 1915,* Berlin 1915, 95.

42. See Liulevicius, *Kriegsland,* 145–51.

43. For instance, in the *Frankfurter Zeitung,* an article appeared as a separate printing, Arthur Feiler, *Neuland. Eine Fahrt durch Ob.Ost.,* [Frankfurt n.d.], and in the *Hannoverscher Kurier,* also as a separate printing, Fritz Hartmann, *Ob-Ost. Friedliche Kriegsfahrt eines Zeitungsmannes,* Hannover 1917.

44. See Carl Strecker, *Auf den Spuren Hindenburgscher Verwaltung. Erlebnisse und Ergebnisse einer Studienfahrt in Ob. Ost,* Berlin 1917.

45. Ibid., 7.

46. Ibid., 13.

47. Ibid., 472.

48. Hartmann, *Ob-Ost*, 30–36.

49. Quoted in Anne Lipp, *Meinungslenkung im Krieg. Kriegserfahrungen deutscher Soldaten und ihre Deutung 1914–1918*, Göttingen 2003, 216.

50. See ibid., 51, 75.

51. See, e.g., Otto Hoetzsch "Der russische Imperialismus." In: *Deutsche Kriegswochenschau*, no. 20 of 22/4/1917, 267f.; Christian Krollmann, "Ostpreussens deutsche Geschichte." In: *Deutsche Kriegswochenschau*, no. 37 of 19/8/1917, 537f.; J. Lulvès, "Die Beziehungen des Grossen Kurfürsten zu Kurland." In: *Deutsche Kriegswochenschau*, no. 83 7/7/1918, 1270f.

52. See Brackmann, "Die Russengreuel"; Albert Brackmann, "Der deutsche Ritterorden und seine östliche Kolonisation." In: *Deutsche Kriegswochenschau*, no. 48, 4/11/1917, 714f.; Leutnant d.R. Kassebaum, "Das Deutschtum in den Ostseeprovinzen." In: *Mitteilungen für den Vaterländischen Unterricht*, no. 11, 6/3/1918, 8–11; Leutnant d.R. Kassebaum, "Die deutschen Bauernkolonien in Russland." In: *Deutsche Kriegswochenschau*, no. 66 of 10/3/1918, 1002–5: Otto Krauske, "Die Tataren-Einfälle in Ostpreussen. Eine zeigemässe Erinnerung." In: *Deutsche Kriegswochenschau*, no. 37, 19/8/1917, 550f.; Gerhard Mueller, "Die Ukraine." In: *Deutsche Kriegswochenschau*, no. 58, 13/1/1918, 875f.; Fritz Braun, "Land und Leute in den besetzten Gebieten des Ostens." In: *Deutsche Kriegswochenschau*, no. 58, 13/1/1918, 868–71.

53. See *Das Land Ober Ost. Deutsche Arbeit in den Verwaltungsgebieten Kurland, Litauen und Bialystok-Grodno*, published under the auspices of Oberbefehlshaber Ost, edited by Presseabteilung Ober Ost, Stuttgart, Berlin 1917.

54. Ibid., 19.

55. Ibid., 11.

56. See Rudolf Mitzka, "Die K.u.K. Militärverwaltung in Russisch-Polen." In: *Die Militärverwaltung in den von den Österreichisch-Ungarischen Truppen besetzten Gebieten*, edited by Hugo Kerchnawe et al., Vienna, New Haven 1928, 8–52.

57. See Hugo Kerchnawe, "Die K.u.K. Militärverwaltung in Serbien." In: ibid., 53–269.

58. On Brückner, see *Aleksander Brückner zum 60. Todestag. Beiträge der Berliner Tagung 1999*, edited by Alicja Nagórko, Frankfurt 2001. Brückner's first name is correctly spelled *Aleksander*, the spelling used here.

59. See Aleksander Brückner, *Die Slawen und der Weltkrieg. Lose Skizzen*, Tübingen 1916.

60. Ibid., 132.

61. Ibid., 36.

62. Ibid., 35.

63. Ibid., 155.

64. Max Friederichsen, *Die Grenzmarken des Europäischen* [*sic*] *Russlands. Ihre geographische Eigenart und ihre Bedeutung für den Weltkrieg*, Hamburg 1915, 56.

65. Max Sering, "Einleitung." In: *Westrussland in seiner Bedeutung für die Entwicklung Mittel-europas*, Leipzig, Berlin 1917, xiii–xxxii, here xxvii.

66. Ibid., xxxii.

67. Despite the implications in the title, the book by Brücker's colleague at the University of Graz, Matthias Murko, *Das serbische Geistesleben*, Leipzig, Munich 1916, contains only literary historical description that is objectively based.

68. See Günter Ramhardter, *Geschichtswissenschaft und Patriotismus. Österreichische Historiker im Weltkrieg 1914–1918*, Munich 1973, 13, 56f., 110f.

69. Ibid., 49.

70. Ibid., passim.

71. Ibid., 52.

72. Ibid., 63f.

73. Lammasch served in office between 27/10 and 11/11/1918 as minister president of the monarchy, which was in the process of being dissolved.

74. See Ramhardter, *Geschichtswissenschaft*, 65–72.

75. Reinhard Nachtigal, "Die Kriegsgefangenen-Verluste an der Ostfront. Eine Übersicht zur Statistik und zu Problemen der Heimatfronten 1914/15." In *Die vergessene Front. Der Osten 1914/15*, edited by Gerhard P. Gross, Paderborn 2006, 201–15; and Uta Hinz, "'Die Deutschen 'Barbaren' sind doch die besseren Menschen.' Kriegsgefangenschaft und gefangene Feinde in der Darstellung der deutschen Publizistik 1914–1918." In: *In der Hand des Feindes. Kriegsgefangenschaft von der Antik bis zum Zweiten Weltkrieg*, edited by Rüdiger Overmans, Cologne, Weimar, Vienna 1999, 340–61.

76. See Andreas Peter, *Das "Russenlager" in Guben*, Potsdam 1998, 64–73.

77. See "Achtet auf die Kriegsgefangenen! Ein Mahnruf an Landwirte und Gewerbetreibende." In: *Deutsche Kriegswochenschau*, no. 32 of 15/7/1917, 471f.

78. See Georg Wurzer, "Das Schicksal der deutschen Kriegsgefangenen in Russland im Ersten Weltkrieg. Der Erlebnisbericht Edwin Erich Dwingers." In: *In der Hand des Feindes*, 363–84.

79. See Aribert Reimann, *Der grosse Krieg der Sprachen. Untersuchungen zur historischen Semantik in Deutschland und England zur Zeit des Ersten Weltkrieges*, Essen 2000, 210–22, here 215.

80. "Als Stabsarzt im Osten. Anfang Oktober." In: *Von Flandern bis Polen*, 401–5, here 404. See also Rapeutkow, "3. Oktober." In: ibid., 380f.

81. See Bernhard Chiari, "Geschichte als Gewalttat. Weissrussland als Kind zweier Weltkriege." In: *Erster Weltkrieg–Zweiter Weltkrieg. Ein Vergleich. Krieg, Kriegserlebnis, Kriegserfahrung in Deutschland 1914—1945*, published under the auspices of the Militärgeschichtliches Forschungsamt, edited by Bruno Thoss and Hans-Erich Volkmann, Paderborn 2002, 615–31, here 626.

82. This is according to Brückner, e.g., *Die Slawen*, 84–93; Hartmann, *Ob-Ost*, 79. On anti-Semitism, see, e.g., the ethnicity-minded member of the governing council, Georg Fritz, who feared a large wave of immigration by the eastern Jews into the German Empire but also had a strong desire for an improvement of living conditions and the elimination of discrimination against the Jews in Poland and Russia. He was also enthusiastic about Zionism. His work in the previously mentioned volume of collected articles on western Russia is characterized by a mixture of anti-Semitic stereotypes and (feigned?) empathy; see Georg Fritz, "Die Ostjudenfrage." In: *Westrussland*, 239–55. More clearly anti-Jewish is his brochure *Die Ostjudenfrage. Zionismus und Grenzschluss*, published by J. F. Lehmanns-Verlag, Munich 1915, in which he refers to the "acknowledgment of the race and cultivation of the race issue as the foundation of all policy"

(4). He interpreted the world war as a battle of the Germanic peoples "against the Mongolized Slavs and the 'Roman,' or so-called free peoples of the race-chaos of the Midland" (ibid.). He believed the eastern Slavs had increasingly lost their Indo-Germanic character and were now "permeated and flooded with the blood of Finns and Tatars, vanguards and trail blazers" (6). Fritz speaks of "poor, embattled eastern Jews" (48), but puts a positive slant on anti-Semitism and declares himself to be in favor of governmental protection against the immigration of the east European Jews. There were no doubt anti-Semitic stereotypes present among the military, but at the same Jews were also viewed positively. The occupation authorities cooperated with the Jews in many ways, and Jewish political and cultural life flourished, in sharp contrast to the economic situation. The recollections by the inner Jewish community of experiences with the Central Powers the time between the wars can be quite idealized. See Frank M. Schuster, *Zwischen allen Fronten. Ost-europäische Juden während des Ersten Weltkrieges (1914–1919)*, Cologne 2004, 458–89.

10

All Quiet on the Eastern Front

German Literature and the Eastern Front of the First World War

Eva Horn

The title of Erich Maria Remarque's novel, *Im Westen nichts Neues* (All Quiet on the Western Front), was wrong. "Nichts Neues" (nothing new) refers to the sort of messages that came in all too often from the Army High Command announcing that no breaches had occurred on the western front. This kind of situation, in which a front barely changed at all after years of the most intensive fighting, actually was something new that had arrived with modern warfare. Remarque's novel was and still is considered one of most impressive witnesses to this harrowing new characteristic of war. The war on the western front, which was irreparably traumatic, turned the First World War into the "great seminal catastrophe" of the twentieth century.[1] By the same token, the experience of a static battle tactic that was completely dominated by technology not only affected the image of modern war and warriors but also brought forth a unique kind of literature: the world war novel and world war poetry. With this, the First World War became an event whose historical form and remembrance are essentially defined by its literary representations. In a manner unique in literature and history, the experiences on the western front generated a flood of personal war memoirs with distinctive aesthetics, unusual narrative strategies, and an entire pantheon of literary characters who then returned to haunt the Weimar Republic. These figures ran the gamut from Ernst Jünger's *Stahlgestalt* (Figure of Steel) to the nationalistic warlike figures found in the works of authors like Schauwecker, Zöberlein, and Remarque; Paul Bäumer, the narrator-protagonist in Remarque's *All Quiet on the Western Front*, and like characters are representatives of the lost generation that never found its bearings in postwar society. The line stretches further to Ernst Toller's tortured and despised "war cripple," Hinkemann (whose surname means "limping man").[2]

But this image of the First World War and its cast of characters is the result of a systematic cover-up that is rarely scrutinized. It was the specific experience of the western front that became imprinted into the memory of the war, and therefore this experience became a metaphor for modern warfare. Germany's war in the east, the occupation that followed, and the military administration of the territory of Ober Ost did not appear in the afterimages of the First World War. But although the conduct of war in the east, the occupation and, of course, the subsequent battles by the Freikorps in Upper Silesia, Lithuania, and Courland are all documented in journals, letters, wartime memoirs, and novels, the eastern front has neither an Ernst Jünger nor a Remarque. What has persisted is the "inner experience," as Jünger termed it, of the western front, not the eastern. As a result, one can contemplate the military, historical, and literary "forgotten" eastern front only against the backdrop of that flood of stories and reminiscences inspired by the experience of the western front.

This prompts the question as to why there is a never-ending need to discuss and justify the front experience of the west while examination of the east is restricted to a couple of conventional war memoirs or journals, the usual letters and newspaper reports from the field, and (as I extensively examine in this essay) the power and fantasies of superiority found in the Freikorps novels. If getting to the essence of the eastern front experience and its literary treatment is to be more than a matter of simply closing a "gap in research," then we must ask why the war in the east has been overshadowed in the public consciousness by the western front. Why does it not fit into the modern discourse about the war? And which aspects of the war are ignored in its portrayal?

The war in the east is the "blind spot" in the discourse about modern war and its aesthetic representation, as if it were something too insignificant, uninteresting, or perhaps too threatening and overwhelming to be transformed into an adventure or literary narrative. It seems that no one has come upon the idea that the battles in Poland or Romania, Lithuania or Russia might contain the stuff of "inner experience." This becomes evident even in documentary materials. The thirty-six-volume series *Schlachten des Weltkrieges* (Battles of the World War), which appeared under the auspices of the Reichsarchiv starting in 1921, devoted twenty-six volumes to the western front, only five to the eastern front, four to the Balkan front, and one to the Italian.[3] And in 1931, Winston Churchill published a book on the course of the war in the east under the title *The Unknown War.*[4] It is not so much that the eastern front has been forgotten as that it appears to have fallen victim to an economy of attention: the waging of war in the west has always been the standard and norm for that which was "modern" about the war. At the same time, however, the logical question arises as to what sort of modernity is defined by concentrating on the war in the west while to a large degree ignoring the one in the east.

The relative nebulousness of the enemy to the east can be seen in the total mobilization of publicity that became known as "Die Ideen von 1914" (The Ideas of 1914) or "Der Krieg der Geister" (The War of Minds) which has a more warlike sound to it. The key words in this rhetoric famously identify the military enemy as the archenemy in the intellectual sense—and they refer to the enemies to the west. Thomas Mann poses a dichotomy between German "culture" as opposed to the "civilization" of France and England; German "soul" as opposed to French "intellect" and English "profit-seeking": "Culture," he wrote, "is unity, style, form, attitude, taste, and is a certain intellectual organization of the world. . . . Civilization is wisdom, enlightenment, placidness, having mannerly qualities, skepticism, solution, dissolution—spirit."[5] Werner Sombart pits "heroes" against "merchants"—an organic and organized community of Germans against a capitalistically designed, individualistically scattered society in England, the "perfidious Albion."[6]

The construction of the western enemy is little more than a projection of what had been criticized within German culture before the war: exaggerated individualism, the loss of genuine values, cultural frivolity, and an all-dominating rationality.[7] Western Europe, at least according to the general diagnosis in Germany, suffered from all the pathologies of modernity, but when war came, this discourse implied, Germany's misdirected society returned to being a community and the overly refined modern human being returned to simplicity and genuineness. The enemy in the west has a face, the all too well-known face of one's own illness.

The east remains strangely underilluminated in this discourse. While the enemy in the west is stylized with great philosophical extravagance into a distorted image of the Germans' own pathologies, there are mainly blanket judgments about the Russian enemy. The Russia of the czars was characterized as culturally backward, barbaric, and primitive, as an empire of despotism, ubiquitous secret police, and political censorship under the exploitative and wasteful government of a decadent ruler. It is not surprising that the view of Russia as a political and cultural enemy originated primarily from the pen of Socialist journalists. "Russian czarism," writes Wilhelm Herzog, "is the enemy of all western peoples, even the middle class of these peoples. Should the czar's hordes come to Germany, they would not bring freedom but slavery, not development but desolation, not progress but brutality."[8] And Otto Braun already envisioned the "half-Asiatic, schnapps-filled Russian Cossack hordes stomping across German fields, martyring German women and children, and trampling German culture."[9]

As an enemy the Russian is not simply a cultural opposite; he is a cultural zero, a savage. In the semantics of the hostilities as they were expressed at the beginning of the war this meant that Russia is in fact a highly dangerous enemy in military terms because of its superior troop numbers, but on an intellectual level not an equal and worthy opponent. As for the western European nations, Germany had a long intellectual and dynastic kinship with them, yet in the discourse of enmity, they were still made out to be the absolute enemy. The east was not any less enmeshed with the European royal families and not any less present in the European consciousness through its literature; nonetheless it appears too foreign culturally and politically and even too indistinct to become the object of that kind of enmity. The enemy in the east, according to Bernd Hüppauf, "was an image that blended both fear and fantasies of superiority, which was different, and for a war that was stylized as a worldwide historical victory from the start, it was peripheral."[10] Yet as early as 1914, this enmity was vigorously depicted as an insurmountable cultural difference to the extent that it almost represented a difference in terms of the human race. It was less about concrete war aims than about existential dichotomies; it was a "struggle between peoples" (as it was expressed at that time) that was to bring forth not only the victory of a nation but the birth of a "new" kind of human being. In this respect the enemy in the east occupied the role of the absolute loser: it was not so much a being that had to be conquered as it was one that had long since been left behind, an anachronism to modern times.

The military operations in the west were characterized by such experiences as the fronts at Verdun and Douaumont, the dogged persistence of static warfare amid nerve-racking artillery bombardment. After an interval of about ten years these experiences led to a wealth of novels, first-person accounts, and essays about the western front. The traumatic quality of the western front experience was perhaps described most accurately by Walter Benjamin in his essay "Erfahrung und Armut" (Experience and Poverty): "Wasn't it noticed at the time how many people returned from the front in silence? Not richer but poorer in communicable experience. . . . A generation that had gone to school in horse-drawn streetcars now stood in the open air, amid a landscape in which nothing was the same except the clouds and, at its center, in a force field of destructive torrents and explosions, the tiny, fragile human body."[11]

A generation had expected to be healed from a lifeless and overly refined culture; it had expected an actual "adventure"; and it expected to return from the environment of the war to an organic community. But they had stood on an empty battlefield scarred by mortars, had fought against an invisible and yet all too familiar western European enemy, and had seen and experienced nothing but the destructive, and yet completely inefficient violence of modern industrialized war. The trauma of the western front consisted of a complete blackout of all experiences and adventures in the confrontation with the technological destruction of man, material, and landscape.

Ernst Jünger confronts this blackout in an early work in which he makes battle into an "inner experience" by transforming the overwhelming, destructive experience of trench warfare into the transcendent metaphors of a "storm of steel" and a "God of War" who daily, with new force, voraciously "gorges himself on . . . blood, peace and human strength."[12] The war is a mythical juggernaut that the technology makes into an anthropomorphic power, the warrior a completely functional, completely sovereign, unshakeable steel figure. After the war, Jünger turns this warrior-worker into a "New Man" of a future society in which social organization follows the model of total mobilization.[13] Remarque approaches this problem the same way, even though his hero, Paul Bäumer, is a completely different protagonist: an average man. Here, too, the precarious experience of modern technological warfare completely transforms the perception of the individual subject. For Jünger it is the sphere of the victor; for Remarque, Renn, Köppen, and others it is the sphere of the defeated in the experience of war. Still others, such as Franz Schauwecker, take the chaos of the front experience and distill it into the order of a nation that will be born anew: "We had to lose the war in order to win the nation."[14]

One commonality, nevertheless, is that all these texts focus on a protagonist—whether he is tragically broken or celebrated and distinguished—who in the postwar period steps forward to build a new community that is even more warlike, more heroic.[15] This heroism, imbued with adventure but cleansed of the trauma, forms the nucleus of the discourse on the western front. And precisely for that reason this war, and this particular aspect of the war, can become the primal scene of that high modern fixation with technology, organization, and productivity, which Heinz Dieter Kittsteiner called the "heroic modern." A historical character who will withstand the forces of history certainly has options open to him, and these are the same ones portrayed by the authors of the western front genre: "persistence marked by heroic suffering—or a final attempt to overcome by means of superhuman powers."[16]

The discourse of the western front, then, is the discourse of the heroic modern, a discourse in which "characters" and "creatures" think and narrate in forms that are tailored to a single perceiving figure. The heroism of this figure rests on his ability to describe. The unimaginable aspect of the modern battlefield may thus be made imaginable, and ultimately perceivable, through the medium of the narrative. Still today the idea of modern war is dominated by the image of this empty battlefield that has been transformed by weaponry itself, something comprehensible only through technical media. In other words, this discourse of the western front stresses the idea of that which is specifically *modern* about wars—the dominance of the technology over the "human factor." The "field" becomes invisible, dominated by highly developed technology. With this, the enemy moves to an unbridgeable distance; he becomes abstract, like the aiming point of a ballistic calculation or a small spot on the lens of an air reconnaissance camera. The experience on the western front is, as Bernd Hüppauf recently argued, to a large extent the birth hour of a "cool" war, a clean, technologized, and ideally human-free war whose most recent state is illustrated by the perfecting of air reconnaissance by means of satellite images and the idea of the precisely calculated surgical strike.[17] This cool, abstract war of machines reflects a rather gruesome but also comforting image of a modernity that is the embodiment of foundational ideas such as domination, reliability, order, and cleanliness.

While it is possible to identify a discourse on the western front, all that can be verified for the eastern front is its existence. There are, of course, certain episodes in autobiographies such as Victor Klemperer's *Curriculum Vitae* or the journals of Hans Carossa. There are conventional war memoirs such as Walter Bloem's *Sturmsignal* (Storm Signal) or the nightmarish wartime journal of Edwin Erich Dwinger about his Russian war captivity, *Armee hinter Stacheldraht* (Army behind Barbed Wire). Not forgotten is the popular Walter Flex book *Wanderer zwischen beiden Welten* (The Wanderer between the Two Worlds), which describes a rather homoerotic war comradeship and is reminiscent of the literature of the *Wandervogel* youth movement of the Romantic period. And finally there is Arnold Zweig's novel about the administrative territory Ober Ost, the German occupation zone in the Baltic states, *Der Streit um den Sergeanten Grischa* (The Case of Sergeant Grischa).

But there is no Jünger of the eastern front. The war in the east is not comprehensible in the modernist heroic perspective of the western front experience. In comparison to the traumatic trench war in the west, the campaign against Russia was completely conventional. It was a mobile war with major gains in territory and direct contact with the enemy. In comparison to the "homogenous" western front, the eastern front was monstrously long and diffuse. It encompassed just as many occupied areas as direct battle zones. Those who participated in the war confronted impassable terrain, described by many as desolate and primitive, prone to extreme weather conditions, and filled with a confusing multiplicity of ethnicities and languages.

In the vast areas that were affected by the war, far more than simply battles took place. Michael Geyer described the conduct of war in the east as a "wild war," in which the desolation and depopulation in the areas surrounding the battles were as dramatic as the direct battle operations themselves.[18] This war involved masses of refugees and deportees, the violent recruitment of slave labor, the misery of prisoners of war on both sides, as well as lands made uninhabitable by plundering, pogroms, and epidemics. This war also meant extreme frost and deep mud, miserable roads, insufficient medical care, illness, and language barriers. In contrast to the west, national stereotypes do not play a role here, only ethnicities and their different languages, religions, and mentalities.[19]

In the west, the experience and the interaction with the latest weapons technology formed the nucleus of the war experience; in the east, only one-third of the weapons used on the western front were available. Soldiers in the east lacked tanks and heavy artillery, and in addition there were logistical problems due to bad roads and missing rail networks. The war on the eastern front was seen not only as a "primitive" war (Hüppauf) but as a confrontation with a world that was essentially "premodern."

While the shock of the western front experience had more than a little to do with the horizons of expectation of a great adventure, a notion that fell away after experience of the reality of battle, this sort of expectation is noticeably absent on the eastern front. In his memoirs, Norbert Elias sums it up succinctly: "The Czar and the Cossacks—barbarians, all of them. The barbaric East—it exceeded our ability to imagine."[20] The literary texts circumvent this gap, using concepts and images of vagueness, insubstantiality, and eeriness. We sense that from the east there emanates a horror that can hardly be expressed. It can be both sinister and familiar: German soldiers come face-to-face with Germany's own past in the form of architecture that they vaguely recognize as "old Germanic," or in the sound of Yiddish, which is often described as *putzig,* or "cute"; it is quite understandable to a German speaker but at times it also seems shockingly archaic, odd, dirty, primitive. Walter Bloem, a very popular author in the Wilhemine Empire, reported to the front voluntarily at the age of forty. Like Elias, he admitted that he had not the slightest notion as to what he would encounter. "The people of Turgenev, Tolstoy, Gorky, although familiar to me from their literature, are yet strange and incomprehensible. I love France, I love Belgium, I feel rage against England—the Russian is for me a concept with no form."[21]

The landscape is perceived in a similarly indistinct manner by the German soldiers who traveled day after day until they arrived at their final posts. Describing their arrival in the east, Bloem writes: "Dirt, rubble, horror everywhere. . . . We stumbled over . . . roads between mud huts to a hovel in Ziegelrohbau . . . millions of flies coated every object like a black crust. . . . At a snail's pace we rolled toward the south, onto a gray and eerily vast plain. . . . This is the east—this, the land of the Steppes, of sorrow and of sacrifice . . . a landscape [of] gloomy forest and meadowlands."[22]

Again and again there is the topos of desolation and the horrifying monotony of the landscape. Sometimes it appears as if melancholy readings from Chekhov had been inserted directly into the perception of the land. In the eyes of the Germans the traces of the war, such as the destruction of settlements by the scorched-earth policy, the dirt, the ruins, and the misery of the plundered population became the specific character of the region. The east is unearthly; it appears as a bizarre mixture of cultures, languages, and religious affiliations, partly homey and comforting, partly exotic, revolting, and incomprehensible.[23]

From a literary standpoint, this unearthly quality of the east can go two ways. On one hand the blanket description of the barbarian that existed at the beginning of the war now finds its refinement by emphasizing the primitiveness, backwardness, and brutality of the enemy. This ranges from the condescending, amused view of a Bloem or Carossa of wailing and begging villagers to descriptions of Russian dim-wittedness and brutality in the prisoner of war camps that appear in Dwinger's work all the way to the extreme power fantasies of the Freikorps novels, which strike an explicitly racist tone.

On the other hand, the literature can also evoke the Romantic period by focusing on the themes of melancholy and a connection with nature. In this case the east becomes a stronghold of authenticity and integrity that had been lost in modernity. Arnold Zweig discovered in the Hasidic Jews of the east an unadulterated down-to-earth piety that he documented in 1922 in his book *Das ostjüdische Antlitz* (The Face of East European Jewry). In the encounter with the wretchedness and hideousness of this war, in confronting the projections of an unknowable enemy, Zweig states, "the Jew of the East maintains his face."[24] And in his autobiographically inspired novel, *Das Gesicht der Etappe* (The Face of the Occupied Territory) (second edition 1919), Victor Jungfer describes the chauvinism of the German administrators of Ober Ost but also narrates the gradual enchantment of his hero by the fairy-tale quality of the Lithuanian language and heritage.

This mélange of fascination, longing, and bewilderment becomes complicated when it is bundled into one single, highly ambivalent figure. The Freikorps novels in particular showcase this ambivalence, crying out against the "Reds," "Bolsheviks," "Polacks," and so on in fantasies of racist violence, yet on the other hand, in the countryside in the east, be it Upper Silesia or the Baltic countries, they depict a pristine landscape reminiscent of the homeland that offers hope. Ernst von Salomon encapsulates this paradox in describing the odor of the ground of Courland: "I knew exactly at that time that for me this smell seemed to encapsulate all things, which moved me to hope and danger in Courland. I was enchanted by the dangerous strangeness of this country to which I stood in a unique proximity. It was just this feeling, while in the middle of this sweet landscape, of actually always standing on an uneasy swamp ground that constantly released its bubbles, which had indeed given the war up here its stirring, constantly changing character."[25]

In the Freikorps novels the ambivalence between longing and alienation, supremacy and threat that afflicted the occupiers and later the Freikorps fighters with respect to the cultures of the east is transformed into fantasies of violence that they wildly acted out and proudly reported.

The clearest manifestation of this "unearthliness" of the east comes in the form of the enemy. While in the west, the soldiers' enemy is technology itself, in the east the enemy is an actual human creature, one with an endless number of faces who wishes to be recognized and understood—that enemy may also have no face at all. Walter Bloem tells of one episode that vividly evokes the figure of the eastern enemy:

> We had to ride through a huge pine forest. Our cigars burned, the hooves clip-clopped on the excellent army road. . . . Suddenly, from the right, out of the darkness of the forest came a noise—anyone who heard it cannot forget it. The sound had something evil about it. Körstein, he knew the east, he knew that sound . . . 'the whistle of the Cossack!' he stammered hoarsely. In the same moment our horses broke into the most insane gallop. Did they know that whistle too—or was it the incomprehensibly delicate sensitivity of the horse, in which he overwhelms his rider? As if being chased, we swept through the darkness of the forest—listening, panting. Wasn't there a shot? Weren't there hoofbeats coming after us? Nothing. It is said that the Cossack is a coward. Yet never in my life have I experienced such an attack of nerves.[26]

Swept with panic, the human comes face-to-face with a kind of danger so unfathomable that it can be sensed only with the instinct of an animal. Bloem is describing an instinctive, unfounded, and untamed fear. This is the nucleus of the construct of the enemy in the east. It is a fear or a horror whose cause is ultimately a mystery. It remains an open question as to whether the danger is real or originates within the person himself.

The task of literature, as Bloem and many others understand it, is on one hand to transpose this horror, which the individual experienced as something diffuse and opaque, into images and narratives that give a face to one's own fears, such as that of the brutal, cowardly Cossack; on the other, it is to translate the individual's disorientation into the familiar tune of Russian melancholy.

A few authors, however, are haunted by the suspicion that this war cannot be grasped in this way. In his book on Ober Ost, Victor Jungfer portrays a character who explains what a novel about the eastern territories must actually strive for. "It must be just like our life out here. It must contain many plots, but none that are resolved . . . people would have to appear and disappear. Everything would be like a kaleidoscope—lighting up in a flash, then disappearing. The image would fit together like a mosaic." As the novel's protagonist says to a comrade, "They and I would be the heroes . . . but the main character must be life itself, duress, unrest, the futility of all action and the ridiculous efforts of small humans to escape all of that which is pushing them."[27] In the confusion and complexity of the diffuse war and occupation, according to Jungfer, a living and narrating hero, a man, can no longer be the main character of the story. Instead, the war itself must become the actor and hero of the story.

Ultimately Victor Jungfer did not write that story, but Arnold Zweig did. His is one of the most intelligently written and well-informed books about the First World War. At one time it was used in school lessons in East Germany, but in West Germany it was forgotten, overshadowed by the volubility and celebrity of the heroes of the western front in the works of such authors as Remarque and Jünger. Like Jungfer's *Das Gesicht der Etappe*, Zweig's *Der Streit um den Sergeanten Grischa* also plays out in the German administrative area Ober Ost. The action begins in March 1917, when the former sergeant Grischa Paprotkin, a prisoner of war with the Germans, breaks out of a prison camp and finally makes it home to his family in the administrative territory of Ober Ost. Suspected of being a spy, he is taken prisoner. Although it becomes clear that he is neither deserter nor spy but an escaped prisoner of war, the court case against him cannot be stopped—after much back-and-forth by the authorities and against the entire body of evidence, Grischa is sentenced to death and shot.

Thus, this is not a novel about the front featuring heavy artillery and brooding battle descriptions; it takes place in the rear and focuses on an event that is unimportant to the overall war. Unlike nearly all western front novels, *The Case of Sergeant Grischa* is not a description of the experience of one single hero, his inner or external adventure, but a highly detailed and knowledgeable analysis of the war administration, encapsulated in one court case in which the administrative apparatus commits "judicial murder" through its incompetence and lack of impartiality.

The case file of Grischa Paprotkin follows a path through the authorities of the legal system in the eastern territories, accompanied by quarrels between the high commander and the division-level commander: a narrow-minded major general versus an "Old Prussian" division commander. Here the organizational structure of the war unfolds not as a battle landscape but as a network of political interests, twisted career paths, personal animosities, differing mentalities, and a blind, malevolent raison d'état. By focusing on one tiny detail of military history, the injustice committed against a prisoner, an individual with the absolute least importance in the war and the fewest legal rights of any participant in the war, Zweig reveals the entire bureaucratic organization of the war as a network in which coincidence and inevitability, the interests of the individual, and grand strategies are inseparably interwoven. The protagonist of the plot is not Grischa, nor is it the many more or less integrated, more or less powerful figures who willingly and unwillingly exert influence on Grischa's fate. Instead, it is the case file itself. Unread, it was coincidentally handed forward and then, through a new coincidence, declared to be a test case; finally, despite various objections, a verdict is handed down in a decree from above.

The case provides a view into the conditions of the war and its restricted possibilities, revealing more about the organizational structure of the war than about experience in battle. This organizational structure is all-encompassing. It applies to the civilian population of the occupied zone, Ober Ost, just as it does to the division officers. The wife of Private Bertin delivers the case file to the war tribunal council, a factor that plays just as crucial a part as the telephone connection to Merwinsk or the war profiteering agreements between Major General Schieffenzahn (aka Ludendorff) and the big industrialist Schilles (aka Stinnes). The war as an organizational structure encompasses both homeland and front, economy and administration, civilians and soldiers, men and women, Jews, Russians, and Germans. Most important, the court case of Grischa Paprotkin demonstrates that everything is connected to everything else, and that in this system, which is closed and opaque, life and death are determined by tiny coincidences.

Zweig succeeds in his depiction of this labyrinth by means of a narrative technique that avoids placing one single protagonist in the foreground or casting an all-seeing glance down onto the events from above. Instead, he presents a kaleidoscope of introspections. What unfolds are Grischa's wishes and insights and his gradual uncomplaining acceptance of his death, interwoven with the history and perspective of each person who enters the sphere of the action. These histories range from the sad childhood of Major General Schieffenzahn and his social resentment toward the aristocratic division commander von Lychow to the much biased judge in the military court-martial to the inner perspective of lynx, who at the beginning of the novel stalks Grischa as he flees into the forests. In Zweig's story, the never-ending network of the war is broken up into segments that touch upon each other coincidentally, yet no matter how random, they wield the power of life and death. The war is an overwhelming experience not because of weapons technology but due to its paradoxical mixture of extreme planning and absurd coincidences. It is the breakdown of the telephone connection to Merwinsk, which delays the retraction of the order until the following day, when Schieffenzahn has second thoughts. And it is the indecisiveness of the division officers around Lychow who do not dare to protest the obviously unjust verdict. And finally it is Grischa, who has simply had enough of life with his "strain and anger" and spurns efforts by the woman he loves to help him escape.

The execution of Grischa Paprotkin in the stone quarry near Merwinsk has as many "fathers and mothers" as the novel has characters. What emerges in this novel is not just the organizational dimension of the war—which, by the way, is authentic. The injustice that befalls Grischa through the justice system exposes a form of violence that is different from destruction through technology. It is injustice in the sphere of law; it is the reduction of the state to the element that actually holds it together, pure power. As Major General Albert Schieffenzahn, who represents the hub of the organizational structure of the war, proclaims to the legalistic Lychow, "The state creates the law, and the individual is but a louse."[28]

In the chapter "Bildnis eines Selbstbeherrschers" (Portrait of a Disciplined Man), the figure of Schieffenzahn expresses the powers and interests of the war in the form of a psychological puzzle. "In reality he carried the brain of the entire territory between the Baltic Sea and the Carpathians in his shorn skull—not one transcendent, brilliant instinct, but rather the enlightened center point, the place where all consciousness, insight, will, and command was located. Behind his forehead was systematically categorized a monstrous amount of knowledge. Since he had predetermined on every map each material depot, every field hospital, each railway or road that was to be constructed, he commanded these details, in the manner in which one plays with intellectual property."[29]

Schieffenzahn, alias Ludendorff, is the embodiment of what Vejas Liulevicius has called the "military utopia of the administration of Ober Ost." This utopia, according to Liulevicius, essentially exists in cultural fantasy: what was perceived as the chaos and disorder of the east must be countered with German order and planning.[30] Victor Jungfer, however, contests this notion of a central German fantasy about the cultivation of the east. "What is the essence of the war? Destruction. And the occupation? Grafted as a headstrong national structure on top of another with completely different life issues and reasons for existing, it creates compromise filled with evil."[31] In reality, he maintains, the war was about exploitation by the Germans, not about cultivation of the eastern territories, although he concedes that both the cultural mission and exploitation could be considered an expression of the same sense of superiority, which saw nothing in the other culture but a backward, rather primitive stage of modernity.

Unlike the traumatic but always coherent "war experience" on the western front, Zweig's war dissolves into an entanglement of endless perspectives and versions that are both coincidental and inevitable. Within the war's endless "adventures," the main focus ultimately becomes the way in which these perspectives are configured and connected. Zweig's east is not *the* monolithically simple and nonconceptual east but the mixture of people as they actually exist, with very different mentalities, horizons of development, interests, and cultures, a hypertrophic system that, in the final analysis, proves to be chaos.

At the same time, the indigenous population is depicted through portrayals of individuals, and the depiction of the German occupiers is spread across a multitude of types—from ordinary dogged soldiers from Eberswalde to the idealistic Jewish judge of the court-martial, Posnaski to the old-style Prussian general, von Lychow, and the corrupt and brilliant social climber, Schieffenzahn. In the quarrel over the file of an insignificant prisoner of war, Zweig explores the infinite diversity of the events of the war, expanding the concept of war far beyond the battlefield. His understanding of the war includes the occupation, and his novel reflects the administration's grand scheme for the overall control of the Baltic states under German rule as a kind of war by other means.

Zweig challenges the purpose and consequences of this desire to reorganize the allegedly chaotic east with German discipline and order. It appears that the dream of great order through administration was, in this respect, a side effect of that unearthly quality of the anachronistic and disordered east. Through German organization and work, this primitive landscape on Europe's periphery was to be lifted into modernity. As Liulevicius has pointed out, this dream was de facto a much-expanded system of regulations and a chaos of overgoverning, a government for the benefit of the German Empire and to the detriment of the local population.

The literary treatment of the eastern front of the First World War, be it marked by horror and eeriness, by the defiance and disgust of many war reminiscences and almost all Freikorps novels, from the melancholy, amazed, and romanticized manner of a Victor Jungfer to the analytical lucidity of Arnold Zweig, is a treatment of a war that, when placed side by side with the overpowering technological experience of the western front, can only give the impression of an anachronism. The "wild war" of the east is not a war of machines but a war of bodies and mentalities, not a war of nations but of ethnicities, not a war of destruction from a distance but a dirty, destructive interaction between enemies. It is a war that involved war-torn populations, refugees, epidemics, and plundering. It is a war against the impassability of the terrain, the pitfalls of a poorly defined front; it is death from hunger, frost, and illness instead of from wounds. The "wild war" is a war of excesses large and small, of alienation enveloped in absurd brutalities by unfamiliar cultures, strange dress, poverty such as never before experienced, and languages that are not understood.

In this, the view of the east during the First World War foreshadowed a type of war conduct that ultimately became a reality, and not just during the campaign of annihilation during the Second World War. It prefigured another side and another category of the conduct of war, which modernity in its self-concept of technology and control tended to exile to the realm of the "archaic." Michael Geyer has developed the notion of the "wild war" into a paradigm for a new and different view of the experience of violence of the First World War. This experience with violence has less to do with being overwhelmed by technology than with people having to deal with relocations, depopulation, and cultural barriers; it is much less concerned with the violence of weapons than with what has more recently been called collateral damage, the violence of occupation, plundering, and ethnic cleansing. It happens less often at the front than in the rear, in areas where civilians and soldiers come into contact. Arnold Zweig's novel in particular demonstrates something that became dramatically clear during the US occupation of Iraq after 2003: that the occupation and governing of a conquered nation can be an extended form of war. When these elements of the "wild war" on the eastern front are exposed—and the war literature appears to be especially well suited to do this—this "forgotten front" emerges as a theater of war that is both instructive and eerily relevant.

Notes

1. George F. Kennan, *Bismarcks europäisches System in der Auflösung. Die Französisch-Russische Annäherung 1875–1890,* Frankfurt, Berlin, Vienna 1981, 12; in the original (*The Decline of Bismarck's Order: Franco-Russian Relations, 1875–1890,* Princeton, NJ 1979), it is called "the great seminal catastrophe of this century."

2. Ernst Jünger, *In Stahlgewittern,* 1919; Franz Schauwecker, *Der feurige Weg,* 1926, *Aufbruch der Nation,* 1929; the National-Socialist author Hans Zöberlein, *Der Glaube an Deutschland,* 1931; Ernst Toller, *Hinkemann,* 1922.

3. *Schlachten des Weltkrieges.* In individual descriptions edited and published on behalf of and in cooperation with the Reichsarchiv, 36 vols., Oldenburg, Berlin 1921–1930. See also Markus Pöhlmann, "'Das Grosse Erleben da draussen.' Die Reihe Schlachten des Weltkrieges (1921–1930)." In: *Von Richthofen bis Remarque. Deutschsprachige Prosa zum I. Weltkrieg,* edited by Thomas F. Schneider and Hans Wagener, Amsterdam 2003 (= *Amsterdamer Beiträge zur neueren Germanistik,* 53), 113–31.

4. Winston Churchill, *The Unknown War: The Eastern Front,* New York 1931.

5. Thomas Mann, "Gedanken im Kriege." In: *Neue Rundschau,* 25 (1914), 1471–84, here 1471.

6. Werner Sombart, *Händler und Helden. Patriotische Besinnungen,* Munich, Leipzig 1915.

7. The war texts by Georg Simmel exemplify this. *Der Krieg und die geistigen Entscheidungen,* Munich, Leipzig 1917.

8. Wilhelm Herzog, "Der Triumph des Krieges." In: *Das Forum,* issue no. 5/6, 3/10/1914, 268.

9. Journal entry of Otto Braun, 5/8/1914, quoted in *"Vaterlandslose Gesellen." Sozialdemokratie und Nation 1860–1990,* edited by Dieter Groh and Peter Brandt, Munich 1992, 160.

10. Bernd Hüppauf, "Der Osten als Bild und Bilder vom Osten. Spuren der Phantasie und des Lichts in Kriegsfotographien," manuscript of journal article for the conference "Foto-Krieg. Österreichische Kriegsfotografie 1914–1918: Wahrnehmung, Erinnerung, Politik," held at the IFK—Internationales Forschungszentrum Kulturwissenschaften, Vienna, 14–15/5/2004. I owe several key ideas in my own text to this article. My thanks to Bernd Hüppauf for the generous access to his manuscript.

11. Walter Benjamin, "Experience and Poverty" [1933], In: *Selected Writings,* vol. 2, Cambridge 1999, 731–36, here 732–33.

12. Ernst Jünger, "Der Kampf als inneres Erlebnis." In: Ernst Jünger, *Sämtliche Werke,* vol. 7, Stuttgart 1983, 28.

13. Ernst Jünger, "Der Arbeiter. Herrschaft und Gestalt." In: *Werke,* vol. 8, Stuttgart 1981.

14. Franz Schauwecker, *Aufbruch der Nation,* Frankfurt 1930.

15. I have proposed a typology for the narrative model of world war novels in Eva Horn, "Erlebnis und Trauma. Die narrative Konstruktion des Ergnisses in Psychiatrie und Kriegsroman." In: *Modernität und Trauma. Beiträge zum Zeitenbruch des Ersten Weltkrieges,* edited by Inka Mülder-Bach, Vienna 2000, 131–62.

16. Heinz Dieter Kittsteiner, "Die Stufen der Moderne." In: *Geschichtsphilosophie und Kulturkritik. Historische und Systematische Studien,* edited by Herta Nagl-Docekal and Johannes Rohbeck, Darmstadt 2003, 108.

17. Hüppauf, *Der Osten als Bild.*

18. Michael Geyer, "Gewalt und Gewalterfahrung im 20. Jahrhundert. Der Erste Weltkrieg." In: *Der Tod als Maschinist. Der industrialisierte Krieg 1914–1918* (catalogue for the exhibition at the Industriemuseums Osnabrück, 17/5–23/8/1998), edited by Rolf Sprilker and Bernd Ulrich, Bramsche 1998, 248f.

19. The eastern front is much less researched in terms of military history as well. A significant exception is Norman Stone's *The Eastern Front, 1914–1917,* New York 1975.

20. Norbert Elias, *Reflections on a Life,* Cambridge 1994, 19.

21. Walter Bloem, *Sturmsignal!* Berlin 1935 (1st ed. 1918), 85.

22. Ibid., 60–63, passim.

23. The ambivalence of the German point of view of the occupied and administered Baltic is described in the outstanding study by Vejas G. Liulevicius, *Kriegsland im Osten. Eroberung, Kolonisierung und Militärherrschaft im Ersten Weltkrieg,* Hamburg 2002

24. Arnold Zweig, *Das ostjüdische Antlitz,* 2nd ed., Berlin 1922, 14.

25. Ernst von Salomon, *Die Geächteten,* Berlin 1931, 115.

26. Bloem, *Sturmsignal!* 118.

27. Victor Jungfer, *Das Gesicht der Etappe. Ein Kulturroman,* 2nd ed., Berlin, Riga, Leipzig 1919, 195.

28. This aspect of injustice during wartime is the subject of inquiry of the literary scholar and author W. G. Sebald in his article on Zweig's novel. See W. G. Sebald, "Humanitarianism and Law: Arnold Zweig, *Der Streit um den Sergeanten Grischa.*" In: *The First World War in Fiction: A Collection of Critical Essays,* edited by Holger M. Klein, London 1978, 126–35.

29. Arnold Zweig, *Der Streit um den Sergeanten Grischa,* Berlin 1994, 194. Translation from the English version: *The Case of Sergeant Grischa.*

30. Liulevicius, *Kriegsland im Osten,* 72–115.

31. Jungfer, *Das Gesicht der Etappe,* 35.

The Battles in Russian Poland and Galicia in 1914

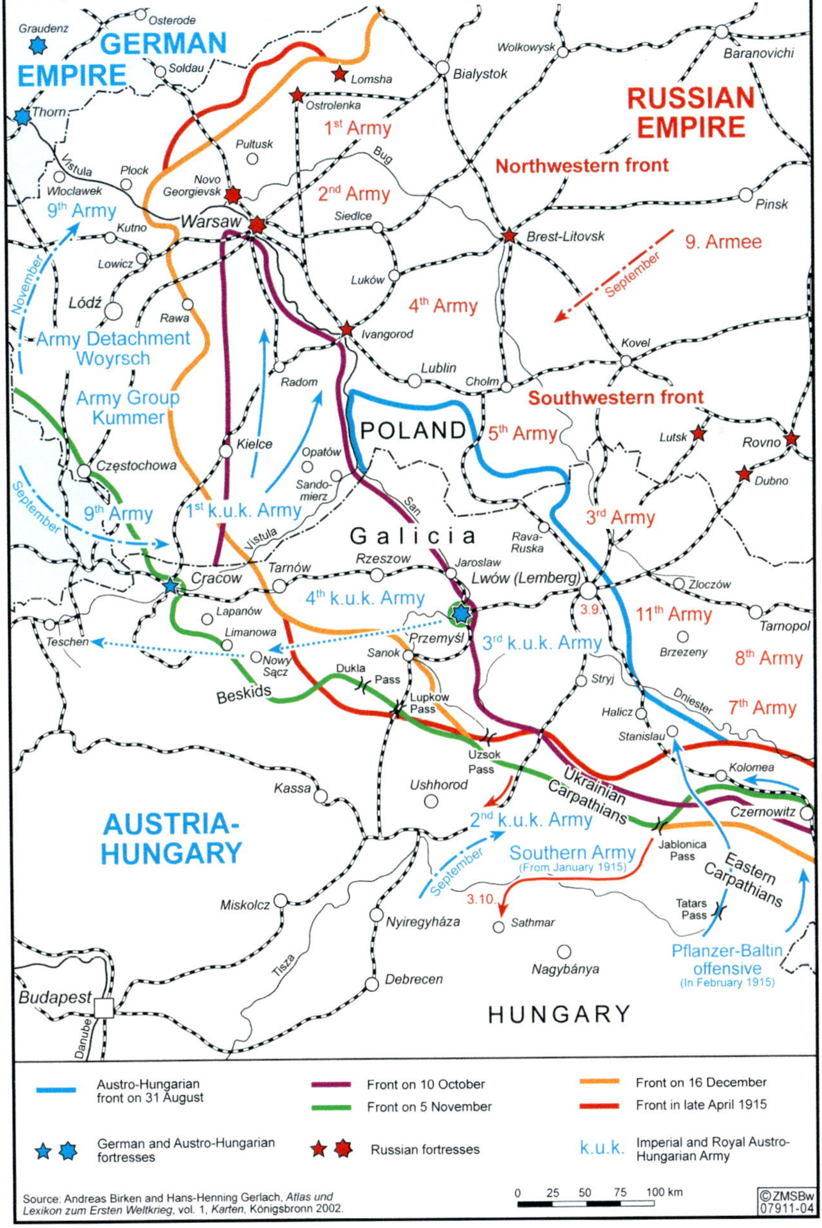

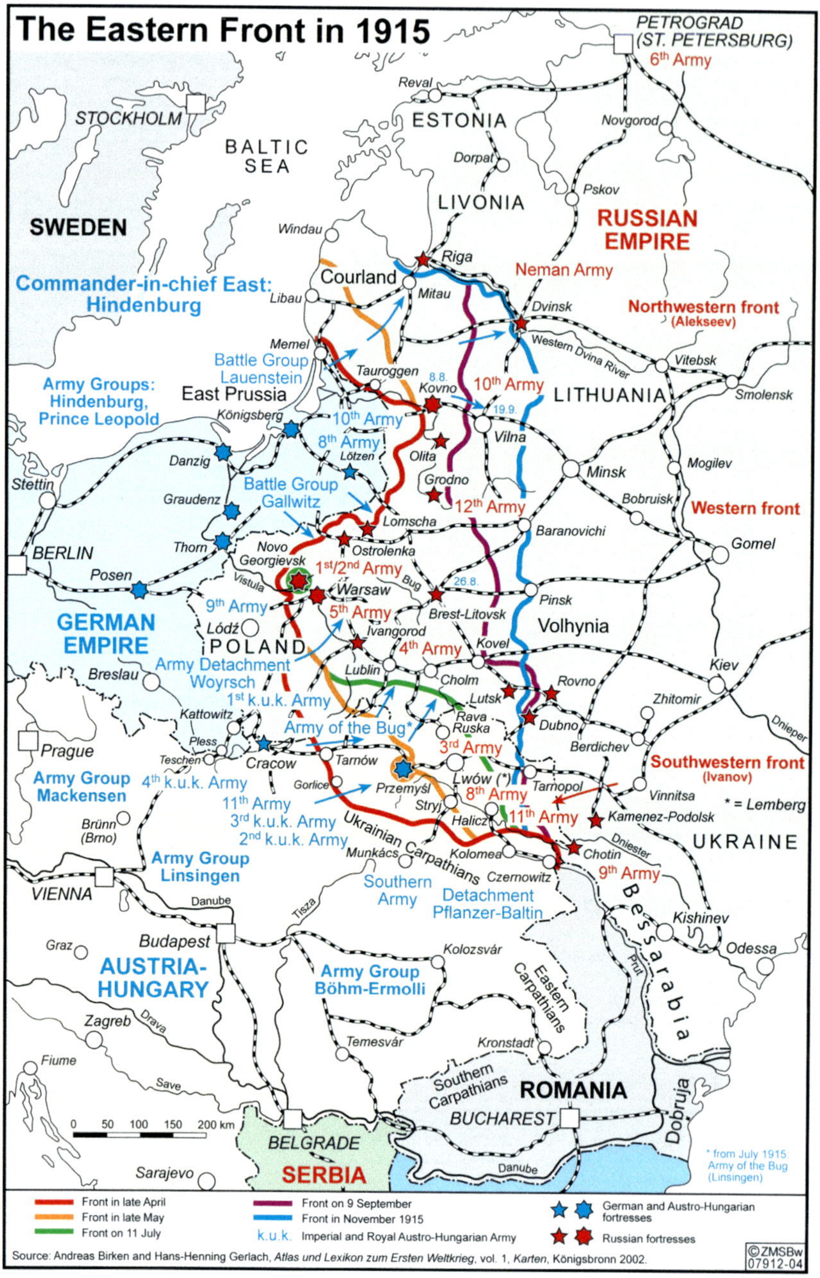

The Eastern Front in 1915
PETROGRAD (ST. PETERSBURG)
6th Army
STOCKHOLM
BALTIC SEA
ESTONIA
Reval
Novgorod
Dorpat
Pskov
LIVONIA
RUSSIAN EMPIRE
SWEDEN
Windau
Riga
Neman Army
Commander-in-chief East: Hindenburg
Courland
Libau
Mitau
Dvinsk
Northwestern front (Alekseev)
Memel
Western Dvina River
Battle Group Lauenstein
Tauroggen
Vitebsk
Army Groups: Hindenburg, Prince Leopold
East Prussia
8.8.
Kovno
10th Army
LITHUANIA
Smolensk
Königsberg
19.9.
10th Army
Vilna
8th Army
Danzig
Lötzen
Olita
Minsk
Mogilev
Stettin
Battle Group Gallwitz
Grodno
Graudenz
12th Army
Bobruisk
Western front
Lomscha
Baranovichi
BERLIN
Thorn
Novo Georgievsk
Ostrolenka
Gomel
Posen
1st/2nd Army
Vistula
Bug
26.8.
Warsaw
Pinsk
9th Army
5th Army
Brest-Litovsk
GERMAN EMPIRE
Łódź
Ivangorod
Volhynia
POLAND
4th Army
Kovel
Army Detachment Woyrsch
Lublin
Kiev
Breslau
Cholm
Rovno
1st k.u.k. Army
Lutsk
Zhitomir
Kattowitz
Army of the Bug*
Rava Ruska
Dubno
Dnieper
Pless
Prague
3rd Army
Berdichev
Teschen
Cracow
Tarnów
Southwestern front (Ivanov)
Army Group Mackensen
4th k.u.k. Army
Gorlice
Przemyśl
Lwów (*)
Tarnopol
Vinnitsa
* = Lemberg
11th Army
8th Army
Stryj
3rd k.u.k. Army
Halicz
11th Army
Kamenez-Podolsk
Brünn (Brno)
2nd k.u.k. Army
Ukrainian Carpathians
UKRAINE
Dniester
Chotin
Munkács
Kolomea
9th Army
Army Group Linsingen
Czernowitz
VIENNA
Southern Army
Detachment Pflanzer-Baltin
Danube
Tisza
Bessarabia
Kishinev
Budapest
Graz
Odessa
Kolozsvár
AUSTRIA-HUNGARY
Army Group Böhm-Ermolli
Prut
Eastern Carpathians
Zagreb
Drava
Temesvár
Kronstadt
Fiume
Save
Southern Carpathians
ROMANIA
0 50 100 150 200 km
BUCHAREST
Dobruja
BELGRADE
* from July 1915: Army of the Bug (Linsingen)
Sarajevo
SERBIA
Danube
Front in late April
Front in late May
Front on 11 July
Front on 9 September
Front in November 1915
k.u.k. Imperial and Royal Austro-Hungarian Army
German and Austro-Hungarian fortresses
Russian fortresses
Source: Andreas Birken and Hans-Henning Gerlach, Atlas und Lexikon zum Ersten Weltkrieg, vol. 1, Karten, Königsbronn 2002.
©ZMSBw 07912-04

Winter Battle of the Masurian Lakes
(7 to 21 February 1915)

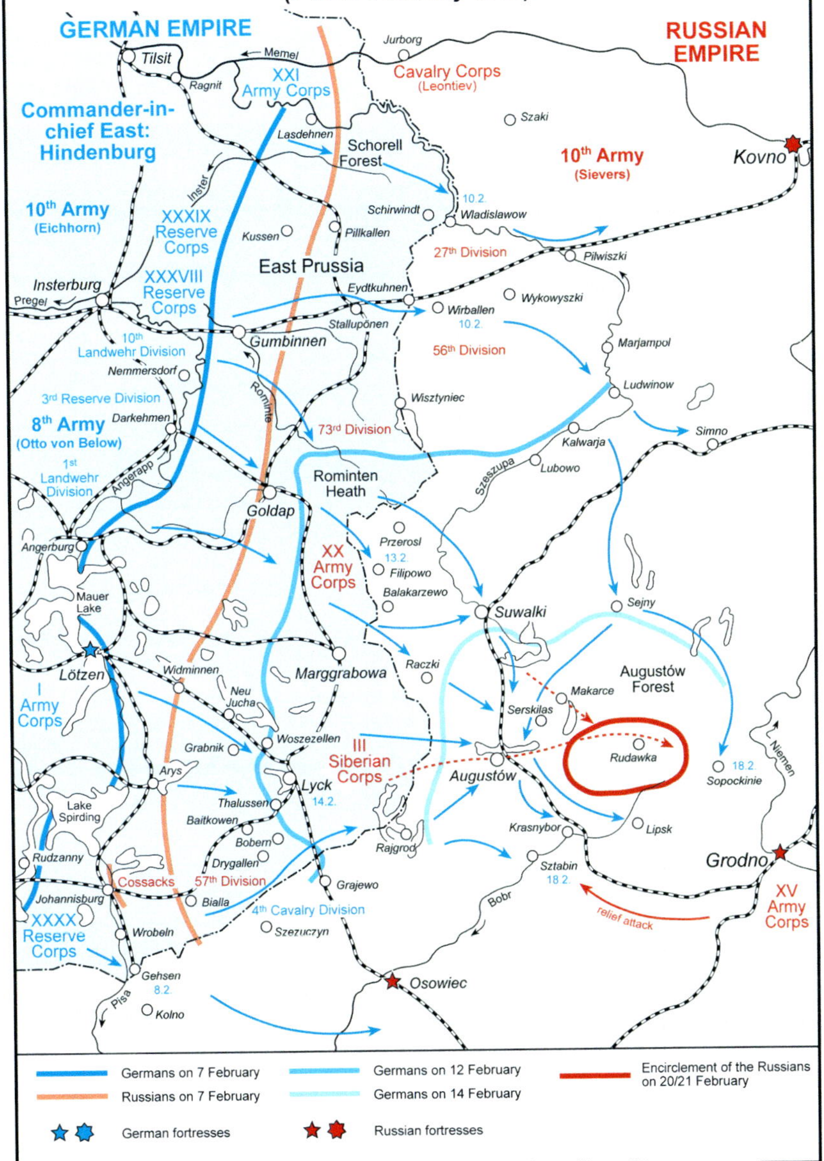

Source: Andreas Birken and Hans-Henning Gerlach, *Atlas und Lexikon zum Ersten Weltkrieg*, vol. 1, *Karten*, Königsbronn 2002.

The Breakthrough at Gorlice in May 1915

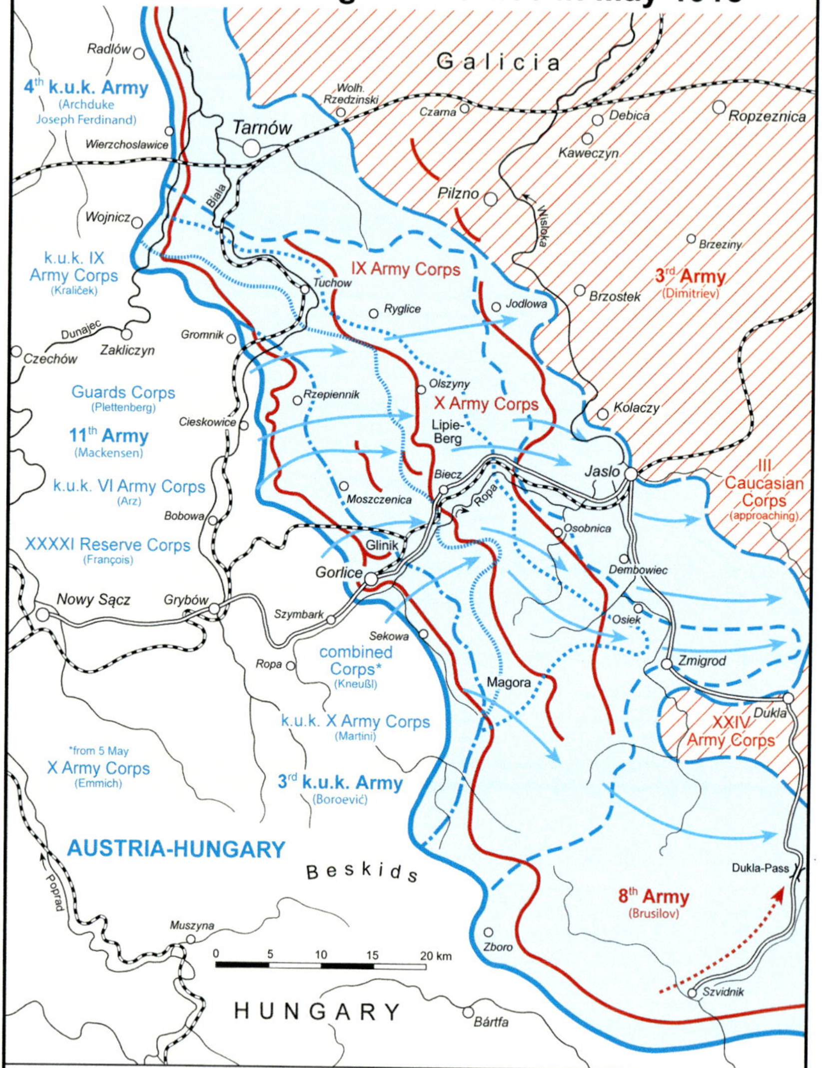

German and Austro-Hungarian positions in the morning of 2 May

Russian positions in the morning of 2 May

Russian-occupied territories in Austria-Hungary

k.u.k. Imperial and Royal Austro-Hungarian Army

Lines reached in the evening: 2 May; 3 May; 4 May; 5 May; 6 May

Source: Andreas Birken and Hans-Henning Gerlach, *Atlas und Lexikon zum Ersten Weltkrieg*, vol. 1, *Karten*, Königsbronn 2002.

11

August 1914

Alexander Solzhenitsyn and Russian Wartime Literature of the Early Years of the War

Birgit Menzel

The First World War has been described as both a challenge to modernism and a reaction to it. Modris Eksteins, in his *Rites of Spring: The Great War and the Birth of the Modern Age,* makes a first attempt to synchronize modern culture with modern conduct of war, a perspective of more recent cultural history.[1] Here, the outbreak of the war and the artistic avant-garde are described as *one* radical revolt against the existing system, a system whose proponents were not only the cultural and intellectual elite but also fundamental social and political forces within mass culture:

> The term *avant-garde* has usually been applied simply to artists and writers who promoted experimental techniques in their work and urged rebellion against established academies. The notion of *modernism* has been used to subsume both this avant-garde and the intellectual impulses behind the quest for liberation and the act of rebellion. Very few critics have ventured to extend these notions of the avant-garde and modernism to the social and political as well as artistic agents of revolt, and to the act of rebellion in general, in order to identify a broad wave of sentiment and endeavor. This book attempts to do so. Culture is regarded as a social phenomenon and modernism as the principal urge of our time. The book argues in the process that Germany has been the modernist nation *par excellence* of our century.[2]

Thus a line of continuity is drawn here from the modernism of the artistic realm and the modernist impulse of the First World War to the establishment of the totalitarian dictatorships that ultimately led to the catastrophe of the Second World War.

Modernism in Art and War

The outbreak of the First World War has generally been experienced and described as both an opportunity for radical change and an opportunity to validate the existing—that is, aristocratic—system of government within the European nations. In his attempt to connect war with the avant-garde, Eksteins begins with the understanding that both are deeply ambivalent reactions to modernism—to such things as solidified social constraints, rationality, Western civilization, middle-class norms, and all types of hypocrisy, especially regarding middle-class sexual mores. At the same time, in Germany the notion of Western civilization was understood primarily to be the civilization of the English and French, which, because of its long tradition of dominance, was reproached for its arrogance and superficiality.

This revolt against the cultural norm was carried out with a warlike militancy in the name of elemental, irrational impulses. Germans saw a particularly strong synergy in the combination of nationalism and culture—in other words, in the criticism of civilization. This synergy was intended to mobilize mythical and archaic forces in battle against the perceived evils of the civilizations of neighboring countries.

In Eksteins's view, however, this revolt was a reaction to the impositions of modern technology to which humans had been exposed on a massive scale inside of a few decades, in the form of mechanization, rationalization, individualization, and alienation. Eksteins names four features that war has in common with modernism: introspection, primitivism, abstraction, and myth creation.

Introspection in the realm of art encompasses a penchant for psychological self-examination, that is, the cult of the aesthetic, which was not infrequently associated with a tendency toward narcissism. Introspection can be seen in the metaphysical motivation for the war, especially the second phase, when the earlier optimism had disappeared. Slogans—such as this quote from Bismarck's contemporary Emmanuel Geibel, "Am deutschen Wesen soll die Welt genesen" (Germany's soul will heal the world)—invoked ideas cloaked in mystery and romanticism of the inevitability of war as an inner necessity, of Germany's mission as a nation of culture, and of the conflict as a fight for truth and self-actualization. Even at the bitter end, this slogan served as a vitalistic justification for the necessity of war as an experience of such heightened intensity as to liberate the world from banal materialism and hypocrisy.[3]

Primitivism in art is illustrated by the paradigm of Igor Stravinsky's symphonic poem *The Rite of Spring*. This piece celebrates a heathen and archaic rite of spring in which the unrestrained sensuality of the music reaches its crescendo with the offering of a virgin in sacrifice. Its 1913 debut in Paris, attended and talked about by many personalities of rank and name, was received internationally as a scandalous sensation, largely due to the extremely liberal choreography of Sergei Diaghilev's Russian Ballet Company, with its emphasis on the body.[4] In painting and fine arts, fascination for primitive cultures other than European, in combination with the bursting of moral fetters, led to unusual innovations. The conduct of the war was also associated with a gradual reduction to elementary, primitive forms of life—static warfare in trenches, the abandonment of patterns of behavior instilled by civilization, total war against military and civilian populations and the use of barbaric weapons of death.

In the years prior to the First World War abstract painting became popular internationally, something the futurists described as a "major breakthrough," which was viewed as a declaration of independence, as it were, of language from content and the ultimate rejection of mimetic art.

Abstraction as a characteristic of the war found its real and gruesome expression in the deformation and dismemberment of the body through newly designed weapons—fragmentation bombs, mines, and flame throwers—and in the surrealistic pictures of soldiers in gas masks. The First World War was even spoken of as "cubist war."[5]

Myth creation included key concepts of total art as seen in the Wagnerian cult or the myth of Germania which, combined with the cult of the hero, were also used effectively as a means of waging war.

What is described here for the western European nations in general and for Germany in particular can also essentially be applied to Russia. Both Germany and Russia exhibit parallels in such areas as social development and cultural self-reflection. Although these parallels exist, there were also concepts specific to Russia.

Unlike Napoleon's campaigns, the Revolution of 1917–1918, and the Second World War, the First World War is not a prominent theme in Russian literature or in western European literatures.[6] Until recently only a small amount of attention has been given to its research.[7] This can be partly explained by the fact that the historical memory of the Russian intelligentsia of the First World War was dominated by the October Revolution; the world war, in the manner of a mere prelude, was lost in the undertow of events that followed. In Russia the basis for a unified national loyalty was weak because at least since 1905 the intelligentsia, as representatives of society, had opposed the czarist regime.

Nevertheless, testimonials from that time as well as documents written later about this war reveal some remarkable details that had been kept hidden by Soviet historiography until recently. It is worthwhile to consider them more closely, as they point out some of the ambivalent reactions to modernism in Germany and western Europe mentioned earlier. To the same extent, they confirm that in Russia, too, there was a connection between war, modernism, and the avant-garde.

This chapter will begin with a thematic overview of reactions to the war by contemporary Russian intellectuals and artists, at least to the extent that one can speak of a common position held by the symbolists. Representing the avant-garde, the voice of the most prominent poet among the futurists, Vladimir Mayakovsky, will be heard through his 1915–1916 poem "Voina i mir" (War and the World). The essay concludes with an exploration of the foundational theses of Alexander Solzhenitsyn's novel *August 1914* (1971/1983), the only substantial work by a well-known author about the First World War.

Russian Symbolists and the War

The symbolist writers and philosophers—Fedor Sologub, Nikolai Gumilev, and even Andrei Belyi, Nikolai Berdyaev, Petr Struve, and Fedor Stepun—reacted to the outbreak of the war with a literary and journalistic outburst of passionate patriotism and an unaccustomed unity. This essay will examine these poets, philosophers, and writers of modernism, that is, the symbolists and post-symbolists. The findings here do not apply to the whole body of literature: realists like Maxim Gorky and Alexander Kuprin, the literature of the proletarian worker, and popular literature have been omitted.

Most of the symbolist poets and philosophers welcomed the outbreak of the war, seized with a wave of patriotism for their own country and hatred for Germany. Even the most atheistic members of the Decadent poetry movement were in agreement with the general topos of religious justifications and meaningful purpose to this war, regarding it as a "crusade by holy Russia against godless Germany." Fedor Sologub, one of the most internationally known Decadents, immediately pledged himself to a glowing patriotism, and wrote many propaganda poems. In his 1914 poem "Na nachinaiushchego Bog" (God against the Aggressor), for instance, he used biblical allusions to summon forces against the enemy:

> God against the aggressor!
> Believe the proverb.
> Anyone who causes evil death to his neighbor
> He will die ahead of his time . . .
> His supports will turn to dust . . .
> He who creates the uproar,
> God will damn to unconsciousness
> If his fist is also armed with iron
> shattered to death before our unshakable house.[8]

Sologub published an article in 1916 entitled "Why Symbolists Support the War." It professed a unity within the symbolist movement that never existed, not that year, nor ever. Valerii Bryusov had expressed an extravagant taste for destruction and war as early as the start of the Japanese War in 1905: "I am for these barbarians, the Huns, the Russians." In his poem "Posledniaia voina" (The Last War), he described the war in 1914 as a theatrical drama and as a struggle of the old world, which had been "immersed too long in its Babylonian orgy," cowering in fear against the attack by the Germanic tribes. But now the iron hand would wipe out the old regime with one swipe, "in one horrifying year of fighting." But he views it as a chance for total transfiguration: "Everything we had dreamed of, as if it were a miracle, might perhaps come true . . . in a bath of fire a new world may arise . . . as a beginning of peace and freedom." Bryusov described himself as being torn between the "Hun" and the "Westerner."[9]

With few exceptions, all modern Russian poets greeted the war as a challenge, seeing in it the possibility of a radical self-purification, a motivation Katerina Clark described as the dominant impulse for the whole prerevolutionary intelligentsia—the opportunity for a religious, or at least a metaphysical, validation of their own greatness as a front against foreign influences and dangers.[10] Within this paradigm, reaction to the war ranged from the tenor of an enthusiastic aesthetic lust for death and destruction, as in the case of Nikolai Gumilyov and Valery Bryusov, all the way to apocalyptic predictions of a massive period of tragic transformation, as with Boris Pasternak and Alexander Blok.

There were, in fact a variety of ideological worldviews: neo-Slavophile philosophers like Sergei Bulgakov, Fedor Stepun, Nikolai Berdyaev, Semen Frank, and others published hate articles against Germany in the periodical *Russkaia mysl'* (Russian Thought). In articles such as one by Vladimir Ern titled "From Kant to Krupp," Germany's culture was now generally depicted as barbaric and godless, rationalistic, power hungry, and aggressive, and was contrasted with the universally pacifist Russian intellectuality.[11] The theme of holy virgin Russia being raped by brutal German maleness was described in a much-cited article by Ern, "The German People Have Made the Abstract Concept of Chauvinism Their Dogma."

Even Germanophile symbolists like Andrei Bely, who was taken with the anthroposophy of Rudolf Steiner, sought refuge in a racist Russian-based mysticism that also encompassed a cultural anti-Semitism.[12] The reaction to the war led to a desire for religious and spiritual national self-determination, which meant a process of making oneself completely separate from the enemy. This enemy was primarily identified as the "inner German," and the process corresponded with the desire for self-purification. The war was seen as punishment for the inner "Germanization" of Russian culture. Russian disassociation from Germany as a representative of the West occurred in some writers and philosophers in the form of a *Selbstorientalisierung* (self-orientalizing), a rejection of the culture of the West and identification with the East. By projecting onto Germany and the West everything about their own modernism they rejected as negative, they sought to elevate themselves through a more positive identification with the East. In the context of the old fight over whether Russia belonged to Europe or to Asia, those incriminating Asiatic characteristics that had once been considered blemishes—uncivilized backwardness, slavish subservience, crude and gruesome customs—were now viewed as positive. This was reflected, for instance, in Eurasian-style works and motifs, the portrayal of Eurasia as "Scythia," the return to Eastern Orthodoxy and, not least, the influence of the theosophy of Helena Blavatsky on the contemporary intelligentsia.[13]

There are three specific elements in the reaction of the Russian symbolists and the post-symbolists that can be tied to the outbreak of the war:

1. Whatever their differences of aesthetics, worldviews, or politics, members of the Russian intelligentsia were bound together by the desire for an anti–middle class revolt and self-purification. By 1914 the intelligentsia's self-criticism and the embittered controversy over the 1909 anthology *Vechi* (Signposts) had been forgotten.[14] The opportunity came for a new national unity with a new metaphysical meaning assigned to the war. Within this can be found a continuity between symbolism and the avant-garde and ultimately between adherents of the modern aesthetic and political modernism.
2. The exceptionally close albeit profoundly ambivalent relationships of Russian artists and intellectuals with Germany made a long-lasting enmity impossible. But during the first months of the war all camps were unified by a patriotic elevation of the self by means of disassociating from the enemy; Russians projected negative stereotypes of the Germans as the cultural root of all evil—commercialization, rationalization, soulless dependence on technology, vulgarity, godlessness, self-indulgence, and a desire for power. This propaganda-based alliance between camps did not last long. Right after the war, Russia and Germany reestablished their close ties. Even though the commonalities reached far deeper with the cultures of, say, the English or the French, and although Russia had been a member of the Entente alliance during the war, there were no indications of growing friendship with Britain or France.[15]
3. Russian poets and philosophers were far removed from political reality, caught in an abstract, apocalyptic, and aesthetic vision of the world. Between the glorification of death and violence and the demonization of tragedy and catastrophe, they nevertheless claimed a privileged access to transcendence, having foreseen this epochal change. The unpredicted destruction of Russia affected them all the more bitterly. Their personal

disillusionment heralded the end of hope and with it the end the symbolist movement. The silence of the symbolists was quickly replaced by the revolutionary clamor of the avant-garde.

The Avant-garde: Vladimir Mayakovsky and the War

Mayakovsky, the best-known representative of the avant-garde, published his first poems in 1912. In his futurist manifestos he called for an aggressive struggle against all traditions and praised technical progress, which he equated with artistic progress. But at the heart of his early poems, in which he experimented with language, stood the human figure oppressed by the abysses of the modern large city. Although it did not explode into a rude public scolding of the middle class, this figure is nevertheless shown as a victim of the coldness and loneliness of life in a metropolis, a figure transformed and restored in the dramatic, tragic sense.[16]

Politically active early on in the underground circles of the Communist movement of 1914, after a short enthusiasm for the war—he even volunteered for military service but was rejected—Mayakovsky took a clear position against the war, which he wanted to turn into an anti-imperialist revolt through his propagandistic poems and posters.[17] Along with poems and two prose skits that are scathing attacks on the hated petty bourgeoisie on the home front, in particular his poem "Voina i mir" is dedicated to the theme of world war.[18] Here, in a firework of metaphors, the war of the people of Europe is depicted as the result of the failure of politics. Addressing those who stayed home, the author-as-himself shouts at his reader: "Listen here! Everyone, even the most unnecessary person, should live; one can't bury a man alive in the grave of the dugouts—you murderers."

Mayakovsky's poem contains characteristics of symbolist war poetry, such as its depiction of the war as a theatrical performance: a Roman gladiator fight takes place "in the theater of war"; "the whole world is a coliseum"; "all Europe hangs in the sky like a fire-red chandelier." Also present is the Nietzschean hyperbole of self-creation and anti–middle class revolt.

Nevertheless, Mayakovsky's reaction to the war, along with that of the avant-garde, is essentially different in content and in its formal aesthetics. The lyrical subject expresses its rejection of the war as an imperialistic world theater, satirically exposes the insanity of the enthusiastic masses, "massomiassaia bykomordaia orava" (a horde of human flesh and ox meat)—"Bravo! Braa-vo! Bra-aa-vo! Bra-a-a-a-vo!" At the same time, the poem identifies itself with militant violence as a rebellious destruction of the fossilized modernism that is permeated with rotting middle-class decadence. Adopting the pose of the representative victim of mankind gone crazy, the martyr role of the crucified Christ, the narrator cries: "You take on the sin of the world, let it increase."

Here he is adapting the biblical Christian metaphor to his own circumstances.[19] The brutality of the war was never before portrayed in such shockingly graphic images. We see bodies tossed into the air by bombs, soldiers sunk in filth and swamps, rotting, stinking corpses, clumps of flesh and blood on the battlefield, an army of legless cripples: "for forty men, four legs remained rotting in the wagons," "torn-off heads call their names. On one skull hangs a piece of hacked-off scalp."

In the same way, the decadent habits of bourgeois society in the rear area are depicted as repellant and disgusting. Both the events of the war and bourgeoisie debauchery are described in sexually explicit images; battle and the act of sex are juxtaposed:

> At the beginning of the bloody game,
> A moment's standstill, tense,
> Like an act of sex,
> Breath halted,
> Suddenly,
> The seconds fragmented,
> The arena exploded with smoke into the abyss.
> The sky—pitch black
> The seconds race and race—
> An explosion,
> roaring,
> ripping,
> One frothy shot after another into the
> Bloody wall.
> Forward![20]

Mayakovsky, too, depicts the war in a way that is far removed from experienced reality, above all as a linguistic and aesthetic gesture. The same is true of technical advances. Herein lies a typical trait of Russian futurism in contrast to Western avant-garde. The machine age, which was enthusiastically vaunted for its civilizing and technologizing results, still did not represent a real experience of mass industrialization and its impact for backwards Russia. In Germany, its witnesses were the artists. The skyscrapers described by Mayakovsky in the futurist manifesto *A Slap in the Face of Public Taste* did not yet exist in Germany in 1913, only in America. But the Russian poet evoked the attributes of the machine age primarily metaphorically, and all the more radically, by presenting imagined images without referencing actual objects. In Germany, the breathtaking technological industrialization was a real societal experience for everyone.

What distinguished Mayakovsky from the symbolists and other contemporary poets was the language he used to describe the war. As shown in the above examples, his art expressed a mimetic adaptation of violence. To this extent, one can confirm Eksteins's thesis that modernism is fully accepted here in its *gestus*, or embodiment of promise and destruction, including the destruction of self.

Alexander Solzhenitsyn and the First World War: *August 1914*

Solzhenitsyn wrote the only Russian novel of substance about the First World War from a historical distance of twenty to fifty years after experiencing the Russian Revolution, the Stalinist dictatorship, and the Second World War. He wrote it under Cold War strictures that governed production and reception in a time of increased ideological East-West polarization. What does his literary reaction to the war offer as an interpretation of the events of the war, the role of Russia, and Russia's relationship to Germany and to the West?

Scholarly treatment of Solzhenitsyn has been distorted by exceptionally strong ideological stances, such that to date there has been no unbiased analysis of his literary texts either in Russia or the West. The ideological context of the genesis and reception of Solzhenitsyn's novel *The Case of Solzhenitsyn*, although it is genuinely important and could contribute something to the understanding of his work and person, will largely be excluded here.

First, some explanatory notes on his text are needed. The novel *August 1914* was published in two editions. The first appeared in Paris in 1971 and consisted of sixty-four chapters; in 1983 an expanded and substantially revised second edition, with eighty-two chapters, was published. The creation of a second edition grew out of the author's own political and biographical situation. Having been freed from a prison camp, Solzhenitsyn was censured and forced to emigrate in 1974. Further, for three decades Solzhenitsyn had been collecting and storing source material in archives in Russia, America, and Switzerland.

The novel is the first part of a trilogy. The whole work, referred to by the author as his "uzel" (knot), consists of several volumes and thousands of pages on the history of the Russian Revolution and the Civil War that followed. This work was first published in the West from 1983 to 1991 under the title *The Red Wheel* (*Krasnoe koleso*). The beginning of Solzhenitsyn's planning and collection of materials goes back to the years 1936–1937. Even before the Second World War, which the author actually spent as an officer in the East Prussian Army in the same location as his novel's setting, he had composed its first chapter. It was not until approximately 1969 that the first edition was finalized, along with the conceptual design for the entire trilogy. Because Solzhenitsyn was aware that decades would pass before the completion of the trilogy, he agreed to an independent publication of the novel, *August 1914*. It was a shortened version that was missing the chapter "Lenin in Zurich," a portrait of Vladimir I. Lenin, which was published separately later. In 1972 a German translation was published, followed by numerous editions in other languages.[21]

In the afterword of the Paris edition, Solzhenitsyn described the novel as his main work, something he needed to accomplish because Russian authors, the older as well as the younger generation, were being forced to silently ignore this most important topic of recent history. As he had refused to comply with the censors and had included the word *bog* (God) in lowercase, he knew it would have been impossible to publish in the USSR.[22]

In the second two-volume edition, the order of the chapters was substantially altered, and some chapters were rewritten. In addition to the new Lenin chapter, other material was added about the czar between 1899 and 1911 (more than one hundred pages), Russian domestic politics, especially the murder of the minister of the interior, Petr A. Stolypin, and the fate of several radical and terrorist members of the opposition. This edition of the novel is much more specific as an introduction to the year 1917, with the war as mere prelude to the Revolution. The author's basic statements remain intact, however; they have simply been strengthened.

The novel deals with the outbreak of the war and the progression of the East Prussian campaign. It continues up to the annihilating defeat of the 2nd Russian Army by the materially superior 8th Army under Generals Erich Ludendorff and Paul v. Hindenburg in the battle near Tannenberg on 28 August 1914. The commander of the 2nd Russian Army, General Aleksandr Samsonov, subsequently committed suicide. A large portion of the more than five-hundred-page novel consists of several individual stories of military operations, described in detail. The work does not feature a conventional plot line that revolves around a few characters; there are a confusing number of both fictional and historical characters, mostly the latter. Except for the main characters, all the military leaders are authentic. Solzhenitsyn also weaves in some autobiographical information, along with that of some contemporaries and family members. Thus, for example, the figure of the student Isaaki "Sanya" Lazhenitsyn is recognized through his similar name as Isaj Solzhenitsyn, the author's father, who was an artillery officer at the battle of Tannenberg.[23] At the start of the novel, there is a meeting between Isaaki/Sanya and Leo Tolstoy at the latter's country property, Yasnaya Poliyana. The meeting and the student's veneration for the highly regarded older man are historically authentic. Only a few of the characters in the novel are of central importance to the story: General Aleksandr Samsonov, Colonel Vorotyntsev, and the colonel's constant companion Private Arseni Blagodarev, who is also a peasant and who maintains a respectful distance. Like Vorotyntsev, he is a fictional character.

There is a series of second-tier characters, from Count Nikolai Nikolaevich in the upper ranks to the simple privates of low ranks. In the beginning part of the story, which takes place in peacetime shortly before the outbreak of the war, several families with different ideological social and worldviews are introduced so that the reader sees a cross-section of the generations, lifestyles, and viewpoints of the times: students, revolutionaries, intellectuals, people from the large metropolises, people from the small cities of the south, simple peasants, and rich property owners.

In its structure, *August 1914* breaks several traditional literary conventions of the historical novel. Besides multilevel interconnected narratives, there is a chronologically ordered succession of historical overview chapters, or daily reports, that are introduced in individual time frames and chapters; these are pure documentaries that contain no fictional characters. The events are depicted from several different perspectives. Numerous documents, newspaper clippings, song texts, postcards from the front, telegrams, and flyers are presented between the chapters as collages, graphics, and stylistic facsimiles. Under a heading reading "Film Screen" are melodramatic word images and other insertions, similar to what one would see in a movie script, depicting events such as battle scenes taking place simultaneously somewhere outside the narrative. Chapters frequently open with slogans and close with aphorisms, poems, and common sayings. These kinds of techniques, devices meant to disrupt continuity, were typical of avant-garde prose writers of the 1920s such as John Dos Passos. Introduced as a means of dissolving the border between fiction and documentary, the techniques were not new as hallmarks of the modern novel, though they were not typical in Solzhenitsyn's works.[24]

In its stylistic speech, the novel offers many barriers to comprehension even for contemporary Russian readers. At first glance, these processes could be understood as the avant-garde strategy of literary estrangement. In any case, a closer evaluation of the author's intent indicates that he avoided traditional speech patterns in order to preserve the reputed richness of the Russian language. Solzhenitsyn's project was to breathe life into the Russian language beyond the prescribed Soviet "newspeak." His style often appears stilted, artificial, and overdone. The vocabulary includes a wealth of uncommon, sometimes antiquated or bizarre, often newly fabricated words and compounds. Along with stylizations of all types, the author uses a syntax filled with breaks and ellipses.[25] All these techniques remain superficially decorative and have no counterpart in the deeper structure. They cannot disguise the fact that overall this novel is derivative of the conventional realistic novel of the nineteenth century. It falls into the genre of the monumental times and morals novel. Much of its structure and content, especially its historical and philosophical aspirations and the moralizing stance of the author, point to Leo Tolstoy's historical novel about the Napoleonic campaign, *War and Peace,* as a concrete model. As a German reviewer noted, Solzhenitsyn writes implicitly and explicitly for the Russian reader, in "grandiose misjudgment of Western literary taste."[26] Despite the novel's semi-modern multiple perspectives, one can identify the auctorial narrator's perspective, as the characters can be placed into clear positive or negative categories. Social or psychological categories have no role to play here, and no role as an interpretive tool. General Samsonov, for example, is on top of the social hierarchy and is an absolutely positive character type, as is the peasant Private Blagodarev, who stands at the lower end of the hierarchy. The deciding criterion is much more about the inner attitude of the figures toward the Russian nation.

The main point of the novel is to investigate the reasons for the annihilating military defeat.[27] These justifications are explained from the auctorial perspective and developed and evaluated most visibly at the level of the action. Foremost is the inability and failure of the Supreme Command, of Generals Zhilinsky, Januskevic, Oranovsky, Danilov, and Rennenkampf, and along with them, the political leadership of the czar. Disorder and chaos, personal vanity, addiction to power and image, bureaucratic stagnation of the organization: in other words, the inability to confront the challenge of an effective, rational, and technically highly developed—that is, modern—military. According to the understanding of history expressed in Solzhenitsyn's novel, personalities help shape history. In failing because of their lack of modernism, they shared responsibility for the nation's defeat and thus paved the way for the Revolution, which the author perceives as a catastrophe.

The revolutionaries shared responsibility for the defeat, with their speeches that subverted battles and the defense force, especially the naïve populist and activist Yaroslav Kharitonov, who in moments of dramatic battle mobilization or after a defeat called out to his comrades: "The more dead, victims, and defeats on the Russian side, the sooner the opportunity will come when all soldiers refuse to fight and demand revolution" (chapter 14).[28]

The characters in the novel with radical viewpoints, such as the student Jude Galperin, the high school teacher Tolstoyan Lenartovich, and the mother of activist Kharitonov, however, express strongly simplified, abstract, and unrealistic views about the Revolution's ability to transform the masses. Their positions in the novel appear as satirical exaggerations. Some of the revolutionaries, such as Kharitonov, in crucial moments of existential need and military preparedness, join in the common spirit (*sobornost*) of the Russian nation, when the destructive propaganda is at the peak of cynicism. All of this is to guide the reader to an understanding that the revolutionaries played a historically negative role in these war years, but that they do not bear the main responsibility. Here one can argue against contemporary literary critics who, comparing Solzhenitsyn's earlier anti-Stalinist and anti-Communist works and statements, believed the author was positing that a main reason for the military breakup of the Russian Army was the revolutionary propaganda.[29]

It is striking to note that among the intellectuals in the novel, there is not a single completely positive figure. Almost all express extreme opinions, which in view of the author's value system appear egotistical, morally reprehensible, or destructive. In the novel, the term *folk* is used exclusively by intellectuals in all variations of their idealizations.[30] In this critical attitude toward all representatives and orientations of the Russian intelligentsia there can be seen in Solzhenitsyn a continuity with his criticism of the Russian intelligentsia in the 1909 collected volume *Vechi,* where he contended that the intelligentsia's own radical extremism was the precursor to intellectual decay and the Revolution.

The actual reasons for the total military defeat are not dealt with specifically in the novel. They are implied in the background, revealed through occasional comments by the narrator, in symbolically loaded speeches, and in a few key scenes. As a result, they appear less as part of the plot than as elements of narrative, symbolic, and figurative representation. One of the key scenes is found in chapter 42, in which the old librarian Varsonofief, a marginal character who appears only briefly, engages in a philosophical discussion with the two students Sanya and Kostya in which they address the fallacy inherent in their worship of the people. To Kostya's question of whether it is even possible to have an ideal social order, the older, superior Varsonoviev responds as the voice, or alter ego, of the author himself: "There was originally a better meaning for the word *order:* it was 'inner order' (*vnutrenii poryadok*). And for humanity, there is nothing more important than the order of the soul, not even the well-being of the next generation. . . . History is not rational, my young friends. It is its own organic web, not transparent to us. History grows like a living tree. And reason is an ax, and with reason you will not encourage growth. . . . The laws of the best human order can only be based in world order. In the idea of a total world. And in the determination of humanity. That is it, of course, the task before us—to complete the order within" (*August Vierzehn,* 367).[31] According to Solzhenitsyn, this order essentially rests in the collective experience and collective consciousness of entrenched national Russian Christian thinking. Through the action and comments of the characters we are shown that in Russia, this order has fallen into ruins.

A second key scene of the novel is in chapter 50, set in the middle of the catastrophic chaotic retreat of the scattered surviving troops through the Grünfliess woods after the battle. Some of the soldiers drag their dead second lieutenant along, risking themselves to bring the body out of the battlefield, which seems an absurd undertaking to others. This depiction of the fleeing men lost between fronts, able to find an hour's shelter in the very surreal fog that surrounds them, evokes the mythological concept of the woods as a "no-man's land." In the coincidental presence of Colonel Vorotyntsev and under the guidance of his peasant companion Blagodarev, the only person familiar with Orthodox burial rituals, the soldiers bury their lieutenant. Through this scene, in which ordinary soldiers and a colonel, simply through the ritual of honoring the dead, are bound by brotherly love in the existential dimension, the idea is posited of a transcendent Christian metaphysical unity providing a deep source of national strength in the "community of faith" (*sobornost*). It is a repeal of the sociopolitical and military hierarchy, a unifying of all humanity, a substantiation and strength through a metaphysical connection with Christian roots. The scene concludes without direct words from the narrator-author to disrupt the moment: "And soaring higher than the sun, higher than the sky, directly to the throne of the All-High, from fourteen men's voices the familiar chant arose, not in supplication but in sacrificial offering, in renunciation: 'To Thee, O Lord . . .'"[32]

As has been pointed out, there are a great many connections, parallels, and contradictions between *August 1914* and Tolstoy's novel *War and Peace*. A close comparison of the works shows that the key scenes depicted here express a clear correspondence with Tolstoy's historical philosophical beliefs. Both novels are, in any case, connected by the theme of existential threat caused by wars provoked from outside. There is direct homage to Tolstoy in Solzhenitsyn's depiction of his meeting with the students at the beginning of the novel, in which he specifically mentions the author and his works, especially *War and Peace*. In chapter 53 General Blagoveshchensky is an explicit imitation of General Kutuzov from Tolstoy's novel, and the reader will recognize that his theory of historical fate attempts to legitimize his cowardice and inability to cope. Further parallels lie in the interweaving of private fates or family histories and historical and sociopolitically relevant events and personalities, in the combination of real and fictional characters, in the composition of a many-layered array of plot threads, and in the representations of the characters, such as General Samsonov, General Kutuzov, Blagodarev, and Platon Karataev.

There are also distinct differences, however. Solzhenitsyn does not share Tolstoy's pacifism. In his novel he accepts the necessity of defending the nation, that is, preparation for force and the readiness to make sacrifices, as a positive trait for his characters and their membership in the national community. This position contradicts Tolstoy's radical Christian teachings, according to which man "should resist evil." A further difference concerns Tolstoy's concept of history. In *War and Peace* Tolstoy provides every opportunity for the individual to shape history and to exert influence, which was a radical shift in his thinking. He expresses this in the novel by showing that it was the power of the people, the masses of fighting soldiers, not the generals, who won the battle of Borodino against Napoleon. In Solzhenitsyn, on the other hand, the responsibility for victory or defeat is vested in the leaders and the commanders, and it is these individuals who are granted the opportunity to shape "great history." A third difference is that Tolstoy's characters, despite their moral rigidity and use of ideological monologues, are basically conflicted and torn, while the characters in Solzhenitsyn's novels, although they have inner soliloquies, are never divided within themselves, and the judgmental narrator maintains his auctorial perspective.[33] Tolstoy's characters, in contrast to those in Solzhenitsyn's war novel, are shown with a larger aesthetic and literary complexity that affects both message and literary quality.

To return to the theme stated at the outset of this chapter, taking into consideration the reasons given in Solzhenitsyn's novel for the Russian defeat at the beginning of the First World War and placing them in context with modernism in art and culture, it can be said that in his critique of disorganized bureaucratic ineptness, personal power struggles, and the rigid backwardness of the Russian Army, Solzhenitsyn represented a primarily modern position. Through his fictional character Vorotyntsev, he promulgated rational reforms in the technical and administrative conduct of war.

This is reflected in a third key scene shortly before the end of the novel, as Vorotyntsev passionately accuses the generals of their mistakes and failures. The prince allows him to do so openly and in the presence of military leaders after the lost battle. The inferiority of the Russian Army rested on the partly age-related refusal to commit to a necessary strategic, technical, and administrative modernization of the military apparatus. Some analyses claim that this novel has a broader, primarily anti-Communist account to settle with revolutionary ideologies and their proponents, who represented several contemporary critics of his emigration.[34] But such interpretations miss the point. What Solzhenitsyn argues here is that this war brought the Russian Army face-to-face with modernity. The challenge before them was the need to adapt, but the responsible parties in Russia, whether political or military, were not up to the task.

As a solution to this problem, he offers a vision of national unity in Christian belief, a society in which the moral steadfastness of the individual flows together with the collective religiously rooted *Volksgemeinschaft,* or ethnic community. The deeper reason for the defeat, an essential part of his message, was the disintegration of the metaphysical "spiritual order" of the nation. This expresses an impulse that is directed against modernism in the most profound sense. Solzhenitsyn, in a prophetic gesture, envisions a conjuncture of Orthodox belief and ritual with the metaphysical force of national strength. Despite his argument that this aspiration is about humanity's existence, however, in my view it is a perpetuation of the myth of the Russian *Sonderweg,* or special path to modernism.[35]

Notes

1. Modris Eksteins, *Rites of Spring: The Great War and the Birth of the Modern Age,* Boston 1989. German version: *Tanz über Gräbern. Die Geburt der Moderne und der Erste Weltkrieg,* Reinbek bei Hamburg 1990.

2. Eksteins, *Rites of Spring,* xv–xvi.

3. See Rudolf Euken, *Die sittlichen Kräfte des Krieges,* Leipzig 1914, quoted in Nikolai Plotnikov and Modest Kolerov, "'Den inneren Deutschen besiegen.' Nationalliberale Kriegsphilosophie in Russland 1914–1917." In: *Traum und Trauma. Russen und Deutsche im 20. Jahrhundert,* edited by Dagmar Herrmann and Astrid Volpert, Munich 2003, 15–59, here 16. According to Eksteins's argument, the endurance of the German troops, considering the catastrophic depravations and defeats, was not about national defense as it was in England, where it was a matter of life and death. It can be explained only by an irrational sense of duty to higher goals. He quotes the statement from a student recruit: "Poetry, art, philosophy and culture—that is what this war is about." Eksteins, *Tanz über Gräben,* 93.

4. Ironically, the tumultuous scandal broke in the French-Russian artists' ensemble, of all things. The star dancer of the group, Vaslav Nijinsky, and the famous choreographer Sergei Diaghilev made no secret of their homosexuality.

5. Eksteins, *Tanz über Gräben,* 164.

6. In Russia, in fact, in the beginning phases of the war, there was an abundance of texts about the war, even in the high literature. (Ben Hellman discusses over 270 works from the symbolist authors; see Ben Hellman, *Poets of Hope and Despair: The Russian Symbolists in War and Revolution, 1914–1918,* Helsinki 1995). The Petersburg printing house of Ivan Sytin published more than 50 collected volumes and war speeches in the series Voina i kul'tura. See Plotnikov/Kolerov, "Den Inneren Deutschen besiegen." Popular folk literature also offered many texts referencing the war. See also Hubertus F. Jahn, *Patriotic Culture in Russia during World War I,* Ithaca, NY, London 1995; Werner Benecke, "Kopekenliteratur für Russlands Wehrpflichtige. Die 'Soldataskaja Biblioteka' 1896–1917." In: *Jahrbücher für Geschichte Osteuropas,* 50 (2002), 246–75. But in Russian literature, in comparison to literature on the Revolution, the Civil War, and the Second World War, the First World War theme is less frequent and of lesser quality. This can also be said of German and English literature. (On German literature, see the essay by Eva Horn in the present volume. For English literature, see Paul Fussell, *The Great War and Modern Memory,* New York, Oxford 1975.)

7. Strongly ideologically biased articles from Soviet literature of the 1930s to the 1970s include Orest Tsekhnovitser, *Literatura i mirovaia voina 1914–1918;* Moscow 1938, Anatolii A. Volkov, *Poeziia russkogo imperializma,* Moscow 1935; Raissa Messer, "Russkie simvolisty i imperialisticheskaia voina." In: *Leningrad,* 7 (1932), 65–74; Vladimir Piskunov, *Tema o Rossii: Rossiia i revoliutsiia v literature nachala XX veka,* Moscow 1983. For more background materials, see *Revoliutsiia 1905–1907 godov i literatura,* edited by Boris A. Bialik, Moscow 1978. Only since the 1990s have there been some pioneering studies on this subject, such as Hellman, *Poets of Hope;* Ben Hellman, "Kogda vremia slavianofil'stvovalo: Russkie filosofy i pervaia mirovaia voina." In: *Studia Russica Helsingiensia et Tartuensia,* vol. 1, *Problemy istorii russkoi literatury nachala XX veka,* Helsinki 1989 (= *Slavica Helsingiensa,* 6), 211–39; Plotnikov/Kolerov, "Den inneren Deutschen besiegen"; Michail Bezrodnyj, "Zur Geschichte der russischen Germanophilie. Der Verlag Musaget." In: *Zauber und Abwehr. Zur Kulturgeschichte der deutsch-russischen Beziehungen,* edited by Dagmar Herrmann, Munich 2003, 319–56; Ronald E. Peterson, *A History of Russian Symbolism,* Amsterdam 1994; Avril Pyman, *A History of Russian Symbolism,* Cambridge 1993. Some contributions from cultural historians in literature include Raymond Pearson, *The Russian Moderates and the Crisis of Russian Tsar-*

ism, 1914–1917, London 1977; Heinz-Dietrich Löwe, *Antisemitismus und reaktionäre Utopie: Russischer Konservatisvismus im Kampf gegen den Wandel von Staat und Gesellschaft 1890–1917,* Hamburg 1978.

8. Fedor Sologub, "Na nachinaiushchego Bog." In: Fedor Sologub, *Sobranie sochinenii,* vol. 4, Moscow 200, 106.

9. Valerii Bryusov, "Posledniaia voina." In: *Valerii Briusov, Stikhotvoreniia,* Leningrad 1959, 354; "Griadushchie gunny" (1905). In: *Valerii Bryusov, Sobranie sochinenii,* vol. 1, Moscow 1973, 433; Tevtonu (1914), ibid., 157, first in: *Russkaia mysl'* 10 (1914), 166. See also Hellmann, *Poets of Hope,* 33–37.

10. Clark refers among other things to the poetic leitmotif of the snowstorm. Katerina Clark, *Petersburg–Crucible of Cultural Revolution,* Cambridge, MA 1995, 54–65. Warning voices existed, as well as those that championed a connection with Germany, such as the St. Petersburg symbolist Dmitrii Merezhkovskii with his wife, the poet Zinaida Gippius (Plotnikov/Kolerov, "Den inneren Deutschen besiegen") and Boris Pasternak ("Brief an die Eltern 19.7.1914." In: *Boris Pasternak, Aus Briefen verschiedener Jahre,* Berlin 1992, 10ff.). Pasternak had studied in Marburg, and others such as Anna Akhmatova ("July 1914") and Osip Mandelshtam sensed the coming catastrophe. See also Galina Belaja, "Die gesprengte Welt. Der erste Weltkrieg in der Russischen Dichtung." In: *Berlin-Moskau-Moskau-Berlin 1900–1950,* exhibition catalogue, Munich, New York 1995, 105–9. On other critical voices among disseminators of culture, see Ernst Metner, "V. Fiwer, Leonid Slonimskij, Moisej Rubenstejn." In: *Bezrodnyj, Zur Geschichte,* 319–56.

11. Vladimir Ern, "Protestantizm kak kontrast. Ot Kanta k Kruppu." In: *Russkaia mysl'* 12 (1914), 2, quoted in Plotnikov/Kolerov, "Den inneren Deutschen besiegen," 24f. This interpretational stereotype, however, was not limited to Russia but was used by the various camps. Thus, an article appeared in Paris in 1915 by Léon Daudet entitled "De Kant á Krupp"; see also Bezrodnyj, *Zur Geschichte,* 51. The feminizing of Russia influenced the genderizing of the cultural contrasts. This genderizing was introduced into Russian religious and philosophical discourse by Nikolai Berdyaev, among others. See Nikolai Berdyaev, "O 'vechno-bab'em" v russkoi dushe." In: *Nikolai Berdyaev, Filosofiia tvorchestva kul'tury i iskusstva,* Moscow 1994, vol. 2, 290–300.

12. See Bezrodnyj, *Zur Geschichte.*

13. The ancient Slavic nomadic peoples of the steppes of Scythia, a kind of eastern version of the Celts, had become a mythologem of Slavophile self-definition by the beginning of the century and were often treated in the poetry of the symbolists. See Nikolai Gumilev's poem "My—skify" (1916), and Alexander Blok, "Skifi" (1918). The theosophical teachings combined elements of the eastern, i.e., Indian, religion and philosophy of Buddhism with western European science or gnoseological traditions; the influence of these teachings on the Russian intelligentsia and their development during the war years were long underestimated, according to Maria Carlson, *No Religion Higher Than Truth: A History of the Theosophical Movement in Russia, 1875–1922,* Princeton 1993, 76–80.

14. See the collected volume published by literary historian Petr Struve: *Vekhi. Sbornik statei o russkoi intelligentsii,* with essays by Nikolai A. Berdyaev et al., Moscow 1909. Philosophers of various religious and political orientations, such as Mikhail Gershenzon, Sergei Bulgakov, Nikolai Berdyaev, and Semen Frank, contributed essays criticizing the radical intelligentsia and their utilitarian maximalism, holding the intel-

ligentsia partly responsible for the catastrophic defeat of the Revolution of 1905 and the ensuing political repression. The volume met with rejection and protest on all sides. The five editions that quickly followed prompted more than 300 news articles within a year, and six collected volumes in the ensuing years with polemic responses. See *Wegzeichen. Zur Krise der russischen Intelligenz,* introduced and edited by Karl Schlögel, Frankfurt 1990 (= *Die andere Bibliothek,* 67).

15. See Plotnikov/Kolerov, "Den inneren Deutschen besiegen."

16. See, e.g., Vladimir Mayakovsky, "Der Morgen/Utro" (1913); "Die Hölle der Stadt/Adishche goroda" (1913); "Und trotzdem/ A vse-taki" (1914). In: *Vladimir Mayakovsky, Polnoe sobranie sochinenii,* 13 vols., vol. 1, Moscow 1995.

17. This is mentioned in his autobiography "Ich selbst/Jas am." Vladimir Mayakovsky, *Jas am. Stikhotvoreniia,* Moscow 1965 (= *Sochinenijaia,* vol. 1), 22–25.

18. The word *mir* means both "world" and "peace." See Vladimir Maiakovskii, "Voina ob'iavlena" "Mysli v prizyv"; "Ia i Napoleon"; and the sketches "Shtatskaia shrapnel" I and II.

19. See Jurij Striedter, "Poesie als 'neuer Mythos' der Revolution am Beispiel Majakovskijs." In: *Terror und Spiel. Probleme der Mythenrezeption,* edited by Manfred Fuhrmann, Munich 1971 (= *Poetik und Hermeneutik,* 4), 409–34.

20. Mayakovsky, *Polnoe sobranie sochinenii,* 222 (see also 216, 226).

21. Aleksandr Solzhenitsyn, "*Avgust chetyrnadtsatogo,* Paris 1971." In: *Sobranie sochinenii,* vol. 11, 12, Paris 1983; *Lenin v Tsiurikhe,* Paris 1975; Aleksandr Solženicyn, *August vierzehn,* translated by Svetlana Geier, Darmstadt, Neuwied 1972.

22. "Nachwort." In: Solzhenitsyn, *Avgust chetyrnadtsatogo,* Paris 1971, 572; Paris 1983, 595f.

23. Russian names from Solzhenitsyn's work cited in this chapter have been rendered in accordance with the English version of *August 1914,* translated by Michael Glenny (Farrar, Straus and Giroux 1972).

24. Some Russian critics of this, so to speak, cultural emigration praised this technique as especially innovative, but others found it an artistic failure. In the Soviet press, bad reviews appeared although the book was banned. But it was accepted by Samizdat (an underground publishing organization) and especially by the intelligentsia of large cities right after it appeared, and two years after the Paris publication a collected volume appeared with critical articles by the Samizdat. *Avgust chetyrnadtsatogo chitaiut na rodine,* Paris 1973. See, e.g., the article (which, like most contemporary literary criticism and literary scholarship, is strongly apologetic), by iurii Kuplanovskii, "Stil' i istoriografiia 'Krasnogo kolesa' A. I. Solzhenitsyna." In: *Materialy konferentsii A. I. Solzhenitsyn i ego tvorchestvo,"* edited by Aleksandr D. Glezer, Paris, New York 1988, 58–69.

25. On Solzhenitsyn's use of language, see Laszlo M. Tikos, "Stilistische Beobachtungen zu August 1914." In: *Über Solschenizyn. Aufsätze, Berichte, Materialien,* edited by Elisabeth Markstein and Felix Philipp Ingold, Darmstadt, Neuwied 1973, 209–57; V. B. Bolan, "Language and Style in A. Solzhenitsyn's *August 1914.*" In: *Slavic and East European Journal,* 21 (Fall 1977), 3, 344–53; Una Patzke, "Zwischen Mythos und Erneuerung. A. Solzenicyn und die russische Sprache." In: *Russische Emigration im 20. Jahrhundert. Literatur, Sprache, Kultur,* edited by Frank Göbler, Munich 2005.

26. Helen von Ssachno, "Ein Roman emigriert." In: *Die Zeit,* 2/7/1971, 14.

27. See Patricia Blake, "Solzhenitsyn and the Theme of War." In: *Solzhenitsyn: A Collection of Critical Essays*, edited by Kathryn Feuer, Englewood Cliffs, NJ 1976, 84–90.

28. Translator's note: This quotation is translated from the German. Chapter 14 of English versions of *August 1914* contains no corresponding statement by the figure Yaroslav Kharitonov.

29. See Jochen-Ulrich Peters, "Die Rezeption von August 1914. In: *Über Solschenizyn;* Nikita Struve, "The Debates over *August 1914*." In: *Solzhenitsyn*, 71–83; John Dunlop, "The Debate over *August 1914*." In: *Alexander Solzhenitsyn: Critical Essays and Documentary Materials*, edited by John B. Dunlop, Richard Haugh, and Alexis Klimoff, Belmont, MA 1973.

30. See I. Tropinin, "Avgust chetyrnadtsatogo i russkoe istoricheskoe samosoznanie." In: *Avgust chetyrnadtsatogo chitaiut na rodine*, 83–99.

31. Translator's note: Translated here from the German. In the two English translations of *August 1914* that I researched, Varsonofief's discussion with the students differs. Neither version shows an exact correspondence to the first two sentences on "inner order." In the electronic version of *August 1914* (The Red Wheel, Knot 1) translated by H. T. Willets, the closest match is as follows: "History grows like a living tree. Reason is to history as an ax is to a tree. It will not make it grow. . . . That is our whole vocation . . . to perfect the order in our souls. . . . The laws for constructing the best social order must be inherent in the structure of the world as a whole. In the design behind the universe and in man's destiny" (8008, 8033). In the Michael Glenny translation of *August 1914*, the pertinent parts of the conversation (pp. 403–11) are only slightly differently translated, but these comments are not one long lecture but part of a longer conversation, and do not match up exactly enough to use here.

32. Quotation taken from Glenny's translation of *August 1914* (pp. 492, 437 in German version).

33. "Moral rigidity" and "ideological monologues" both refer to the theoretical explanations by Michail Bachtin, *Probleme der Poetik Dostoevskiis*, Frankfurt 1985.

34. See Struve, *The Debates over August 1914*.

35. The main concern is not the "de-mythologizing" process, as Alexander Schmemann maintains: he is referring to the traditionally disseminated myth of the Russian suffering masses and gives reasons—rightly—as to why this critical revelation by Solzhenitsyn, that the urgent national defense prevented lethargy, is false. Schmemann, however, sees significant perpetuation of the myth elsewhere. Alexander Schmemann, "Der Russland-Mythos und August Vierzehn." In: *Über Solschenizyn*, 94–101.

12

The Reality of War and the War Experience of Russian Soldiers on the Russian Western Front, 1914–1915

Igor Narskij

The process of reconstructing the reality of war and the war experience of Russian soldiers presents several challenges that, although they have become quite familiar, bear mentioning briefly here. These challenges primarily involve the methodological issues that accompany any attempt to research reality and experience from the perspectives of sociology of knowledge, living environment, or cultural history. With this in mind, the terms in this essay will be defined as follows: *reality* will refer to a socially constructed phenomenon that is formed by culture.[1] *Experience* will denote the aggregate of techniques used in the construction and processing of reality as defined above.[2] At the same time it should always be kept in mind that the war experience (like all other experience) exists in a permanent, long-lasting, and open process in which the reality of war continues to be constructed and interpreted after the war.

The case of Russia represents a rapid and radical reinterpretation of war reality and war experience during the war and in the postwar era. The First World War did not become integrated into the Russian culture of remembrance but was instead submerged by the Revolution of 1917 and the Civil War of 1918–1920. Against this backdrop, we are well advised to approach the subjective reality of Russian soldiers in the world war on the basis of their direct personal accounts. The source material for this particular area, however, is wanting. Most of the sources relating to daily life during the war came into being after the fact, and with the passage of time and its tendency to deform memories, it has become impossible to consistently and precisely separate the adventures and experiences of the first two war years from those experiences that took place at other times, whether earlier or later. Moreover, the voices of (former) Russian soldiers come to us from indirect sources. Their daily life is primarily described in a fragmented manner by high-ranking officers and commanders of the Russian Army.[3]

But even these kinds of descriptions are relatively rare. In Russia, in contrast to Great Britain or France, the culture of war remembrance was underdeveloped, and postwar events did nothing to encourage that genre of writing. But more important than the scarcity of such memorials is the question of their quality. Their weak point lies in the cliché-ridden preconceived notion that Russian soldiers were backward and uncultivated. This interpretive pattern applied to material that should serve as one of the most important motivations for a memoirist has clouded the view of several generations of historians.[4]

Russian soldiers, incidentally, left behind more personal testimonials than one might expect, assuming a lack of cultivation. These personal accounts are, however, idiosyncratic in nature and their function as a source for researching the war reality and war experience of the soldiers is limited. In terms of personal testimonials, such soldiers' memoirs are not only a rarity but for the most part are heavily politicized. In contrast, letters from soldiers, tens of thousands of which are kept in Russian military history archives and which for the most part remain unpublished, represent a massive resource.[5] Nevertheless, they served as a basis for the regular morale reports from the military censors from 1915 to 1917, which, rather than reflecting the daily life and living environment of the soldier, reflect more about the culture of censorship and the preferences of censors, who were educated and belonged to a different social strata. The same is true of works of Russian high literature that are completely or partially based on the personal accounts of soldiers.[6]

Thus, it is still a challenge to present a convincing description of the reality of war for the Russian soldier. Even when dealing with the available primary resources, it is difficult to identify experiences that are specific to the individual as opposed to those of the group. This is due partly to the quality of the information, as cited above, and partly to historians' limited progress so far in deciphering the information in soldiers' letters and personal accounts.[7]

Thus, for the purposes of this chapter it is necessary to find a common denominator for the multiplicity of experiences filtered through numerous group-specific and individual prejudices and situations. This is by necessity one-sided and simplified. This essay will further attempt to outline the most important singular qualities of the war on Russia's western front that influenced the way the soldiers constructed and processed the realities of the front. Social and cultural circumstances such as age, ethnicity, or the soldier's origins will not be taken into consideration. Among the particular characteristics of the "Russian" world war, the factors that had a particular influence were the vast area covered by the war in eastern Europe, the unique civilizing mission of the war, the sharp contrast between the front and the rear, and finally, Soviet Russia's accelerated collective amnesia about the First World War.

Expanses, Mobile War, and Violence

A unique characteristic of the war on the Russian front is the interplay between its vast size and the elements of mobile war; neither feature was an attribute of the war in the west. At a rough estimate, the surface area of the theater of war in the east was four times the battle area of the western front in France and Flanders. The relative vastness of the area was both a cause and a result of the mobile war in the east. The static phases of the war came after the offensives and counteroffensives of the enemy from August to October 1914, from May to November 1915, and from May to September 1916, which in each case continued for several months and led to considerable shifting in the front line. The mobile war phases on the eastern front brought the Russian Army extremely high casualties; the number of dead, wounded, and captured climbed quickly each time. As is evidenced by the ultimate stabilizing of the front in fall 1914, 1915, and 1916, however, these losses did not have an immediate demoralizing effect on Russian soldiers. This is why historical research on the Russian Army during the First World War should not focus solely on its gradual demoralization and inevitable collapse.

The characteristic feature of the war in the east, mobile warfare, had a considerable effect on the way the war was perceived as well as on the way Russian soldiers formed *experience* in the sense of our present definition. In the trench war, which was typical of the front in the western Europe, the soldier felt more like a defenseless victim of violence rather than its cause or instrument. Thus, the static war in the west produced massive numbers of pacifists rather than militarists. It was different in the east, where cavalry and infantry attacks played a major role and great emphasis was placed on the bayonet and fighting at close quarters. This could contribute greatly to the brutalization of the soldiers.[8] In this respect, the mobile war experience of the war was a legacy handed down to the Russian Civil War of 1918–1920. The Civil War, too, was characterized by the major significance of cavalry among all warring parties as well as by direct physical killing.[9]

In contrast to the experiences of the mobile war, the static war and its military strategies evidently had negative connotations and were thus extensively suppressed. It was not until the official end of the Civil War that these experiences were put to direct use, when from 1920 and 1921, the Red Army deployed gas and airplanes against the insurgent peasants and the insurgent army staffs improvised trenches.

The expansiveness of the theater of war was certainly only one of the reasons for the mobile war on the Russian front. A further cause lay in the limited technical abilities of Russia to conduct a long-term war, which increasingly became a duel of heavy artillery. A not insignificant reason for the mobile war ultimately lay in the strategic concepts of the Russian generals, who remained loyal to the military science of the nineteenth century. The majority of them conducted extravagant campaigns featuring frontal attacks with heavy casualties and inefficient cavalry, disdaining modern technology and the building of trenches.[10] But it was these same higher-ranking officers and politicians who complained about the backwardness of the soldiers.

Russian Soldiers: Unsuited for Modern Warfare?

The poor state of Russia's readiness for the First World War was the subject of criticism by contemporaries, and such criticism has been further passed down by historians. The criticism was aimed at three conditions in particular. First was the poor organization of the Russian Army, resulting in insufficient administration and spotty logistical support. This in turn led to extreme overextending of soldiers and a senseless sacrifice of human life, not to mention miserable conditions in their daily lives. Finally—a criticism that will be put to rest here—were allegations that the Russian soldiers were "unfit human material," peasant soldiers of a "backward," premodern mentality who were unable to cope with the challenge of modern warfare. This collection of traits allegedly led directly to their disastrous failure in battle and the army's ongoing demoralization and irreversible collapse. The beginning of this disintegration process has been placed, depending on the author, between summer 1915 and spring 1917.[11]

The notion of "backwardness" needs to be placed into perspective at this point. Most arguments in favor of this idea could actually apply to all countries participating in the war. At the beginning of the First World War, no state or general staff was prepared for a long war of this dimension. No existing conscription system could keep supplying enough soldiers for a war of attrition; recruiting systems had to be modified everywhere during the course of the war. Even that German reservist system admired by Russian experts and adopted by Russia proved to be a *stumpfe Waffe* (blunt weapon) because of the poor preparation of the reservists.[12]

To varying degrees, the same was true of the resupplying of all the participating armies of the war. While it was true that in 1915 the logistical support of Russian soldiers came to a standstill, leaving them without needed weapons and munitions, clothing and boots, ultimately this crisis was largely solved. According to the opinion of eyewitnesses and experts, the food supply for the

Russian Army was much better than that of its enemies, and in 1914 and 1915 it was even "absurdly wasteful."[13] Certainly there were dramatic situations in which, for a period of time, the soldiers were without weapons or remained barefoot. But much evidence points to the fact that such episodes were overemphasized and overstated by historians, perhaps in the light of Russia's pitiful collapse that followed.

Also dubious are other arguments that would place the responsibility for Russian catastrophic failure in the war on its soldiers' low level of social cultivation, their allegedly premodern mentality, and their patterns of behavior. The crisis of disorientation due to the sudden uselessness of earlier learning amid the new reality of war was not unique to Russia; it was manifested on an international scale. Familiar to the physicians of all countries participating in the war was the widespread incidence of what they called "shell shock," "battle neuroses," or "moral shock" caused by artillery bombardment and other terrors of the war.[14]

For some time now it has been doubted that the delayed nation formation in Russia can be considered a manifestation of Russia's underdevelopment or as an important cause of the Russians' defeat in the First World War.[15] Alleged Russian expressions of weak national identity, such as the nebulousness of their image of the enemy and fraternization incidents, are on record for all armies in that war. If Russian soldiers described the artillery bombardment with metaphors taken from nature, religion, or agriculture (thunder, earthquake, hell, Last Judgment, thrashing, harvest time, and so on), it was probably less an expression of their premodern culture, as has been maintained in the most recent academic literature, than an attempt to connect something unknown and unusual with something familiar.[16] The "more advanced" Germans, French, or English soldiers used a similar vocabulary. Even the soldiers' tendency to describe in detail the landscape in which their unit was stationed, something the army censors deplored, was an international phenomenon. Thus there is little reason to believe that the mental structure of Russian soldiers caused them to place greater significance on local identity than did soldiers of other nationalities.[17]

The Russian military was therefore not so very primitive, and the soldiers were not "premodern" to the point that this quality could satisfactorily explain the military defeat of the Russians during the First World War. On the front, the Russian soldiers saw themselves confronted with the same problems as the soldiers in the west European and central European armies, and they behaved similarly. They lived under constant danger to their lives; they died by the hundreds of thousands, especially during the mobile phases of the war; they killed the enemy; they were eyewitnesses to the death of friend and foe; and they suffered from great deprivation, injuries, and shell shock.

Nevertheless, the everyday life of the Russian soldier between 1914 and 1916 was much less affected by the difficulties and plagues of the "imperialist" war than contemporary witnesses and (above all) Soviet historical writing depicted, as they had a tendency to ascribe the conditions that existed at the end phase of the First World War to the first year of war. As has been pointed out, at the level of soldier, the Russians experienced the static war at a much more modest scale than did the armies in western Europe. The logistical problems of the army were not as acute as those in the early Red Army, and it was not until 1917 that the morale reports from the Russian Army and the military censors reported alarming massive dissatisfaction and resentment against the war among soldiers.

The Russian soldiers appeared to German eyewitnesses to be well nourished. In the static war period of 1914–1916, they were supplied with generous portions of bread (one kilogram daily), meat (the meat ration was doubled at the beginning of the war and reached four hundred grams per day), fat (one hundred grams daily), dehydrated vegetables, and other foods.[18] When Russian prisoners who complained about hunger in their army were searched, they were always found to have a cache of bread on them.[19] The food supply allowed the soldiers to send zwieback and sugar to their families in the rear, and during the first two years of the war their modest pay (75 kopeks a month) allowed them to invest in reserves of sugar, tea, or tobacco.

Even the everyday life of the soldier did not look as desolate and boring as many sources would lead one to suspect.[20] The trenches of the static war phases were built solidly. These were not the often described individual *jamki* (ditches) typical of the summer mobile war; they were reliable shelters with deep, well-protected earthen dwelling places, roofed with three to four layers of timbers and featuring communication trenches that branched out in all directions. During pauses in the fighting, younger soldiers played *gorodki* (a type of dice game) and older ones played checkers. It was during these moments that the camaraderie of the trenches was cultivated. The soldiers further filled their leisure hours with handwork and trading; the trading brought up issues concerning fraternization, as the Russian soldiers would trade their bread to the enemy for cigarettes and schnapps.[21]

The Civilizing Mission of the World War

As cynical as it may sound considering the hundreds of thousands of deaths, the millions of wounded and crippled, and the atrocities bordering on barbarianism that occurred during the Civil War period, the war experiences of the Russian soldiers who survived the years of world war can be judged as having had a significant civilizing and disciplining effect. The war of attrition required self-discipline, endurance, and discipline of the soldiers as a group, especially during the static war phases in which they had to participate in the regular collective work, which must have offered little in terms of immediate satisfaction.[22]

A high degree of discipline is shown in soldiers' letters from 1914 to 1916. The censors categorize the majority of them as either "neutral," "balanced" or "happy."[23] Furthermore, the low level of desertion in the Russian Army from the outbreak of the war to the February Revolution of 1917 (an average of 6,300 deserters per month) was also indicative of good discipline. The considerable decrease in the proportion of prisoners among the losses of Russian troops as of the end of 1915 can also be interpreted as resulting from disciplinary measures.[24] Cases of surrender, marauding, and pogroms against Jews increased symptomatically in the army during the retreat due to the chaos and the slackened control by the officers.

The war also provided a massive impetus to the forming of the nation. It created a mobilized community that developed an identity extending beyond the local level that was prepared to work toward a single goal, whatever this goal was understood to be.[25] Thus, a para-public body had come into being that demonstrated the population's preparedness to cooperate with the state.[26]

In the beginning, Russia's personnel replacement system, which was adopted from Germany, was territorially linked and thus respected the soldiers' identity with a locale. With the continuation of the war, however, this system began to show signs of breaking down. In both Germany and England, the army units began taking recruits from the whole country, which inevitably led to the transformation of a soldier's local identity into the supralocal.

The dynamic of how the image of the enemy developed may also be examined in the context of military discipline. After all, it is doubtful that the negative connotation of the image of the German in Russia arose during two hundred years of living together and their shared bond through Christianity. Germans occupied relatively high social positions in the Czarist Empire and for this reason were culturally less foreign to the majority of the Russian population than the Jews, who were segregated. For centuries, every central European had been labeled with the term *nemec* (German). The image of the German that remained in the ethnic Russian perspective was a mixture of ironic tolerance ("What is healthy to a Russian is fatal to the German"), respect for German scholarliness ("The German is so sly, he even invented the ape"), and admiration for the German's workmanlike skills ("The German has an instrument for everything").[27] In Russia the outbreak of the First World War had initially incited great fear because of Germany's alleged invincibility. One factor that contributed to these fears was the mood of the officer corps, which was made up to a considerable extent of Germans, most of whom considered themselves students of the German art of war. Among the soldiers at the front, however, this fear gradually gave way to admiration for German technology, staying power, and discipline. This respect, in my opinion, can be read as indicative of the peasant soldiers' increasing openness to the concept of European progress.[28]

The civilizing role of the First World War ultimately found expression in the soldiers' accelerated secularization. Practical concerns, such as the difficulty of adhering to fasting times and the performance of other religious rites to the fullest extent under conditions at the front, diluted the soldiers' faith to a great degree.[29] It also meant a weakening of moral qualms with respect to the necessity of killing.

Conflict between the Front and the Rear

As was demonstrated above, the cause of the military disaster in the Russian Army cannot be seen in isolation from problems on the national front. The military front was no hermetically sealed world. It was closely linked to the political and social situation at home, and from there came early signs of decay in the army. Interruptions in the supplying of the army with weapons and ammunition awakened rumors that were recorded by the letter censors as early as mid-1915. There was "betrayal" by higher-ranking officials as well as by unscrupulous businessmen on the home front. Such upsetting rumors came via letters from home, soldiers returning from leave, and replacement personnel. Other rumor factories were the field hospitals, field stores, and field kitchens. These pieces of information spread with lightning speed by "soldier telegraph."

Recruits and reservists brought to the front the loose discipline that had been increasing in the rear, just as they brought a disregard for the nation's assets. On the way to the forward positions the illegal sale of boots and clothing was common practice. This "illness" was of course quickly over after the arrival of the replacement troops in the field army.[30] The reality of war exerted its own form of discipline.

There is evidence that the disciplining process among Russian soldiers at the front took place faster and differently than in the rear, which had become increasingly consumed by economic and political chaos.[31] Soldiers who went home on leave no longer seemed to recognize the country, and by 1915 their dissatisfaction with the rear had increased. The front soldier denounced Russian society for its apparent frivolity, its insufficient interest in the problems at the front, its lack of any sense of solidarity, cooperation, and justice. They were primarily dissatisfied with the unjust distribution of the burdens of war. The targets of their resentment were the deserters and workers, reservists of the "second draft," and the soldiers in the garrisons—that is, all of those who evaded conscription or deployment at the front. Soldiers were incensed about their own wives, who supposedly carried on with prisoners of war and demanded too much power in the village; about greedy merchants, landowners, and farmers who profited from the war; and about the government, which had supposedly betrayed its own army. The soldiers now saw the primary enemy, the "interior Germans," attacking them from the rear. There was a growing readiness, upon returning home, to restore justice through the use of violence and to punish those they considered responsible for the suffering of the soldier at the front.[32] This conflict between the front and the rear echelon was much more pronounced than in Germany, not to mention in France and England. Here, in my opinion, lies the actual manifestation of Russia's lack of preparedness in the First World War. Men who had been changed returned home to a country that had also changed.

The Collective Amnesia of the First World War

All deep breaks with continuity and tradition can lead to new images of the past.[33] The reinterpretation of the First World War in the Soviet Union is an example of such a process. In the memories of contemporaries, the war was transformed within a few years—in both the late czarist period and the beginnings of the Soviet regime—to the point of unrecognizability.

The mechanism of this process can be described as resocialization, which in this case consisted of a radical transformation of subjective reality as human beings "switched over" from one world to another.[34] In Russia the repression of the past took on the character of a collective amnesia. The collapse in civilized order experienced by the Russians during the revolutionary period destroyed the structures that would normally function to maintain a genuine image of the past. The Revolution scattered the "significant others" (relatives, friends, neighbors) who would normally have served as protectors of subjective reality, making communication about the past enormously difficult. Each regime in revolutionary Russia attempted to legitimize its activity as a creation of a true order out the chaos of anarchy. None of the political leaders were at all interested in cultivating positive memories of the prerevolutionary past.

The reinterpretation of the recent past also took place "from beneath." It allowed individuals to find sense in a life that had suddenly become senseless and helped to decode and render heroic personal experiences and biography. Because the First World War did not officially end for Russia but instead progressed seamlessly into the Civil War of 1918–1920, the Civil War became the interpretive paradigm for all events from the beginning of the First World War, which by then had been reinterpreted as the "War of Imperialism." The period from 1914 to 1922, that is, from the beginning of the First World War to the end of the famine in 1921 and 1922, was considered by the Russians of that time to be a continuation of a "seven-year war" whose apex occurred during 1918 and 1920.[35] This allowed the Bolsheviks to shift the blame for their own mistaken decisions onto the czarist government. But many veterans of the First World War, which had been a failure for Russia, had to struggle alone all of their lives with their individual memories and experiences.[36]

Although the First World War disappeared from Russian history in official and public discourse, this war left behind traces in the patterns of thought and conduct of the Russian population. At the latest by the end of the "black land distribution" in 1917 and the signing of the peace treaty with Germany in the spring of 1918, the majority of the former front soldiers noticeably developed a "without me" mentality, which had enormous significance during the Civil War. Most of those eligible for the draft took every opportunity to avoid military service with either the "Reds" or the "Whites."

Even earlier, soldiers began to become "habituated" to war. The fact that military force was considered by broad circles of the civilian population to be a particularly effective means of solving problems and conflicts became noticeable even in the spring of 1917, but primarily during the Civil War and the period of War Communism from 1919 to 1920. This conviction was embodied in the peasant uprisings of 1919–1921 as well as in their suppression, in the increasing militarization of the government, in the language, and in the culture, not to mention in everyday behavior patterns.[37] Paradoxically, the very rapid militarized tempo of the culture can be ascribed to the absence of reflection about its genesis during the First World War.

Among the results of the First World War from a historical and experiential perspective, the most significant for the subsequent development of Russia was probably the emergence of a relatively large group of former front soldiers who embodied a new sort of archetype of the Russia soldier: these were the apparently cold-blooded, ambitious, socially rootless newcomers, mostly those who could read and write, who later found careers in the Red Army and the Cheka (secret police).[38] This soldier type, who viewed "war as the ultimate expression of modern life," was a product of the world war that appeared in all the countries involved in the war, but certainly not to the same degree as in Russia.[39] Socialized during the war, these men were usually more keenly affected by the propaganda about coming to terms with the "backward" past as well as by visions of an "enlightened" future.

The Russian Army cultivated massive numbers of enemies of the "antiquated" agricultural way of life, which was apparent in the unprecedented brutality against the peasantry (and the church) during the Civil War and the Bolshevist's War Communism. In the trenches of the front, soldiers dreamed of returning after the end of the war to settle accounts with the traitors and cowards in the rear area. After the first two years of the First World War, their goal was to restore justice by disciplining their civilian fellow countrymen in military style, that is, by turning the rear echelon into a front.

And that is precisely what they did.

Notes

1. Peter L. Berger and Thomas Luckmann, *Die gesellschaftliche Konstruktion der Wirklichkeit. Eine Theorie der Wissenssoziologie*, Frankfurt 1998.

2. Here I follow the same approach as the special research area of the University of Tübingen, "War Experience: War and Society in the Modern Era."

3. See, e.g., A. A. Brusilov, *Moi vospominaniia,* Moscow 1963; A. I. Denikin, *Ocherki Russkoi Smuty. Krushenie vlasti i armii, fevral'–sentiabr' 1917,* Moscow 1991; N. N. Golovin, *Voennye usiliia Rossii v mirovoi voine,* Moscow 2001.

4. See J. Sanborn, "Besporiadki sredi prizyvnikov v 1914 g. i vopros o russkoi natsii: novyi vzgliad na problemu." In: *Rossiia i Pervaia mirovaia voina* (*materialy mezhdunarodnogo nauchnogo kollokviuma*), St. Petersburg 1999, 202–14, esp. 202–5.

5. Only a small number of these letters have been published, mostly from 1917 as an illustration of the "revolutionizing," demoralization, and collapse of the army. See "Soldatskie pis'ma 1917 g., Moskva, Leningrad 1927; Soldatskie pis'ma v gody mirovoi voiny (1915–1917 gg.)." In: *Krasnyi archiv,* vols. 4–5, Moscow 1934.

6. See, for example L. Voitolovskii, *Po sledam voiny. Pokhodnye zapiski,* vols. 1–2, Moscow, Leningrad 1927–1928; S. Fedorchenko, *Narod na voine,* Moscow 1990; "V. P. Kataev, Iunosheskii roman." In: V. P. Kataev, *Sobranie sochinenii v 10 tomakh,* vol. 7, Moscow 1984 (German edition: Valentin Katajew, *Die Bekenntnisse meines alten Freundes Sascha Pischolkin. Roman einer Jugend,* East Berlin 1984).

7. Considering this challenge it is understandable that the research into the war reality and war experience of Russian soldiers remains in its infancy. See, e.g., V. P. Buldakov, *Krasnaia smuta. Priroda i posledstviia revoliutsionnogo nasiliia,* Moscow 1997, esp. 119–39; *Rossiia i Pervaia mirovaia voina;* E. S. Seniavaskaia, *Psikhologiia voiny v XX veke: Istoricheskii opyt Rossii,* Moscow 1999; O. S. Porshneva, *Mentalitet i sotsial'noe povedenie rabochikh, krest'ian i soldat v period pervoi mirovoi voiny* (*1914-mart 1918 g.*), Ekaterinburg 2000.

8. As Dirk Schumann remarks on this subject: "The 'materiel battle' on the front in France and Belgium that presently defines the general perception of the First World War, in which the individual soldier saw himself as victim of an uncontrollable machinery of annihilation, did not usually instill in him a long-term capacity for violence. In the east, on the other hand, the war was a mobile war to a much higher degree, in which the 'agency' of the soldiers was less hampered, and their individual weapons use was more significant than in the west. . . . [It] was . . . the killing and wounding by one's own hand and the awareness of its central military significance that led to a barbarization of the soldiers, that is, those who were primarily active, not those who participated passively in the event." Dirk Schumann, "Europa, der Erste Weltkrieg und die Nachkriegszeit: eine Kontinuität der Gewalt?" In: *Journal of Modern European History,* 1 (2003), 24–42, here 32.

9. Dietrich Beyrau, "Der Erste Weltkrieg als Bewährungsprobe. Bolschewistische Lernprozesse aus dem 'imperialistischen' Krieg." In: ibid., 96–123, esp. 106f.

10. Orlando Figes, *Die Tragödie eines Volkes: Die Epoche der russischen Revolution 1891 bis 1924,* Berlin 1998, 275–94, esp. 282f. Even a progressive commander such as General A. Brussilov was convinced at the beginning of the war that most of the blood spilled by the soldiers was for the sake of victory. In a letter to his wife he writes: "As you see, blood flows in streams all of the time, but without this, war cannot be waged. The more that is spilled, the better the results, and all the sooner the war will end. As you see, it is a difficult and bitter duty, but without it there will be no victory." Ibid., 277.

11. See, e.g., Richard Pipes, *Die Russische Revolution,* vol 1, *Der Zerfall des Zarenreiches,* Berlin 1992; Figes, *Die Tragödie;* V. P. Buldakov, *Krasnaia smuta.*

12. Dennis E. Showalter, "Niedergang und Zusammenbruch der deutschen Armee 1914–1919." In: *Deutsche Umbrüche im 20 Jahrhundert,* edited by Dietrich Papenfuss and Wolfgang Schieder, Cologne 2000, 3–61, here 41. See also David G. Herrmann, *The Arming of Europe and the Making of the First World War,* Princeton, NJ 1996.

13. Golovin, *Voennye usiliia,* 244–50.

14. See, e.g., K. Friedlander, "Neskol'ko aspektov shell shock'a v Rossii 1914–1916." In: *Rossiia i Pervaia mirovaia voina,* 315–25.

15. See Hubertus F. Jahn, *Patriotic Culture in Russia during World War I,* Ithaca, NY 1995; Peter Holquist, *Making War, Forging Revolution: Russia's Continuum of Crisis, 1914–1921,* Cambridge, MA 2002; Joshua A. Sanborn, *Drafting the Russian Nation: Military Conscription, Total War and Mass Politics,* 1905–1925, De Kalb, IL 2003.

16. A. B. Astashov, "Russkii krest'ianin na frontakh Pervoi mirovoi voiny." In: *Otechestvennaia istoriia,* 2003, no. 3, 74–86, esp. 74f.

17. Ibid., 83.

18. Golovin, *Voennye usliia,* 250.

19. Seniavaskaia, *Psikhologiia voiny,* 261.

20. Complaints by the soldiers about their boredom that were picked up by the military censors may not have accurately characterized the situation at the front, but could simply have reflected the emotional state of the letter writers.

21. Kataev, *Iunosheskii roman,* 337, 339, 341, 395; Astashov, *Russkii krest'janin,* 79f.

22. V. Kataev's novel, based on authentic letters from 1916, describes among other things the everyday business of the static war, which consisted of organized, difficult cooperation. In a letter dated 7/(20)3/1916, reproduced by Kataev, a volunteer wrote to his girlfriend about the western Russian front: "The region around is literally packed with troops, as well as with artillery of all calibers, machine gun commandos, mortars and flame throwers. . . . And during a walk during daylight one can believe it is an uninhabited island; everything has gone underground, everything is carefully camouflaged and masked from the greedy telescopes of observers. Someone who knows nothing of this (and perhaps even someone who does know) can pass by the battery without noticing them. The picketers on horseback are in hidden the forest thicket. The infantry sits in deep, narrow trenches, which are surrounded with barbed wire that is so covered with pine branches that there is nothing to see. The ground is cut up with covered up, contorted communication trenches. The artillery stands behind the hills, surrounded by a whole forest of cut-down pine trees, so that it is very difficult to discover them. . . . Nights, however, everything is transformed. Infantry columns appear to grow out of the earth, the field kitchens drive, machine guns, baggage and medical vehicles, two horse carts, and the artillery batteries move. The soldiers appear in their field gray clothing . . . they form an endless mass. They look alike. Even their faces look alike. All of this is in motion all night long. At first light, the area transforms again, however, as if with the wave of a magic wand, back into the deserted island." Kataev, *Iunosheskii roman,* 315f. My thanks to J. J. Chmelevskaja for the reference to this source.

23. Golovin, *Voennye usiliia,* 323; V. L. D'iachkov and L. G. Protasov, "Velikaia voina i obshchestvennoe soznanie: prevratnosti indoktrinatsii i vospriatiia." In: *Rossiia i Pervaia mirovaia voina,* 58–67, esp. 62f.; Astashov, *Russkij krest'janin,* 75, 82.

24. Golovin, *Voennye usiliia,* 130–36, 181–87.

25. Sanborn, *Drafting the Russian Nation.*

26. Holquist, *Making War.*

27. The adage regarding the invention of the ape was noted by W. Dal' in the mid-nineteenth century, when the main work of Charles Darwin on the origins of humans had not yet been published. It suggests a certain familiarity of the Russian underclass with the accomplishments of European science, which stands in opposition to the traditional image of their ignorance.

28. See Fedorchenko, *Narod na voine,* 24–28, 61–67; Iakimovich, "1914–1918 gody: U istokov totalitarizma i 'massovoi demokratii.'" In: *Pervaia mirovaia voina: Prolog XX veka,* Moscow 1998, 221–35, esp. 232; D'iachkov/Protasov, *Velikaia voina i obshchestvennoe soznanie,* 64f; Porshneva, *Mentalitet i sotsial'noe povedenie,* 228–30.

29. The church service on the front at Easter 1916 was described by V. Kataev: "There was no actual confession. A pure formality. Everything was done quickly, as if on the march. There we received forgiveness for our sins! And which sins, actually? What sins does a soldier commit? After confession and a quarter of an hour's wait, the priest spoke for a short time, Father Arkadij, and right after, without hesitation, communion began, which took place just as quickly and automatically as the absolution." Kataev, *Iunosheskii roman,* 323.

30. Golovin, *Voennye usiliia,* 263–66, esp. 264.

31. It is probably no coincidence that the First World War is hardly noticeable in the firsthand accounts or memoirs of civilians during the period between the summer of 1914, with its patriotic euphoria, and the last months of the year of 1916, a period burdened with growing supply problems. See D'iachkov/Protasov, *Velikaia voina i obshchestvennoe soznanie,* 62.

32. Seniavaskaia, *Psikhologiia voiny,* 256–63; Astashov, *Russkii krest'ianin,* 81–83; Beyrau, *Der Erste Weltkrieg,* 102f.

33. "All deep breaks in continuity and tradition can lead to the reemergence of the past, if after such a breach a new beginning is attempted. New beginnings, renaissance, restoration always appear in the form of a reaching back into the past." Jan Assmann, *Das kulturelle Gedächtnis. Schrift, Erinnerung und frühen Hochkulturen,* Munich 1999, 32.

34. "During resocialization, the past becomes reinterpreted in order to fit with the present reality, and in doing so, elements are smuggled into the past that during that period were not subjectively possible." Berer/Luckmann, *Die gesellschaftliche Konstruktion,* 167–74, here 174.

35. For more detail, see Igor Narskij, "Bürgerkrieg–zur Konstruktion eines Gründungsmythos im frühen Sovietrussland (Ural 1917–1922)." In: *Der Krieg in den Gründungsmythen europäischer Nationen und der USA,* edited by Nikolaus Buschmann and Dieter Langewiesche, Frankfurt, New York 2004, 320–30.

36. This is illustrated in the *Jugendroman* (novel of a youth), for instance, written in the years 1980 and 1981 by Valentin P. Kataev, which conveys the impression that the images of war at the time of the writing still stood vividly before the author's eyes and haunted him. Kataev, *Iunosheskii roman,* 376f.

37. See Orlando Figes and Boris Kolonitiskii, *Interpreting the Russian Revolution: The Language and Symbols of 1917,* New Haven, CT 1999; Beyrau, *Der Erste Weltkrieg,* 73f., 177–79. Interestingly, expressions from the mobile war vocabulary such as *Vorhut* (vanguard), *Attacke* (attack), *Kampagne* (campaign), *Feldzug* or *Schlacht* (battle) had a

positive connotation in the Soviet political language, while still today the verb *okopat'sia* (to burrow in) connotes cowardice.

38. N. A. Berdjaev characterized this level of the early Soviet society as follows: "In Russia a new, not so very social but more anthropological strata has been formed. . . . A young man appeared in a soldiers' jacket cut after the English model, smooth shaven, a military type, very energetic, able, and obsessed with the desire for power; mostly fresh and reckless, he pushed his way into the first rows of life. He was seen everywhere, he dominated everywhere. . . . Something had changed in Russia, in the Russian people, to the point of unrecognizability: the Russian facial expression. In Russia faces like this had never existed earlier. The type of the new young man is not Russian, but international . . . the war had made the manifestation of such types possible, it was the school from which these young people emerged." Nikolaj A. Berdjaev, *Das neue Mittelalter. Betrachtungen über das Schicksal Russlands und Europas,* Darmstadt 1927, 91f. See also Figes, *Die Tragödie,* 286f.

39. Showalter, *Niedergang und Zusammenbruch,* 52f.

13

The War in the East of 1914–1915 and the Experience of the German Military

Hans-Erich Volkmann

Direct experience becomes learning experience by means of memory, and out of this evolves the psycho-historical dimension of the present and the future. The First World War had a long-term impact that extended from the Weimar Republic to the Third Reich and on through the Cold War. The war in the east in particular left its imprint on anyone who participated in it, helped to shape it, or was personally touched by it in any way, to any extent. This imprint often found expression in letters, reports, and memoirs, which are the very kinds of material that present obvious challenges as historical sources. Nevertheless, for our present inquiry they are extremely important, not as a precise reflection of historical reality but as a perception of verified reality. They represent a personal statement and conviction that is conveyed to us in writing and is then transformed politically, militarily, and artistically.

In the war in the east, for the first time, large numbers of Reich German soldiers and officers came into direct contact with Slavs, set foot in the Russian Empire, which naturally included Congress Poland, and came face-to-face with the czarist multiethnic nation, from the Baltic to Crimea. Especially for Germans who came from areas west of the Elbe and south of the Main River, the war in the east opened a window onto an unknown world, a world beyond their imaginations, one for which they had had no mental or cultural frame of reference. While someone from Baden or Alsace, for instance, would have come to some understanding of the reasons for fighting on the western front, this was not necessarily so for those deployed on the eastern front, nor was it for most of the armies deployed there.

In a stereotypical cliché-filled speech from the throne by Wilhelm II to the German Parliament three days after the declaration of war on Russia, the following passage stands out most conspicuously: "The Russian Empire has obstructed the federated monarchy in its pursuit of its rightful interests . . . with heavy heart I have had to mobilize my army against a neighbor with whom it has fought together on so many battlefields. It is with true pain that I have seen the breaking up of a friendship that has been loyally upheld by Germany. The Imperial Russian government has taken to the field . . . on the side of a nation which, through its self-serving criminal attacks, has brought on the evil of this war."[1]

Based on trumped-up charges of terrorism and expounded upon in tones of regret, this flimsy declaration of war failed to inspire the jubilant patriotism that had been typical of the campaign in the west. The further away the German states lay from the eastern border, the greater the need to explain to the public the military conflict with Russia. In Freiburg, for instance, the censored press reported the violations of the border by Russian troops in East Prussia in such a manner as to convincingly show the czar to be the aggressor.[2] Among military leaders there was still a fear that the troops in the war in the east lacked fighting morale and sufficient motivation to achieve victory.

As a military observer during the Russo-Japanese War, Max Hoffmann, the first general staff officer in the High Command of the 8th Army, was touched by the faces of fallen Russians, whose expressions seemed to ask: "How is it I came to die in this place? What concern of mine is this land, this foreign region whose name I had never before heard?"[3] In the brutal fighting that was expected to take place on Russian ground, would German soldiers, he wondered, not ask the same question?

During the war in the east, as Michael Howard notes, it was less a matter of a German-Russian conflict than an Austro-Russian contest for dominance of the Balkan region. German military circles had no indications as to Russian war aims with respect to Germany, no sort of threat could be determined, and therefore an image or concept of Russia as an enemy had to be constructed.[4] Rudolf Alexander Schroeder did so hastily in rhymed verse, simultaneously invoking the Christian duty of the German East Army and Germany's role as a global peacekeeping power:

Toward the gray heap of the east
Attila's barbarian army approaches.
They would set in flames
this house, in which God delights.
Stand, brothers, stand together!
For when we die, the world dies.[5]

"The arsonist: 'Hard times! For four weeks I have set nothing on fire except a bad cigar!'" (*Kriegs-Album der Lustigen Blätter*, 29 [1914], issue 14)

These lines reflect an emotionalized propaganda whose primary underlying element was racial prejudice and an overblown cultural conceit. A Catholic Sunday paper in Freiburg printed a cartoon of a Russian "arsonist."

"Russian Slavism," another publication reads, "with its lack of culture, its rawness and barbarianism, attacks the sacred material of our culture. We are actually waging a cultural war."[6] While the military conflict with France and England had arisen out of hegemony and competition, the war against Russia was portrayed as the defense of civilized Europe against the barbaric Slavic world. This hobgoblin of the past, which was largely without substance, burst onto the scene in East Prussia at an opportune moment, leaving behind it a path of desolation that could not be brought under control until early 1915. Politically hand-selected war reporters, mostly reserve officers, filled the German press with a series of articles about adventures and experiences with Russian troops on German territory. This diverted attention away from the real strategy, which would have created public outcry: years earlier, military strategists had already determined that in the case of a two-front war, they would occasionally sacrifice eastern territories for the benefit of a quick victory in the west. The fact remains that it was the military press that produced a particularly clichéd image of the Russian enemy, denounced the "Russian-Mongolian war operation," and ranted about such things as the "outburst of [the Russians'] latest incendiary incursions into East Prussia."[7] In his memoirs of 1915, a cavalry officer of the Landwehr offered his impression of the conduct of the Russian occupiers after the retreat into Friedland: "Here, too, they had wrought havoc, as only Huns and Cossacks can do."[8]

This kind of thinking is illustrated in another written account, one that appeared in its second edition as early as 1915, describing Russian prisoners of war in East Prussia:

> On shaggy Cossack ponies, some *Unteroffiziere* [noncommissioned officers] of the Landwehr approached, [and] following them, guarded by the Landwehr, were Russian prisoners in a long, long column, more than two thousand in number . . . in the lead, several secular priests, greasy and unkempt, behind them some spies in peasant smocks, their hands bound. O God, how thankful one must be that the terrible handiwork of this horde has been stopped. These Asiatic-looking people, who appear dull and indifferent, with nothing, nothing at all that is soldierly—like our soldiers now demonstrate—what if these robbers and fire starters had invaded German peace! Yes, now one believes everything, everything that we had been told about the Russian brutalities. "They deserve to be hanged; they are gallows birds—arsonists, not soldiers." This is what our Landwehr people tell us, which is reiterated to me later by the officers. "They have rampaged in an unspeakable manner everywhere, raided all the houses, searched through them and carried off valuables, then set the houses on fire. The bullet is too good for these wretches."[9]

Landwehr and troops of the German east armies were the moral backbone of the battles in East Prussia. "For the Russian is *the* enemy here. . . . He is hated with all the strength of the Prussian heart . . . because people know that from over there comes the gray terror, which can only be stopped with powder and lead."[10] While such statements of hatred had no historically proven basis, they were an effective political construct in the interest of the anti-Russian smear campaign. German officers stationed in the east had nevertheless been concerned about Russian pan-Slavism and the Franco-Russian double alliance. After a stay in Russia of several months during the Russo-Japanese War, the Silesian-born general Albrecht von Thaer advised Quartermaster General Helmuth von Moltke to take military advantage of the situation while the Russian Navy and Army were still tied up in East Asia. This Moltke rejected, pointing to the existing alliance with Petrograd, and calling it an act of "disloyalty toward our old most loyal ally Russia."[11] The Göttingen historian Kaehler characterized Moltke's reaction as naïve, given the general world situation and the Russians' emerging policy of encirclement with respect to Germany. But did he concede to Moltke that even the politically experienced Grossadmiral (Grand Admiral) von Tirpitz stood firm in his loyalty to Russia and was proponent of a close alliance with it.

This supports our view that at the beginning of the war, German military officers held no pervasive, pronounced enmity toward the Czarist Army. It is revealing, on the other hand, that at the beginning of the war, east German Albrecht von Thaer had no reticence about attacking Russia. After the battle of Gorlice-Tarnów, he wrote: "Too bad, too bad that I cannot be there, or make a long distance trip to Petersburg by way of Riga."[12] A few days later he writes in his memoirs, "Too bad that I cannot participate in the east!"[13] After the liberation of East Prussia, a war reporter summed up his impressions in this sentence: "From the visible facts, I was able to convince myself *of that which the European absolutely considered impossible.*"[14] This can point to only one thing: in defending the German eastern border, the Germans were allegedly trying to protect Europe from Asia.

It cannot have been easy to take a stand against these kinds of reports and try to correct them, but publications such as the *Vossische Zeitung* (the Voss Newspaper), a prominent Berlin paper, attempted to do so. Various other eyewitnesses also attested to the excellent soldierly conduct of the Russian troops, and attributed most of the atrocities such as arson and plundering to the Siberian Cossacks.[15] As Ludendorf recalls: "Many Russian troops during August and September in East Prussia behaved in an exemplary manner. Wine cellars and supplies were placed under guard. Rennenkampf held strong discipline in Insterburg. . . . The Cossacks were brutal and crude, they burned and plundered. Many of the inhabitants were killed and women were violated, some of the population kidnapped."[16]

In the early 1930s a small collected volume was published by the Wehrkreiskommando I (military district command) about battles on East Prussian soil dating from the era of the German Teutonic Order until the First World War, with a foreword by then Oberst (Colonel) von Reichenau, commander and chief of staff of the 1st Division. Judging by the questions and answers it provided, it clearly set out to create a sense of threat and a desire to defend: "Will the long series of battlefields in East Prussia come to an end? No one can answer [this question], let alone affirm it."[17] What is striking here is that the authors, likely in deference to the secret military cooperation between Berlin and Moscow, refrain from all reference to excessive behavior by the Russians when they invaded East Prussia in 1914–1915.

What did German military leaders know about the Russian enemy at all? The Great General Staff had insufficient information on the fitness and intentions of the Russian Army. Insiders complained of the failure of German military intelligence, which was mostly due to lack of funds. Tradition has it that in 1902 deployment plans were available for purchase from a Russian General Staff colonel. "We only knew that the Russian deployment had changed from that time, but how it had changed was very uncertain for many years."[18] Not until 1910 was information available about the establishment of two armies, one of which was oriented toward East Prussia from north of the Masurian Lakes, the other from the south, but their composition was little known.[19] They had to have come from the military districts of Warsaw and Vilna. Concerning the use of troops from the military districts of Petersburg, Finland, Moscow, Kazan, Caucasus, and the Asiatic areas, the General Staff knew little. There was an assumption, however, that in the case of a military conflict, the Russians would not be able to send large numbers of Eastern Siberian troops to the front against Germany.

Thus, although at the beginning of the war the Germans had little concrete knowledge about the strength of the Czarist Army or about its war preparations, they were certain that the Russians had gained experience from the disastrous conflict with Japan. In an article written after the war, the military attaché at the German embassy in Petrograd declared that his reports transmitted to Berlin between 1912 and 1914 on the Russian mobilization in progress and the mood in general, both at the court of the czar and within military circles, represented a clear warning of Russian aggression. His intention was to emphasize Russia's responsibility for the war. He particularly points to Russia's rash military measures between 24 July and 1 August 1914 as "premature, with nothing to justify them," and as the only thing that prompted the German declaration of war, thereby making the war in the east unavoidable.[20] This raises the question of whether the premature Russian mobilization placed the German military officers in a dilemma.[21] Sources, however, show that the Germans had no knowledge of the Russian preparation for mobilization. The general staffers and military historians claimed otherwise only after the end of the war in order to claim that the German declaration of war against Russia on 1 August 1914 was a preemptive measure. The war propaganda system dealt with the surprise effect of the unexpected Russian deployment with a rationalization bordering

"Russian mobilization." (*Kriegs-Album der Lustigen Blätter*, 29 [1914])

on the absurd. It constructed a mosaic of various hackneyed ideas about the Russian enemy that were meant to expose the dreaded strength of the Russians as little more than a collection of well-concealed weaknesses. The Russian motor pool, the force behind the alleged Dampfwalze, or "steamroller," became an object of ridicule, and the Russian soldier was generally belittled as a weak enemy because of the high rate of alcoholism.

But the memory of Russian mobilization and quick deployment had long-term experiential value. Later, a subpanel of the Reichstag would study it intensively as part of its analysis of the events that had led up to the First World War.[22]

Even after the end of the First World War, the mobilization and deployment remained firmly entrenched in the memory of German military officers. In an effort to conceal the fact that their own attack on the Soviet Union violated international law, National Socialist leaders would later adopt the propaganda used for the eastern front of summer 1914 and call it a preemptive war. When the soldiers of the newly established Bundeswehr were being psychologically prepared for a possible deployment against the Soviet Union as part of NATO, it called to mind the Russian deployment at the beginning of the First World War. In order to avoid creating a sense of insecurity, however, emphasis was placed on the mental weaknesses of the Russian military officers, which was alleged to be typical of their ethnicity and to have been the ultimate cause of Russia's collapse. As an article in the *Wehrwissenschaftliche Rundschau* (Military Science Review) of 1956 reads: "Built on the principle of absolute numerical superiority over the weaker enemy, always ready for the general defensive strategy during counterattacks, the Russian deployment of 1914 lacked that boldness and absolute readiness to attack that could have made it into a destructive weapon against the Central Powers. The Russian military strength, despite its ultimate failure at that time, obviously grew strong even without exhaustive use of its human and material reservoir; and, in an analysis of the present military situation, the Russian Empire should not be overlooked even today."[23]

Since the introduction of universal conscription, the Russian mass army was thought of as a "steamroller." But a steamroller can be set into motion only slowly, and it moves clumsily, especially through the notorious forests and swamps of the Russian Empire. The German general staffers and commanders were all the more surprised that Russia had expanded its sparse rail network for the sake of strategy, and used it for the quick transport of its strongest forces to the Russian western front.

The German camp placed its trust in the superiority of its General Staff and the leadership art of its commanders, and the caricaturists were required to use their talents to foster public confidence in this area.

Nevertheless, during the first confrontation with the Narev Army the highest German leaders in the east reacted with confusion and insecurity. Hindenburg and Ludendorff dismissed and replaced the commander in chief of the 8th Army, Generaloberst (Colonel General) Maximilian von Prittwitz und Gaffron, and Supreme Quartermaster Generalleutnant (Lieutenant General) Georg Graf von Waldersee.

"Petrograd oracle: 'Yes, alright, Rasputin, your cards are good . . . But I am afraid that those of the German General Staff are better.'" (*Kriegs-Album der Lustigen Blätter*, 29 [1914])

The victory at Tannenberg had a psychological effect that extended far beyond its limited military significance. It bolstered the soldierly self-image of the troops and allowed the military leadership to foster the hope that, with a skillfully conducted mobile war, the numerical superiority of the enemy could be overcome and the frequently invoked steamroller would be outmaneuvered.

More than this, however, the field commander, Hindenburg, now became the legendary hero of Tannenberg, which later led to his becoming president of the Reich. As such, he became the gravedigger of the Weimar Republic, as it were, and ultimately a genuinely tragic figure of the First World War. The army of war propagandists portrayed Hindenburg as the "Marshal Forward of the East," "the Terror of the Russians," a man an army could look up to, someone soldiers could follow trustingly, a figure necessary to their cause. The Russian soldiers did manage to gain proper respect from their German enemy. After the battles of Tannenberg and Kutno, Hindenburg displayed his self-confidence by paying tribute to the enemy, although in a backhanded compliment: "The Russians are good soldiers and maintain discipline. Discipline is ultimately crucial to the campaign. But Russian discipline is something different from that of the Germans . . . it is more a mute, blunt obedience. . . . The Russians will not crush us . . . the Russians are fragile."[24]

Still, the experiential world of the German soldier contrasted with the wishful thinking of the military leaders. Young officers in the war in the east were only being realistic when they refused to rank the Russian soldier beneath the French or English. They knew his bravery and obedience, but above all they knew his willingness to risk his life in battle. "The guards, the Siberians, the grenadiers, and the riflemen were the kind of soldiers that could stand up to any comparisons."[25]

One war correspondent had this to say about the German victory over Russian troops in the Augustów Forest on 9–10 March 1915: "Any other army in the world would be completely unable to fight for a long time after a defeat like this, if not for organizational reasons, then certainly for reasons of morale . . . but the [Russian] Army will never be demoralized by defeat."[26] After every defeat the Russians stood ready to attack again in the shortest possible time. Later, in the static war, they charged against the German lines in an inexhaustible desire to fight, exposing the lies of German war propaganda, whose constant theme was that Russian troops were flight prone.

In an effort to strengthen fighting morale, constant emphasis was placed on the superiority of the Germans and their civilizing mission, something that did little to offset the deprivations of the winter of 1914–1915. The propaganda even tried to sell the winter as an advantage, saying that Russians' strongest talent, digging in, could not be put to use in frozen ground.

But as Max Hoffmann wrote, "The great cold was serious. We experienced the greatest losses because of this, almost more than through the enemy."[27] Yet during the Second World War blitzkrieg strategists Guderian and Manstein—who had both experienced the eastern front of World War I—in arrogant overestimation of their technological abilities and their operational capabilities,

"Hindenburg, the terror of Russia: His very glance is: Victory! / His thundering war cry is: Smite them! / The sound of his sword is like the howl of a storm! / The traces of his days on earth shall not perish for eons to come." (*Kriegs-Album der Lustigen Blätter*, 29 [1914], issue 48)

turned a blind eye to this fact as if it were nothing more than a piece of ancient history.

While there were signs of nutritional deficiencies even in the west, real starvation was a problem specific to the eastern front. German war propaganda

“The evil Germans. Everything kaput.” (*Kriegs-Album der Lustigen Blätter*, 29 [1915], issue 34)

spared no effort to show that the Russian soldier lacked readiness to fight as a result of surviving on half the necessary rations and was thus quite willing to be taken captive.

But the German soldier was also affected by considerable shortages of sup-

"Interrogation of prisoners. 'You, you Ivanovitches and Gregorovitches, where is your army located?' 'Father, it is not located anywhere—it is always on the run!'" (*Kriegs-Album der Lustigen Blätter*, 30 [1915], issue 24)

plies, some of which were due to travel and weather conditions inside the Russian Empire. It remains undisputed that starvation did occur on the eastern front. The following letter, written in November 1915, was symptomatic and not unusual: "Every day we cover 22–25 kilometers, packed with gear for the field march, and the fatigue increases day by day because of the 'good' provisioning. On the ninth day, when we arrived at the regiment, almost two hundred men were missing [out of six hundred]. None had died in battle, but were broken heroes because of miserable injustice. One day, the [battalion] com-

"General Winter, our new ally." (*Kriegs-Album der Lustigen Blätter*, 30 [1915], issue 1)

mander said . . . that probably during the course of the day we would be met by Field Marshal Hindenburg. He asked for disciplined conduct. An answer of a hundred voices from the troops: 'Hunger, hunger, bread, food.'"[28] In mid-1917, a flood of complaint letters about the poor supply situation prompted the Postal Inspection Office to inform Ludendorff of the situation.

In the defensive battles of 1914–1915, it was mostly the more motivated east German troops who were deployed. These were gradually replaced over the course of the offensive static war by units filled with older troops, some of whom were from Alsace or southwestern Germany and were often likely to desert, creating weak links in an otherwise stable front. The German soldiers, in general, came to terms with their military task on the eastern front less because of an awareness of intellectual and cultural superiority than because of the discipline achieved by drill in the indoctrinated ideological themes of patriotism, comradeship, loyalty, bravery, duty, and absolute obedience. It was a discipline that, together with an idealized willingness to sacrifice oneself, became the basis for a heroism that was invoked again and again. But it was nevertheless a corrupted one. Understood, or misunderstood, in this manner, this brand of heroism became a leitmotif that ran through the officially appointed war coverage, repeated over and over in many variations, drowning out the cries of pain of the wounded and dying. Only a person who had internalized such a definition of heroism possessed the degree of immunization necessary to cope with the tragedy of a mass war of destruction, an indescribable war that was not discussed as such in the media, whether as a personal, on-site experience or as recollection of that experience.

In journals and memoirs mostly published after the late 1920s, with few exceptions, the horror is hidden beneath the shadow cast by heroism: "The horror. It is the super real, it is the battle in one's own breast, carried out on the level of the soul once more. Demons fight their Catalaunian battle."[29] In these sources there is no shortage of descriptions of battlefields with mountains of torn human bodies and horse corpses; the spectacle could be withstood, or coped with, only through the idea that death in battle was sacred. "The battlefield has its wild poetry, sung by generation after generation. It is the dying from overwhelming force, it is the jubilant commitment to a grand idea. It is the last and great fulfillment of a vehement praising of eternal love for the fatherland."[30] From there it was only one step further to the modern fanatical perpetrator of murder-suicide.

Only rarely were the horror and atrocities of the experience at the front recorded as a visual recollection. For the western front this was done by Otto Dix, and for the eastern front it was the well-known Professor Ludwig Dettmann. He served his duty as a war painter, creating images of badly wounded, dying, and dead soldiers surrounded by a breath of fog. His journal notes provide further contours and room for interpretation. On 11 November 1914 he recorded: "Around me lie many Germans, dead and expressionless. . . . [How] cruelly have the bullets hit, the bayonets stabbed, and the rifle stocks bludgeoned, the mortars exploded. The dark red blood seeps from wounds, seeps across the ground, weapons, and jackets and paints thoroughly, as if trying to suppress all other colors. . . . Hands compressing blood flow are as if covered with red gloves; naked flesh gleams; the wounded straighten themselves up, fall back; eyes stare from shot-up faces, half broken."[31]

"Russian border soldiers. 'Dimitri, I have an excellent war plan: throw the gun away, run across, get myself captured, get something good to feed on!!'" (*Kriegs-Album der Lustigen Blätter*, 29 [1914], issue 33)

Aware of the advance of the Russian military steamroller on the broad front against the German eastern border and the two attacks by Russian troops in East Prussia, the average soldier on the eastern front had come to the conclusion that he was in a proper war of defense, and the war propaganda supported him in this conviction. But while pushing forward onto Russian territory under the banner of annexation, it seemed to him that his military deployment was becoming increasingly questionable. If war newspapers dealt with the possible war aims in the east as a subject in and of itself, it was more to explain what was militarily necessary for implementing the political goal than to stimulate the goal-oriented desire for victory. Looking back after the war, a front doctor wrote: "The only war aim that he [the soldier] . . . could recognize and feel with his whole being was the slogan: We are conducting a war of defense. But soon, in wider circles, those not belonging to the front, the desire for defense became a will to conquer. . . . By and large, the troops behaved in a way that opposed the striving for 'strategic security and border revisions in the east and west.'"[32] In particular, during the advances into the Russian Baltic Sea provinces, great efforts were made to create a bond between the individual interests of the ordinary soldier and the imperialist, annexationist, and security policy of the national and military leadership by offering him settlement opportunities, a program that met with only very modest success. In the First World War, as in the Second, the conditions in eastern Europe were such that the area held little attractiveness as a place to carry out a settlement policy.[33]

There were also adverse conditions in the rear echelon, as is reflected in Arnold Zweig's character Landsturm Private Birkholz from Eberswalde. Not surprisingly, his thoughts flowed "ceaselessly toward the west . . . over there, where wife and child waited for him in some boxlike rooms of a brick house . . . he is pulled to them with force, but something has burst in between them which has great power: an order."[34]

With the inner collapse of the Imperial German Government, the eastern front collapsed. Released from their oath to their supreme commander, war weary and infected with revolutionary spirit, the soldiers of the army headed home. The memory and experience of the Russian adventure had been indelibly etched into their consciousness.

The war in the east, other than the defense of East Prussia, had made both the average soldier and the officer corps doubt that their personal commitment, deprivations, and loss of friends and relatives had been of value. Yet the experience became idealized, especially after the Treaty of Brest-Litovsk. The experience of the eastern front was for the most part reduced to the memory of male comradeship, welded together in a storm of steel, bound in shared heroism. It was a life experience that, because of its uniqueness, could not be re-created, nor would it ever be permitted now that such terror had become taboo.

There is now increasing evidence to support the opinions, given in retrospect in personal sources, that there was an essentially more harmonious relationship between soldiers, noncommissioned officers, and officers on the eastern front than in the west, where the rear echelon had become extensively demoralized. Much evidence points to the idea of the brotherhood of the trenches and an easing of the formalities that had previously formed barriers between ranks. While many reports do reflect a kind of calculated optimism in this regard, something further whitewashed by ideology, there was also visible evidence: "They did not stand together as superior and subordinate but, with all due maintenance of military discipline, as man to man. They suffered the same deprivations, were exposed to the same dangers, squeezed together into the same cramped shelters, and came to know and appreciate one another better."[35]

While the trench created a long-lasting impression as a substitute homeland, Russian war imprisonment, mostly in Siberia, became a metaphor for desolation and existential threat. Many soldiers of the eastern front reflected on whether they would choose death over Russian captivity, and many escaped the feared internment through suicide. At the beginning of the Russian campaign in 1941, many soldiers imagined the fate of German prisoners of war at the hands of the Russians to be a scene of horror of the kind described by bestselling author Edwin Erich Dwinger.[36]

The war experience was not confined to military action or the personal circumstances endured by the soldier. The soldier was also conscious of the foreignness of his environment. While German intellectual and cultural superiority was repeatedly suggested to him, the German soldier also became conscious of this on his own because of the primitive agricultural conditions that predominated in the Czarist Empire. He sometimes experienced these conditions in a state of culture shock. A flood of printer's ink filled military satire papers and trench newspapers with verses and illustration concerning the Polish economy and conditions in Russia. Lice and bedbugs took center stage and became important components of the writers' experiences and recollections, as exemplified is this field mail postcard, which uses rhymed verse to satirize a mouse hunt by soldiers billeted in Russia:

Of culture
Not a trace.
Every night,
Great hunting.[37]

For the German soldier, the cultural domain was commonly considered as important as German order and cleanliness. There were regulations about bathing and haircuts, and the German soldier brought this culture to the east in the same manner that American GIs in 1945 brought chocolate as a token of their occupation power.

For the German soldier, the cities of France, the pinnacle of which was Paris, were associated with the idea of spirited, beautiful, and elegant women, a subject that needs no further mention. "Beautiful Polish ladies" also had a reputation that preceded them. But when it came to femininity on Russian territory, the fantasies of the German ground troops showed some gaps. Military

"That is the war. 'A kiss must be paid for, Maruschka; if you require it, afterward I can fill you out a requisition certificate for it.'" (*Kriegs-Album der Lustigen Blätter*, 29 [1914], issue 50)

propaganda found this a challenge to overcome but was not shy about declaring the girls of the east as requisition items.

The First World War was the first war in which it was possible to capture in photos a great deal of what happened and what was seen. A cache of these memories, of particular value to historians, exists on film. Even in the best of cases, however, this treasure trove does not contain reality but only excerpts of it, most of which are of the positive aspects. Early research has unanimously shown that in private photos the horror of the war is for the most part taboo; what is captured on film is the foreign "other" and the environment of the theater of war. From the eastern front we have photos of peasant women in regional dress, young Ukrainians, and idyllic landscapes. Here the soldier has declared peace with the enemy and his environment, had conjured a piece of the ideal world, and had preserved them long after the war in a shoe carton or in an album for himself and for the future. Photos were a "means of reconciliation between the soldiers as 'humans' and their mission as 'fighters' and 'victors.'" They could be read as a means of conciliation between the soldiers and the environment into which they had been thrown through their participation in the war."[38]

The situation in Poland was perceived quite differently. Max Hoffmann expressed the reaction of German soldiers in general: "As to the roads, the dirt, the vermin—it was all unimaginable."[39] After the Second World War, one of the most prominent state politicians from southwestern Germany made more careful observations, sketching a detailed image of the "Polish economy." He also reported the infestation of lice, although he found it bearable. He felt the impoverished conditions under which Polish peasants lived might make German soldiers more satisfied with "the living opportunities in Germany." This observer described in great detail the living conditions, but not without goodwill, despite the "incredible filth" everywhere. Locations where Germans were quartered were kept in order by soldiers, and children were taught to wash themselves daily.[40] In Poland the previously cited Landwehr cavalry officer fulfilled an old wish by having himself quartered in the castle of an educated Polish nobleman. There he saw his prejudices about Polish lack of culture confirmed. The furnishings and paintings in the estate imparted the impression of French style, so much so that he asked sarcastically: "What could it have been like in Poland before the French had rococo and if they had not sent furniture to Poland? For with the exception of some ancestral portraits of mustachioed knights in the ethnic costume of Sarmatia, there is nothing to be seen of the old fabled Polish nation. And to see French furniture, one need not come to Poland."[41] One war correspondent who was housed with a Polish farmer remarked with astonishment on the cleanliness, order, and the white cloth on the table, and then learned that the Polish hostess was married to a German who had been abducted by Russian troops. "It was the same poor environment, the same meager lifestyle, but it was as if a whole world separated this room from the surrounding Polish farmhouses forever. Just like the border, here in the east the line doesn't merely separate two countries from one another, it [separates] squalor and constructive work, languishing and a strong, healthy life; this is what the house is like that the German builds here in Russian Poland, like a foreign, happy land, and it is such a strong witness to superiority, such a distinct racial superiority, that it ultimately produces hatred in the other people."[42] But turning to the atmosphere of Warsaw, he notes: "The Polish lightheartedness showed itself here . . . and the fact that in Warsaw . . . the heart of Polish life beats purely and vigorously can be seen by anyone who wanders even a little through the streets full of memories, past these airy palaces, these tasteful houses, these Catholic churches that speak of western culture, and only of this."[43]

In the Imperial German Army there was no lack of anti-Semitism. The fact that Max Bauer and Erich Ludendorff were its main proponents speaks for itself. This makes the reaction of German soldiers all the more surprising, at least as evidenced in their writing, when they encountered eastern European Judaism. This coming together was often recorded as an enjoyable part of the war experience because the Yiddish language enabled conversation and the Jewish business sense offered an improvement in living conditions. While being quartered in a Jewish home, "two daughters, blond Jewish beauties," caught the eye of one observer.[44] The Bavarian regional author Ludwig Ganghofer wrote two war reports noting his observations of eastern Jews, such as this one from the Carpathians: "Among the peasants, one sees groups of Jews in their long, black coats. Should one need to ask directions or any other matter, it is best to turn to these wearers of locks; they are friendly and helpful, answer appropriately, and almost always speak very understandable German. Among them one also sees beautiful, picturesque figures."[45]

Jewish merchants were also sometimes feared, albeit not always respected, but they were indispensable partners of Ober Ost when it came to bringing in raw materials and foodstuffs from the occupied territories of the Czarist Empire. This took place to a large extent through normal processes—that is, by payment—but was nonetheless conducted to the disadvantage of the indigenous population. Hindenburg's occupation authority was focused on the ruthless exploitation of the territories in favor of supplying the Germans at home. The agricultural merchant Kurt Klamroth of Halberstadt, as reserve officer in Grodno responsible for the collection of the necessary goods, had his reservations about the business practices of the local Jews. As business partners he treated them with ruthlessness and discrimination, as revealed in passages from his wartime correspondence: "These eastern Jews have absolutely no feeling for decency in business transactions. What they consider to be skill at business and acumen, we consider to be chicanery. . . . Weissenborn [the mayor of Halberstadt who had been drafted into war service] was very surprised one day when he saw how in dealing with a Jewish merchant who tried to cheat me far too much, I wrote the receipt for his payment on his back with my riding

"The great exhibition of the people of the world: 'It was planned of course for San Francisco—for next year. But the plan fell through because before the people even suspected, they found themselves in Döberitz.'" (*Kriegs-Album der Lustigen Blätter*, 19 [1914], issue 43)

crop. The procedure appeared questionable to Mr. Captain of the City." Yet he thought it worth repeating as a measure to ensure success: "A few days later," Klamroth wrote, "I saw him do the same thing to a fishmonger who was brazenly cheating the poor citizens despite a quite recently announced ordinance." As Klamroth told his family, it was just this mixture of servility and business sense that "made [the Jews] so disagreeable to us."[46]

Even with all his reservations about foreignness, nothing can be found in Kurt Klamroth's letters of racist anti-Semitism. Instead one finds more of a lack of understanding for the living environment of eastern Judaism, which was fundamentally different from the everyday bourgeois existence of the German middle and upper classes. He expresses, however, an admiration for "the Jewish inner family life" and "the strong moral lifestyle of the Jewish women and girls."[47]

Jews served in the Czarist Army, just as they did in the German Army, which was not without discrimination. They appeared from time to time in German war reports when they showed up in prisoner of war camps. Here too, they were singled out from the mass of their Russian fellow prisoners of war, but in a mostly positive manner. Inhabitants of occupied East Prussia had supposedly informed the German troops that the Jews in the Russian Army would behave more correctly than Russians. Wherever possible, out of psychological motives, German war reporting built up the image of Russian Jews in the czar's army to the German Jewish soldiers in the ranks of the German Army. It was also considered remarkable that in East Prussia the Jewish soldiers from the government of Kovno "made a far better impression than the other [Russian] war prisoners, if only in terms of their appearance in uniform and conduct."[48]

It is well known that debates regarding war aims ranged from power politics and strategically grounded territorial amputations to a splintering of the Russian Empire to the principle of nationalities all the way to alliances and European political matters. In the latter two questions, eastern Jewry played no small role. At the beginning of the war, journalist and author Alfons Paquet worked in the intelligence section of the representative Generalkommando (General Command) XVIII. After several trips through Poland and Ober Ost in 1915, he authored his article "Nach Osten!" (To the East!), in which he pleaded for the liberation of certain ethnic groups from the Czarist Empire, such as the Finns, Baltic Germans, Poles, Ukrainians, Jews, and Georgians, who would have most adamantly opposed Russification.

Although inferior materially and socially, the eastern Jews had a certain cultural link to Germany that led Paquet to view them as Germany's natural allies in the creation of a postwar order in the east. During a trip to Palestine, Paquet had admired the accomplishments of Judaism and embraced the ideal of integrating Judaism and Christianity. He felt that the mission of Germany should be to foster and protect Judaism and Zionism. By conquering Poland and Courland, "something like responsibility for the fate of a large part of Jewry was conveyed to the German people."[49] In the "Land of Ober Ost," the quintessence of German administrative ability and economy but also of ethnic tolerance, Ludendorff surrounded himself with liberal and leftist German representatives of culture, even of Jewish descent, while the German occupation power broadcast and professed sympathy for the eastern Jews. The writer Sammy Gronemann, employed in the press staff of Ober Ost, had this to say:

> In the first years of the war . . . there was conceited jubilation and enthusiasm about the discovery of the eastern Jew as the protector of German ways and language. There arose enthusiastic songs of praise to their loyalty, and a series of German literati—and by no means were they only Jews—demonstrated in deeply grounded discourses that the eastern Jew was actually the true German, a carrier of German culture who, with incredible toughness and loyalty, had preserved Germanic ethnic culture through the centuries of Slavic suppression. The imperial headquarters graciously received a memorandum about the subject in a beautifully bound deluxe volume. Kaiser Wilhelm's first impulse was to decree the immediate release of all eastern Jewish pris-

> oners of war. . . . In short, it almost seemed—it was as if Kaiser Wilhelm had called for a levy expressly for the salvation of his greatly loved eastern Jews.[50]

The favorable image of Judaism, which was highly played up mainly through propaganda during the Bolshevik Revolution and among the German Left, may have then triggered an anti-Semitic impulse, especially among the regular troops and Freikorps, who still remained in the east after the Treaty of Brest-Litovsk and after the end of the war as a bulwark against Bolshevism.

Still, propaganda and journalism during the First World War were not free from negative ethnic typological statements. While war correspondents' reports and published journals seldom show any striking traces of anti-Semitism, during the course of the war in the east the Russian soldier was increasingly ascribed more definite Asiatic traits that seemed exotic and that settled into the memory of the German soldier like a kind of racial sediment. In the postwar literature of the so-called Baltikumer (Baltic fighters), such as author Ernst von Salomon, an enemy image evolved out of the symbiotic link between Mongolian barbarianism and expansionist Bolshevism. This image found resonance especially in anti-democratic circles, most strikingly those in which the former front soldiers were found.

Incorporated into the SA by the leaders of the Freikorps, this image wove harmoniously into the aggressive anti-Soviet cliché designed by the Baltic German Alfred Rosenberg, chief ideologue of the early Nazi Party. For years this representation was taught to school pupils, Hitler Youth, students, and young soldiers, and it was adopted by a good portion of the higher-ranking military officers; thus the Wehrmacht, unlike the Imperial Army of 1914–1915, was motivated for war by the time of its attack on the Soviet Union. This image of the enemy now embodied one single consciously held phenomenological explanation for the aggressiveness and stubborn persistence of the Wehrmacht and the various units of the SS. Ultimately the image of the Red Army soldier also acquired a Semitic element, relegating him, as it were, to the rank of illegitimate offspring of the Slavic subhuman.

What united the higher military leaders amid all the experiences, disappointments, and expectations of the war in the east beyond adherence to the official positions and propaganda? As has been mentioned, the rapid mobilization and fast deployment of the Russian troops, whose leaders understood how to skillfully exploit terrain and human material, had truly been a surprise. At the same time the German leaders responsible for the eastern front considered themselves professionally superior and hoped to win the upper hand through a skillful mobile war and encirclement battles. This would be possible only to a degree, and not until far in the future, due to the necessarily divided forces of the Central Powers in the west and the repeated obligation to support the weak

Cover of the brochure *Der Untermensch*, c. 1942.

Austrian Army on its southern front. Ultimately, as German leaders recognized early on, there was no prospect of destroying the enemy militarily.

The war aims had been much discussed since Fritz Fischer's time, but what were they by the time the war began? In their basic outline, they corresponded with the imperialist and annexationist ambitions of the nationalist circles of the Imperial Government, but among the military officers goals were guided by the general war situation. The officers responsible drew from their personal experience and sometimes made far-reaching innovative military decisions that would continue to have repercussions for the structure of German-(Soviet) Russian postwar relationships.

In November 1914, Grossadmiral Alfred von Tirpitz, the secretary of state of the Imperial Naval Office and one of the most politically influential military officers, advised the Prussian minister of war and chief of the General Staff General Erich von Falkenhayn to conclude a separate peace with Petrograd. The results of the war in the east were fully obvious by then, and Tirpitz was confronted with the sobering realization that for Germany, obligated on two fronts, the war in the east could not be won, and it was necessary to concentrate forces against Germany's imperial rival England. This was reiterated in a statement by Falkenhayn to Reichskanzler Theobald von Bethmann-Hollweg: "As long as Russia, France, and England stand together, it is impossible to conquer our enemy in such a way that we can come to a proper peace. We would risk much more danger of slowly exhausting ourselves. Either Russia or France must be put to one side. If we were to succeed in our primary goal of bringing Russia to the peace table, then we would be able to wrestle down France and England enough so that we can dictate the terms of the peace."[51]

Hindenburg finally sketched out a Polish border line for the military security of the Reich in the east, an area that the Germans believed the czarist government would easily relinquish.[52] Vizeadmiral (Vice Admiral) Albert Hopman, acting director of the central section of the Navy Office in the Great Headquarters, recognized that, given the alliance's political situation and the fact that Russia was the main enemy of Germany's ally Austria, a separate peace was out of the question. He therefore wrote to Admiral Eduard von Capelle: "The favorite idea of the secretary of state [Tirpitz] is still a joining with Russia in a vanguard against England. As possible as such a policy might have been five to ten years ago, in my opinion it is now impossible. Aside from the fact that Russia would never be open to this, it would also mean abandoning Austria, which is unthinkable."[53] Yet Tirpitz, like the majority of German military leaders, considered the Austrian ally to be both a political and a military burden, and he doubted its future existence as a sovereign nation outside of the German Empire. Grossadmiral Tirpitz had learned through diplomatic circles that Russia was ready to come to an "understanding" if Germany would break off its Austrian alliance. "We must try," he explained to Hopman, "to come to an agreement with Russia. Our interests have never impinged on one another."[54] Naturally, out of dynastic interests Wilhelm II did not involve himself in such mind games but instead endorsed the high-ranking military officers, such as General Adjutant Generaloberst Hans von Plessen, who were accelerating the war against Russia and trying to force the czarist government to the negotiating table under the pressure of German military successes. This opinion also became the definitive guideline in the Great Headquarters, although informed observers of war events doubted this concept would succeed.[55] In late November 1914 the military delegate from Württemburg, Generalleutnant (Lieutenant General) Friedrich von Graevenitz, called the idea "a catastrophe [for] the Russians, as no longer probable," and he "cursed the Austrians strongly."[56]

Of particular interest in this regard is the opinion of one of the most high-profile officers of the Great General Staff of the eastern front, Max Hoffmann, who for a long time received little recognition for his accomplishments. As the closest colleague of Hindenburg and Ludendorff, he could never step outside their shadow. Although at the beginning of the war he was only a first lieutenant (by 1916 he was a colonel, by October 1917 a major general), he was personally acquainted with Wilhelm II, whose trust and protection he enjoyed. He was respected as a foremost authority on military matters. "Ludendorff and Hoffmann as well—very significant minds," noted Hopman after a conversation with the industrialist Hugo Stinnes.[57]

Max Hoffmann did not lack self-confidence, something fully consistent with his expertise and capability. Unlike Hindenburg, who was born in Posen and the son of a Prussian officer, or Ludendorff, who came from a place near Posen, Hoffmann was from Hesse. He had a neutral opinion of the German and European east, yet he was better versed in its problems than many other officers. Although he had served as a lieutenant and company commander and in various General Staff assignments in East Prussia and Posen, he had also experienced the Russian-Japanese War on the Japanese side as military observer, in which capacity he acquired important knowledge about Russian war operations. Late in 1898, having passed the interpreters' exam for Russian, Hoffmann traveled to Russia for half a year to study, and then served in the Russian Department of the Great General Staff until 1911. He had to have been considered expert. As a congenial coworker of Ludendorff and later as his successor, he was the operational mind for the area of Ober Ost. Hoffmann considered the war against Russia to be one of the greatest military and personal challenges yet. The use of the parade as a way of impressing an enemy who was far superior in numbers was something he understood and designed as practical general staff exercises. The clear awareness of the responsibility conferred on him came together with a commitment to do it justice professionally, and this grew into a passion for being a soldier. After the first failed attempt to conquer Warsaw, Hoffmann wrote: "We have no fear of the Russians, even when they, as now, come in numbers three times higher than ours. But we will not be able to avoid having to relinquish a part of German territory in order to strike somewhere."[58]

The fulfillment of the military mission allowed no room in the exhausting daily events for any possibly annoying reflections about the justification for the war in the east. But Hoffmann criticized this military conflict as an irresponsible military adventure, destined from the start to be a multiple-front war. Again in reference to the first failed attack on Warsaw, he wrote: "I would have considered it more proper first to clear the slate with either France or Russia. If we had sent just two to three more corps, I would have guaranteed success here."[59]

By the time the situation on the western front developed in 1914–1915, he considered it impossible to conclude the war in the east victoriously because of the ratio of forces there; just as impossible was a victory by the Austro-Hungarian Army, which had been far from able to cope with its mission. But he did not believe there would have been a defeat, either. Hoffmann's journal entry in early March reads: "The Russian Army cannot be completely defeated; we could do this only if we waged war with Russia alone. Furthermore, the Austrians are defeated. . . . I consider it impossible that we can be defeated, but also that we will defeat the others so much that we will be able to dictate terms; I also said this to the Reichskanzler."[60] To this end, the war had to be halted militarily and brought to a close diplomatically, sacrificing all eastern expansion by making strategically significant corrections with respect to the Russian part of Poland.

When a pamphlet by the director of general territory of East Prussia, Wolfgang Kapp, called for vigorous action by German troops both in the east and in the west under the precept of annexationist war aims, Hoffmann replied tersely: "The man is completely right, but argues from a false assumption. We have not won as yet and have no prospect of destructively defeating all enemies." Even early in the year 1915 Hoffmann declined all claim to territory of the Russian rim area: "Even here in Russia I am against all major land acquisition. The Baltic Sea provinces cannot come under discussion—because we did not conquer them and we cannot conquer them. Furthermore, the population there is not German and wants nothing to do with us: Baltic people, Finns, etc. Nor do I want anything from any other of the Russian border countries, we have enough Poles. . . . Kapp lives in Utopia and therefore can only do harm."[61] The military successes on the eastern front in 1915 allowed Bethmann-Hollweg and the broad circle of the political public to go back to their plans for a new order that had been discussed at the beginning of the war.[62] This also meant that new issues arose for the local military officers. What was referred to as the issue of the rim countries was finally updated and made concrete, and it was partially realized after the invasion in the Ukraine and in the Baltic. After the experience of the invasion of East Prussia, leading military officers called for a territorial *cordon d'avant postes* (military outpost), contemplating introducing annexationist measures in support of their necessary or supported acts of hegemony. Ludendorff specified that "Poland must not be given back to Russia under any circumstances . . . that it had to become part of a more or less independent conglomerate of nations under German supremacy. We must go safely for the sake of the future, which will be a difficult one for us, and all the more difficult the less we weaken Russia."[63] Thus, for Ludendorff both motives seem to have flowed together. The much-discussed continental imperialist plan for eastern annexation came primarily under the category of military strategy and was endorsed by a no less credible figure than Fritz Fischer.[64]

Seen thus, after experiencing two invasions of East Prussia by the Russians, there was a need for a politically stable territorial buffer, be it in the form of annexed territory or an independent conglomerate of nations closely connected to the German Empire. Ludendorff's annexationist policy met its limitations when it touched on the vital interests and the national sensitivities of czarist Russia.

Max Hoffmann reenters the picture from time to time in the annexations issue, due to the military successes that occurred thanks to the unexpected turmoil of the Russian Revolution. Early in 1917, he pleaded for an annexation of Lithuania and Courland as well as the expansion of a militarily secured border facing Poland in whichever form it existed. "The issue is . . . how we will implement these terms. I stand on the opinion that it is possible to wrestle down Russia, if the necessary troops are made available."[65] Four weeks later he returned to his former stance on relinquishing annexations, due to the cumulative experiences with the population and their national representatives and ambitions. He tried to make it clear to a delegation from the Reichstag that the Germans, Poles, Lithuanians, and Latvians, all competing for power in Ober Ost, hated the Imperial Germans, something that could not realistically be bridged by politics. He recommended abandoning military action against Russia under a strict policy of political neutrality.[66] For the sake of peace terms and future alliances with Russia, and considering their analysis of the military situation and its possible development both in the west and the east, the more influential military officers wanted to settle for borderline regulations that accommodated their security considerations. These included complete forced relocations of the population. In the fall of 1915 von Thaer, an *Ostgrenzler* (champion of the eastern zones), disagreed with the minister of war, Wild von Hohenborn, and spoke out against a more or less independent Poland bordering directly on the Reich. He argued instead in favor of a wide band of land between the nations, settled purely by Germans. He claimed that his opponent was sympathetic to this idea.[67] The idea of the Polish border strip, he said, came from his father; the younger Thaer then reworked the plan and submitted it to Hindenburg and Ludendorff. He favored the Germanizing of Posen and West Prussia, for instance, which meant removing Poles and Jews from this and other territories to be settled elsewhere into a more or less independent area, with the main body of Poland awarded to Russia under certain circumstances, with Warsaw and Kattowitz (Katowice) as centers.[68] What is unmistakable here is the line of continuity from the First to the Second World War: the National Socialist policy of remaking the ethnic culture of an area through resettlement processes (*Umvolkungspolitik*) acquired further significance in the annihilation of Jews.

The Bolshevik Revolution was accelerated by the Reich when it repatriated Lenin, opening the possibility of an armistice and a peace settlement amid the well-known military and diplomatic turbulence in Brest-Litovsk. The representative of the OHL (German High Command) in the German negotiation delegation was Max Hoffmann. Regardless of the revolutionary unrest during the course of 1917, he had already come to the opinion that after the war it would be worthwhile to ally with Russia to create a counterbalance against a British-American alliance, above all in the area of economics.[69] As a prerequisite for this, Hoffmann probably visualized a non-Bolshevist Russian postwar settlement. This was because he hated the Bolsheviks that now sat opposite him at the negotiations table and probably counted them out as heirs to the czarist government. The major topic in the peace negotiations of Brest-Litovsk was the right to self-determination—this was something, however, that each party in the negotiation understood differently, and the general had to advocate for the border countries in this regard.[70] The border state settlement that finally resulted was one that Hoffmann helped to establish, but even today his personal convictions on the matter are unclear. What is known was that Hoffmann fell out with Ludendorff over the Polish issue when in a personal presentation to the kaiser he rejected the annexation of Polish territory beyond what was needed for border security.[71] Early in 1919 the Munich historian Karl Alexander von Müller met Max Hoffmann—the man whom the press claimed had pounded on the table with his fist in the effort to rein in the Bolshevist delegation in Brest-Litovsk. "What remained with me from his statements," noted von Müller after the conversation, "is that in all of the war aims he was much more reasonable than the supporters of the Army High Command at home had been. . . . Also in Brest-Litovsk, he said he had sympathized much more with the secretary of state von Kühlmann than with the guidance from the Great Headquarters."[72]

The general staff officers who were familiar with the war in the east had already formed a "Russia faction" during the campaign. In taking stock after Compiègne and Versailles, military experiential values took a back seat to political and strategic considerations. They feared a French-Polish or French-Russian postwar alliance, a danger that ultimately could be averted long term only by means of a German-Russian federation at the cost of Poland. As early as 1919, Oberst Max Bauer, as former director of the deployment division of the OHL and as someone directly occupied with the war in the east, publicized his own conclusions on the subject. As one of the inaugurators of what became known in German as the *Dolchstosslegende,* or "stab-in-the-back myth," he blamed the democratic parties for even the machinations of the war in the east, accused the Center Party of hatred for the Orthodox Church and the Social Democrats of hatred for absolute czarism. Even in 1915 Bauer had been plagued by doubts about a victorious ending to a war on all fronts.[73] In his *Erin-*

nerungen und Betrachtungen (Memoirs and Observations) he once more voiced this opinion explicitly. Taking into consideration the given ratio of forces, it seemed fruitless to him "in the east and the west to try to defeat both enemies at the same time." Even if delayed war operations in the west had made it possible to deploy an additional six to eight army corps in the eastern war, in his opinion these reinforcements would not have been sufficient to destroy the Czarist Army. His experience in 1914–1915 made his assumption more of a certainty: that the Russians, as masters of retreat and static battles, would have successively retreated while fighting, who knows how far and how long. "We would have ended up with endless rear lines and in the best case, by winter 1914, we could have been in the place we stood in summer of 1915."[74] Bauer cautioned about the immeasurable size of Russia, about the inadequate notions that western Europeans had about the significance of time and distances in this land, and about the particular difficulties of occupying and pacifying it. In 1918 there was a German occupation soldier for every twenty square kilometers.

The experiences of the war in the east left Bauer with only one conclusion: that there needed be a return to a traditional German-Russian friendship.[75] "Never have the two empires needed to confront one another with weapons, and there will be still less reason in the future."[76]

The ultra-monarchist Bauer could imagine the restoration of a German-Russian partnership, but only after the restitution of the Hohenzollern and czarist rule. The former chief of the general staff on the Russian southern front, now chief of the Army High Command of the Reichswehr, Seeckt, together with Schleicher, laid the foundations for German–Soviet armament cooperation. In this, they paved the way to Rapallo and the secret military cooperation that would follow. Seeckt wrote a tactics manual for the Red Army, which it adopted in 1925. And it was fitting that the onetime chief of the field rail system and chief of the general staff of Army Group Kiev, Wilhelm Groener, now minister of transport, sat at the cabinet table when the Rapallo treaty was approved. In September 1922, Seeckt wrote to Reich President Ebert: "Poland's existence is unbearable. . . . It must disappear and will disappear by means of its own inner weakness and through Russia—with our help."[77] On the basis of the German-Soviet Federation, the structural framework of the Versailles Treaty was to be nullified.

Notable general staffers may well have assigned the war in the east to the evidence room of history as no more than a historical intermezzo, sparked by political blunders. But for many front officers of the German Army, it still held a powerful existential significance. Some continued the eastern campaign as annexationist knights errant, so to speak, or as fighters against Bolshevism in the Freikorps, demonstrating a militancy that disparaged civilization and flouted democracy. The Baltic fighters left the memory of the deployment on the last front of the First World War to the National Socialist regime as a historical legacy of sacrifice. In a widely read book of 1936, their former commander in chief, General Rüdiger von der Goltz, expressed it as "the great inheritance of the world war and . . . key to the future of the Third Reich."[78] By 1933 he was director of the Vereinigten vaterländischen Verbände (Federated Associations of the Fatherland) and from 1934 to 1938 director of the Reichsverband deutscher Offiziere (Reich Association of German Officers). Von der Goltz had learned to be proactive in spreading his ideas, which found expression in his publications such as *Darstellungen aus den Nachkriegskämpfen deutscher Truppen und Freikorps* (Descriptions from the Postwar Struggles of German Troops and Freikorps), published by the Research Institute for War and Army History. Other of his writings were published through the Military History Research Office of the Army, and were thereby learned as doctrine by the ordinary soldiers. "Anyone who stepped in at that time to protect our borders with their blood and life, with knowledge and ability," assured the Reich war minister von Blomberg in his preface to von der Goltz's *Darstellungen* (Descriptions), "may count himself with pride among the predecessors and pathfinders of a better future."[79] Behind such comments is buried a latent revanchism that was revitalized when Hitler seized power, especially for the Freikorps fighters who had been seasoned by war in the east and who had an influential literary lobby, not the least of which came from their own ranks. One of their best-selling authors, Ernst von Salomon, in a collected volume by Ernst Jünger, gave birth to a popular saying that targeted the Versailles Treaty and summed up the world war: "Even the phrasing that had been found for this peace without victors and without vanquished proves that the conclusion of the war is not considered final anywhere in the whole world."[80]

Still, during the period of German-Soviet military cooperation, Blomberg and later other high-ranking military officers commented enthusiastically on the technological progress and the armaments-related economic capability of their Russian partner. They were impressed with the speed of the Red Army's transformation in terms of leadership concepts and tactical doctrine. Guderian, because of the promise of gaining settlement land in the east, continued there on his own initiative as Freikorps soldier. As a Reichswehr officer, he also remained involved in the secret military cooperation. Because he had traveled in the Soviet Union for study purposes, he was very well informed on the military situation there, and even as early as the 1930s, he cautioned against underestimating the Soviet potential.

Yet in light of the Russian-Finnish War and the euphoria of the German victories in the west, military wishful thinking quickly won the upper hand over a fundamental sense of reality. This influenced perceptions as to Hitler's sudden decision to attack the Soviet Union. Just as in 1914, neither the German generals responsible nor the expert general staffers of 1940–1941 believed that a war with the huge neighbor to the east had any militarily-based urgency. Nevertheless, from Hitler's perspective, the war appeared inevitable; it served anti-Bolshevist sentiments and was therefore accepted by a large portion of German high-ranking military officers as well. This was the manner of its conception against the experiential backdrop of the First World War.

But just who was the enemy? This question was just as essential in this second Russian field campaign of the century as in 1914–1915, for both campaigns involved a reliance on troops who were not exactly motivated.

On the eve of Hitler's seizing of power, a National Socialist author wrote a kind of military science book that reflected back to the First World War and drew a sketch of the character and mentality of the Russian soldiers in which they appeared as an ethnic and typological constant. It intended to show "that the Russian character is neither quick nor tough, that his intellect is not purely occidental but Asiatic in nature, not very versatile, but on the other hand it is persistent in nature, waiting, thoughtful, doubting—in short, it should have been clear from the beginning that the Russian, without underestimating him, is not an equal opponent and is much less dangerous than an enemy from the west would be."[81]

What in 1914–1915 had been implanted into the consciousness of the soldier as a purposely clichéd and falsely painted image of czarist Russia was later adopted by the military top leaders of the Third Reich as an image of the reality of the Soviet enemy. After the liquidation of important top military leaders by Stalin, the new leadership was thought to be just as inexperienced, overextended, and inept as the troops overall. What had been feared in 1914–1915 as the Russian steamroller was now looked upon as a colossus standing on the clay feet of the Stalinist rule of terror. Just as the czarist government had crumbled under the events of the Revolution, so would the Stalinist empire crumble under the anti-Soviet forces during the German invasion through the weak areas of its western national borders.

In the Second World War, the same controversy arose that had raged on after the First World War: should Germany have first sought victory in the east in order to defeat the west with the newly available troops, or would it have been more effective to limit the war in the east to delay tactics with limited forces in order to enable an early victory on the western front? But by 1941, after the blitzkrieg over France, this argument no longer had any relevance to the situation at hand.

In any case, Russia had already lost its halo of invincibility by 1914–1915. All of the responsible military officers of Hitler's Wehrmacht were in agreement on this and were concerned only about a multiple-front war. The strategic military situation of 1941 appeared to represent a logical conclusion based on accurate inferences drawn from the First World War. The Hitler-Stalin Pact was an extremely politically skilled delay tactic that had been implemented in order to be able to force the enemy in the west to its knees quickly. The members of the highest level of generals and admirals as well as expert general staff officers thereby declared a military operation against the Red Army, which seemed to be winnable in a few weeks with the help of the obvious technological, operational, and tactical superiority of the Germans. The lessons from the previous confrontation with Russia's massive array of military, the unreliability of the infrastructure, and the climatic conditions in the eastern theater of war were not considered pertinent. Guderian, too, adopted this opinion and line of argument. As chief of the General Staff of the Army between July 1944 and March 1945, and having been given an estate in the east, he could be counted among the influential and loyal generals who adhered to Hitler's order to persist at any cost, and who had shut themselves off from practical military insight and responsibility.

Thanks to their technological progress and high degree of modernization, used in combination with blitzkrieg style attacks and encirclements (which in turn would open up the possibility of exploiting a large operational area) and deployed against an enemy whom they viewed as indolent and inflexible, the Germans expected a quick and victorious conclusion to the Russian campaign.

The technological aspect underscores a particular element of the First World War. During the period between the First and the Second World Wars, technology had gained significance beyond its military value in the conduct of war; it had grown into a literary, even philosophical category. Particularly in the west, all war romanticism had been buried in shell craters. Amid shattering metal and poison gas vapors, the soldier saw himself condemned to being "a defenseless victim of chance and the machine." The brotherhood of the trench had degenerated into an emergency association that was devoid of soldierly qualities, as was the fight in the static war, in which "in the end, neither courage nor intelligence, neither heroism nor cowardice were of any use."[82]

Ernst Jünger, like other intellectuals who had participated in the war, lamented the loss of a basic soldierly quality—the sense of what one was fighting for—as a result of the nascent "industrial mass killing" during the First World War on the western front. This could also be said of the war in the east, although in a slightly different way.[83] The conduct of war in the east was in fact different from in the west. Here, too, artillery dominated, but the war in the east, as one contemporary described it, was "richer and more colorful, and the element of adventure that for ages deceived us as to the nature of war was not completely taken away."[84] The expanse of the area and the numerically superior Russian mass army demanded and allowed the German leaders operational and tactical creativity, yet the German infantry often conquered the trenches of the Russian enemy with their bayonets, man against man, and sometimes munition was not handed out at all. Cavalry attacks retained characteristics similar to those of the nineteenth century. The cavalry exerted a nostalgic fascination as a symbol of all that was soldierly. It skillfully survived clear into the Second World War, although with considerable reductions in extent and function, despite the protests of modernization-obsessed critics who tried to threaten its existence.

Nevertheless, even Ernst Jünger, an often-heard voice in military matters, proclaimed the technologizing of war to be a chance for the reindividualizing of the soldier, for instance, as a machine gunner, tank leader, pilot, or U-boat commander. These represented his belief in a revitalized, modern image of the soldier and hero, which was ultimately manifested by the heroes who filled such duties during the Second World War. Yet their personal military significance should not be given too much weight in view of the dimension of the war against the Soviet Union. Considering the unique qualities of this total war, in 1941 the defining structural conditions for the German defeat were comparable with those of 1914. They consisted of the almost inexhaustible reservoir of Russian human material, their bold willingness to sacrifice their lives, and the expanse of the area, which could not be overcome by the Germans under the difficult conditions of climate and insufficient material resources. There was also the same kind of delusion that they could break down the (Soviet) Russian multiethnic nation, and the same underestimation of the leadership capability of the Russian officer corps—an officer corps that during the secret cooperation with the Reichswehr had been able to gain practical experience with modern war technology and had mastered German tactical doctrine.

The outcome might have been different if the memory of the eastern front during the First World War had still been alive and intact in 1941, handed down like a unique and treasured possession. Instead, its effectiveness as historical experience was lost.

Notes

1. Quote from *Kriegs-Almanach* (1915), 167–69, here 168.

2. See also Christian Geinitz, *Kriegsfurcht und Kampfbereitschaft. Das Augusterlebnis in Freiburg. Eine Studie zum Kriegsbeginn 1914.* Diss., Freiburg i.Br., Essen 1998, 116–25.

3. Max Hoffmann, *Die Aufzeichnungen des Generalmajors Max Hoffmann,* edited by Karl Friedrich Nowak, vol. 1, editions 4–6. Berlin 1930, xiii.

4. Sir Michael Howard, "Der Erste Weltkrieg—eine neue Betrachtung." In: *Der Erste Weltkrieg und das 20. Jahrhundert,* edited by Jay Winter, Geoffrey Parker, and Mary Habeck, Hamburg 2002, 19–33. See William C. Fuller Jr., *Die Ostfront.* In: ibid., 34–70, esp. 38f.

5. Rudolf Alexander Schroeder, "An die deutschen Krieger, 1. August 1914." In: *Kriegs-Almanach* (1915), 9f., here 10.

6. *Sankt Lioba Blatt,* 23/8/1914, quote from Geinitz, *Kriegsfurcht,* 117.

7. *Deutsches Offizierblatt,* 13 (1914), 982.

8. Friedrich Franz von Conring, *Mit der Division "Graf Bredow" unter Hindenburg,* Berlin 1915, 15.

9. This is according to the war correspondent with the High Command of the East Army, Paul Lindenberg, *Gegen die Russen mit der Armee Hindenburgs,* 2nd ed., Leipzig 1915, 36.

10. Rolf Brandt, *Fünf Monate an der Ostfront. Kriegsberichte,* 4th ed., Berlin 1915, 5.

11. Albrecht von Thaer, *Generalstabsdienst an der Front und in der OHL. Aus Briefen und Tagebuchaufzeichnungen 1915–1919,* edited by Siegfried A. Kaehler, Göttingen 1958, 7.

12. Notes from 4/5/1915. In: ibid., 33f., here 34.

13. Notes of 10/5/1915. In: ibid., 34f., here 34.

14. Brandt, *Fünf Monate,* 28.

15. See *Deutsches Offizierblatt,* 13 (1914), 982. Here the war correspondent von Koschützki from the *Vossische Zeitung* writes: "I have so far put down false rumors about any brutal war conduct of the Russians, as soon as I could determine the facts."

16. Erich Ludendorff, *Meine Kriegserinnerungen 1914–1918,* Berlin 1919, 53.

17. *Schlachtfelder in Ostpreussen,* edited by Wehrkreiskommando I., 2nd ed., Königsberg i. Pr. 1932, 3.

18. Hoffmann, *Die Aufzeichnungen,* vol. 1, 13.

19. On the Russian deployment plans in the prewar period, see the essay by Boris Khavkin in this volume.

20. Bernhard von Eggeling, *Die russische Mobilmachung und der Kriegsausbruch. Beiträge zur Schuldfrage am Weltkriege,* Oldenburg i. Gr., Berlin 1919, 22.

21. For completely different perspective, see Gunther Frantz, "Der russische Aufmarsch gegen Deutschland im August 1914." In: *Wissen und Wehr,* 1 (1920), 212–22; Gunter Frantz, "Die Entwicklung des Offensivgedankens im russischen Operationsplan." In: ibid., 5 (1924), 373–92.

22. Reichstag, 12th Panel. Documents from the stenographic reports on the public hearing of the subpanel (1st Subpanel): *Zur Vorgeschichte des Weltkrieges,* issue 2, *Militärische Rüstungen und Mobilmachungen,* Berlin 1921, 29–39.

23. Hermann Hammer, "Die russischen Aufmarschpläne gegen die Mittelmächte." In: *Wehrwissenschaftliche Rundschau,* 6 (1956), 165–76, here 176.

24. "Hindenburg über die Russen." In: *Granat-Splitter,* 1914, 15, 3f., here 3.

25. Max Wild, *In geheimem Auftrag an der Ostfront. Aufzeichnungen eines deutschen Nachrichten-Offiziers,* Berlin 1931, 6. Wild was initially battle ordinance officer of the AOK 8 in East Prussia and Poland, then, because of his Russian-language ability, served in espionage and counterespionage.

26. "Die Psyche des russichen Soldaten." In: *Deutsches Offizierblatt,* 14 (1915), 326f., here 326.

27. Hoffmann's notes dated 13/3/1915. In: *Hoffmann, Die Aufzeichnungen,* vol. 1, 65f., here 65.

28. Quote from *Frontalltag im Ersten Weltkrieg. Wahn und Wirklichkeit. Quellen und Dokumente,* edited by Bernd Ullrich and Benjamin Ziemann, Frankfurt a.M.1995, 127.

29. Ferdinand Bringolf, "Das Grauen." In: *Das Antlitz des Weltkrieges. Fronterlebnisse deutscher Soldaten,* edited by Ernst Jünger, Berlin 1930, 12–15, here 12.

30. Conring, *Mit der Division,* 19.

31. Ludwig Dettmann, *Ostfront. Ein Denkmal des deutschen Kampfes in Bildern und Tagebuchblättern,* Berlin 1938, 44.

32. Eugen Neter, "Der seelische Zusammenbruch der deutschen Kampffront 1918. Betrachtungen eines Frontarztes." In: *Süddeutsche Monatshefte,* 22 (1925), 1–46, here 31f. See also treatment of this issue by Anne Lipp, *Meinungslenkung im Krieg. Kriegserfahrungen deutscher Soldaten und ihre Deutung 1914–1918,* Göttingen 2003, 174–205.

33. Lipp, *Meinungslenkung,* 212–21.

34. Arnold Zweig, *Der Streit um den Sergeanten Grischa,* Potsdam 1928, 10.

35. Kurt Floericke, *Die Masurenschlachten,* Stuttgart 1916, 7.

36. Edwin Erich Dwinger, *Die Armee hinter Stacheldraht. Das sibirische Tagebuch,* Jena 1929.

37. Original German reads "Von Kultur, Keine Spur. Jede Nacht, Grosse Jagd." Quoted in Hans-Erich Volkmann, "Das Russlandbild in der Schule des Dritten Reiches." In: *Das Russlandbild im Dritten Reich,* edited by Hans-Erich Volkmann, 2nd ed., Cologne, Weimar, Vienna 1994, 225–55, here 228.

38. Bodo von Dewitz, "Schiessen oder Fotografieren? Über fotografierende Soldaten im Ersten Weltkrieg." In: *Fotogeschichte,* 12 (1992), 43, 49–60, here 56, quoted in Daniela Neuser, "Der Krieg als Reise—Private Fotografien und Feldpostkarten." In: *Der Krieg als Reise. Der Erste Weltkrieg—Innenansichten,* edited by Daniela Neuser, Siegen 1999, 86–103, here 100f.

39. Hoffmann's notes, 29/10/1914. In: *Hoffmann, Die Aufzeichnungen,* vol. 1, 59f., here 59.

40. Letter of 11/4/1915. In: Reinhold Maier, *Feldpostbriefe aus dem Ersten Weltkrieg 1914–1918,* Stuttgart 1966, 63–66.

41. Conring, *Mit der Division,* 58.

42. Rolf Brandt, *Der grosse Vormarsch 1915. Kriegsberichte,* 2nd ed., Berlin 1915, 20.

43. Ibid., 164.

44. Ibid., 13.

45. Ludwig Ganghofer, *Die Front im Osten,* Berlin, Vienna 1915, 21.

46. Quoted in Wibke Bruhns, *Meines Vaters Land. Geschichte einer deutschen Familie,* 9th. ed., Munich 2004, 63.

47. Quoted in ibid., 64.

48. Lindenberg, *Gegen die Russen,* 87.

49. On the eastern Jews in the First World War, see Gerd Koenen, *Der Russland-Komplex. Die Deutschen und der Osten 1900–1945,* Munich 2005, 66f., 73–75; quoted in ibid., 67.

50. Quoted in ibid., 74.

51. Letter from Bethmann Hollweg dated 19/11/1914 to the undersecretary of state in the Foreign Office, Arthur Zimmermann. In: *Deutsche Quellen zur Geschichte des Ersten Weltkrieges,* edited by Wolfdieter Bihl, Darmstadt 1991, 91–93, here 91. See also Holger Afflerbach, *Falkenhayn. Politisches Denken und Handeln im Kaiserreich,* Munich 1994, 259–65, 286–313.

52. See also Fritz Fischer, *Griff nach der Weltmacht. Die Kriegszielpolitik des kaiserlichen Deutschland 1914/18,* 4th ed., Düsseldorf 1971, 223–31.

53. Letter from Hopman, 3/10/1914, to von Capelle. In: *Albert Hopman. Das ereignisreiche Leben eines "Wilhelminers." Tagebücher, Briefe, Aufzeichnungen 1901 to 1920,* edited by Michael Epkenhans, Munich 2004, 451–53, here 451.

54. Hopman's notes, 7/11/1914. In: ibid., 486–88, here 488.

55. Hopman's notes, 10/11/1914. In: ibid., 492f., here 493.

56. Hopman's notes, 25/11/1914. In: ibid. 507f., here 507.

57. Hopman's notes, 6/9/1916. In: ibid., 868–70, here 870.

58. Hoffmann's notes, 29/10/1914. In: *Hoffmann, Die Aufzeichnungen,* vol. 1, 59f., here 59.

59. Hoffmann's notes, 21/10/1914. In: ibid., 58f., here 59.

60. Hoffmann's notes, 6/3/1915. In: ibid., 64f., here 64.

61. Ibid., 64f.

62. On 3 June, Przemyśl; 22 June, Lwów (Lemberg); 1 July, start of offensive from Baltic Sea to San and Bug; 5 August, capture of Warsaw.

63. Ludendorff's letter, 20/10/1915, to undersecretary in Foreign Office, Arthur Zimmermann, quote in Fischer, *Griff nach der Weltmacht,* 257.

64. Ibid., 309.

65. Hoffmann's notes, 9/1/1917. In: *Hoffmann, Die Aufzeichnungen,* vol. 1, 153f., here 154.

66. Hoffmann's notes, 28/2/1917. In: ibid., 158f.

67. Letter by von Thaer, 16/10/1915. In: *Thaer, Generalstabsdienst,* vol. 1, 42.

68. Ibid., 204–6; see also Imanuel Geiss, *Der polnische Grenzstreifen 1914–1918. Ein Beitrag zur deutschen Kriegszielpolitik im Ersten Weltkrieg 1914–1918,* Hamburg, Lübeck 1960.

69. See note of 8/6/1917. In: *Hoffmann, Die Aufzeichnungen,* vol. 1, 186.

70. See Hans-Erich Volkmann, *Die deutsche Baltikumpolitik zwischen Brest-Litovsk und Compiègne. Ein Beitrag zur "Kriegszieldiskussion,"* Cologne, Vienna 1970, 12, 16, 32, 34f., 40, 46, 50, 70–73, 76f., 95f., 98, 212, 216.

71. See *Hoffmann, Die Aufzeichnungen,* vol. 1. Here, see the biographical outline of General Hoffmann, xxiv; entry of 18/8/1918. In: ibid., 205; *Hoffmann, Die Aufzeichnungen,* vol. 2. Berlin 1930, 195–218.

72. Karl Alexander von Müller, *Mars und Venus. Erinnerungen 1914–1919,* Stuttgart 1954, 309f.

73. See also Adolf Vogt, *Oberst Max Bauer, Generalstabsoffizier im Zwielicht 1869–1929,* Osnabrück 1974, 503.

74. Oberst [Max] Bauer, *Der grosse Krieg in Feld und Heimat. Erinnerungen und Betrachtungen,* 2nd ed., Tübingen 1921, 41.

75. Ibid., 289.

76. Ibid., 302f.

77. Memorandum, Seeckt, 11/9/1922, quote from H. R. Berndorff, *General zwischen Ost und West. Aus den Geheimnissen der deutschen Republik,* Hamburg n.d., 121–29, here 125f.

78. Graf Rüdiger von der Goltz, *Meine Sendung in Finnland und im Baltikum,* Leipzig 1920; 2nd rev. ed. titled *Als politischer General im Osten (Finnland und Baltikum) 1918 und 1919,* Leipzig 1936, 6; for historiographical viewpoint, See Hans-Erich Volkmann, "Das Deutsche Reich und die baltischen Staaten 1918 bis 1920." In: *Von den baltischen Provinzen zu den baltischen Staaten. Beiträge zur Entstehungsgeschichte der Republiken Estland und Lettland 1918–1920,* edited by Jürgen von Hehn, Hans von Rimscha, and Hellmut Weiss, Marburg 1977, 378–408.

79. *Darstellungen aus den Nachkriegskämpfen deutscher Truppen und Freikorps.* 3 vols., Berlin 1936–1938, here "Zum Geleit."

80. Ernst von Salomon, "Hexenkessel Deutschland." In: *Der Kampf um das Reich,* 2nd enlarged ed., Essen n.d., 13–38, here 13.

81. Ewald Banse, *Raum und Volk im Weltkriege. Gedanken über eine nationale Wehrlehre,* Oldenburg i.O. [1932], 158.

82. Wild, *In geheimem Auftrag,* 6.

83. See also Markus Pöhlmann, "Von Versailles nach Armageddon: Totalisierungserfahrung und Kriegserwartung in deutschen Militärzeitschriften." In: *An der Schwelle zum Totalen Krieg. Die militärische Debatte über den Krieg der Zukunft 1919–1939,* edited by Stig Förster, Paderborn 2001, 322–39, here 339.

84. Wild, *In geheimem Auftrag,* 6.

14

From Ober Ost to Ostland?

Vejas Gabriel Liulevicius

This essay will focus first of all on the German conception of the future of the occupied territories in eastern Europe during the First World War, in particular the plans for what was known as Ober Ost (today, Lithuania, Latvia, Estonia, parts of Poland, and White Russia). This conception will be examined in the context of the discussion on war aims. Further, this chapter will trace possible continuities that extended into the period of the Second World War. Finally, it will look at the Reich Commissariat Ostland (Eastland) and the National Socialist policy in the east, including the genocide and plans for extensive ethnic resettlements.

The question of continuities must be treated with care and approached separately.[1] Thus, I wish to begin by stating clearly that the German occupation policy in the First World War was aimed at ethnic manipulation, something that stood in sharp contrast to the homicidal campaign of annihilation in the east during the Second World War. Nevertheless, there are important historical connections between the two events. In other words, it is fully legitimate to pose the questions: How did the expulsions and ethnic resettlements (which, as Norman Naimark has argued, ultimately turned into genocide) become thinkable?[2] And when did these policies become thinkable—was it not until 1939 to 1941, in the 1930s, or much earlier?

Beginning in 1914, three distinct stages of a process of radicalization can be identified. Initially, the experience of occupying the east during the First World War opened new vistas in terms of expectations and opportunities for action. Military leaders now looked upon lands and peoples as objects of modern population policy. The practice of colonial authority in the occupied territories made new possibilities for exerting control conceivable.

The second stage began as a result of the defeat of the Central Powers in 1918, which sparked the beginning of the process of radicalizing German perceptions of eastern Europe. As a reaction to the confusion of the ethnic mélange, people now tended to react and argue in racist categories. The failure of the *Ostpolitik* (German policy in the east) of the First World War was now blamed on the ethnic populations with whom one had had to work. Entire peoples were labeled "filthy," "unhealthy," and "dangerous." People spoke less often of "land and peoples" and increasingly of "space and race." Hitler and the National Socialist government were able to build upon this for their own specific aims.

The National Socialist regime shaped the third stage of the radicalizing process: a virulent, fanatical anti-Semitism and a radical biological racism merged with the determination to restructure eastern Europe. Supposed "lessons learned" or conclusions from the experiences of the First World War were combined with racist imperatives, which then led to the determination not just to win a war but also to bring about a "final solution."

Ober Ost

By 1915 Germany and its ally Austria-Hungary had conquered large territories in eastern Europe, wresting them from the Czarist Empire. Under the direction of the military leaders of the German Empire a curious governmental structure evolved, a military state called Ober Ost. The policy there seemed very much a result of improvisations. Because German dominance over parts of eastern Europe had come as a surprise even for the occupiers themselves, their occupation policies became characterized by adaptations to local conditions.

To trace this development more closely, however, one must first look back onto the first year of the war and the unexpected events experienced by the Germans (the collapse of the attack in the west, the trauma of the invasion of East Prussia, and the later major German conquests in eastern Europe) that formed the backdrop for later political developments. While the mass of the German Army was deployed in the west in accordance with the Schlieffen Plan, a scheme that quickly turned out to be unrealistic, the eastern provinces of the Reich were to a large extent left on their own and unprotected.[3] Because the Russian armies had mobilized and marched into East Prussia more quickly than expected, this calculated risk proved a mistake. It resulted in panic among the German civilian population and the flight of hundreds of thousands in order to escape the Russian invasion. In two major battles, the battle of Tannenberg and the battle of the Masurian Lakes (August and September 1914), General Paul von Hindenburg and his chief of staff Erich Ludendorff beat back the Russian troops, and in the early months of 1915 drove them permanently out of East Prussia. Hindenburg and Ludendorff were soon elevated to the status of national heroes.

This early event of the war was of crucial significance. The results of the two battles appeared to support the claim by the Reich government and the official propaganda that Germany was fighting a war in its own defense. The Russian threat contributed greatly to the fact that the Social Democrats cooperated in the sense of *Burgfrieden,* or truce agreement between factions. The invasion of East Prussia also seemed to have a significant impact on the home front from the perspective of mass psychology. The capture of two-thirds of the province of East Prussia proved to be the only significant instance during the war in which Imperial German territory was conquered. Although more historical research is needed to determine precisely how this invasion actually played out, German propaganda disseminated shocking images. The list of Russian crimes against civilians read as follows: thousands of deportations to Siberia, killings, rapes, arson, plundering, and executions of civilians accused of spying. By describing it as a wave of Slavic barbarism and brutality against the German homeland, the invasion was made out to be an ethnic invasion. This account prompted the petition by German intellectuals of 4 October 1914, the *Manifesto of the 93,* also known as the Appeal to the World of Culture. The signatories railed that in the east "the earth was soaked in the blood of the women and children executed by Russian hordes."[4] This image of the enemy was epitomized in the frightened cry "Cossacks are coming!" The damages suffered by East Prussia were not attributed to the war itself but to the purported mania for destruction on the part of an enemy that had ravaged occupied areas and shown excesses in the waging of war.

When German armies victoriously invaded the territories of the Czarist Empire, an event remembered afterward as the Great Advance, many of these prejudices were even further validated. Over half a million German soldiers flooded into new areas. The Central Powers experienced victories to an extent previously unknown. Galicia was reconquered, and in August and September, Warsaw, Kaunas, Brest-Litovsk, and Vilnius were taken. The front stabilized in September 1915 in front of Riga. The Russian troops were thrown back five hundred kilometers and lost all of Poland, Lithuania, Courland (southern Latvia), and western Ukraine—an area about the size of France.[5]

The actual sight of the destruction of these newly conquered countries made a deep impression on German soldiers. The region had suffered badly in the war. The Russian scorched-earth policy (which meant the conquered territories were to be left to the enemy in a chaotic condition, as in the times of Napoleon's invasion of Russia in 1812) and the mass flight of the population had laid waste to the territories in the east to an extent that had never before been seen. The wave of refugees was spurred on partly by fear of the conquerors, but also to some extent by official ethnic policies. Governmental statistics estimated that by the end of 1915 the number of refugees came to at least 3.3 million. Yet this movement of refugees was only the prelude; expulsion and flight were to become characteristic of the entire war in eastern Europe. This was also a harbinger of tragedies still to come in the twentieth century. The philosopher Hannah Arendt saw it as the Century of the Displaced Person—of the uprooted, the exiled, and the refugee. Other reports from that period estimate that in 1917 in Russia there were more than 6 million refugees (including those of the Caucasus)—that is, some 5 percent of the total population.[6] The countries that had been sacrificed now appeared mostly empty and depopulated.

German sources and reports, even those of ordinary soldiers, refer to the scorched-earth policy in particular. The infrastructure had been destroyed with an incredible thoroughness. Train tracks were torn up, rail stations burned down, telegraph lines cut, bridges blown up, fields set afire, government offices and archives evacuated. It is likely, however, that the allegedly systematic nature of this destruction was somewhat exaggerated in the reports, while the "normal" damages of war were simultaneously underestimated. Drawing attention to the Russian scorched-earth policy served a purpose in the German conduct of the war. On one hand it confirmed the enemy's brutality, and on the other it could be cited as proof that the Russian government had relinquished its claim on the area. As a poem in a German Army periodical expressed it:

> I still hear the threat of heavy steps,
> in the ruins of the city, I hear human cries,
> the sigh of villages sacrificed to fiery death,
> all around, my eyes still see the sorrow
> invoked by the infamy of the Russian Army
> against my own land, against the workings of nature!

Still, the amateur poet closes with optimism:

> That which seems forever lost,
> the German battalions
> will create anew.[7]

Ludendorff expressed the situation in a more practical manner when he wrote that in this region, "we were faced with an appalling task. We had to construct and organize everything afresh."[8]

For many German soldiers it was in this context that the first direct confrontation with the areas and people of the east took place. The first impressions were of great importance to later German perceptions of this region.[9] One particularly important insight was how different these territories were from one another, and that although they represented one unified land, the Russian Empire, that unification was only superficial.

Many German officers and soldiers perceived the countries as very primitive, seemingly out of an earlier era. The Germans had the sense of having marched into the past. The relatively primitive methods of agriculture, the lack of a forest industry or utilization of the primeval forests, and the bad condition of roads, buildings, and villages left a permanent impression. A further factor was the amazing variety in the ethnic makeup of these regions: here one found Lithuanians, Jews, Poles, Latvians, Russian, Ukrainians, White Russians, and Tatars. Later on, they came upon Estonians and indigenous German minorities, especially the Baltic German upper class of the Baltic provinces, who appeared to be related to the Reich Germans yet remained foreign. But ethnic identity was malleable and changeable—there were people who were not entirely certain which nationality they were, and others changed their national allegiances.

The first priority after these unexpected conquests had been to create and maintain "orderly circumstances," but soon new ambitions evolved in addition to this minimum requirement. While the southern part of Poland was placed under a civilian administration, all policy in the northern part was dictated by Hindenburg and Ludendorff. Their sphere of influence was called "the Land of Ober Ost" after Hindenburg's title *Oberbefehlshaber Ost* (supreme commander of all German forces in the east). Ludendorff, whose temperament and technocratic ambitions were of a completely different nature from those of his rather traditionally minded superior officer, expressed a "firm determination to create something whole."[10] Later he would write in his memoirs with an almost godly self-assurance: "My will penetrated the administration and maintained the joy of creation within it."[11] When one considers the monopoly of power held by the army and the civil servants in field gray, the resulting state can be characterized as a military utopia. It is also worth noting that the administration was not made up of average soldiers, but rather of those who had been selected by Ludendorff. His selection criteria included expertise, energy, and a technocratic ethos. As Ludendorff later wrote, he had decided "to take up the cultural work in the occupied countries that the Germans had done over many centuries. The population, made up as it is of such a mixture of races, would never accomplish anything of its own accord, and left to itself would succumb to Polish domination."[12] Consequently, the administration had to be exclusively German. A central ideological catchphrase of the state of Ober Ost was the term *Deutsche Arbeit* (German work).[13]

"German work" in this context meant a kind of administrative genius; German officials were to channel the diffuse energies of the indigenous population in service to productive goals. One of these was a predetermined goal that even during the war, new structures were to be created, and the countries were to be developed in a way that would ensure close ties with Germany in the future. Two additional areas of policy in Ober Ost were also controlled from higher up: a *Verkehrspolitik,* or movement policy, was intended as a means of bringing together the populace and economy. A comprehensive cultural program was established to guide the development of the ethnic groups, or *Völkerschaft,* as they were termed.

The movement policy was an attempt to control the region with such methods as surveillance and information gathering. To comprehend the magnitude of this self-appointed mission, one must bear in mind that Ober Ost was the size of East Prussia, West Prussia, Posen, and Pomerania combined. It held a population of 3 million people who, as previously mentioned, belonged to different ethnicities. During the battles approximately 1 million fled further east, leaving parts of the region depopulated. Now the entire migration and economic activity in Ober Ost was to come under intensive control. An administrative network was spun across the entire region. Police surveillance methods were used to enforce a system for issuing personal passes. Then the populace had to be forcefully convinced to grow used to carrying passes and being controlled. Other methods of control included population censuses and new administrative borders that could not be crossed without permission, not even in cases where villages and neighborhoods that belonged together were cut off from one another by artificial boundaries. The governmental orders were extraordinarily detailed and had to be followed absolutely. Because some of the native languages lacked the words that would enable the German administrative ordinances to be communicated, the occupiers even created new words. Generally speaking these strategies could be compared to those used in European colonies overseas, but in this case they were being applied in Europe itself. Economic control over the territory was enforced by strict ordinances. Entire harvests were confiscated, horses requisitioned, and raw materials important to the war effort collected. The rich forest assets of the region, especially in the primeval forest of Bialowieza, were exploited intensively, and forced labor battalions were conscripted. The results of these economic measures were two-sided. The goals of autarchy for the administrative territory and relief for the home front were in fact fulfilled, but because many of the bureaucratic measures came into conflict with the requirements for economic success, the price had to be paid by the native population, whose sympathies, along with any possible economic upswing, were lost.

The control over the population had a further important basis: the fear of contagious illnesses that haunted eastern Europe, such as typhus, malaria, cholera, and typhoid spotted fever, as the epidemics occurring in the civilian sector endangered the troops at the front.

While people were thus turned into objects of organizational policy, they also saw very useful improvements with respect to public health and hygiene. Among the authoritarian measures carried out were such things as forced immunization vaccinations, forced disinfections, inspections during the building of toilets and sewers in the cities, and the establishment of bordellos for soldiers. *Seuchentruppen* (epidemic units) would seal off and disinfect areas where epidemics had broken out. A network of laboratories and examination centers was created in the occupied territories, scientific outposts in a biological war in the middle of the world war. This work was useful but also dangerous: ten of the fifty German medical officers in Poland died of typhus.[14] Overall, this occupation policy led to a situation in which the officials of Ober Ost became accustomed to a particular kind of administrative thinking that merged with the categories of people and places.

This kind of thinking was an integral part of the German extensively specialized and comprehensive cultural program, a truly amazing plan in its scope considering the tremendous material demands of a total war. Periodicals were published in the languages of the various ethnic groups, museum exhibits were organized, and archeological excavations and archival research were undertaken in order to bring the indigenous population closer to the history of the region (with particular attention given to purported signs of earlier German cultural influences).

The native population welcomed the founding of schools with instruction in their native languages, although from the first grade on, the German language was taught as a school subject. It was often taught by older, authoritarian German soldiers with the goal of bringing the various local ethnic groups closer to the superior German cultural sphere. Critics in field gray attended theater performances of the different ethnic groups in order to evaluate them. Rigorous censorship measures forbade any discussion of political themes. The local people were encouraged to adopt the best of German culture, and therefore German theaters were allowed to stage only the classics, not light entertainment dramas. Schiller's *Wallenstein* was especially popular among the German audiences, perhaps because it was set during the Thirty Years' War and seemed to parallel the current grave world situation. The cultural program was aimed at defining ethnic blocs that would be suitable for further German mentoring in the future. The political goals remained firm: in the future eastern Europe the Lithuanians were to form a counterweight to the Poles, a role that even the White Ruthenians would be able to fulfill after their expected renaissance. But ultimately these schemes came to nothing. Overall the cultural measures from above had little influence on the consciousness of the civilian population.

A further important dimension of the occupation in the east was the German soldiers' experience on the front, which had a profound impact. Approximately 2 to 3 million German soldiers served in the east (an average of 1.3 million per year, about half as many as on the western front). A key aspect of their experience was the sense of disorientation in an unfamiliar environment and the very understandable human desire to return to one's homeland as soon as possible. The American military historian Dennis Showalter termed them "conscript conquerors," for whom any sort of conviction as to the meaning of their sojourn far from Germany was always mixed with homesickness. The region itself was perceived as dangerous and primitive. In the famous declaration "Ideas of 1914," numerous German thinkers and propagandists advanced the thesis that Germany was fighting a war against the artificial values of Western civilization in the name of genuine German culture. In the east, however, this was not the case: here the German soldiers were confronted instead by *Unkultur*, or barbarism, a word often found lurking in the historical source materials. The German soldiers obviously ranked the folk of the east into a hierarchy at whose apex (no matter what the hierarchy might have looked like further down the scale) stood the Germans themselves, independent and separate from the local turmoil of nationalities and ethnic groups. This sense of being of a superior rank was wholly consistent with good intentions and compassion. Here it was not about racism as an ideology of hatred but about the conviction that these people were not equals. This attitude was not unique to the Germans—it was commonly held by all Western nations at that time. In any case, there was an entire spectrum of reactions to the indigenous populace, ranging from compassion to appreciation for their respective cultures all the way to a purported validation of prejudices and negative images of foreigners.

The encounter with the eastern Jews in the cities, villages, and shtetls was of great significance. The Jews were among the few groups who, through Yiddish or other languages, could communicate with the Germans. Yet even in this case there was no monolithic reaction. In Schaulen (Šiauliai, Lithuania) the mayor, a German soldier appointed by the occupiers, ordered Jewish women to clean the market square. While some of the German soldiers laughed at the women, others were enraged over this degrading treatment and harshly condemned the mayor. It was a scenario with ambivalent meanings, prompting varying reactions. Anti-Semites within the administration protested that that their comrades did not sufficiently acknowledge what they considered to be the danger presented by Jews. They considered it delusional to think that the Jews were a German-friendly element in the country. For German-Jewish soldiers, however, contact with eastern Jews held a special significance, as their own self-image was often affected by their acquaintance with kindred communities.

From the perspective of a history of mentalities, it can generally be said that the experience of German soldiers, officers, and civil government employees in the occupied east was essentially an experience of spaces. The east was perceived as a land of war: bleak, depopulated, and underdeveloped. It represented a tabula rasa for the Germans, ready to be written upon, especially with a view to later wars.

The Discussion of War Aims

The history of Ober Ost is also inherent to the discussion of war aims that holds so prominent a position in historiography, particularly within the context of the fierce ongoing debates in the wake of the 1961 publication of Fritz Fischer's work *Griff nach der Weltmacht* (Germany's Aims in the First World War).

During the war there arose a broad consensus in German society regarding extensive changes in the political map of Europe: German influence would have to be extended into neighboring countries. In favor of this argument was Germany's strategic situation: since Germany was fighting in its own defense, the supposedly vulnerable position of the country had to be strengthened for the sake of the future. The effective British blockade underscored the vulnerability of the Reich at that time. This position met with general approval, and while it was less a factor among the ranks of the Social Democrats, not everyone among them appeared immune to this line of argument. There were, however, different ideas about how this geopolitical transformation was to be achieved. Two variations were up for debate. On one side, the military authorities and pan-German and conservative parties favored the direct annexation of large territories (or the creation of a personal union with the House of Hohenzollern). They argued that the expected large territory gains in the industrialized lands such as Belgium and northern France made it necessary to acquire agricultural lands in the east in the interest of economic balance so that the character of German society would be preserved. To this end, plans for German settlements were already being circulated. On the opposing side of this argument there were political groups that proposed a less radical course. A chain of satellite states was to be established; these states would maintain their national autonomy and cultural uniqueness but would be integrated into a kind of central European union with Germany as the geopolitical center of power. While no decision was reached, the two separate concepts evolved further on their own, in concert with the events of the war and changes within Germany. But above all, the increase of authority of the 3rd OHL, or Army High Command, led to a new situation: in August 1916 Hindenburg and Ludendorff were promoted to its top leadership (afterward, the administration in Ober Ost continued working in their spirit). The fact that these two victors of Tannenberg still did not succeed in translating the discussion of war aims into a successful war policy can be seen in the example of Poland. In fact, in November 1916, at Hindenburg and Ludendorff's insistence, Poland's future independence was proclaimed. However, the Polish armies that were expected to be deployed alongside the troops of the Central Powers did not appear, and therefore the prospects of peace negotiations with Russia were simultaneously eroded.

What had been envisioned for the future of Ober Ost came to light particularly after the Kreuznach War Aims Conference of 23 April 1917. Courland and Lithuania were to come under German control, as were the Baltic provinces, while the future Poland was to be held by German allies as leverage. This strategic vision was based on key considerations as to further future conflicts. A map showing the distribution of ethnic groups reveals how very much blended the settlement territories of these groups were, and moreover, they were in no respect closer to the Russians mentally than they were to the Germans. "Plan Neuland" (the plan for establishing a new territory) was prepared in the fall of 1917 for the purpose of gathering information on how future economic controls could be achieved and German settlements established in order to implant a living defensive line of model settlements composed of fighting farmers, or *Wehrbauern*.

One related project shows a further push toward a new population policy—the plans and preparations for the creation of a Polish border strip. This border strip was more than just modest border realignment; several variations of the concept also provided for ethnic resettlements, something that Ludendorff characterized as a "generous settlement policy backed by powerful intentions."[15] These plans, researched by Imanuel Geiss, show how popular such concepts were: "The government of the Reich, the Prussian state government, the general government in Warsaw, and the German Supreme Command were occupied with these kinds of deliberations."[16] The plans had their roots in the prewar period, in the anti-Polish sentiments of the All German Party, and in the settlement policy of the Prussian settlement commission. The war, however, accelerated the wishful projections of colonialism and smoothed the way for more radical methods, which had now become thinkable and worth considering.

A particular detail found in one of these proposals clearly revealed how earlier events in the war could influence this development. In a memorandum to the Reich government on 20 December 1914, the governor of East Prussia, von Batocki, proposed, among other things, the acquisition of virgin territory in the east, a total of thirty-six thousand square kilometers having an existing population of 2 million, and promised the prospect of "resettlement." Von Batocki's line of reasoning is of special interest here because his ideas for resettlement draw on Russian ethnic migrations of the prewar era and, in an unexpected manner, on the German evacuation of East Prussia in 1914: "If Russia, despite the deficiencies in its administration in recent years, managed to transplant a peasant population numbering upward of a hundred thousand per year across hundreds of miles without difficulties and hardships; if in East Prussia in August 1914 it was possible that far more than one hundred thousand countrymen could, without the possibility of any sort of official organization, manage the flight overland by wagon with horses and cattle, covering thirty to forty miles going out and the same during the return journey in the six weeks following without suffering essential damage to persons and living property, then this is evidence that with proper preparation, resettlement is possible for the most part without damage to the rural population."[17]

Later plans, such as those championed by Ludendorff himself, envisioned resettlement and expulsion. While the possibilities for the deportation of Poles and Jews were being contemplated, there was hope of being able to resettle Russian-Germans or Germans living in other foreign countries in these territories. Nevertheless it must be stated that in most of these designs, the promised resettlement was supposed to be voluntary (how unrealistic this expectation was is anyone's guess) or compensated (mostly in the form of an expansion of Polish territory toward the east). It is also of key importance that the plans for a border strip were not, in fact, implemented—as much out of practical considerations as concern for the consequences of such a policy in terms of international law and worldwide public opinion. As Geiss notes: "One must not fail to recognize that prior to 1918, despite any radicalism in their rhetoric, the leading German classes at that time still were bound to legal norms . . . when it came to an open breach of international law through the annexation during the war, no one had been able to make that decision."[18]

In any case, it is worth noting that such settlement plans were considered at all. The "radicalism of the rhetoric" and, to paraphrase Hegel, of the intellect, could and should have consequences, even if no deeds are involved. During the war, countries and people appeared to the occupiers as objects of modern population policy; new possibilities for control were conceived. The categories of "land and peoples" able to be remodeled at will found increasingly broader application and differed in subtle ways from the categories of "country and population," a formulation that still expressed a certain justification and recognition of earlier circumstances. As the popular slogan of that time expressed it, "War is war." Actions that were hardly reasonable earlier were now justified by the extraordinary circumstances. This dialectic was celebrated by the cultural policy in Ober Ost, although it had found expression much earlier in literature, for instance, in the previously mentioned Schiller trilogy *Wallenstein.*

> Easily side by side the thoughts reside
> yet hard in the area
> the objects push themselves
> where one takes a seat, the other must retreat
> whichever one does not want to be pushed away, must push:
> This is where conflict reigns and only the strong are victorious.[19]

Deliberations over possible resettlements were in no way unique to the Germans; this was a global phenomenon, as evidenced by the "scorched-earth" policy (which was often aimed against Jews and other minorities of the czarist government) or the policy of the Ottoman Empire, where the deportation of the Armenians in 1915 led to a genocide in which 1 million men, women, and children died—an intensification of total war never before imagined.

The discussion of war aims in the east appeared to have come to an end when, on 3 March 1918, the Peace Treaty of Brest-Litovsk was signed with Lenin's Bolsheviks, who had come to power in Russia. It was a bitter peace, one that wrested Poland, Lithuania, the Baltic provinces, Finland, and Ukraine from the Russian state. Although there was still no victory in the west, this was nevertheless an hour of triumph in which the war aims in the east appeared within reach.

Collapse

The collapse of the German war efforts in the fall of 1918 was all the more difficult to accept because it directly followed the apparent victory in the east. Once the victors became the vanquished, the priority in eastern Europe was a disciplined retreat. Eastern European peoples like the Poles now demanded their national sovereignty.

The end of the war triggered veritable streams of refugees pushing toward Germany: 150,000 German prisoners of war, 10,000 deportees from East Prussia, and 120,000 refugees of German descent from Russia and the former Baltic provinces.[20] In addition, there were Germans who had resettled there from the eastern territories that had fallen to Poland. These migratory movements were an actual modern *Völkerwanderung,* or mass migration, with all of the usual side effects—that is to say, enormous political, economic, and hygienic problems.

The November 1918 armistice in the west did not put an end to the clashes in the east. In the Baltic region, the brutal fighting continued in the Freikorps battles of 1918 and 1919. The Freikorps, or German volunteer units, moved eastward. The so-called *Baltikumer* (Baltic fighters) about twenty thousand to forty thousand men, continued fighting against the advancing Red Army and the weak military forces of the Baltic republics. This undertaking had no realistic political goals but was instead a violent extension of the world war, and one that was more than ever without constraint. As Rudolf Höss, who was later the commandant of Auschwitz, explained: "The battles in the Baltic states were of a doggedness and ferocity that I have never experienced in any Freikorps battles before or since. There was no actual front, and the enemy was everywhere. And when a battle took place, it became butchery to the point of total destruction. . . . I believed at that time that there could never be a more extreme human mania for destruction."[21]

Evidence left behind by the Freikorps fighters reveals exaggerated images of the enemy based on the ideas harbored by ethnic groups in those areas who no longer wanted to tolerate their earlier subordination. Along with these images also came the fear of Bolshevism, which became widespread in the middle-class society of Europe.

The lost war developed into a deep trauma, and the defeat, especially with respect to the eastern front, was difficult to grasp. As Golo Mann noted: "The Peace of Brest-Litovsk has been called the forgotten peace, but the Germans have not forgotten it. They know that they defeated Russia and sometimes they look upon that proudly as the real, if unrewarded, European achievement of the war."[22] After the war, several former Ober Ost officials came to the conclusion that it was not their plans that had been worthless but the "human material" they had had to work with. The achievements of the occupying government would now pass to others, although it appeared doubtful whether these products of German work could actually be preserved. From the German perspective, the eastern European ethnic groups had demonstrated that they were immune to culture. Stereotypes were disseminated of an east without culture, one that could not be cultivated but instead had to be cleansed. Fears of Bolshevism were equated with the chaos of the east. Many of these fears, worries, and concerns of the postwar era were reduced to one common denominator. Germany's loss of about 13 percent of its territory and the "bleeding borders" of the country were issues utilized by right-wing radicals in order to portray the Germans as a "people without space."

The National Socialists' Ostland

The rising National Socialist movement, as is well known, gained strength from the events and experiences of the First World War. In Munich, Hitler and his early comrades were part of Ludendorff's circle, along with former Ober Ost officials and veterans of the wars for independence in the Baltic regions. The ideology of the Nazis merged radical racism and anti-Semitism with claims on *Lebensraum* in the east. In the National Socialist worldview, Communism plus Jewish identity equaled "Judeo-Bolshevism." Members of eastern European ethnic groups were categorized as *Untermenschen,* or subhumans. After 1933 these delusions were being put into practice. The attack on Poland followed the "ethnic reallocation" of areas that were to come in direct contact with Germany: by spring 1941, 365,000 Poles and Jews were resettled elsewhere, replaced by "ethnic Germans." In his function as "Reich Commissioner for the Strengthening of the German National Character," Himmler organized vast new colonization and resettlement programs. His aides were proud of the "tough" and "realistic" ethos of these programs. Operating simultaneously was "Operation Tannenberg," in which as many as 50,000 Poles and Jews fell victim to death squads, an action intended to disempower Poland's society.

In June 1941, the invasion of the Soviet Union followed, and with it an enormous wave of murders in what was known as the "final solution"—the genocide against the Jewish communities of eastern Europe, in which millions of victims lost their lives. This war of extermination was a conscious act. Just how consciously the National Socialists proceeded is clearly evidenced in the criminal orders from the Reich commissioner (Himmler) mandating the murder of civilians and hostages and the abuse of prisoners of war, who died by the millions. These orders presupposed an image of the enemy as Untermenschen. The brutality was rationalized by claims that it was done in order to preempt atrocities by the enemy. August 1941 saw the establishment of Reich Commissariats in the occupied territories: the Reich Commissariat of Ukraine under Erich Koch and the Reich Commissariat of Ostland under Hinrich Lohse, the latter consisting of Lithuania, Latvia, Estonia, and White Russia. This occupation, too, was one of appalling brutality—in White Russia alone, the deaths came to approximately 1 million.[23] While the government of Ober Ost had had to improvise, this occupation had been prepared well in advance ideologically. Relevant works by members of the Ober Ost administration were quoted and circulated as an orientation to their own brutal occupation policy in these areas. There were also cases of continuity of personnel within the administration, especially in the case of former Baltic Freikorps fighters.[24] The propaganda slogans of the Reich Commissariats in Ostland were "Aufbau und Kultur" (Development and Culture) or "Aufbau im Osten" (Development in the East), but in later times they acquired a completely different meaning than in the First World War. Culture was no longer something that could or should be conveyed; it was considered to be an attribute of "ethnicity," a characteristic of racial and biological value.

At last the "General Plan for the East" was developed, which outlined a vision for the future of eastern Europe twenty-five years after the end of the war. It described a radicalized idea of the area of the east. Produced by the planning authorities of the SS, the design of the plan was presented to Himmler in June 1942 and was developed further in the following years. Among other things, it provided for the resettlement of more than 30 million Slavs to Siberia and their "decimation." A purely Germanic master race was to settle the areas and rule over a slave population. Even this was not final, because they also imagined pushing the ethnic borders further east through future wars in case more Lebensraum should become necessary. Hitler himself insisted that the indigenous populace was not to be cultivated, civilized, or Germanized but rather kept in a primitive condition and be thereby doomed to extinction. These plans for eastward expansion were part of a still larger project, racial selection among the Germans themselves.[25]

Discontinuities and Continuities

In conclusion I would like to address the issue of discontinuities and continuities. "Continuity," as Ian Kershaw has defined it, "is, in fact, the historian's abbreviation for the persistence, survival, or retention of the *dominant* strains and features of a social and political system."[26] It is understood that continuity is not the same as identity or conformity. Ober Ost cannot be placed on the same plane as National Socialist Ostland. Nor does continuity necessarily imply any teleology—history might also have followed a different course than it did. The concept of continuity should instead be used to investigate historical events to determine whether they can be interpreted as stages of an evolutionary process. In a comparison between Ober Ost and Ostland, the differences are clear. While the cultural policy of Ober Ost was aimed at ethnic manipulation or Germanization, in their war the Nazis committed premeditated murder. A further point of contrast between the radical anti-Semitism of the National Socialists and in the nationality policies of Ober Ost is that in the latter there were guidelines for the equal treatment of all ethnic groups. As previously mentioned, the reactions of German soldiers to their encounter with the eastern Jews were ambivalent, but in no respect were they all marked with anti-Semitism. Finally, Ober Ost differs from Ostland in the area of planning. The administration of Ober Ost was improvised and developed step by step as reactions to the pressures of the circumstances, while the National Socialists (despite all strategic changes of direction toward the end of the war, as they tried to win over the eastern Europeans for a defense against the Soviet Union) stepped forth consciously in pursuit of an ideology and as champions of a worldview. A further essential difference is that in the Second World War the level of violence acquired a dimension hitherto unknown. The emphasis of the differences is not to say that during the First World War no ideological aims had been developed. As I have demonstrated, the case is quite the opposite. The radicalization by the Nazis was not "simply" a quantitative intensification of the First World War—their consciously implemented atrocities had a completely new quality. It is the sudden changeover from quantity into a new quality that makes the answer to the question of continuities so complex. Possibly it would be better to speak of lines of development in this case, whether this development was intended or not.

In this essay I have attempted to address the patterns of interpretation and action that made the policy of resettlement and expulsion of entire peoples—in other words, the ethnic population policy in eastern Europe—increasingly conceivable and reasonable. Although these ideas were not realized during the First World War, the National Socialists took them up with enthusiasm and carried them further. The results of the latter of these two lines of development were no less fatal. The representatives of Ober Ost as well as those of the Reich Commissariat of Ostland drew on the concept of culture as a means of bolstering the mission in the east. Yet their respective understandings of culture were contradictory: in the first instance, culture was used as a method of education for domestication—through performances of Schiller, newspapers, and the creation of a professional terminology in the local languages for administrative structures. In the second instance, Himmler maintained that the master race needed slaves for its culture—culture was now understood as a racial characteristic that could not be passed on. A dialectical process had run its course. Drawing on Ian Kershaw, it can also be argued here that the continuities harbored discontinuities within themselves that would later come to fruition.[27] The Nazis used continuities in order to cause breaches. While they skillfully understood how to maintain the appearance of continuity, their policy was nonetheless a breach with the Great War that had preceded them.

Notes

1. See also Bruno Thoss, "Die Zeit der Weltkriege—Epochen als Erfahrungseinheit? In: *Erster Weltkrieg-Zweiter Weltkrieg: Ein Vergleich. Krieg, Kriegserlebnis, Kriegserfahrung in Deutschland,* published under the auspices of the Militärgeschichtliches Forschungsamt der Bundeswehr, edited by Bruno Thoss and Hans-Erich Volkmann, Paderborn 2002, 7–30.

2. Norman Naimark, *Fires of Hatred: Ethnic Cleansing in Twentieth-Century Europe,* Cambridge, MA 2001.

3. On German war planning in 1914, see Terence Zuber's chapter in the German edition of this book.

4. "Aufruf an die Kulturwelt vom 4.10.1914," reprint. In: *Aufrufe und Reden deutscher Professoren,* edited by Klaus Böhme, Stuttgart 1975, 48.

5. Peter Gatrell, *A Whole Empire Walking: Refugees in Russia during World War I,* Bloomington, IN 1999, 31.

6. Ibid., 3.

7. Max Hamm, "Ein Rückblick." In: *Wacht im Osten. Feldzeitung der Armee-Abteilung Scheffer,* 819, 28/2/1918, BA-MA, PH 8/73.

8. Erich Ludendorff, *Meine Kriegserinnerungen 1914–1918,* Berlin 1919, 146.

9. Vejas Gabriel Liulevicius, *Kriegsland im Osten. Eroberung, Kolonialisierung und Militärherrschaft im Ersten Weltkrieg,* Hamburg 2002.

10. Ludendorff, *Meine Kriegserinnerungen,* 145.

11. Ibid., 161.

12. Ibid., 138.

13. It originated with an author from the German Romantic period of the nineteenth century, Wilhelm Heinrich Riehl, also known as the Vater der Volkskunde (Father of Folk Studies).

14. Paul Weindling, *Epidemics and Genocide in Eastern Europe, 1890–1945,* Oxford 2000, 78.

15. Quoted in Imanuel Geiss, *Der polnische Grenzstreifen 1914–1918. Ein Beitrag zur deutschen Kriegszielpolitik im Ersten Weltkrieg,* Lübeck 1960, 11.

16. Ibid., 5.

17. Quoted in ibid., 76.

18. Ibid., 149.

19. Friedrich Schiller, *Wallensteins Tod,* act 2, scene 2, lines 788–92.

20. Weindling, *Epidemics and Genocide,* 112.

21. Rudolf Höss, *Kommandant in Auschwitz. Autobiographische Aufzeichnungen von Rudolf Höss,* Stuttgart 1958, 34.

22. Golo Mann, *Deutsche Geschichte des 19. und 20. Jahrhunderts,* Frankfurt 1958, 665. (*History of Germany since 1789.* Praeger 1968, 33.)

23. Bernhard Chiari, *Alltag hinter der Front. Besatzung, Kollaboration und Widerstand in Weissrussland 1941–1944,* Düsseldorf 1998 (= *Schriften des Bundesarchivs,* 53).

24. Hans-Heinrich Wilhelm, "Personelle Kontinuitäten in Baltischen Angelegenheiten auf deutscher Seite von 1917/19 bis zum Zweiten Weltkrieg?" In: *The Baltic in International Relations between the World Wars,* edited by John Hiden and Aleksander Loit, Stockholm 1988 (= *Acta Universitatis Stockhomiensis.Studia baltica Stockhomiensia,* 3), 157–70.

25. Götz Aly, "Bevölkerungspolitische Selektion als Mittel der sozialen Neuordnung." In: *Der nationalsozialistische Krieg,* edited by Norbert Frei und Hermann Kling, 137–45, Frankfurt 1990.

26. Ian Kershaw, "1933: Continuity or Break in German History?" In: *History Today,* January 1983, 13f.

27. Ibid., 18.

Part 3

The Culture of Remembrance of the First World War

15

Introductory Remarks

Rainer Rother

The war that began in 1914 was a European war between major powers that were locked in alliances against one another. It was a war that quickly spilled over onto large areas of the globe, which in many respects was a first for the twentieth century. Militarily, with the mobilization of armies of millions, with new kinds of weapons such as U-boats, airplanes, and tanks, with the use of gas and bombardments of enemy cities, it was the first "modern" war, at least on European ground. It forced the organization of the economy into serving the needs of waging war. Further, this war had a new character in which propaganda played a part, for without support or at least cooperation from the inhabitants it could not have been carried on for such a long time. The populations of the involved countries reached the point where they could no longer delude themselves that the war would end within a short time frame, nor could they continue to believe that they would remain untouched by war events.

For many countries the war ended a long period of peace, in some cases an interlude of more than forty years. Some members of the population and many cultural institutions coped with the war in the manner of museum curators, in a sense, by investing in collections. A series of illustrated war chronicles was available by subscription, and such a collection could be expanded with a special series of books on world war topics or with various postcard series about the Great War. Almost immediately upon the outbreak of war, the public counterpart of collector mania in the private sphere began. The flowering of museums of that time carried the seeds of later national museums. Inspired by the certainty of being witness to an event whose future impact could not be overestimated, private individuals, libraries, and museums reacted with an almost unprecedented degree of collecting. In her chapter, Christine Beil focuses on the example of the German Reich and the considerable energies it devoted to its genre of war exhibits. Through these various displays, the exhibits created an emotional bridge between the battle front and the home front. They responded to the growing need to know what it was actually like at the front, which they accomplished with their displays of tangible three-dimensional objects. As a form of propaganda, these exhibits were unique and especially impressive compared to simple words and slogans. The exhibits were an effective cultural weapon whose purpose was to strengthen the visitors' self-concept and their concept of the enemy, although over the duration of the war, amid the ever-increasing desire for peace, they proved to be no more effective than most other forms of propaganda.

When the fighting came to an end, there was no immediate, generally accepted form of commemoration in Germany. Commemorations were often controversial, even contested. The other countries involved in the war, however, developed their own unique cultures of remembrance. These forms of remembrance rested for the most part on the question of whether the respective country counted itself among the victors or the vanquished. The latter had a more difficult task of developing a culture of remembrance that would be accepted by a large part of the populace. For central and eastern Europe in particular, the fighting did not end in 1918 but instead continued on in the form of interstate war, civil war, and revolution. In terms of remembrance this meant that any dates these countries settled on for commemorations were problematic. From the perspective of some countries, such as Poland and the Baltic states, however, these dates also brought them their own nationhood and for them, they would always be defining moments.

With the Second World War, the memory of the First World war did not merely fade—in most cases it lost its potential function as a central episode in the collective memory. The Holocaust and war of extermination, even in comparison to the events between 1914 and 1918, clearly represented a breach in what we know as civilization. In Germany, after a weary, decades-long, and much-contested process, something like a collective memory of the crimes of the Second World War has gradually evolved. In the process, however, the First World War, the "great seminal catastrophe" of the twentieth century, became a pale memory. Similarly, in the Soviet Union, the second War of the Fatherland was officially interpreted as a legitimization of its system, while references to the First World War lost all significance in the collective memory. Using the Moscow City Fraternal Cemetery as an example, Kristiane Janeke illustrates the way in which a memorial site established at the start of the First World War became devalued after the victory of the Russian Revolution. This military cemetery, intended as a structure of world war remembrance, was forgotten, just as such remembrance in general has been buried in the process of "deconstruction." A parallel "new construction," as it were, was created in the collective memory from completely different material. It was only after 1989, and now once more under the auspices of politics, that attempts could be made to reestablish practices of remembrance in the former Soviet Union. These practices attempt to associate themselves with the earlier culture of remembrance, although it is no accident that they often do so in a parochial and obtrusive manner.

Yet even where the First World War is still present today in various forms of commemoration, such as in France and Great Britain, one can hardly assume that there has been a continuing remembrance without a break in continuity. The successful founding of new museums about the First World War—such as the Historial de la Grande Guerre in Péronne (opened in 1992) or the In Flanders Fields Museum in Ypres (1993)—is certainly more of an expression of a new way of thinking about the events of 1914–1918 than it is a result of an unbroken tradition. Nevertheless, on the part of the former Western Allies, continuities can be found that have no counterpart in either the cultures of the Central Powers or in those of Russia. One example of a newly created culture of remembrance, which even after the First World War sometimes proved to be an example worth following, is the laying to rest of the Unknown Soldier, the first occurrence of which I treat in my essay in this section. This ritual of laying to rest of an anonymous body may be especially appropriate for the "short" twentieth century. It began as a form of commemoration of the immense losses of the First World War and was adopted by the Soviet Union in 1967 to honor the dead of the Second World War. With the later successful identification of the Unknown Soldier from the Vietnam War (entombed in 1984, identified 1998), the practice became, as it were, an anachronism.

The culture of remembrance represented by the Unknown Soldier comes under the heading of communicative memory, meaning that it is a kind of memory that is least partially transmitted orally. Gundula Bavendamm points out in her chapter that with the advent of internet, an essentially globally available platform is offered today, which is quite worthy of respect from the standpoint of the culture of remembrance. Websites of museums, archives, organizations, and private individuals concerning the First World War attract great numbers of visitors. Bavendamm, following the ideas of Aleida and Jan Assmann, finds that these websites are rightly categorized under the heading of cultural memory. In proportions similar to existing remembrances of historical science and popular historiography, the German-language internet websites are fewer in comparison to those in French and particularly English. The wealth of English-language websites on the First World War in this very modern information medium bears witness to the general observation that nowhere is the fostering of remembrance of the war as ardent as it is in Great Britain, Canada, Australia, and New Zealand. As Kristiane Janeke notes, even the tendency toward historical remembrance on Russian internet sites can be categorized under the rubric of the "new construction" of historical remembrance.

Yet it can be concluded that the culture of remembrance of the First World War is gradually becoming integrated into the context of remembrance of the twentieth century as a whole. This was apparent in 2004 in the exhibit by the German Historical Museum, *The World War, 1914–1918: Event and Remembrance.* While ten years earlier, the exhibit *Die letzten Tage der Menschheit: Bilder des Ersten Weltkrieges* (The Last Days of Mankind: Images from the First World War) was almost the only platform that dealt with the First World War, the year 2004 saw something of an upswing in First World War remembrance in Germany, including special issues of periodicals, magazine series, television documentaries, and commemorative articles in newspapers. It now appears that the First World War is beginning to acquire more priority in the creation of historical continuities. This increased attention is not because changes have taken place in the German culture of remembrance but because after the events of 1989, changes have occurred in the historical perspective.

16

War Exhibitions

Forms of Presentation of the World War for the Homeland Front

Christine Beil

From the very beginning, the First World War was put on exhibition. Be it in Great Britain, France, or in the German Empire, the outbreak of the war set off a virtual collecting mania that lasted through its final days. In Paris, one of the most famous of the contemporary war exhibits was opened by a married couple named Leblanc; in London in the spring of 1917, the Imperial War Museum was established, one of the largest war museums in Europe.[1] But nowhere else did the collecting and exhibition of war-related items reach the intensity or extent associated with German war exhibitions.

While German soldiers fought on the front, senior citizens' organizations, soldiers' associations, schools, business concerns, small local museums, welfare agencies, other public institutions, and private individuals began collecting and putting on display everything having to do with the war. And although a great portion of the civil population was starving, their lives defined by shortages, Germans could attend exhibitions and gape in astonishment over weapons, spoils of war, ration coupons, and ingredients used as food substitutions or extenders (*Ersatzmittel*). War was *the* subject of the day, one that drew in hundreds of thousands of visitors.

New exhibition pieces from the current theaters of war constantly arrived at museums and exhibitions, making these venues increasingly important sources of news coverage on the war. These exhibitions appeared to be one of the most useful forms of media at that time for making war-related events comprehensible to the home front. Civilians saw "a fascinating supplement to the abstract reporting from the theater of war" or "a visual representation of the horrors and dangers . . . that their father or brother confronted on the field of battle."[2] This addresses a particular feature of the exhibitions that acquired vital importance at that time: their ability to engage the senses and create an emotional bridge between the experiential sphere of the front and the society of the home front, two realms separated by space but parallel in time. The items on display from the front made it possible to bring the distant military experiential world closer to those who remained at home. When the German war exhibition visited Berlin, one journalist wrote: "From now on, with our deeper knowledge, we will understand much more of what [the soldiers] have to write and to say."[3] In view of the enforced separation, whose duration only increased, of the soldier from his family members, the power of these exhibitions must not be underestimated.

This essay will explore some of the most important war exhibits and war museums in the German Empire. In keeping with the thematic focus of this volume and in view of the wealth of material offered by these exhibits, this chapter will focus on two areas: the image of the German east and the image of the enemy as they were propagandized in museums and exhibits.

The Berlin Zeughaus as a Medium of Reassurance

Unlike the image portrayed in the propaganda, the military museums of the German Reich did not reflect a nation united. Prussia, Bavaria, Wurttemberg, and Saxony paid homage to their armies in their own respective military museums.[4] For decades the Zeughaus in Berlin, today the seat of the German Historical Museum, held a special status among all of these others due to its close connection to the kaiser.[5] While the army museums in Munich, Stuttgart, and Dresden only occasionally received items captured from the enemy, throughout the war years the Zeughaus was supplied with large inventories of enemy weapons, uniforms, and pieces of equipment from collection points for captured goods at the front as well as from the Friedrich Krupp AG.

Once the Zeughaus had become a museum, trophies of war were its primary focus. Further, the overall sculptural design of the building carried allegorical representations of triumph, from the superstructures on its battlements in the shape of trophies to the Schinkel-style vitrines.[6] Further, most of the specimens the museum contained were captured pieces of equipment from victorious battles of the Prussian-German Army from the Wars of Unification up to the Boxer Rebellion in China. Beginning in August 1914 war trophies from the world war were lined up for display. Individual pieces were shown in a manner that represented the chronological and typological development of weaponry. Despite the fact that this war had expanded into an industrial mass war, and the huge quantities of captured equipment allowed the press to deduce

During the war the exhibition at the Berlin Zeughaus was constantly supplied with new pieces of captured goods from all fronts. (Bibliothek für Zeitgeschichte Stuttgart, Neg. No. 570/8a)

that Germany was on the road to victory, the guidelines for curating the collection still adhered to traditional forms. The meticulous selection of individual weapons in the exhibit was not intended merely to further understanding of the complexities of this mass war but also to place the chaos of war into an orderly system, to show war as having evolved into a traditional, historically legitimized pattern.

This is not to say that there was an attempt to cover up the destructiveness of the war and the disintegration of civilizing strictures. In fact, nearly all objects on exhibit bore evidence of destruction and violence. The producers of these exhibitions found these signs of battle important in helping to "bring the events of the battle closer to the viewer's understanding and sensitivity."[7] However, to avoid undermining people's acceptance of the use of violence as a necessary means of conducting the war, the conflict's horrors could be displayed only to a limited extent. The process of constructing the desired image of war entailed downplaying elements that did not fit into the representation the museums intended to convey. The damaged captured equipment sent an unmistakable message about the military superiority of the German Army. These visible traces of use and destruction meant that there was no need of the written word for further verification of German victory. By putting these objects on public display, it was as if the military enemy was defeated once more, symbolically, before the visitors' own eyes. As to the strength of the German weapons, however, visitors had to use their own imagination or information gathered from the press—military secrecy guidelines forbade showing German war equipment in the Zeughaus or other war exhibits.[8]

The character of the war as an industrialized mass war was conveyed to visitors not through any special form of presentation but simply through the display of new kinds of weapons such as machine guns, hand grenades, mines, and artillery shells. Along with these, by decree of the Kaiser, the Focker aircraft flown by fighter pilot Oswald Boelcke was placed on display in May 1917 in the inner courtyard of the museum. Because of its novelty and destructive potential, it was an object of great fascination. Displayed amid a collection of historical cannons and against the backdrop of the classic architecture of the museum, this exhibit gave all the more impression of being a foreign object.

While anonymity and chaos reigned on the battlefield, the image of the war projected in the Zeughaus was one of individuality and order. The orderliness of the individual objects made the idea of reindividualization possible, even in the era of the mass armies and weapons of mass destruction. Amid the complexity of this modern war, such presentation had a calming effect on the visitor. Typical war trophies, such as flags, uniforms, rifles, and cannons captured from the enemy, took up a large part of the exhibition area, often put together in artistic arrangements.[9] The flags in particular gave the impression that face-to-face confrontations continued to play a large role in combat, even in the age of technologized warfare. In contrast to the anonymity of the modern mass war, these kinds of exhibits represented a familiar aspect of war in which the boldness and courage of the individual still had a major significance.

The longer the war lasted, the more the Zeughaus became a means of reassurance to a German society for whom the conflict had slipped away into increasingly distant lands. The war trophies also continued to focus on the German Army's victories at a time when defeat and stagnation had become defining characteristics of the war. Against the background of a radicalized war and disintegration of strictures, the museum took on the character of a counter-image to the reality of war; and in the face of the modern mass war, war of destruction, and the urgent situation on the home front, the exhibits enabled the museum to endow the actual day-to-day world of war with a sense of order. In so doing, the Zeughaus became a place apart from the visitor's own experience and living environment. For many visitors, the attractiveness of the museum, especially during the second half of the war, may have been due to its role as a place of refuge.

National Plans: The Imperial War Museum

Under the assumption that the German Reich would emerge from the great battle as the celebrated victor, planning began for a national war museum. At the beginning of the war museum experts debated whether the Zeughaus in Berlin would be suited for this purpose. Wilhelm Pessler, the folklorist who originated one of the most sophisticated contemporary concepts for the establishment of the world war museums, was not the only one to see the Zeughaus as "an already existing, natural focal point for that sort of Reich museum."[10] The publisher of the periodical *Museumskunde* (Museum Studies) and director of the Düsseldorf Historical Museum, Karl Koetschau, was also in favor of this choice, noting in a memorandum "that the Zeughaus would be well regarded as a central collection of all war collections."[11] He felt that particularly important captured pieces could attain their full effect "only in the Royal Zeughaus in Berlin, as an institution that came under Royal Ministers of War" and as a facility with a unique national and historical significance.

This project was abandoned in late 1916 by the Ministry of War. The kaiser was in favor of a national German Imperial War Museum in Berlin, an idea put forward in a memorandum by the art historian and director of the Berlin National Gallery, Ludwig Justi.[12] There were several reasons for the decision against the Zeughaus. To begin with, it offered insufficient space and capacity for personnel. The most important factor, however, appeared to be that the director of the Zeughaus, Julius Binder, educated as an art historian, had no desire whatsoever for an Imperial War Museum.[13] Furthermore, many experts felt that the Zeughaus was simply too much of a "Prussian museum," and instead wanted a museum established just for German military history.[14] Justi's maniacally outsized concept of an "Imperial War Museum celebrated the world war as a unified accomplishment of the German people."[15] This museum was to be more than an exhibition hall, it was to be a symbol of a nation united and strengthened by war. To this end Justi intended to present the war as a modern, industrialized, and total war. The events of the war on both the battle front and the home front were to be equally represented. His notes reveal a profound fascination and enthusiasm for the war, which he portrays as succession of challenges that could be overcome by military and logistic strategy.[16]

The idea for the proposed museum reveals the extent to which the emphasis had shifted from the traditional image of war and the soldier to the modern conception of war. Its first hall was to be a gigantic, stark space set up as a hall of fame; the upgraded social status of the simple soldier with respect to the military leaders would be shown as it evolved in concert with the expansion of the army into a mass army. In other words, this space would not be like the halls of fame in most military museums, which were normally devoted to the memory of political and military leaders. Instead, focus was on the German Army's achievements in war. There was to be a Hall of the Field Commanders, but only as an adjoining area in the form of a domed chamber with a sacred, muted atmosphere. There, instead of a statue of the kaiser as the highest-ranking military commander, would be a likeness of Hindenburg, surrounded by portraits

Photo of the model, which is no longer in existence, for the Imperial War Museum by Ludwig Justi and August Endell, 1917–1918. (Ludwig Justi, *Werden—Wirken—Wissen. Lebenserinnerungen aus fünf Jahrzenten* [Berlin, 2000], 384)

of other field commanders.[17] A widespread cult had grown up around the popular field marshal Hindenburg after the battle of Tannenberg, and as a result he had become a notable part of the German national identity. But another driving point was Justi's fervent hero worship of Hindenburg, with whom he had personally discussed his museum project.[18]

The statue of the kaiser on horseback, on the other hand, would be located not inside the museum halls but outside over the entrance to the building. This may be a reflection of the power situation of that era, as by this time Kaiser Wilhelm II had taken on more of a representational function, while the conduct of the war had been taken over by the military elite. Nevertheless, it is not likely that Justi had purposely intended to make this kind of statement.

In his design, architect August Endell interpreted Justi's concept as a winged, two-story structure. Its unadorned modern design, reminiscent of architect Peter Behrens's factory buildings or of large, contemporary railway stations, was a distinct departure from the usual elaborately decorated museum architecture. Endell's design proclaimed, as it were, that only the elements of objectivity, simplicity, practicality, and monumental size could appropriately summarize and reflect the historical significance, the totality, and the industrial character of the war. At the same time, the contemporary mythical elevation of the world war experience to a key national experience found its expression in gothic architectural elements such as church-like windows and high, pointed arches, which were intended to create a religious atmosphere within the gigantic exhibition halls.[19] With a floor area 26,000 square meters (279,864 square feet), this museum structure would have been of a size that was not attained until twenty years later by the National Socialists.

For Ludwig Justi, the defeat of the German Army and thus the end of his museum project came as a surprise. Any further work on it was impossible, for with the downfall of the monarchy and the dissolution of the Ministry of War, he lost all his supporters and with them his financial support. Within a short time the collection of world war items had been distributed among various museums.[20] Only after the seizure of power by the National Socialists were the museum plans taken up once more. Now Justi's design became the basis of a German World War Museum, reworked with a historical image containing National Socialist ideology.[21]

The Exhibition as a Means of Strengthening Public Will

To exploit public interest in the war, the government staged a large number of exhibitions as instruments of propaganda. These government-sponsored exhibitions corresponded to the course of the war and its developments. Only a few months after the beginning of the war, for instance, faced with public unrest over hundreds of thousands of war wounded, the government responded with exhibitions on wartime welfare. Mockups of trenches were built, so that those on the home front could take away their own impressions of the harmless nature of the new trench warfare.[22] It was particularly through such models and mockups that the attempt was made to convey an authentic and yet reassuring image of the front to the civilian population.

The most successful and probably most elaborate series of exhibits were the *Deutsche Kriegsaustellungen* (German war exhibitions). In 1916 and 1917, in conjunction with the Red Cross (and in cooperation with the Wurttemberg, Saxon, and Bavarian War Ministries) the Prussian War Ministry staged large exhibits of captured equipment in more than thirty cities of the German Empire, in Turkey, and in Poland.[23] An appeal to the visitor read: "Stand fast until the victorious end!"[24]

This message was desperately needed by now, for the mass battles on the western front were devouring humans and material, and the military leadership increasingly needed to validate its actions.[25] Disillusionment and weariness regarding the war spread relentlessly. It was not until the end of 1916 that the government organized professional and centralized national propaganda measures as such, yet as early as January 1916, when the German war exhibitions first opened, strategies for encouragement and slogans to urge people to stand fast had already been found to be of crucial importance.[26]

There was a now rush on the part of the government to develop teaching and entertainment events in the style of the popular world, country, and trade exhibitions of the nineteenth century.[27] Along with the captured equipment, uniforms, and pieces of equipment, which were displayed in the manner of consumer articles, the German war exhibitions displayed war-related texts, photographs, art, medical items used in treating the sick and wounded, and handicrafts from pris-

Main room of the German war exhibition, which was located in Berlin from 8 January to 24 April 1916 in the Exhibition Hall in the Zoological Gardens. (Reclams Universum, 13.1.1916, H. 15)

oner of war camps. These exhibits were accompanied by a comprehensive program of military concerts, lectures, film presentations, and theater performances. The visitor could also step into a mockup of a trench and pin on emblems of combat. There were even vendors selling war souvenirs and postcards, not to mention garden pubs for relaxation. Here, the war became an adventure.

The public paid a fee for entry, and therefore the German war exhibition, with its concept of rich diversity and appeal to the senses, proved to be a profitable source of money for war welfare programs. In Berlin, the German war exhibition hosted 500,000 visitors within three months, in Karlsruhe about 95,000 in a month, and in Frankfurt am Main the attendance came to 150,000 over a two-month period.[28] All visitors were given the message that providing for the German Army logistically was an easy matter, that its destructive potential could be kept in check, and that a victorious end to the war lay within close reach.

The Image of the German East

In the wartime exhibitions, the western and eastern fronts were presented in equal measure. It was, after all, important to prove that the enemy stood along all the borders of the Reich, and that the German Army had prevailed on all fronts: "Herded in rank and file, the Russian, Belgian, Serbian, French riflemen, our enemies from all four winds, captured by German courage in Russian snow, in the burning glow of the sun across the plains of Flanders, [and] on impassable mountain paths of Serbia."[29]

At this time the war in the east was only one topic of interest among many others. The proposed Hindenburg Museum in Posen was intended to offer a detailed image of German life in the east.[30] This little provincial museum, supported by an association and a committee under the chairmanship of Margreth Ludendorff, began building its collection in the summer of 1915. It opened on 2 October 1918, shortly before the end of the war, on the occasion of Hindenburg's seventy-first birthday.[31] But when the war ended just eight weeks later it had to be closed. The museum association intended to reopen it after the "return of quieter times." It would, however, always stand as a token of what the local German population considered to be the illegal usurpation by the newly founded Polish state of German cultural sites.[32]

In the Hindenburg Museum in Posen, the worship of Hindenburg and Ludendorff occupied a great deal of space. Posen was, after all, the "father city of the field marshal." His headquarters had been located here for months, and nearby was the birthplace of Ludendorff.[33] According to its thoroughly nationalistic-minded business leader, Heinz Bothmer, the museum's goal was "to illustrate the meritorious actions of our armies in the occupied territories" and "to secure the already present influence of German spirit in the east."[34] German culture in the east, as the exhibit was supposed to portray it, was all about creative power, cultural accomplishments, orderliness, organization, and clarity. Only the ideal and the idyllic aspects of German culture were featured. Proclamations, wall posters and circulars, programs of theater performances, and even German wartime postage stamps were proclaimed as evidence of the "organizational talents of our authorities in the land of the enemy" as well as their "high cultural spirit, which directs all of its energy toward stemming the misery of war."[35] As a symbol of the German triumph over Russia, the original furnishings from the hall in which the peace negotiations of Brest-Litovsk had taken place were put on display.[36]

Since 1917 the Hindenburg Museum had received its support from the western part of the Reich. The German Foreign Area Museum and Institute, founded in Stuttgart, also had the function of legitimizing the claims of the German population in Poland and Russia and directly supporting their activities. According to Martin Roth, it was one of the first museums founded exclusively on the basis of political intentions, something that forged a new direction for the business of museums. When the National Socialists came to power, this idea experienced a resurgence in the form of the propaganda museum.[37]

These museums were supposed to convey to the visitors an impression of

German cultural superiority. By 1916 German expansionist ambitions had increasingly become an open topic of discussion, and the catchphrase "German culture" was part of the attempt to justify these ambitions to Germany's own population as well as to those abroad. Thus the German claim to territory in the east was represented as being justified. After the German defeat, the Stuttgart museum appealed to Germans' sentiment toward their homeland by showing that German culture was still present in Poland and Russia even as the museum denounced its suppression. Thus, amid the anti-democratic and revisionist trends of the Weimar Republic, the same line of thinking was able to take hold.

Images of the Enemy

In order to allow German war achievements to shine all the more brightly, designers of the exhibits developed a frightening image of the enemy. The exploiting of enemy images was generally part of the basic patriotic mobilization strategy of government propaganda. Its purpose was to create a polarization between Germany and its allies on one side and the allied enemy countries on the other. While during the beginning phase of the war images of the enemy had served to lend credibility to the notion that it was a war of defense, over the course of the war these images increasingly became a surface onto which prejudices, fears, and stereotypes were projected in order to justify continuing the war.[38] Particularly on the home front these images were considered effective means of encouraging the civilian population to stand fast. Here the images were effective because, as Bernd Ulrich notes, "the reality of the front was filtered through the organs of public opinion and passed on in a distorted way" and could not be compared to an individual's own experiences.[39]

The enemy stereotype propagandized in the exhibitions was conveyed by means of the rhetoric of marginalization, an approach that the media knew how to use and one that had taken on an increasingly ideological and racist radicalization from the time the war began. The catchphrase used against France and England was "culture versus civilization." The war in the east was portrayed a battle of "German culture" against the "barbarity" of the eastern European peoples. In contrast to consumers of other media, visitors to a German war exhibition were confronted not only with verbal descriptions of the enemy but with original objects that they could see for themselves, "pieces of evidence," as it were, along with three-dimensional displays that substantiated the propagandized enemy stereotype.

An article in the *Schwäbische Kronik* (Swabian Chronicle) of 25 May 1916 about the Wurttemberg war exhibition in Stuttgart took a snide, chauvinistic view: "From old ceremonial cannons converted to grenade launchers to the *Stockgewehr* of the Belgian snipers, from the knife of the ethnic Indian to the

Exhibition room showing uniforms of the Austro-Hungarian Army in the Württemberg war exhibition in Stuttgart. (Bibliothek für Zeitgeschichte, WK I 130, No. 577/36)

grandiloquent French proclamations and the dum-dum bullets of Longwyi, everything is represented and neatly arranged."[40]

These pieces of evidence were provided as proof of the unfair fighting methods of the enemy soldiers, their allegedly base motives for military action, their military inferiority, and their cultural backwardness. Many of the approximately six thousand exhibition specimens in the Hindenburg Museum were intended to expose the Russian Army as a horde of uncivilized, dishonorable, and inferior soldiers.[41] Primitive wooden rifles "after the Potemkin style" were presented instead of genuine weapons; a large oil painting with the title *The Destruction of the Russians in Tapiau* by the painter Koch-Hanau was intended to document the destructive rage of the enemy.[42] Other pieces of "evidence" were a large club carved from larch wood on display in the Zeughaus in Berlin, supposedly taken from a Russian soldier, and a "barbarian Cossack dagger."[43]

Even more than the weaponry, the uniform was considered a measure of the cultural status of a nation. In the traditional style of military and homeland museums, the uniforms of the enemy and the German Army along with their allies were displayed in rows of figurines and mannequins. The mannequins wearing the uniforms of the enemy had racially stylized heads to assist in identifying the nationality of a given soldier represented there.[44] The complete array of like-new uniforms worn by the Central Powers were displayed in an orderly manner next to the uniforms of the enemy, which were worn out, cobbled together, and battle torn. These were often treated with derision by the press: "Next up are the enemies uniforms, which . . . are now clean (and thoroughly deloused!) and displayed on wax figures."[45]

The most spectacular of all were life-sized representational mannequins arranged in realistic front scenarios in the manner of ethnological exhibits and wax museums, complete with weapons, barbed wire, wood, dirt, trees, and shrubbery. There were about seventy of these wax mannequins in Stuttgart, Dresden, Leipzig, Frankfurt am Main, Munich, and Hanover, which had been manufactured by the firm of Umlauff-Hagenbeck in Hamburg. The figures dressed in the uniforms of the enemy armies were shown in battle or engaged in some other activity: "French mortar in a trench, mountain infantryman camouflaged in a tree nest, Russians performing their national dance, colored and white Englishmen, Indians with hand grenades in a Flanders trench!"[46] In Frankfurt an entire hall and in Stuttgart an entire section was devoted to a model of a sector of the front. Andrew Zimmerman had made reference to such examples in the Ethnological Museum in Berlin, maintaining that such imitations of reality were very popular with visitors because of their vivid nature, although museum experts usually objected to them because of their unscholarly methods of representation.[47] But the producers of the German war exhibitions were confident of the believability and popularity of this kind of display, using it to showcase enemy stereotypes in the most graphic, effective manner possible.

The mannequins' accessories and the way their conduct was portrayed were determined by their nationalities. Clothing, appearance, utensils typical of their nationalities, even the stance of the body were part of the visual image of the enemy, invested into the design of each mannequin. The non-European and Russian soldiers in the displays were made to look upon their Western contemporaries with a mixture of arrogance and curious awe. The scenario with the Russian soldiers depicted all the clichés of an uncivilized horde. Their faces had "Mongolian" features, they drank, performed wild dances, wore grimy clothing and, on top of everything else, resided in a burned-out barn. In exhibits in Stuttgart, Dresden, and Leipzig, they were shown as guards of Polish and Russian refugees: on foot or on small ragged horses, Cossacks accompanied a group of refugees who had piled their few possessions into a cart.[48] The intent behind these scenarios is obvious: they were meant to evoke both pity and revulsion in their audience. They denounced the treatment of the civilian population by Russian troops and at the same time attempted to gain support for German war policy in the territories in the east. Such exhibits and

A Polish refugee troop in the Russian section of Dresden's German war exhibition, which could be viewed between 1 June and 25 October 1916 on the Brühl Terrace in the Albertinum. (*Die Woche*, 1916, 1005)

scenarios were also intended to provoke fear. Their vivid depictions warned of the kind of fate that awaited the German homeland should it fail to defend against the enemy.

The portrayals of Asiatic and African soldiers who fought on the side of France and Great Britain had a similar aim. The producers of the exhibitions massively condemned their deployment. According to their racist point of view, these soldiers occupied the lower end of the scale of respectability, and as such they were considered not to be *ebenbürtig*, or worthy combatants.[49] Their deployment was therefore construed as a sign of military and moral weakness on the part of England and France. In the German war exhibitions, this deprecation of soldiers from non-European nations found expression in the slovenly clothing and dirty faces of their representative mannequins and in the animalistic manner in which they were portrayed. Thus a Ghurka, for instance, was shown with a knife clenched in his teeth.

Public interest in the "allied foreign soldiers" was also an expression of the ethnological interest and curiosity about foreign people and countries that had increased since the end of the nineteenth century and its colonial wars. Researcher Britta Lange speaks of an "ethnographic view" of the enemies.[50] The mannequins and objects became something beyond the context of the war, beyond the notion of the enemy at arms, in that they represented the foreign and exotic. Because museum dioramas merged various military resentments, racial stereotypes, and national attributions into one image, the vision of the enemy ultimately emerged into something clear and distinct.

Conclusions

On the home front during the First World War, museums and exhibitions took on the function of a cultural weapon. The unique aspect was not so much the pattern in which the war, the notion of the self, or the image of the enemy was portrayed. It was more a matter of the multiplicity of exhibition forms and aesthetic designs that were used to create a visual mode for strategies of self-reassurance, comfort, and mobilization. Although the press disseminated these same messages, the exhibits did not simply broadcast the dull platitudes normally found in the daily press; instead, they issued an appeal for perseverance in a much more subtle manner. Producers of the exhibitions used thousands of captured items as proof of the German troops' superiority and success, even at a time when the war had already been lost. By portraying enemy stereotypes through visual images, the defamation, mockery, and racial disparagement of enemy soldiers acquired a new quality. Simultaneously, because these kinds of "realistic" scenarios interpreted the real horrors of war through easily comprehensible, memorable scenes, the civilian population was able to soften its perception of the actual extent of the atrocities of battle and the chaotic conditions at the front, at least for a certain amount of time. And just as important, to a large extent, events like the German war exhibitions made the war into a source of recreation or diversion, and this diversionary aspect was given legitimacy by their humanitarian purpose, as many of the exhibits had the outward appearance of being charitable efforts or service to the community and the "Fatherland."

It is difficult to determine whether the images conveyed by these exhibitions held up against the reality of the war and whether visitors considered them credible. There is no record of contemporary public opinion other than the voice of the press, which was for the most part enthusiastic. What strongly supports the persuasive power of these exhibits and their version of the war, however, is that behind the exhibits stood members of the military, charitable organizations, and representatives of societal groups with credibility and respect among a large sector of Wilhelmine society.[51] This aspect was possibly enhanced by the ostensible charitable purpose of the exhibits. Since war exhibits were still a relatively fresh approach to propaganda, they probably were perceived less as a state instrument to manipulate public opinion than as places of education or diversion.

But the longer the war lasted and the more the resulting sociopolitical crisis intensified, the more the war exhibits lost credibility. This was evidenced by the fact that in the second half of the war no mockups of trenches were in evidence, and by 1917 several homeland museums had begun to close down their world war sections and return to "civilian" themes.[52] The idealized reality of war seen in the simulated trenches and staged displays of idyllic scenes, battle front, and home front could not endure against the process of disillusionment that increasingly defined perceptions among the German population.

In the battle that began later, however, that is, the battle for remembrance of the war, the museum-style images of the front and the enemy that were disseminated during the war continued to play an important part. These images set the stage, as it were. The material stood ready in the wings, in the manner of theater props and sets, waiting only to be rediscovered and pulled back onto the stage.[53] The Weimar Republic, in its own struggle over meanings and interpretations of the "proper war adventure," was able to take advantage of these old props. And seamlessly, or so it appears, this material was then taken up by the National Socialists.

Notes

1. On the war museums in France, see Daniel J. Sherman, "Gegenstände des Erinnerns. Geschichte und Erzählung in Französischen Kriegsmuseen." In: *Geschichtskultur in der Zweiten Moderne,* edited by Rosmarie Beier, Frankfurt, New York 2000, 207–36, here 211f.; and Susanne Brandt, "Kriegsmuseen in Deutschland, Frankreich und Grossbritannien im Ersten Weltkrieg und in der Nachkriegszeit" (master's thesis, Düsseldorf 1989)), 67f. On the Vienna exhibit: Maureen Healy, "Exhibiting a War in Progress: Entertainment and Propaganda in Vienna, 1914–1918." In: *Austrian History Yearbook,* 31 (2000), 57–85. On Great Britain: Eva Zwach, *Deutsche und englische Militärmuseen im 20. Jahrhundert,* Münster 1999, 51f.; and Sue Malvern, "War, Memory and Museums: Art and Artefact in the Imperial War Museum." In: *History Workshop Journal,* 49 (2000), 177–203.

2. *Ludwig Justis, Memorandum of April 1916,* GSt-Archiv PK (Geheimes Staat-Archive PK), Berlin, repository 89, no. 3225, 9–13; *Katalog Deutsche Kriegsausstellung* (in cooperation with the military administration for the benefit of the Red Cross), Leipzig 1916, 5.

3. *Berliner Tageblatt,* 6/1/1916 (evening ed.).

4. After renovations the Zeughaus in Berlin was newly opened in 1881 as a hall of fame and army museum. The army museums in Munich and Dresden were opened in 1880 and 1894 respectively. In the castle in Stuttgart a small army museum was set up as a part of the State Museum. See Eugen Lisewski, "Deutsche Heeres-und Garnisonsmuseen bis 1945" (thesis, Abschlussarbeit der Fachschule für Museologie, Leipzig 1990).

5. Heinrich Müller, *Das Berliner Zeughaus. Vom Arsenal zum Museum,* Berlin 1994, 168f.; Regina Müller, *Das Berliner Zeughaus. Die Baugeschichte,* Berlin 1994, 214f.

6. R. Müller, *Das Berliner Zeughaus,* 98f.

7. *Kriegsministerium/Zentralstelle für Kriegsbeute an die Kriegsbeutesammelstellen, Frankfurt/Oder, Stettin, Münster, Darmstadt, Kassel, Berlin,* 30/09/1914, HStArch Stuttgart, M 1/9 Bü 110, vol. 1, sheet 18f.

8. Duplicate of the *Änderung der Verfügung des Chefs des Stellvertretenden Generalstabes,* Berlin, 27/3/1916: *Gründsätze für die Handhabung der Bilderzensur,* HStArch Stuttgart, M1/9, Bü 110, vol. 1. These censorship regulations applied equally to film, the press, and exhibitions.

9. *Grosser Bilderatlas des Weltkrieges,* edited by Hermann Konsbrück, vol. 1, Munich 1915, 124f., 130.

10. Wilhelm Pessler, "Das Historische Museum und der Weltkrieg." In: *Museumskunde,* 1915, 2:68–75, 3:143–55; 1916, 2:91–104, 3:199–203; 1917, 52–82, here, *Museumskunde,* 1915, 72, 150.

11. *Denkschrift vom 12.9.1915 über die Kriegssammlung des Düsseldorf Stadtmuseums,* DHM-Hausarchiv, repository Z 205, 4.

12. Ludwig Justi, "Das Reichskriegsmuseum." In: *Ludwig Justi, Im Dienste der Kunst,* Breslau 1936, 272–91: *Denkschrift Ludwig Justis vom April 1916,* GStArch PK Berlin, repository 89, no. 32257; Ludwig Justi, *Werden–Wirken–Wissen. Lebenserinnerung aus fünf Jahrzehnten,* edited by Thomas W. Gaethgens and Kurt Winkler, vol. 1, Berlin 2000.

13. In the files of the Zeughaus there is no evidence of intentions to expand the museum into a world war museum.

14. See the collection in honor of the founding of the Verband deutscher Kriegssammlungen (Society of German War Collections), HStArch Stuttgart, M1/9, Bü 58, sheet 180f.

15. *Konzeption von Ludwig Justi vom April 1918,* HStArch Stuttgart, M 1/9, Bü 58, sheet 155–69, sheet 157f.

16. Even twenty years later, in his memoirs, Justi characterizes the First World War as "the incomparable accomplishment of the German peoples." See Justi, *Werden,* 374, 388.

17. *Konzeption Justis vom April 1918,* HStArch Stuttgart, M 1/9, Bü 58, sheet 158f.

18. In his memoirs Justi dedicated an individual chapter to this visit with Hindenburg on the western front in 1917. Justi, *Werden,* 348–52.

19. R. Müller, "*Das Berliner Zeughaus,* 218; see also "Zwei Fotografien des Modells von August Endell." In: Justi, *Werden,* 384, 387. The plans are reproduced in Ludwig Justi, *Im Dienste der Kunst,* Breslau 1936, 284.

20. The Zeughaus also received some paintings and models that the director, Dr. Julius Binder, had stored away in the depot, arguing that the Zeughaus was a "weapons collection" point and not an institute for national instruction in military history. On the dissolution of the museum, see the memorandum by Oberstleutnant D. Sterzel (ret.), coauthor of Referates V. der Armee-Abteilung im Kriegsministerium: *Die Zukunft des Reichskriegsmuseums.* December 1918, 3, DHM-Hausarchiv, repository Z 237; H. Müller, *Das Berliner Zeughaus,* 202f.

21. Gerhard Peers, "Plan für ein deutsches Weltkriegsmuseum." In: *Zeitschrift für Heeres-und Uniformkunde,* 10 (1938), 22–31, here 22; Gerhard Peters, "Das ehemalige Reichskriegsmuseum in Berlin." In: *Zeitschrift für Heeres-und Uniformkunde,* 9 (1937), 99–101.

22. See Christine Beil, *Der ausgestellte Krieg. Präsentationen des Ersten Weltkriegs 1914–1939,* Tübingen 2004, 129–53; Susanne Brandt, *Vom Kriegsschauplatz zum Gedächtnisraum. Die Westfront 1914–1940,* Baden-Baden 2000, 79–88; Britta Lange, *Einen Krieg ausstellen. Die "Deutsche Kriegausstellung" 1916 in Berlin,* Berlin 2003, 74–88.

23. See Beil, *Der ausgestellte Krieg,* 160–207; Lange, *Einen Krieg ausstellen,* and Britta Lange, "Die Deutsche Kriegsausstellung 1916 in Berlin." In: *Kritische Berichte. Zeitschrift für Kunst-und Kulturwissenschaften,* 2 (2001), 43–55.

24. From the *Schwäbische Kronik*, 26/5/1916, quoting the chairman of the Württemburg Red Cross, Dr. von Geyer, at the opening ceremony of the Stuttgart war exhibition.

25. Anne Lipp, *Meinungslenkung im Krieg. Kriegserfahrungen deutscher Soldaten und ihre Deutung 1914–1918*, Göttingen 2003, 174f.

26. Gunther Mai, "'Aufklärung der Bevölkerung' und 'Vaterländischer Unterricht' in Württemberg 1914–1918. Struktur, Durchführung und Inhalte der deutschen Inlandspropaganda im Ersten Weltkrieg." In: *Zeitschrift für Württembergische Landesgeschichte*, 38 (1979), 199–235, here 203f.

27. On the connection between entertainment and propaganda, see Gary D. Stark, "All Quiet on the Homefront: Popular Entertainments, Censorship, and Civilian Morale in Germany, 1914–1918." In: *Authority, Identity and the Social History of the Great War*, edited by Frans Coetzee and Marilyn Shevon Coetzee, Providence, Oxford 1995, 57–80.

28. In Berlin there was a net profit of almost 95,000 marks. See *Bericht der Sitzung des Centralkomitees der Deutschen Vereine vom Roten Kreuz*, Berlin, 24/6/1916, HStArch Stuttgart, M 1/9 Bü 110, vol. 2, sheet 180f.; *Karlsruher Zeitung*, 1/3/1916; Detlev Hoffmann, "Die Weltkriegssammlung des Historischen Museums Frankfurt." In: *Ein Krieg wird ausgestellt. Die Weltkriegssammlung des Historischen Museums (1914–1918). Themen einer Ausstellung, Inventarkatalog*, Frankfurt 1976, 63–74, here 71.

29. *Illustrirte Kriegschronik des Daheim*, issue no. 35, 1916, 157.

30. Arthur Kronthal, "Das Hindenburgmuseum in Posen." In: *Museumskunde*, 15 (1920), issue no. 3–4, 152–59.

31. Heinz Bothmer, "Das Hindenburg-Museum in Posen." In: *Museumskunde*, 14 (1919), issue no. 1, 29–38.

32. Kronthal, "Das Hindenburgmuseum," 155f. It is unclear what became of the museum's inventory.

33. Bothmer, "Hindenburg-Museum," 29f.

34. Ibid., 30, 38.

35. Ibid., 34.

36. Heinz Bothmer, "Hindenburg-Museum. Erwerbungen von Oktober 1917 bis April 1918." In: *Archiv für Waffen-und Uniformkunde*, 1 (1918), issue no. 2–3, 105f.

37. Martin Roth, *Heimatmuseum. Zur Geschichte einer deutschen Institution*, Berlin 1990, 157–68.

38. *Feind-Bilder, Begleitheft zur Ausstellung: 1914–1918*, Frankfurt 1994.

39. Bernd Ulrich, "Kampfmotivationen und Mobilisierungsstrategien: Das Beispiel Erster Weltkrieg." In: *Töten im Krieg*, edited by Heinrich von Stietencron and Jörg Rüpke, Freiburg, Munich 1995, 399–419, here 405.

40. *Stockgewehr* = "stick guns," rifles, primitive or otherwise, or actual dummy weapons used in training.

41. Kronthal, "Hindenburgmuseum."

42. Bothmer, "Hindenburg-Museum," 31.

43. *Illustrirte Kriegschronik des Daheim*, no. 35, 1916, 158.

44. "Württ. Kriegsausstellung in Stuttgart, IX." In: *Schwäbische Kronik*, 20/6/1916.

45. *Deutsche Tageszeitung*, 9/1/1916.

46. *Schwäbische Kronik*, 25/5/1916.

47. Andrew Zimmerman, "Science and '*Schaulust*' in the Berlin Museum of Ethnology." In: *Wissenschaft und Öffentlichkeit in Berlin: 1870–1930*, edited by Constantin

Goschler, Stuttgart 2000, 65–88. Zimmerman defines this need of the visitor as the "illicit desire for a spectacle," 65.

48. "Ein Bild der Dresdner Ausstellung." In: *Die Woche,* 1916, no. 28, 1005.

49. Lipp, *Meinungslenkung,* 226–32.

50. See Lange, *Die deutsche Kriegsausstellung,* 48; and Lange, *Einen Krieg ausstellen,* 40–63.

51. See Christa Berg, Christoph Schubert-Weller, Heinz Stübig, and Ulrich Hermann, "Militär und Militarisierung." In: *Handbuch der deutschen Bildungsgeschichte,* edited by Christa Berg, vol. 4, *1870–1918. Von der Reichsgründung bis zum Ersten Weltkrieg,* Munich 1991, 501–27.

52. An example of this is the Erkenbert Museum in Frankenthal. See *Monatsschrift des Altertumsvereins,* 25 (1917), issue no. 9–10, 32.

53. On the postwar era, see *Krieg im Frieden. Die umkämpfte Erinnerung an den Ersten Weltkrieg. Quellen und Dokumente,* edited by Bernd Ulrich and Benjamin Ziemann, Frankfurt 1997. On war exhibitions and antiwar exhibitions, see Beil, *Der ausgestellte Krieg.*

17

Suppressed Remembrances

On the History of the Moscow City Fraternal Cemetery

Kristiane Janeke

In which of the three wars of the twentieth century did Russia experience the most losses in its history? In the 1990s very few Russians came up with the First World War as the answer.[1] This points to a striking difference between Russia and western Europe in the culture of remembrance with respect to the Great War. On the ninetieth anniversary of the beginning of the war, the United Kingdom, France, and Belgium saw a great number of memorials in the form of exhibitions, films, and publications. In Russia, in contrast, the program was quite modest. What can account for these "suppressed memories" in Russia?

This essay will explore this question as it relates to the fate of the Moscow City Fraternal Cemetery.[2] To trace the life of this cemetery is to follow the evolution of traditions surrounding First World War remembrance in Russia. The first part of the chapter will address the history of the cemetery from its beginnings during the First World War to its disappearance from memory in the Soviet Union. The second part will attempt to identify the reasons for this development, showing that the memory of the First World War had been consciously dismantled. The third part will address the debate over the restoration of the cemetery since the collapse of the Soviet Union. This conflict illustrates how arduous a process it has been to reconstruct memories against the backdrop of the Russian search for a new national identity.

History of the Fraternal Cemetery

The Moscow City Fraternal Cemetery consists of a small memorial zone with about twenty memorial stones and crosses. It is located next to a church, wedged between the metro entrance at Sokol station, apartments, storefronts, and a movie theater called Leningrad.

There are a range of inscriptions commemorating the fallen of many conflicts: "soldiers, officers, generals of Serbia, Belgium, France, England, and the USA who fell in the war from 1914 to 1919"; nurses, Junkers, and student military cadets from Moscow who perished during the October Revolution of 1917; and causalities of the Crimean War of 1856, the Russian-Turkish War of 1877–1878, the Russian-Japanese War of 1904–1905, the First and Second World Wars, and the Chechen War of 1994–1995. Generals of the Imperial Army are also celebrated. On one cenotaph, a memorial for a German cavalry corps, lies a wreath with the words: "To our forgotten comrades."[3]

At length one comes upon a cenotaph with the following inscription: "Moscow City Fraternal Cemetery. Pan-Russian Memorial to the War of 1914. Citizens! Do not forget that here lie the ashes of our fallen brothers who gave their lives in defense of the homeland."

This, the Moscow City Fraternal Cemetery (Moskovskoe gorodskoe bratskoe kladbishche), was founded on 15 February 1915.[4] Later, more fraternal cemeteries were built across the whole country.[5] In 1915–1916 a fraternal cemetery was established in Kiev, followed by others in Vologda, Kursk, Tambov, and Ekaterinoslav. In September 1916 an organization was founded in Riga under the name Committee for the Establishment of the Riga Fraternal Cemetery for the Fallen Defenders of the Homeland and Perpetuation of Their Memory by Building a Church, whose cemetery still exists today. In many cases, brothers' cemeteries and burial sites were annexed to previously existing cemeteries. This was the case in Petrograd (today Saint Petersburg), where a piece of ground was designated for the dead of the First World War, and at the Mironositskii Cemetery in Pskov, where another area was set aside for soldiers' graves. This kind of expansion or establishment of new cemeteries usually took place through a public tendering process.

The initiative for the founding of the Moscow City Fraternal Cemetery was begun by the Grand Duchess Elizaveta Fedorovna.[6] The issue had already come under discussion as early as 6 September 1914 in a joint meeting of the Moscow city government and the Commission for War Measures. Under the direction of physician Sergei Vasil'evich Puchkov, chairman of the board of the Moscow Association of Sisters of Charity, a subcommission of six members was formed. Puchkov was later elected by the Moscow City Duma as curator of the cemetery. The subcommission declared its "great moral duty to do everything we can to have a sacred location established, one for all Russians . . . to instill in future generations the love of the homeland and the firm desire to serve the well-being of the Fatherland."[7]

Through newspaper announcements the city sought a piece of ground suitable for the cemetery. The property of A. N. Golubitskaia was chosen. It lay five kilometers from the Tver city gate in the village of Vsekhsviatskoe on the Petersburg chaussee—a large park ground with lime, birch, pine, spruce, and fir trees; today the grounds belong to the City of Moscow. The city bought the twenty-two-hectare property in July 1915 for 271,000 rubles, expanding it further by eight hectares with property belonging to the government.[8] Financing for the cemetery came from other city and community governments and private donations. A. N. Kelch was appointed landscape architect and S. S. Sestakov chief engineer.[9] They wanted the cemetery to have a restrained design, with modest graves. These were furnished with wooden crosses and placed in straight lines.

At the opening ceremony on 6 August 1915, attendees included Elizaveta Fedorovna, members of the military, various representatives of the City of Moscow, and diplomatic representatives of England, France, Belgium, Japan, and Serbia.[10] Initially, it was possible to build and dedicate only a temporary wooden chapel, but in August the cornerstone was set for the Church of the Transfiguration of the Savior by the architect Aleksei V. Shchusev, whose design was selected in a separate, open competition. The church had five domes and was built in the so-called Russian Style, which was typical of Shchusev's style between 1910 and 1920. The building of this church was financed by A. M. and M. V. Katkov, citizens of Moscow, whose sons Mikhail and Andrei had fallen in battle in East Prussia on 6 August 1914; the laying of the cornerstone took place on the first anniversary of their deaths. In their memory, the two secondary altars of the church were dedicated to Archangel Michael and Saint Andreas.[11]

In the same year, a brochure on the cemetery was published.[12] Texts explain the history of its foundation, photos show the views of the grounds, and in the appendix there are plans and reproductions of the official decrees by the responsible committees of the City of Moscow. Also in 1915, the construction of a streetcar line to the cemetery was begun and plans were made to erect a memorial designed by the sculptor Ivan D. Shadr on the cemetery grounds.[13] The City Duma of Moscow launched a design competition for a monument in honor of the victims of the 1915 sinking of the Russian hospital ship *Portugal* by the Germans. Shadr entered with a very innovative design, a project that took him several years and played a crucial role in his artistic development. It is likely that he had already developed the design in 1912 in the aftermath of the Italian-Turkish War. Shadr wanted his monument dedicated not just to the victims of the *Portugal* but to all victims of the war, and he therefore named it "Monument to the Suffering of the World." The design sparked great controversy but was finally accepted. Among the artist's champions were the architect Shchusev and Maxim Gorky. The concept for the project was Shadr's first great artistic success, but unfortunately, with the course of war and the ensuing political changes, the project could not be completed.

Puckov, the curator of the cemetery, came up with idea of expanding this into a pan-Russian war memorial.[14] The whole area would be turned into a military city, featuring a war museum, the soldiers' cemetery, a place of refuge for veterans of the Russian-Japanese War, a school for the children of soldiers, and a military training site.[15] On 24 April 1917 Puckov turned to the duma with this proposal. His plan included not just the cemetery but also captured war equipment and fortifications surrounded by trenches. "In short," Puckov summarized, "the museum will be arranged in such a way that visitors will have the opportunity to gain a very vivid image of what the defenders of our homeland are experiencing and have suffered in this war."[16]

It was never possible to carry out these plans. Yet the cemetery did evolve into a site of shared remembrance as the initiators had planned. The Easter celebrations on April 1916 offer an example of how the fallen were honored. On 9 April, Easter Vigil, several thousand Moscow residents arrived at the cemetery; a special train was even arranged for celebrants.[17] The church gave out six thousand candles that had been made by volunteer workers. In addition, money was donated for grave decorations and wooden crosses.

The cemetery became a symbol of the great "brotherhood in death." It stood open to all victims of the war regardless of religious affiliation or social origin, with designated areas for Catholics, Muslims, Jews, Protestants, and Buddhists.[18] Soldiers of the First World War, the Revolution and the Civil War, the White and Red Armies, and members of the "Latvian Riflemen" found their final rest here. French and English pilots were also interred here alongside members of the Russian Expeditionary Corps in France, Germans, members of the Austro-Hungarian Army, and Turks who had died in prisoner of war camps. Civilians, too, were buried here.[19] The first soldiers and one nurse were laid to rest on the day of the dedication of the cemetery.

Between 1915 and 1919 a total of 17,500 soldiers, 581 officers, 51 Sisters of Charity, 20 public figures, and 14 physicians were buried in the Moscow City Fraternal Cemetery.[20] Located in the archives of the Historical Museum of the City of Moscow are consecutively numbered cards of all the dead, giving personal data such as name, age, religion, rank, birthplace, time and place of death, cause of death, day of burial, and gravesite number. There are still even photos available.[21]

In 1918 the main altar of the Church of the Transfiguration was dedicated, and by 1923 burials took place on a specially built avenue in honor of the airmen. But early in the 1920s, as the country began to recover from the effects of the Civil War, the gradual disintegration of the cemetery began. In 1925 the State Soviet of Moscow issued a plea to its citizens to "beautify the city." What this meant for the cemetery was a decrease in size and an increase in its use as a "recreational zone." Eventually, after the Second World War, the grounds were built over with residential buildings, and in the 1950s a movie theater appeared.

There were various initiatives, above all by historians and archivists, to contest the destruction of the cemeteries. Thus, in 1926, in a commission called Old Moscow (Staraia Moskva), a subcommission for cemetery affairs, was founded for the purpose of photographing and recording all graves before they were demolished.[22]

In 1956 the artillery specialist Vladimir Grigorievic Fedorov, recognized for exceptional service in his development of the machine gun, wrote to Marshall Malinovskii asking permission to erect a small monument at his own expense in remembrance of soldiers buried in the cemetery.[23] The initiative drew support, but after Fedorov died, the matter was not pursued further.[24]

These few attempts to keep the cemetery intact were not enough to preserve its memory, and thus, except for the previously mentioned memorial zone, there is now no trace to be found.

Remembrance of the First World War in Russia

The history of memorials to those who fell in the First World War in Russia has taken a varied path. During the war, the practice of remembrance was constructed through propaganda; after the war, it was purposely dismantled by the Soviet Union. Today, it is being reconstructed slowly and amid controversy. Nevertheless, the question remains of how a war could simply pass into the realm of the forgotten, a war in which 1.7 million soldiers died, almost 5 million were wounded, and 2.5 million were imprisoned.[25] For those who lived it, it was still the Great War, the European War, the German-Russian War, or even the Second War of the Fatherland.[26] As in other countries, contemporaries in Russia sensed the significance of the event and wanted to preserve its memory for posterity. Even in the first months of the war, many museums, libraries, archives, academic societies, and war collections were established.[27] Regional and private initiatives across the country aimed to bring the war to life for those on the home front. Thus in Russia, as in all of the warring countries, the attempt was made to foster remembrance. To this end, along with the staging of war exhibitions, the Russians built cemeteries, monuments to heroes, and churches.[28]

The October Revolution, which brought the Bolsheviks to power in 1917, also brought a paradigm shift that led to the First World War's gradual disappearance from the Russian collective memory. In Germany, there was a continuity of interpretational patterns concerning the war years that influenced remembrance practices in the postwar era; the Soviet regime, in contrast, did everything to dismantle remembrance.[29] It was considered ideologically necessary to break with the traditions of the Czarist Empire and create a new foundational myth.[30] As a war that belonged to the old system, the First World War had to be replaced in the collective memory. The Bolsheviks wanted to break the association with the old regime and start something very new; what they did not want was to continue the war being waged by the provisional regime, which initially had taken power after the fall of the czar in March 1917, on the side of the Entente. The first foreign policy act of the Bolsheviks was, therefore, to declare the exit of Russia from that conflict, which they viewed as an imperialist war. From then on, the fallen soldiers of the First World War were replaced in the collective memory by the heroes of the Revolution and the Civil War.

According to the Marxist-Leninist interpretation that was now in place, the First World War was the result of an imperialist power struggle. It had expedited the growth of the proletarian revolution and had at last ushered in the victory parade of the new Socialist social revolution.

The Bolsheviks were able to eliminate the practices of remembrance of the Great War for the sake of their ideology, but how were they able to suppress, at an individual level, the actual memories of countless victims who had suffered and lost loved ones in this war?

One explanation is in the way that Bolsheviks treated death and its related rituals. Among the central objectives of the new regime was to ignore death as much as possible.[31] This may sound absurd considering that between 1914 and 1922 in the region of the later Soviet Union, 23 to 26 million men lost their lives through war, civil war, hunger, and terror.[32] But that very circumstance of massive death made it important that the new regime be legitimized. Changing the rituals surrounding death offered one way to create a new identity. For the funerals of 238 "heroes" who had died for Moscow in the Revolution, the Bolsheviks understood they needed to separate themselves from the traditional death rituals and replace them with new ones.[33] Using ceremonies and music, familiar traditions in czarist Russia, they attempted to construct a new continuity in peoples' awareness by linking the old and familiar with the new Communist government. In the place of religion and tradition came the military and police. By using familiar rituals for the new ideas, they fought against superstition and religion and attempted to replace the mourning over the losses of the world war with enthusiasm for the accomplishments of the Revolution.[34] This was the beginning of the forgetting of the victims of the First World War.

The 1924 funeral of Lenin exemplified the new ceremonies at their peak. While other countries at that moment were observing the tenth anniversary of the outbreak of the war, the Soviet Union was involved in the most important occasion of official remembrance of its early history. A memorial associated with the world war would no doubt have represented a reason for mourning, but Lenin's funeral, in contrast, afforded the opportunity to renew and solidify the population's bond to the new regime. A bond formed according to this new worldview was cause for joy. Parades and ceremonies in military style helped to alleviate personal mourning, elevating it into the realm of patriotic glory.

Under these new circumstances, the death of the average person, including wartime casualties, was hardly given any attention.[35] Lenin attracted the worship that in other countries was paid the Unknown Soldier (that is, the "ordinary soldier"). The funeral ceremonies staged at the time of his death offered people the opportunity to work through their personal grief for their own years of ongoing sorrow and lost family members. Thus, it is not surprising that a memorial site in the Soviet Union for the Unknown Soldier did not appear until much later.[36]

The Bolsheviks were able to combine their own approach in this respect with traditional practices because even during the war a large majority of soldiers were not buried under their names. In fact, in many other countries the practice of burying fallen soldiers under their name did not start until January 1915.[37] To accomplish this, sections of the Red Cross were reorganized into commissions for grave registration. Thus, citizens whom the state sent to their deaths on a massive scale were now granted the right to an individual burial.

In Russia, however, this was not the case. It is true that the Pan-Russian Society for Remembrance of the Fighters of the Russian Army Fallen in the Current War had existed in Saint Petersburg since 23 April 1915. Its mission included searching for graves, ascertaining the names and families of the fallen, transporting the fallen to their homeland, and maintaining the cemeteries.[38] Yet the dead continued to be buried in mass graves—an indication of the lack of democratization of the country and the deficient civic consciousness of the populace.[39]

A further explanation for the disappearance of the world war from the collective memory of the Russians has to do with the actual sites where battles took place, sites that would become memorial sites.[40] For Russia, the remembrance of the First World War was bound to the theaters of war where Russian soldiers had fallen and to regions of the country that had suffered from enemy occupation. Although Russian soldiers were deployed under the command of the Entente in France, for instance, other sites lay in the western Soviet Union, that is, White Russia, Ukraine, and the western portion of Russia, the Baltic, Poland, Romania, the German Empire, and Turkey. Because of the horrors and losses of the Civil War, the few former theaters of war on Russian home territory were soon filled with memories of more recent events. The areas that lay outside Russia, especially Turkey, were inaccessible to the population. And from then on, the collective memory was occupied exclusively with the remembrance of the heroes and dead of the new regime.[41] In fact, in Russia, not one single national monument or cemetery commemorates the First World War, and not until well into the 1990s was there an organization dedicated to its remembrance.[42] Only a few small memorial gravestones at sites in Ukraine and White Russia admonish us not to forget the fallen of the First World War.

Despite the conscious suppression of the memory of the First World War and its having been overshadowed by the Revolution and Civil War, in the

Soviet Union there was still a certain form of remembrance that was systematically exploited for the benefit of the new regime.[43] Many memoirs and other publications that dealt with the war were published in the 1920s and 1930s, particularly in 1924 and 1934, the tenth and twentieth anniversaries of the outbreak of the war.[44] Every year on the first of August, *Pravda* published a related article. Understandably, the date being observed was not the anniversary of the end of the war which, although it had ushered in the victorious Revolution, had also placed Russia on the losing side. Instead, the newspaper observed the date of the entry into the war by what was now referred to as Imperial Russia. Both in the articles in *Pravda* and in *Bol'shaia Sovetskaia Entsiklopediia* (The Great Soviet Encyclopedia), which at first glance looked amazingly long, there was less emphasis on the remembrance of the war than on interpretation of the current political situation according to Marxist-Leninist historiography.[45] In this interpretation, the world war was a historical symbol for the enemy's capitalist, imperialist, or fascist war, against which the population had to continue to mobilize.[46]

The 1928 publication by historian Mikhail Pokrovskii also fits into this category.[47] Pokrovskii argued that Russian imperialism and the foreign policy of the Czarist Empire had essentially been responsible for the outbreak of the war. He concluded that if the Bolsheviks had succeeded in destroying imperialism not only in their own country but in the whole world, the First World War in Russia would then have had the same historical significance as the war against Napoleon. He considered himself part of the undesirable world of imperialism and thereby lacking the necessary scholarly objectivity to study and write about his own country's history. This included memorializing the war. In other countries, he believed, war remembrances served to legitimize regimes that were still imperialistic.[48]

After Russia's victory in the Second World War, however, this type of ideological analysis of the First World War lost its impact.[49] After 1945 the First World War played absolutely no role in the collective memory of the Soviet citizens and was never turned to as a source of ideological inspiration.

The Soviet culture of remembrance represents a departure from that of other countries.[50] England and France, as well as Romania, Serbia, Greece, and Montenegro, which entered the war as independent states, emerged as victors, and later on were able to make rational sense of the world war. This was also true for newly established or reestablished states such as Poland, Czechoslovakia, and the Baltic states, which, in light of their newly gained sovereignty, were able to give a positive interpretation to the high losses and integrate them into the collective memory. Finally, even for the defeated countries of Germany, Austria, Hungary, Bulgaria, and Turkey, there was an aspect that helped define national remembrance of the war, as these states continued working on the revision of the new peace agreements.

Although Russia had entered the war on the side of the victorious Entente, it pulled out of the alliance amid the 1917 October Revolution and, as a result of the 1918 Treaty of Brest-Litovsk, joined the list of defeated countries. During the Civil War the Red Army did in fact reconquer many of the lost territories and was ultimately able to successfully integrate even more countries that had been independent for a short time, like Ukraine, White Russia, Georgia, Armenia, and Azerbaijan, into the new federation of states of the USSR. Even so, it was neither possible nor desired to build on any connections with the Russia of the prewar era. Instead, it had become necessary to create a new national identity, one that would excise the collective memory of the prewar era and the early years of the war.

This rupture affected not only the way that war remembrances took place in Russia itself, but also the manner in which the other formerly warring countries related to Russia. One outcome was that unlike in the western countries, no agreement was made between the German War Graves Commission and the USSR. Therefore, the graves of the soldiers who fell in Germany could not be visited by family members, something that was taken for granted in the west. In the west, amid the processes of rebuilding, cleaning up war damage, and creating sites of preservation, a "memorial area of the western front" came into being. This was not possible for Russia and the Soviet Union.[51] While in the west, traces of the war were purposely preserved, cemeteries maintained, and ruins kept in place so that they could serve as places of remembrance, these sites were either neglected or completely destroyed in the east.[52]

The conscious dismantling of remembrance of the world war in the Soviet Union is especially striking compared with the practices of Russians who emigrated.[53] Out of protest against the new political circumstances in their homeland, they were determined to maintain the traditions of old Russia at any price, and this persistence also meant holding onto their Russian identity. This form of remembrance kept connections intact between the conservative emigrant circle and intellectuals of the European host country, particularly in France, where the cultivation of remembrance of the First World War created a bond between the émigrés and the local populace.[54] Anniversary days were opportunities for the veterans to gather at commemoration ceremonies or to publicize their memoirs.[55] Even a special periodical was published, the *Russkii invalid* (Russian Invalid). In France, the veterans formed the Fédération des invalides mutilés de guerre russes á l'etranger (Federation of Russian War Disabled Abroad) and looked after cemeteries for members of the Russian Legion or for soldiers of the Czarist Army, such as St. Hilaire-le-Grand at Reims.[56] In Gallipoli a monument was made for fallen soldiers of the Civil War who had belonged to the Wrangel Army expelled from Russia in 1920. The monument was destroyed in 1930, but there are now initiatives for its restoration. A copy of the monument can be found at the St. Genevieve cemetery in a suburb of Paris. In San Francisco the Society of Russian Veterans of the Great War even opened a museum.[57]

In the early 1990s the idea of emigration and its implications began to attract interest in Russia once more. As a result of the collapse of the Soviet Union, the historical continuity of political and societal development in the twentieth century had been interrupted for a second time. Once more the population faced the task of defining a new collective identity. Unlike the period following 1917, however, today it is possible to engage in open debate on the content and characteristics of this new identity.

To this end, there is now an effort to build on national traditions of the old Russian Empire. This has brought the First World War back into the purview of the historian. Although it is still true today that the remembrance of the world war remains closely linked with the Revolution and Civil War, since the early 1990s the interpretive approach to the First World War has changed completely. In contrast to the situation of historians in western Europe, however, there is more to the issue than simply following new trends within world war research. In eastern Europe, effort is made to approach the world war for the first time in a manner that does not reduce it to a mere backdrop to the ensuing events. Only now has it become possible to view the war not just as an engine of the Revolution but simply and literally as a national catastrophe, the only path by which the Bolsheviks could win.[58]

Public memorial ceremonies have so far involved only outstanding events or personalities, and the fallen soldiers are not commemorated in the context of these events.[59] This is shown, for instance, in the debate over the 1998 canonizing of Czar Nicholas II and the transferring of his remains to Saint Petersburg in 2000, and the canonizing of Grand Duchess Elizaveta Fedorovna, the founder of the Moscow City Fraternal Cemetery.[60]

In 1994 Moscow's State Central Museum of Contemporary History held an exhibit on this subject. In 2004 the Saint Petersburg Museum of the Political History of Russia put on a special exhibit entitled *The First World War: Prologue to the Twentieth Century* in cooperation with the German Historical Museum.[61]

Moreover, in the 1990s newly formed military clubs began commemorating the First World War through reenactment events. These are staged not only for the sake of historical remembrance but also as an admittedly vague social protest. Another group active in these reenactments is the Dobrovol'cheskii Korpus (Dobrovol'cheskii Society), which distinguished itself by promoting the remembrance of the Moscow City Fraternal Cemetery.

The Debate on the Reestablishment of the Moscow City Fraternal Cemetery

The members of this Dobrovol'cheskii Society tried in vain over several years to have a memorial created on the grounds of the Moscow City Fraternal Cemetery. In 1994, the eightieth anniversary of the 1914 outbreak of the war, on their own initiative they installed a commemorative stone in a small grove of fir trees next to the Church of All Saints, near the Sokol metro stop. In 1995 this stone was destroyed, but one year later the Dobrovol'cheskii Society replaced it.[62]

This vandalism was a clear statement of protest from those who object to memorials of this kind.[63] And when the commemorative stones and crosses on the cemetery grounds were reinstalled and religious memorial services began to be held there from time to time, the district government of Sokol stepped in. This sparked a dispute over the creation of a memorial area in which even today the Cemetery Council, the Parish Council, and the Dobrovol'cheskii Society stand on one side and the district administration of Sokol stands intransigently on the other.[64]

The Proponents

The driving force behind initiatives for the reestablishment of the cemetery is the Dobrovol'cheskii Society. Its members also created a group called the Social Committee for the Rebuilding of the Pan-Russian War Fraternal Cemetery.[65] Captain Janis Arturovic Bremzis serves as its chairman, and its members include V. S. Petuhov and V. Ju. Kaulbars. Both the committee and the society itself have been very successful in popularizing the subject, although it is likely that their efforts on the part of the cemetery are related to other, more far-reaching political goals. The society's homepage is decorated with photos depicting the patriarch of the Russian Orthodox Church and Czar Nicholas I. Banners with inscriptions such as "For the Russian Nation" and a link to the Pan-Russian Monarchist Center are indicative of the political disposition of the society's membership.

The committee has campaigned since 1998 for the rebuilding of the Moscow City Fraternal Cemetery. An activity report lists the stages of the project, which consist mostly of the installation of large numbers of memorial stones.[66] Some of these have already been destroyed, supposedly by city authorities and the civilian police. Most of the memorial stones were paid for with money from the socicty or individual members. This could often be a significant sum (about 1 million rubles or, according to the exchange rate of April 1994, close to 300 euros). The next project planned is the installation of a monument commemorating the Red Terror of 1918–1920. A common thread liking all of the various monuments is their opposition to the Bolsheviks and the altered political conditions after the First World War.

Along with the installation of memorial stones, the committee is active in arranging religious memorial services and collecting documents and materials for the rebuilding of the Moscow City Fraternal Cemetery.[67] The aim is to reconstruct the graves on the entire grounds.

While the committee has its own homepage, it makes no reference to the website of the Dobrovol'cheskii Society. Its events are sometimes announced on a site that deals with military history and the army in Russia.[68] To the annoyance of the Central Museum of the Military, the webpage makes conspicuous reference to the museum, possibly in the hope of acquiring a more legitimate and official appearance. But the museum expressly distances itself from the Dobrovol'cheskii Society.[69] In a letter to the patriarchs the members of the committee asked for support for their project, citing the 17,500 Orthodox soldiers buried there. Very wisely, they did not mention the soldiers of other religious affiliations included in this number.

In the process of researching material for a planned exhibition at the German Historical Museum this author attempted to establish contact with the Dobrovol'cheskii Society.[70] It turned out to be very difficult.[71] Simple inquiries via email went unanswered. The society did, however, offer photos and objects from private collections, although access to these required payment. Despite intensive efforts, no meeting took place in Moscow with representatives of the society and Major General Aleksandr Valentinovic Kirillin, the director of the Remembrance Center of the Defense Ministry; the planned exhibit by the German Historical Museum received no support from them.

The Opposition

The committee accused the city authorities of blocking its efforts and of wanting to destroy the cemetery grounds. Admittedly the responsible cemetery staff members do not conduct themselves much more professionally in this dispute.

Since the time of the official recognition of the memorial zone in 1995, the Moscow City Fraternal Cemetery has been administered by the Cultural Department of the City of Moscow. The district administration of Sokol has further jurisdiction. The Sokol district administrators respond to inquiries in a rather distanced manner, hiding behind the Moscow Cultural Administration.[72] They are evasive with respect to the official plans by the City of Moscow. Prior to the ninetieth anniversary of the outbreak of the war, it was announced that the cemetery would be rebuilt, but this still has not taken place. The Committee for the Preservation of Monuments of the City of Moscow is preparing a large project for the cemetery, which officially has the status of a "historical landmark." Currently excavations are taking place on the grounds, and the building of a monument is planned for 2005. But as of September there was no sign of this either. The reopening of the cemetery was planned for February 2005, ninety years after it was first opened.[73] Furthermore, the historical museum was given the task of listing all 17,500 names of those buried in the Moscow City Fraternal Cemetery and recording them in a memory book. This is to contain photos, plans, and a text on the history of the cemetery.[74]

The activities of the Dobrovol'cheskii Society have prompted a rather negative response. Its members, it is said, stand for an old, "imperialist" Moscow. Thus, it almost sounds as if little has changed since 1991. While there is little argument that the First World War must be remembered, it is looked upon more as a necessary evil than as a political mission. The city administration holds the attitude that the term *hero* absolutely does not apply here. This is also the position of one particular delegate to the duma, for instance, who appealed to the patriarch against the creation of a monument.[75]

The Sources

In the midst of this controversy, the only neutral zone appears to be the documents section of the National Historical Museum.[76] Here lies the largest portion of the cemetery archives, along with a collection of written materials, newspaper clippings, and photos documenting the debate since the beginning of the 1990s. Also stored here are sixteen thousand alphabetically organized data cards with specific information on the burials, as well as the death register of 1915.

As was previously mentioned, the archives' staff members are currently working to publish all the names of the fallen in a memorial book. This was first attempted in 1992 in a publication by the Culture Ministry in cooperation with the Academy of Sciences and the Historical Library. Data was collected on 356 names drawn from press articles dated from 1914 to 1918, not from the death register.[77]

Publications based on primary historical materials and the open debate concerning the rebuilding of the cemetery offer some evidence that since the collapse of the Soviet Union, remembrance of the First World War is gradually returning. The fact that the memorial zone was given recognition in 1995 is also a positive sign. All of this must be welcomed as a first step on the way to recollection of this history.

Nevertheless, the sometimes questionable political orientation of the proponents of reconstruction of the cemetery on one hand and the lack of understanding by its opponents on the other show that there is still a long way to go before the First World War becomes a part of Russian collective memory.[78]

Notes

1. Catherine Merridale, *Steinerne Nächte. Leiden und Sterben in Russland*, Munich 2001, 141.

2. The term "fraternal cemetery" refers to a soldiers' war cemetery. Fallen soldiers are called "brothers" in Russia, based on their equality in death. The Russian *bratskoe kladbishche* means both "fraternity graveyard" and "common graveyard." In the case of soldiers' war cemeteries, both meanings apply.

3. Quoted material comes from the archival material in the State Historical Museum of Moscow, Section for Written Source Material (abbreviated SHM), fol. 402.

4. On the history of the cemetery, see also M. Katagoshchina and N. Zubova, "Pamiatnik velikoi voiny." In: *Moskovskii zhurnal* (1994), 52–55.

5. Mariia V. Katogoshchina, "Pamiatniki velikoi voiny." In: *Voennaia byl,'* 3 (132), 14–17, and 4 (133), 16f., 21f.

6. Elizaveta Fedorovna was the daughter of Ludwig IV, the Grand Duke of Hessen-Darmstadt. After the death of her husband, the Grand Duke Sergei Aleksandrovich Romanov, a son of Czar Alexander II, she founded a nun cloister and during the First World War cared for wounded soldiers. In 1918 the Bolsheviks had her executed as a member of the czar's family. Several years ago she was made a saint, and there is a monument to her in the center of Moscow. See the speech by Russian president Vladimir Putin in the German Parliament, 25/9/2001, in which he cites Elizaveta Fedorovna as a basis of the historically close German-Russian relations. http://www.documentarchiv.de/brd/2001/rede_putin_bundestag.html.

7. Quoted in Katagoshchina/Zubova, "Pamiatnik velikoi voiny," 52.

8. According to Katagoshchina/Zubova, "Pamiatnik velikoi voiny," 52, the land measured eleven *desiatiny* and 279 square *sazhen* (obsolete Russian area measurements).

9. Katagoshchina, "Pamiatniki velikoi voiny," 15.

10. *Moskovskoe gorodskoe kladbishche,* Moscow 1915, 10. The brochure is located in Archive of the SHM (State Historical Museum), f. 402, e. ch. 265, 1, 22–24.

11. The church was named after them, as 6 August is the day of Transfiguration of the Savior.

12. *Moskovskoe gorodskoe kladbishche,* Moscow 1915, SHM, f. 402, e. ch. 265, 1, 22–24.

13. Ivan D. Shadr, "K proektu 'Pamiatnika mirovomu stradaniiu.'" In: *Tvorchestvo,* 5 (1918), 22–24, reprinted in: *Shadr. Literaturnoe nasledie. Perepiska. Vospominaniia o skul'ptore,* edited by O. Voronova, Moscow 1978, 70f.

14. Mariia V. Katagoshchina, "Mesto, sviashchennoe dlia kazhdogo russkogo. Sud'ba Moskovskogo bratskogo kladbishcha." In: *Russkaia mysl,'* 3909 (20/12/1991), 14, Katagoshchina, "Pamiatniki velikoi voiny," 15.

15. Ibid., 15f.

16. SHM, f. 402, e. ch. 264, 1, 50.

17. SHM, f. 402, e. ch. 264, 1, 117.

18. V. S. Petukhov, Ia. A. Bremzis, and V. N. Chitaev, "Vosstanovit' chest' soldata." In: *Germes,* 5–6 (1996), 13.

19. The burial of Sergei Mamontov, the son of Mäzenaten Savva Mamontov, took place on 11/8/1915.

20. Katagoshchina, "Mesto"; and Katagoshchina/Zubova, "Pamiatnik velikoi voiny," 54.

21. SHM, f. 402, e. ch. 325, 1, 252ff.

22. The Old Moscow Commission was founded in 1909 by the Moscow Archeological Society; in 1923 it was officially closed but was active as a scholarly group in the historical museum, and since 1926, it has been maintained as a section in the Moscow Government Society for Research. See Katagoshchina/Zubova, "Pamiatnik velikoi voiny," 53. The chairman of the commission was V. N. Arnol'd. See SHM, f. 402, e. ch. 351,

f. 54, e. ch. 1126. "Poriadkoi spisok pogrebennykh na Bratskom kladbishche v g. Moskve sostavlennyi po planu 1926 g.," SHM, f. 402, e. ch. 345, 1, 1–14. The 1926 plan worked on by the commission, which recorded all the graves, is still available in the archive.

23. Rodion Malinovskii fought in the First World War in France, among other places. In 1918, he returned to Russia and entered the Red Army. Later he became director of the Frunze Military Academy. In the Second World War he was appointed marshal, and in 1957 he replaced Georgii Konstantinovich Zhukov in the office of the Soviet Defense Ministry.

24. Petukhov/Bremzis/Chitaev, "Vosstanovit' chest' soldata."

25. Christoph Mick, "Der vergessene Krieg: Die schwierige Erinnerung an den Ersten Weltkrieg in Osteuropa." In: *Der Weltkrieg 1914–1918. Ereignis und Erinnerung,* edited by Rainer Rother under the auspices of Deutschen Historischen Museums, Berlin 2004, 78. On the numbers of casualties see also Merridale, *Steinerne Nächte,* 137.

26. Initially the war, even in Russian literature, was called the Great (European) War; later it was called the Imperialist War or the First World War. See the bibliography of V. N. Babenko and T. M. Demina, *Pervaia mirovaia voina: ukazatel' literatury 1914–1993 gg.*, Moscow 1994. The "First Fatherland War" refers to the war against Napoleon in 1812.

27. Mariia V. Katagoshchina, "Muzei Velikoi voiny. Razyskaniia arkhivista." In: *Moskovskij žurnal,* 5 (1992), 39–44, here 39. On the war exhibitions in the German Empire, see the essay by Christine Beil in this volume.

28. Katogoščina, "Mesto." A first civilian memorial stone for the heroes of the war was unveiled on 16/6/1996 in Viaz'ma in Gouvernement Smolensk. (Katagoshchina, "Pamiatnik Velikoi voiny," 23): It was an obelisk on which were engraved the names of the czar, his family members, high-ranking military officers, the nurse Rimma Ivanova—a Russian heroine of the First World War—and city residents who fought in the war. Today there is a car factory here, with no trace left of the monument or of the cemetery. Consider also the following example: On 8/5/1916 the city of Bugulma in Gouvernement Samara began the construction of a park "in honor of the current Great War" and of a museum, for which the Bugul'minskii Infantry Regiment 319 provided forty captured items. Katagoshchina, "Pamiatnik Velikoi voiny," 23.

29. Susanne Brandt, *Die Westfront 1914–1940. Vom Kriegsschauplatz zum Gedächtnisraum,* Baden-Baden 2000, 14.

30. See Igor Narskij, "Bürgerkrieg—zur Konstruktion eines Gründungsmythos im frühen Sowjetrussland (Ural 1917–1922)." In: *Der Krieg in den Gründungsmythen europäischer Nationen und der USA,* edited by Nickolaus Buschmann and Dieter Langewiesche, Frankfurt, New York, 320–30. The author's thesis is that the successful implementation of the new myth was not solely the work of state propaganda "from above," but that "contemporaries, participants and eyewitnesses of the events intensively participated in the construction of a civil war as a foundational myth."

31. Daniel Orlovskii, "Velikaia voina i rossiiskaia pamiat.'" In: *Rossiia i pervaia mirovaia voina,* St. Petersburg 1999, 49.

32. Catherine Merridale, "War, Death and Remembrance in Soviet Russia." In: *War and Remembrance in the Twentieth Century,* edited by Jay Winter et al., Cambridge 1999, 61–83, here 64. Narskij points out that the period of 1914–1922 in Russia was perceived as a "continuum of a 'seven-year' war." Narskij, "Bürgerkrieg," 322.

33. Merridale, "War," 67; Narskij, "Bürgerkrieg," 327f.

34. Merridale, "War," 70. The first Soviet decree for cemeteries was issued at the time of the typhus epidemic of 1918–1919. This marked the beginning of increasingly regulated secular funeral practices.

35. Ibid., 71.

36. Not until 1967 was an Unknown Soldier of the Second World War interred in the Alexander Garden at the Moscow Kremlin. On this subject, see also the essay by Rainer Rother in this volume.

37. Orlovskii, "Velikaia voina," 50. In the founding ceremony, he also referred to the "democratization of the memories" in the tradition of the French Revolution and made reference to Jürgen Habermas.

38. Izvlechenie iz Ustava Vserossiiskogo Obshchestva pamiati voinov Russkoi Armii, pavshikh v tekushchuiu voinu, SHM, f. 424. Katagoshchina, "Pamiatniki velikoi voiny," 21.

39. Orlovskii, "Velikaia voina," 50. The low value placed on a single soldier is reflected in a quotation from a Russian general in connection with the shortage of munitions: "We fight with human bodies." Quoted in William C. Fuller, "Die Ostfront." In: *Der Erste Weltkrieg und das 20. Jahrhundert,* edited by Jay Winter, Geoffrey Parker, and Mary R. Habeck, Hamburg 2002, 34–70, here 47.

40. Brandt, *Die Westfront,* 20.

41. Merridale, *Steinerne Nächte,* 139f.; Orlovskii, "Velikaia voina," 49.

42. Merridale, *Steinerne Nächte,* 136; Orlovskii, "Velikaia voina," 52.

43. Ol'ga Nikonova, "Instrumentalizatsiia voennogo opyta v SSSR v mezhvoennyi period." In: Ch*elovek i voina. Voina kak iavlenie kul'tury,* edited by Igor' Narskii and Ol'ga Nikonova, Moscow 2001, 376–98. On the specific processing of military experiences of the First World War, see Olga Nikonova, "' . . . Der Kult des Heldenmutes ist für den Sieg notwendig . . . ' Sowjetisches Militär und Erfahrungen des Ersten Weltkrieges." In: *Kriegsniederlagen. Erfahrung—Erinnerung,* edited by Horst Carl, Hans-Henning Kortüm, Friedrich Lenger, and Dieter Langewiesche, Giessen 2004, 185–200.

44. See Babenko/Demina, "Pervaia mirovaia voina"; and B. D. Kozenko, "Otechestvennaia istoriografiia pervoi mirovoi voiny." In: *Novaia i noveishaia istoriia,* 3(2001), 3–27.

45. In the first edition of the encyclopedia, the "First Imperialist World War" was given 124 pages (vol. 44, 1939); the entry for "Revolution," however, only had 20 pages (vol. 43, 1939).

46. Aaron J. Cohen, "Oh, That! Myth Memory, and the First World War in the Russian Emigration and the Soviet Union." In: *Slavic Review,* 62 (2003), 69–96, here 79f.

47. Mikhail N. Pokrovskii, *Imperialisticheskaia voina*: *Sbornik statei, 1915–1927,* Moscow 1928.

48. Orlovskii, "Velikaia voina," 52.

49. Cohen, "Oh, That!" 83.

50. Mick, "Der vergessene Krieg," 75, 78f.

51. Brandt, *Die Westfront,* 127, 9.

52. Ibid., 18f.

53. In detail on the remembrance of the world war among Russian emigrants, with source references, see Cohen, "Oh, That!" 72–78.

54. Connected to this was an anti-German attitude due to support of the Bolsheviks by the Germans.

55. Worth mentioning here are the memoirs of the former senator Baron Taube (Michael von Taube, *La politique russe d'avant-guerre et la fin de l'empire des tsars, 1904–1917*, Paris 1928). He propounded the Russian myth of betrayal, which claimed the Bolsheviks obstructed the victory (ibid., 408). This interpretation was the basis for the interpretation of the war by the emigrants. (Cohen, "Oh, That!" 69.)

56. http://crdp.ac-reims.fr/memoire/lieux/1GM-CA/cimitieres/russes/saint_hilaire.htm; http://www.russie.net/franc/cim-hislaire.htm; see also Cohen, "Oh, That!" 69; http://members.aol.com/begemot/legion/. On the Russian Legion see Jamie Cockfield, *With Snow on Their Boots: The Tragic Odyssey of the Russian Expeditionary Force in France during World War I*, New York 1998.

57. http://www.armymuseum.ru/vetww1_e.html.

58. Mick, "Der vergessene Krieg," 80. This was also treated in a conference on the First World War in 1994. There the argument was made that the majority of the current economic, political, ethnic, intellectual, and moral problems of Russia reach back into the era of the First World War. A. P. Liferov, Rossiia i pervaia mirovaia voina: Aktual'nost' problemy. Rossiia v Pervoi mirovoi voine: Tezisy mezhvuzovskoi nauchnoi konferentsii, 4–5/10/1994, Riazan' 1994. See also Orlovskii, "Velikaia voina," 52.

59. Information on fallen soldiers is available through the search services of the Red Cross and the Volksbund Deutscher Kriegsgräberfürsorge für Russland (German War Graves Commission for Russia), as well as through the Archive of the Battle Medicine Documents of the War Medical Museum in St. Petersburg. There the patients' files of all soldiers are kept, which also contain information as to their later fate.

60. On the beatification and re-interment of the czar, see http://www.bautz.de/bbkl/n/nikolaus_ii_z.shtml.

61. For information on the museum, see www.museum.ru/museum/polit_hist. Brochures are available in Russian and English.

62. "Istoricheskaia spravka po istorii sozdaniia memorial georgievskim kavaleram i vozhdiam belogo dvizheniia," n.d. (after 1995). This document, a press release from the Dobrovol'cheskii Society, is found in the collection of contemporary materials of the Cemetery Archive in the State Historical Museum (f. 402).

63. See Alla Stoinova, "Otdokhnem . . . Na mogilach?" In: *Vechernaia Moskva*, 6/6/1996, 3.

64. Stoinova, "Otdokhnem"; and Ol'ga Malysheva, "Led tronulsia v mae." In: *Sokol* 5, May 1998, 3.

65. See the website of the society at http://www.white-guard.ru/dobr/main.htm. See also Petukhov/Bremzis/Chitaev, "Vosstanovit' chest' soldata." The following material is located in the archive of the Moscow Historical Museum, f. 402: Istoricheskaia spravka, Priglashenie, 1/12/1995 (press release); letter to the Patriarch Aleksei II, n.d. (after 1995); letter to the director of the State Historical Museum, A. I. Shurko, 21/3/1995; Kratkii otchet (directed to the Moscow mayor Iu.M. Luzhkov, 1994/1995).

66. Kratkii otchet. The committee's first meeting took place on 1/8/1988.

67. A church service was held on 9/12/1995 for soldiers of the First World War, for instance. Priglashenie, 1/12/1995 (press release). See also Stoinova, "Otdokhnem"; Malysheva, "Led tronulsia v mae."

68. http://www.armymuseum.ru/; announcement of event: http://www.armymuseum.ru/news_r.html. In the style of the society, but without reference to it, shown here is a message that refers to the first religious service for a White general, Anton Denikin. His daughter, who lived in France, had authorized the long-awaited transferal of Denikin's remains. (He had died in the US and was buried there.) The spokesman for the Association of Russian Aristocrats announced that they wanted to erect a chapel in memory of Denikin, Admiral Aleksandr Kolchak, and General Petr Vrangel in the Moscow Alexander Garden between the grave of the Unknown Soldier and the Manegeplatz. See also *Kathpress*, 9/8/2002, www.katolks.no/nyheter 2002/08/12-0015.htm.

69. Verbal information from colleagues at the museum, October 2003.

70. The name of the exhibit: *Der Weltkrieg, 1914–1918: Ereignis und Erinnerung.* German Historical Museum, 13/5–15/8/2004.

71. Contact with Mikhail Blinov was made via the details on the homepage for Russian Veterans of the First World War, http://www.armymuseum.ru/author_e.html.

72. This happened during a meeting on 6/10/2003 with Gennadij Aleksandrovič Vjazovskij.

73. See Irina Maslova, Zentralrat der Gesellschaft für die Erhaltung von Denkmälern (Central Council for the Society for the Preservation of Monuments), in an interview in *Izvestiia,* 4/9/2002, www.izvestia.ru/community/article/23385.

74. This work is currently under the direction of the Archives staff member Mariia V. Katagoshchina.

75. The letter from this delegate is located in the Document Section of the City Museum of Moscow.

76. Sources include historical documents on the history of the cemetery, data on those buried there, photos, material on the Dobrovol'cheskii Society, and newspaper articles referring to the debate since 1995.

77. *Moskovskoe gorodskoe bratskoe kladbishche: Opyt biograficheskogo slovaria,* by Ministerstvo kul'tury Rossiskoi Federatsii, Rossiiskaia Akademiia Nauk, Gosudarstvennaia publichnaia istoricheskaia biblioteka, Moscow 1992.

78. This chapter presents the status of research in 2004. In Russia in 2014, the official commemoration and social remembrance on the occasion of the one hundredth anniversary of World War I caused a paradigm shift, which seems to be the exact opposite of the Soviet narrative. See Kristiane Janeke, "Russia's Commemoration of the First World War. Remarks on Policy of History and Culture of Memory." In: *Muzeja raksti* (Museum publications), 6 (Riga, 2015), 120–26.

In 2014, many publications and exhibitions were made; in Carskoe Zelo, a museum on World War I was established. The one hundredth anniversary of the revolutions of 1917 has called the Great War to mind once again. Since the revolutionary events were interpreted as a tragedy that caused the fall of the Russian Empire, World War I was thus ranked among the wars fought to protect the *fatherland,* and the fallen soldiers were celebrated as heroes. In 2004, the area of the Moscow City Fraternal Cemetery was expanded into a memorial park complex of the heroes of the First World War, and further memorials were erected.

18

The Unknown Soldier

Rainer Rother

Its posthumous journey, in a physical sense, led from a nameless grave on the battlefield to a place in the center of a capital city. At the end of this journey, an extensively decomposed body became the Unknown Soldier.

In a symbolic sense, the journey endowed a unique and exalted status on the One that embodies All. The very absence of identifying markers made the soldier indistinguishable from the masses of the missing. An Unknown Soldier interred on 11 November 1920 in a prominent national memorial site, be it under the Arc de Triomphe in Paris or in Westminster Abbey in London, became a national symbol and, in a sense, an institution.

The final stage of his journey was a powerful confirmation of his status. It was witnessed by masses of his fellow countrymen and affirmed by the prominent status of those who accompanied him to his burial site: statesmen, high-ranking military commanders, highly decorated veterans. In a sense, the procession guaranteed his symbolic importance because both ordinary citizens and officials paid homage together, bringing substance and impact to the Unknown Soldier as a national symbol recognized, even held in affection, by representatives of the nation and its average citizens.

A Heroic Type

The idea of the Unknown Soldier was conceived as a special form of remembrance in response to the First World War. The idea became a reality in the 1920s. Within a few years, following the example set by France and Great Britain, many countries held funerals for their own Unknown Soldiers. These ceremonies were almost always conducted by the former Allied countries. Germany, Austria, and the young Soviet Union did not conduct a ceremonial burial of an Unknown Soldier of the First World War. Hungary, however, did honor an Unknown Soldier of its own, perhaps because with its newly gained sovereignty (although based on losses of territory through the peace treaty), Hungary had achieved its separation from the Austro-Hungarian Monarchy and did not consider the defeat of the Central Powers its own defeat.

Although due to their military defeat, Germany, Austria, and the Soviet Union did not join in the remembrance practices developed by the former Allies, a heroes' monument was erected in Austria by the architect Rudolf Wondracek as a central memorial site for the fallen of the First World War. Intended as a memorial to the Imperial Army's fallen from previous centuries as well, the site contains a monument dedicated to Austria's Unknown Soldier of the First World War along with books listing the names of all those who fell in that war.

Nor did the German Empire memorialize an Unknown Soldier in the same manner as the Allied countries. Even the creation of a centralized memorial site proved to be so complex an issue that ultimately no consensus could be reached. For Russia and later for the Soviet Union, the fighting did not end with the German capitulation and Armistice of 11 November 1918. The ensuing years were defined by the Civil War, so that honoring an Unknown Soldier in this way remained out of contemporaries' range of vision. Moreover, it would have had to be one of the czar's soldiers who, from the Bolshevik point of view, was nothing more than a victim of imperialist politics, not a role model for the new society.

The Soviet Union did join in the tradition after the end of the Second World War. The gravestone of its Unknown Soldier was ceremoniously interred in Moscow on 9 May 1967, 9 May being the traditionally celebrated Victory Day. The German Democratic Republic (GDR) followed the example of its Socialist "Brotherland," but with a visible shift in emphasis: on the twentieth anniversary of the GDR, the country reopened the Memorial to the Victims of Fascism and Militarism. In the remodeled Neue Wache (New Guardhouse), two urns were interred that held "the mortal remains of a resistance fighter and a soldier, along with the blood-soaked earth of fascist concentration camps and the battlefields of the Second World War."[1] Although in Moscow the Unknown Soldier was a natural symbol for the fallen of the Second World War, in the GDR the interment of the urn of the "Unknown Resistance Fighter" stood for the anti-fascist tradition of the state. Thus, while adhering to the official version of history, the GDR was able to form a link with the past in such a way that it did not appear as the heir to National Socialism but instead legitimized itself in a positive way through reference to the Resistance.

The Creation of a Symbol

Reports by those who experienced the beginning phases of this tradition and witnessed the interments on the second anniversary of the Armistice in 1920 provide a genuine view into both aspects of the story.[2] The writers of these reports take pains to point to the general undiluted approval that greeted the ceremonies, from the start of the procession to the interment itself. They recorded in detail both the peaks and valleys in public reception of the newly created symbol. Any controversy, such as difficulty with the pre-published programs for that day, was reported in the closing commentaries, as they could leave out no element of the event in their reports.

What is striking is the detailed manner in which the organization of the parade was described, as if to highlight that the event was actively co-created by all concerned, and that participation helped elevate it into the sphere of the symbolic.[3] Afterward, it was even newsworthy to note the absences of those who could not participate.[4]

In reality the procession in Paris, like that in London, could be viewed as an escalating, ritualistic succession of gestures of tribute. In both cases the coffin reached the capital city by train and temporarily lay in repose at train stations—Denfert-Rochereau and Victoria Station—under the watch of an honor guard. The Unknown was then transferred to the care of a selected escort commando, and in the morning hours of 11 November the last stage of his journey began. Both in Paris and in London, one more symbolically significant stop had been planned before the journey's end—at the Pantheon in Paris and at the Cenotaph in Whitehall in London.[5] From there, now escorted by the highest representatives of the country—in Great Britain by King George V, in France by President Millerand—the Unknown was taken to the site where he would lay in state. This is where the final ceremony, the interment of the Unknown Soldier, took place.

The Unknown Soldier was intended to become a unique national symbol. Select national representatives were to pay him tribute and thereby affirm his elevated status. What the French and British ceremonies had in common was the participation of certain groups: representatives of the state, army commanders, veterans and disabled soldiers, widows and orphans. There were different kinds of representatives in the two ceremonies, however. A specific feature of the French assemblage was the presence of a group from Alsace-Lorraine, serving as a reminder of the most important reason, from an official viewpoint, for the dogged insistence on the restitution of the departments lost during the war years. In Great Britain there were representatives from India, emphasizing the concept of Britain as an empire.

A further difference was the participation of the church. In France, because of its laicism, the church remained clearly and appropriately in the background. The Anglican Church in Great Britain, in contrast, participated on an equal footing with the state, as the Unknown was to be interred in Westminster Abbey. Later, on the initiative of the archbishop of Canterbury, changes were made in the inscription of the sarcophagus.[6] In this, the Anglican Church exerted its sovereignty as an interpreter of meanings, admittedly in the interest of an intensified sense of pathos.

Whose Unknown?

Even the glorified aspects of Unknown Soldier were defined to some extent by national differences. In Britain the Unknown was seen as a means of bridging class differences and was explicitly interpreted as a democratic symbol.

> "The Unknown Warrior" is in a special sense an emblem of "the plain man" of the masses of the people, who in every age have borne their full share in all our national wars. For the first time in the history of great States, it has been decided to recognize this share by the highest honour which Church and State pay to the illustrious dead. Opinions in all quarters has [*sic*] welcomed the step as appropriate, and as just. . . . In this war, where for the first time we have been compelled to fight as a whole people, where all of us, women as well as men, were either fighting or helping others to fight, the old distinctions have melted away and disappeared. It was the people, the masses, the democracy, who fought it, in a sense and upon a scale never known before.[7]

In France, in contrast, social equality played a smaller role. There, where national issues were not as crucially imprinted by class differences, various political factions debated just how the Unknown was to be honored. The Unknown in France would ultimately play a role in reconciliation across party lines and project an image of France that was acceptable to all sides.[8]

In later versions of the ceremonies, other elements were added. It was in the US in 1921 that for the first time, representatives from other countries were involved in the ceremony. The disarmament conference taking place at the same time in Washington gave foreign heads of state, ambassadors, and military leaders the opportunity to participate in the interment at Arlington National Cemetery. The presence of the representatives of the former Allies was considered a gesture of their appreciation for the crucial contribution of the United States. The list of participants at the burial included such figures as Marshal Foch and Premier Briand from France, Ambassador Geddes from Great Britain, and General Diaz from Italy.

Among the medals awarded to this Unknown were many foreign ones, including the highest service awards from Belgium, France, Romania, Czechoslovakia, Poland, Cuba, and Great Britain. From Britain, the Unknown received "the Victoria Cross, Britain's most prized war decoration, never before placed on the breast of a man not a British subject." As the AP reporter Kirke Simpson pointed out, the awarding of the Victoria Cross was remarkable not only because it was being given for the first time to an individual who was not a British subject but because it was also a late repayment for a gesture that had actually been unwished for to begin with.[9] This unwished-for gesture had come from General Pershing after the war. Having been awarded an unprecedented number of international service medals, Pershing handed out American medals as a benevolent gesture. But when he offered to award the Congressional Medal of Honor to the British Unknown Soldier after awarding it to the French Unknown, the British accepted it with reservations.[10] The British had wanted their Unknown Soldier to remain exclusively their own, an exclusivity that was also a central part of the ceremony in France. But with the burial at Arlington National Cemetery something new was added. This American Unknown became the first—and ultimately the only—one in the world to be expressly honored by the representatives of the Allied countries.

A Ritual

The special appeal of the Unknown Soldier was only partly a response to the grand ceremonies that accompanied his burial.[11] The procedure for funerals of the Unknowns resembled those for especially grand state funerals, but a state funeral is about *one person*. Participation of groups such as veterans or widows would be unusual. In a state funeral, moreover, the basis for the tribute is usually the prominent, generally known deeds of the person being honored. It is known how and by what means the person had rendered outstanding service to his or her country. This is not so for the Unknown Soldier. His tributes are exempt from the rules for military and national recognition. Acts of military heroism, strictly speaking, are required to be provable. Conferral of accolades requires proof of the specific deed that was carried out, where it happened, and the identifiable, proven bravery involved. It implies an action that exceeded the expected, something "above and beyond the call of duty." The military award is therefore usually conferred personally, not collectively (although there are certain exceptions during the First World War in which individual cities and communities were honored), never taking place in absentia, and the award is exclusive, direct, and purposeful.

None of this applies to the Unknown Soldier. His burial transcends the immediate sense and purpose of other state or military tributes. With this burial, the process of the creation of the Unknown Soldier has been completed. The production of this symbol naturally had no precedent from which to borrow. Its impact derives from two sources, the first of which is this highest possible degree of national and military gesture of appreciation; the second is the process of steps that elevated the value of the Unknown to a completely different sphere.

By the time the Unknown entered his respective capital city, he was already the Unknown Soldier. The transformation took place through certain previous steps, steps that had been recognized by a majority of the members of his nation; this was why he was honored unanimously on 11 November 1920. The transforming of a nameless person into the Unknown Soldier is not a matter of the usual governmental or military forms of tribute and honor. In fact, such means would preclude such a transformation because they would require a clear personal service. But the process of transforming a corpse into an Unknown Soldier who is intended to represent all of the fallen essentially corresponds to the concept of a ritual whose binding power follows a different logic than such things as military ceremonies.

Rituals are not usually a topic of historical interest. One could say that the field of ethnography gives such great attention to rituals for the very reason that something is present in them that resists historical change. If the processes associated with the burial of the Unknown Soldier appear to have commonalities with ritual, this is in certain respects problematic. Nevertheless, it appears to me useful to explore the burial of the Unknown Soldier in terms of its connection to ritual as an ethnographic concept.

Initially it would appear that there are more differences than similarities between the historical event (the burial of the Unknown) and the special characteristics of a ritual. The formal ceremonies in London and Paris in 1920 had no historical model to draw on.[12] The events are not rooted in a long-cherished tradition that recurs periodically in the life of a community in which the same actions are carried out in an always identical procedure. Thus, what is missing from the process surrounding the burial of the Unknown is the element most typical of rituals: a traditional, codified structure whose concrete configuration differentiates one's own group from other communities, and in which very comparable actions take place for similar events (such as weddings, funerals, and so forth).

The spectacle surrounding the Unknown Soldier was also not intended—at least originally—to *institute* a tradition for a country's local community. It is not the central message of the ceremony that from now on Unknown Soldiers must be buried in this way and no other. Instead, in analogue to the sobriquet "the war to end all wars," this burial was to be unique, the first and last of its kind. With one—albeit distinctive—exception, the basic intent of the burial of the Unknown Soldier survived. In no country except the United States was there a repetition of the funeral specifically aimed at the Unknown Soldier in the context of other wars. Since the First World War, beginning in 1920, other funerals took place that were intentionally similar to that of the Unknowns, such as in the Soviet Union in 1967 and in Iraq in 1982, in which the fallen of other wars were honored. Yet with the exception of the United States such funerals never took place in countries that had earlier buried an Unknown Soldier of the First World War.

In short, the funerals in London and Paris were conceived as unique events—"one time for all times." In 1920 they were meant to fulfill a perceived need, in certain respects a very urgent one, to pay tribute as a nation to those who had died in the war. This event filled that need with a symbolic gesture centered on one chosen individual, whose name, origins, age, and rank could not be determined, who stood for all of those who died in the war. Even though what is represented by this singular procedure with its highly symbolic activities resembles a ritual, it is distinctly different in its time element. In rituals, the crucial element is not only the series of movements or actions involved but also the fact that such actions, carried out in a particular sequence and with a particular purpose, have been carried out in this way in the past. The collective imagination may even believe it was "always" so. In this way a ritual builds on tradition. Equally important is that this ritual, based on the collective concept of "always and forever," will subsequently be carried out in this and no other way, and that the tradition will therefore extend into future.

Unlike a ritual, the process of creating and interring the Unknown Soldier is not based on the concept of a recurring cycle. Nor was it intended to set in motion such events in other countries, although after the first funerals of the Unknown Soldiers in Paris and London, ceremonies followed in other capital cities that followed the same pattern. In this respect, the practice can be viewed as a triumph. But one still cannot maintain that this event founded a ritual in the strictest sense of the word. While it is true that each society that buried an Unknown after 1920 copied the events in Paris and London, they nevertheless staged the funeral as an exclusively national act. Therefore one can characterize the particular event that took place for the first time on 11 November 1920 and each subsequent one as singular remarkable acts, procedures that are *events* and not rituals, meaning they are not (codified) *responses to a certain event* (for instance, the death of a tribal member).

The difference lies in an understanding of the term *ritual,* the predictable reaction to certain events that were introduced far in the past. Rituals are provoked by these events or set in motion by them, and they serve to keep their effects under the control of the group. The rituals themselves are, however, not an event in this sense, and are thus no new constellation for the community. The funeral of the Unknown, then, was an unprecedented event, but not a ritual.

Nevertheless, an understanding of ritual is helpful, if not essential, to an appreciation of the significance of the funeral of the Unknown. The sense of meaning that the Unknown Soldier brought to large portions of each respective society obviously lies in his importance as a symbol. But the ceremony itself is more than simply a protocol that was created at this particular point in history in response to the needs of the moment. Rather, it is a specific type of ritual known as the rite of passage.

Rites of Passage

In his 1909 book *The Rites of Passage,* Arnold van Gennep regards such practices as a particular form of ritual, or "ceremonial sequences . . . that accompany the passage from one condition to another or from a cosmic or social world into another." Further, he writes: "Because of the importance of these transitions, I think it is legitimate to single out rites of passage ('rites de passage') as a special category, which on further analysis may be subdivided into rites of separation ('rites de séparation'), transitional rites ('rites de marge'), and rites of incorporation ('rites d'agrégation'). . . . Thus, although a complete scheme of rites of passage theoretically would include pre-liminal rites, (rites of separation), liminal rites (rites of transition), and post-liminal rites (rites of incorporation), in specific instances these three types are not always equally important or equally elaborated."[13] It is not their "content" that makes these rites comparable, but rather that "a typical pattern always recurs: the pattern of the rites of passage."[14]

In light of this discussion, the procedure or process of the funeral of the Unknown Soldier can be interpreted and described as an event consisting of all elements of a rite of passage. Like the rite of passage, it involves a three-phased structure entailing the transformation from one condition into another. It fulfills the same purpose that such rituals are intended to do for each of the respective communities. Rites of passage "always have the same function and the same form. Their function is to control the dynamic of social life, their form is the three phase structure. . . . The concept of crossing a border commonly lies at the basis of rites of passage, as van Gennep shows. These kinds of passages from one condition of existence into another, according to van Gennep, are generally understood and symbolically expressed as analogous to dying and being born. A 'border crosser' dies in the old world, and experiences a change of existence and is reborn in the new world."[15]

The process by which the Unknown Soldier was created is therefore "constructed" as a ritual not only in certain elements but in its overall context. Its uniqueness does not lie in the notion that, as a result of the implementation of the ritual a corpse became "something else"; it does not lie in the idea that because of the ritual, the individual was afforded passage into another world; it does not lie in the notion that a potentially sinister corpse was now reintegrated into the community as a spiritual forbear. Instead, it lies in the fact that among many bodies, one was *chosen,* and in the end it was largely due to this that the transformation took place.

The Creation of the Unknown Soldier

There was certainly no lack of unidentified bodies from the First World War. Nevertheless, an arbitrary approach to searching for and selecting one for reburial as the Unknown Soldier, both by France and Great Britain, was ruled out. The intention was not to create the glorified Unknown from the first available, adequate, and unidentifiable corpse.[16] Certainly, from the pragmatic view there was little to say against the idea that one unidentifiable set of remains was just as suitable as any other. Still, the Unknown was not to be just a soldier but a *representative* soldier to the greatest extent possible. In essence this policy made sense, as an arbitrarily chosen, unidentifiable corpse would still have to have come from some named location, and the bereaved family of a soldier who fell at Chemin des Dames, for instance, would not have felt itself addressed in the same way by an Unknown Soldier selected from Verdun.

Ideally, the Unknown would no longer show traces of a previous existence. To this purpose it was deemed appropriate to remove any clues that would lead to knowledge of the location where he was found.[17] This and several additional policies meant there would be a process of several stages in the creation of the Unknown. These would ensure that the Unknown was *featureless* but at the same time embodied certain *qualities*.

The first and most important goal of the selection procedure was to guarantee the permanent anonymity of the chosen body. For this reason, when it came to narrowing down the candidates, all bodies buried anonymously in any of the many soldiers' cemeteries in France or Belgium that still bore traces of their identity were excluded. The progress of decay also needed to be so advanced that the idea of possible identification could be ruled out. Having recourse to many bodies from various battlefields ensured the representativeness of the Unknown. These bodies comprised a basic grouping from which one would ultimately emerge as the Unknown. The number of those who were to be exhumed was determined in different ways. In Great Britain four coffins were brought together; in France it was initially supposed to be nine, corresponding to the number of army commands.[18] "As the *Petit Parisien* reported on 10 November 1920, the ninth coffin was excluded because in that particular sector it was not possible to make a clear determination of nationality."[19]

The ceremonies that took place after 1921 followed the French model in that the entire process from beginning to end was a ceremonial and public sequence of events. But in the case of the British Unknown, the selection did not take place publicly. The coffins from which the British Unknown was chosen held the remains of unidentified British soldiers from the Somme, Aisne, Arras, and Ypres. The respective exhumations were undertaken by four different groups, "each comprising one officer and two other ranks, armed with a shovel and a sack and driving a field ambulance. On 7th of November, on the battlefields which were still marked by thousands of wooden crosses, these groups commenced their task, no group knowing the whereabouts of the others. They had been instructed that the body must be taken from a grave which had been marked 'Unknown British Soldier' and that the soldier must have fallen in the early years of the war, to allow nature to cause sufficient deterioration of the body."[20]

The exhumed remains were brought to Saint-Pol, where the British headquarters were located. There they were received by military chaplains, and the remains were examined once more in order to be absolutely certain of British nationality as well as the absence of any reference to name, regiment, or other means of identification. In order to further ensure the anonymity of the final candidates, the four excavation troops arrived in Saint-Pol at different times and left immediately. Thus, all information as to which remains came from which battlefield remained hidden.[21]

The selection of one of the four British candidates took place on the night of 8 November in a Quonset hut temporarily decorated as a chapel and placed under guard. The four coffins lay on stretchers, draped with British flags. General Wyatt and Colonel Gell entered the hut. "Both officers knew what was required and carried out their task quickly and in a dignified manner. Wyatt simply touched one covered body, and with this, the Unknown Warrior was selected. It was as simple as that."[22] The chosen one was laid in a new coffin brought specially from England, the cover closed and draped with the Union Jack. "According to Wyatt, six barrels of earth accompanied the body," the same French soil upon which the coffin would rest in the ground, the same soil for which so many had given their lives.[23] In this relatively austere transaction, which was characteristic of the British process at this point, the soil was the only other symbolic element. The Unknown had been chosen and was ready for his journey.

Unlike the British procedure, that of the French, even at this stage, was oriented toward creating symbolic meaning. The eight coffins lay in state, and the selection process took place publicly in the casement of the Citadel of Verdun.

> White cloths, decorated with clusters of flags and fir branches, extended the length of the room, which was thirty meters long and five meters wide. Candles and electric lamps spread a subdued red light and transformed the hall into a "chapel of rest" and a chapel of mourning. The wall opposite the entrance bore the slogan: "Verdun! On ne pass pas!" [They shall not pass], the slogan that Marshal Petain had broadcast in February 1916, meaning defense at any cost. Accompanied by the bishop of Verdun, the prefects of the department of Meuse, his cabinet chief, the mayor, and his adjuncts, Maginot appeared in Verdun at close to three o'clock in the afternoon. In the presence of veterans, disabled veterans, widows, and orphans, he handed a young infantryman a spray of flowers picked from Verdun and instructed him to place this bouquet on one of the eight coffins, and in this way designate the Unknown Soldier.[24]

As reported in the newspaper *Figaro,* the spray of flowers was designed in keeping with the occasion: a "bouquet of red, white, and blue."[25]

After the laying of the bouquet, the Regimental Orchestra played the *Marseillaise.* Escorted by troops and veteran units, the coffin was then brought on a *lafette,* or gun carriage, to the city hall in Verdun. Here the first memorials for the Unknown Soldier took place: the mayor attached the Medal of the City onto the coffin, wreaths were placed, and then the coffin was taken to the train station accompanied by Camille Saint-Saens's *Marche héroique.*

If the selection process carried out by the British seemed somewhat impromptu in contrast to that of the French, there were two reasons. First, there was little time to spare for either of the ceremonies, and the main effort of the British ceremonies had to be concentrated on the phase that would follow the selection—the transporting of the Unknown to Boulogne, from there to Dover on the HMS *Verdun,* and from there to London. Second, for the British the selection took place on land other than their own. It was obvious that the headquarters in Saint-Pol offered nothing comparable to the spaciousness of the Verdun site—and nothing at all that carried any symbolic meaning. Still, the important difference here is the extent to which the French actively exploited the full potential of this phase; it was the French model, not the British, that stood as a paradigm for others to follow.

A further notable difference was that the British selection process lacked an intermediary figure. This was the exceptional aspect of the selection made in Verdun. An infantryman, Auguste Thin, appeared predestined for the task, as he was doubly suited as an intermediary. Not only had he fought in the war, he was the son of a *poilu,* an infantryman, who was missing in action on the battlefield; in other words, he was himself the son of an unknown soldier. "An unknown soldier chooses the Unknown Soldier. Thin, whose youth signaled purity and innocence, symbolically affirmed the identity of chooser and chosen."[26] The concept of using an intermediary was later interpreted in various ways. "The Americans . . . decided on a sergeant who would place a bouquet of roses on one of four fallen soldiers. The Italians had the mother of a fallen soldier place white flowers on one of their eleven fallen. In Belgium, the decision fell to a blind veteran, and in Romania, a war orphan pointed to one of the ten coffins and said: 'This is my father.'"[27]

Above all, the different stages of the selection process ensured that the Unknown remained "featureless." This made it impossible to provide any information about him; he had no particular traits, only one general quality, that of being an unidentified soldier. But the selection still obviously involved one factor that had to be determined with certainty, which was nationality. The British process limited the possible candidates to those who had fallen in the first years of the war. This increased the probability that the Unknown came from the ranks of the British Expeditionary Corps and not from the either the Kitchener Volunteers, who had not arrived at the fronts until the end of 1915, or the contingents from the dominions or the colonies.

In France's case, at least one newspaper, *L'œuvre,* protested what must be called the "de-selection" of any fallen Senegalese soldiers.[28] The selection process had, in effect, ensured that no matter what the Unknown was claimed to represent, he was, with a probability close to certainty, a white man. The quality of being representational, it was argued, was also associated with exclusiveness.

The British procedure for transporting the Unknown to his final resting place in the country's capital was found to be the most adaptable by other countries. The French transport phase itself seems to have drawn less attention than that of the British, possibly because of the short distance to Paris. The fanfare was interrupted at the train station of Verdun and began anew in Paris at the Denfert-Rochereau train station. The British transport phase, in contrast, was ceremonious and quite emotionally charged, making up for the stark quality of that nation's selection process.[29] The British had intended this buildup of emotion, especially upon transferring the Unknown to the HMS *Verdun,* a ship of great symbolic meaning. Still, from the moment the Unknown left the headquarters in Saint-Pol, he received salutes from the French, and thus the entire transport phase became a ceremonial procession.[30]

At the end of the journey, the Unknown was ceremoniously received at a nationally symbolic site by government representatives, high-ranking military men, decorated veterans, widows, and orphans. The most traditional elements in the overall process were the reception of the Unknown and the funeral that followed. It was during this phase that the Unknown emanated his most powerful symbolic meaning. Although it may have been overlooked at the time, the metamorphosis of the Unknown into a national symbol rested on the knowledge that each step had been part of a planned ceremonious process.

The process suggests three phases that strongly correlate to the previously discussed rites of passage. The separation phase occurred when a number of unknown soldiers were removed (separated) from different soldiers' cemeteries. These unidentified soldiers formed a representative group. The transitional phase took place when the coffins were brought together in a temporary chapel, and the chosen was selected from these coffins. The physical aspect of the Unknown Soldier was now emphasized through gestures such as the decoration of the coffin (using flags and flowers, or even soil). From then on he "existed." The third phase, that of incorporation or reintegration, began at this point. There would naturally be an honor escort along the entire journey. Before the burial there was a stopover, during which the coffin lay in repose. The procession to the burial site on the following day was designed in a hierarchical manner. The burial site in each case already held distinguished status in the mythology of that nation. For the burial itself, all religious and governmental honors were employed. Above all, the attempt was made to ensure that the community of mourners represented a cross section of loyal patriots. France, for instance, included representatives from the re-won Alsace-Lorraine; Great Britain included the delegation from India; and the US included Chief Plenty Coups of the Crow Indians.[31]

While the stages involved in the creation of the Unknown Soldier may correspond to the three stages of the rites of passage, they do so in an *arbitrary* or incidental manner. There is no indication that there was a plan or an intention that would have placed it in the category of a ritual, but one might gather that it was very much intended to be "worthy" of one.[32] At the same time, one can also speculate that this procedure followed the course of a rite of passage in an almost *instinctive* manner. The forms, movements, and the manner of the selection could not have been drawn from any known prototype (the participants were also aware of this), but they did follow a *pattern*. The assertion that the Unknown Soldier lay in that coffin and that coffin only inevitably had to be based on the pattern that governed the selection. This pattern, or model, is not specifically historical, but it is the kind of pattern that normally historically embodies community-stabilizing events. If one views the selection procedure in terms not of its relevance but of its structure, and if one views it from an ethnographic standpoint, then it has the appearance of a rite of passage.

The idea that the creation of the Unknown Soldier has commonalities with ritual is not at all new. Reports from that time generally characterized the event not only as a ceremony but sometimes as a "rite," albeit in a nonspecific sense.[33] Adrian Gregory compares the funeral of the Unknown Soldier in Great Britain to a certain burial ritual in Borneo:

> The archetypal nature of the ritual was uncanny. Thirteen years previously Robert Hertz had written on the collective representation of death, drawing on studies of secondary burial rites in Borneo. The picture he drew could be applied almost without adaptation to the events of 11 November 1920. Peter Metcalf and Richard Huntington summarize his conclusions: "Many people conceive of a period when the mortal is neither alive or [*sic*] finally dead." This reflects precisely the uncertainty embodied in the words "missing in action." At the end of the "intermidiary [*sic*] period" there is a "great feast" during which "the remains of the deceased are recovered, ritually processed and moved to a new location . . . the irreducible minimum is the time required for the bones to become dry and free of decaying flesh." This accords well with the lapse between the war and 1920, particularly as there was a clear bias in selection for an older body. During the intermediate period, the souls of the dead are an uncomfortable presence in need of propitiation by elaborate ceremonial. Once again there is a parallel, the two minutes silence fits well in this context. The

> dead threaten illness and social strife, which in the context of 1919–20 seems interesting. Finally, "the great feast" terminates this miserable period by honoring the now dry bones of the deceased, confirming the soul's arrival in the land of the ancestors and marking the *reestablishment of normal relations among the survivors.*[34]

Arguments against the ritual thesis underscore that the Unknowns not only died, they became Unknowns under circumstances that had nothing exalted about them and that in fact continued to devalue the dead (for instance, through their months-long decomposition between the front lines). A front soldier could fully appreciate the fact that such a sparse fragment of remains would be unidentifiable. Survivors and bereaved family members, however, found the unprecedented numbers of so-called missing in action to be shocking. Thus, from a political standpoint, these remains acquired a heightened value. But the only way they could be successfully installed as a symbol was through a procedure based on a prehistoric prototype and not on a onetime event. The burial of the Unknown, therefore, was presented both as a ritual and as a means of coping at a time when customary memorial mechanisms seemed insufficient.

The Unknown Soldier

What was known of the Unknown Soldier? This rhetorical question was posed in a British newspaper article by an unnamed author who proclaimed himself "our Special Correspondent on the Western Front 1914–1918." He considered himself qualified to express himself on this topic, an attitude prevalent among those who had been at the ceremony. (The implication was that only those who had been affected by the war should be able to play a role in the ceremony.) "The Unknown warrior! Unknown? His name, indeed, and where he comes from now: such things, perhaps, we do not know, nor do we need to inquire. But him we know and did know well through four long, terrible and splendid years."[35] In a sweeping literary gesture, the author invokes the image of the ordinary soldier: "Rough he was and abrupt of speech, but with a curious gentleness that we had not known in him before, and inarticulately glad to be for a breathing space among his own again." The Unknown was considered to be courageous beyond all doubt: "We knew him when he was wounded—one of his many wounds—and he came back, limping and blood-stained, roughly tied up with his own emergency bandage, in pain and shaken, but helping over the shell-pitted ground another more seriously wounded than himself. And he died in many places. Bravery was his as a matter of course, as much a part of him as his humor, his tenderness, or his discontent. But to be 'unknown' is almost an extra, superfluous patent of gallantry. Not often he was unidentified who fell behind our lines [*sic*]. The unknown were those who died far out." As an Unknown, the body could obviously be anyone, and could have come from anywhere, as this former front correspondent continues elaborately. The idea of being "from everywhere" is a specifically British notion, a theme of the empire, so to speak. The author lists "Ulsterman," "Newfoundlander," "Australian," "Scotsman," "South African," "Welshman," "New Zealander," "Canadian," or "someone from the South of Ireland." This nevertheless suggested one obvious quality, which was that the Unknown belonged to the white race. The expression "he was all," therefore apparently excluded, say, the troops from India.

The Unknown Soldier was not always perceived as the *Times* portrayed him. Nevertheless, the tone of the article shows that in glorifying the Unknown, the attempt is being made to make sense of the war and its massive numbers of deaths. The spectacular ceremony on 11 November 1920 reveals an acceptance of the Unknown as a symbol, something that would not have been imaginable without such interpretations. Similarly, one can assume that many of the ceremony's attendees and much of the country's population were able to grasp the idea of the Unknown Soldier, assimilate it, interpret it, and finally honor it in the way that the British newspaper had spelled it out.

The high-flown literary language of the article is a perfect example of the tradition of pathos that met with scorn from both the war poets and the average front soldier for its inadequate representation of what the war really was.[36] But because of its literary quality, the *Times* article brought forth the kinds of associations the Unknown Warrior (as he is called in Britain) was meant to do. It interpreted the funeral as it was meant to be interpreted, a tribute to reunite a nation that was fully divided, even quarreling, over the commemoration of the war. The Unknown Soldier became the focal point for a remembrance of the war that was cleansed of all controversy, a remembrance that looked beyond the suffering and honored the achievements, looked beyond the futility or even absurdity of so many offensives and honored the victory that was finally won, looked beyond the victims and honored the heroes. It was not that the Unknown represented the least common denominator of various forms of remembrance; as a symbol, it transcended all of these distinctions. The Unknown Soldier, the *Times* wrote, "goes through the streets this morning not as a lowly one uplifted, but as a conqueror and of right." A body doomed to remain unidentified for eternity was thereby endowed with a wondrous impact in the here and now.

This impact was possible only because of the Unknown's transformation. By virtue of the selection process, he was "purified" of all specificity. In his newly acquired—and to some extent intensified—anonymity, he virtually became Everyman, for there was nothing to contradict a supposition he could be any one of the countless missing in action who are commemorated in names engraved in monuments such as in Thiepval or at Menin Gate in Ypres. Unlike the many gravestones of unidentified soldiers—marked with the Christian cross, the Star of David, or the Crescent—that stand in endless gleaming rows in cemeteries mostly on the western front, *the* Unknown serves as a universal remembrance. The importance of this achievement was that he *stood for all of those who died.*

The Chosen One was completely transformed at the moment of his selection. A no one became a "someone." In being discovered, or selected, he was exalted. In the moment of his selection out of the Nothing that he had been, he became a positive, completed Something. The completeness was bestowed upon him when those in his environment affirmed his distinct, now new qualities. Through the act of his appointment, a body previously absent of characteristics became a vessel filled with new characteristics. He is seen as having died for his native land, willingly, even gladly; he is seen as having been courageous, pure and, in a sense, free of sin. The Unknown Soldier was the model soldier and became the ultimate hero not on the basis of his deeds but because of the absence of knowledge about the slightest detail of his deeds. He is usually envisioned as a young man, nevertheless. Absent information on his earlier circumstances, he has inexplicably become the conceptual image of a healthy man standing at midpoint of his life, eagerly looking to the future.

Once interred, the meaning of the Unknown Soldier changed. His grave, having been established by the ritual, now became a ceremonial site. What had been the solution to a crisis now metamorphosed into a vehicle for consolidation. "By definition, ritual stands in close context with social passages, while ceremony, in contrast, stabilizes social conditions."[37] Ritual is based on the activity of the participants, or on their "engagement." Ritual requires that certain gestures and actions be performed. Ceremonies do not necessarily need this kind of participation. They can take place without engaged participants, as needed or on a regular basis, and ceremonies can become "empty" of meaning, taking place repeatedly only out of habit. The ritual, in contrast, cannot be implemented "out of habit," for not only does it mean something, it produces something. The ritual produces the cohesion of the community, and the ceremony invokes this cohesion.

A ritual is an act of creation (of meaning); a ceremony is an act of remembrance (of a meaning) by a community. Both are symbolic, but the ritual is binding for its participants and has consequences for the entire community. The success of the ritual depends on whether the community (still) believes that rituals of this kind have the power to transform, stabilize, or even heal. With respect to the suffering, which had not been previously imaginable, the community must accept the instruction to turn to ritual in order to cope. Its effectiveness further depends on whether members of the community believe that ritual is the only way in which the suffering can be represented, and whether they accept ritual as a means for all forms of coping. At its basis, therefore, lies a situation in which a community is in need of a ritual, or at least essential parts of the effect of such a ritual, whether the effect is viewed as reconciliation, comfort, or "only" symbolization.

Notes

1. Dieter Bolduan, "Die ewige Flamme brennt Unter den Linden." In: *Neues Deutschland,* 24/10/1969.

2. See, e.g., the reports on Armistice Day, 1920. "The Burial of the Unknown Warrior." In: *The Times,* 11/11/1920 (supplement); "La cinquentenair de la République. Hommage au soldat français." In: *Le Figaro,* 12/11/1920, 1. Later, the detailed news reporting by the Associated Press in the US was similar. See the complete document of the AP report and coverage of the Unknown Soldier at www.arlingtoncemetery.net/wwi-unk.htm.

3. See the reports in *The Times* and *Le Figaro.*

4. "Les invitations pour la grande cérémonie au Panthéon furent faites un peu hâvitement et il y eut quelques omissions regrettables. On vit notamment une dame essaye de franchir le barrage et parlementer vainement ave les agents qui lui opposaient une consigne inflexible. Par Bonheur le Préfet de police se trouvait non loin de là et il intervint. Et c'est ainsi que Mlle Déroulède put, grâce à M. Raux, assister à la célébration de ce suprême homage rendu à la memoire du grand tribun q'une amitié si vive liait à l'auteur de 'Chants du Soldat.'" (The invitations for the grand ceremony in the Pantheon had regrettable omissions. Of note is that a woman tried to break through the barrier and tried in vain to be allowed through, although she was opposed quite inflexibly. Thankfully, the prefect of the police, M. Raux, was not far away and intervened. Mlle Déroulède, the daughter of Paul Déroulède, was then able to attend the celebration that also honored her father's much loved *Soldiers' Songs.*) *Le Figaro,* 13/11/1920. Déroulède had published the very popular *Chants du soldat* in 1872. He supported nationalistic policies, was a delegate to Parliament several times, and founded the League of Patriots at Gambetta's wish in 1882, serving many years as its president.

5. The two "in-between stops" had very symbolic but different meanings. On the stopover at the Pantheon station, see Ackermann, "'Ceux qui sont pieusement morts pour la France' . . .: Die Identität des Unbekannten Soldaten." In: *Der politische Totenkult. Kriegerdenkmäler in der Moderne,* edited by Reinhart Koselleck, Munich 1994, 296f. In contrast to the controversial incident in France was the incident at Whitehall, where George V unveiled the permanent cenotaph of Edwin Luyten as well as greeted the Unknown in a sense, which was a generally accepted gesture from the beginning. On the history of the cenotaph, see Jürgen Tietz, "Monumente des Gedenkens." In: *Die letzten Tage der Menschheit. Bilder des Ersten Weltkrieges,* edited by Rainer Rother, Berlin 1994, 397–408.

6. The original inscription on the sarcophagus read: "A British Warrior who fell in the Great War. 1914–1918. For King and Country. Greater love hath no man than this." The next year it was replaced by the following text, engraved in black marble tile: "Beneath this stone rests the body of a British warrior unknown by name and rank brought from France to lie among the most illustrious of the land and buried here on Armistice Day 11 Nov 1920 in the presence of His Majesty King George V., his ministers

of state, the chiefs of his forces and a vast concourse of the Nation. Thus are commemorated the many multitudes who during the Great War of 1914–18 gave the most man can give—life itself. For God, for King and Country. For loved ones home and empire for the sacred cause of justice and the freedom of the world. They buried him among the kings because he had done good toward God and toward his house."

7. "Armistice Day." In: *The Times,* 11/11/1920, 15.

8. See Ackermann, "'Ceux qui sont pieusement morts,'" 297, on the unanimous decision of the Senate on the interment site of the Arc de Triumph and the connecting of the ceremony with the memory of Gambetta: "The death of the soldier appears to be enmeshed in a teleology of the Third Republic, which came into being with the intention of allowing 'France' and 'Republic' to become identical."

9. www.arlingtoncemetery.net/wwi-unk.htm.

10. Compare reports in *The Times,* 11/10. (p. 10), 12/10 (p. 11), and 17/10/1921 (p. 10) on the irritations and the honor that took place despite this.

11. Ken S. Inglis, "Grabmäler für Unbekannte Soldaten." In: *Die letzten Tage,* 409–22, offers an overview of the planned interments of the Unknown Soldiers.

12. On the origins, or the precedents, see ibid., 410f.

13. Arnold van Gennep, *Übergangsriten,* Frankfurt, New York 1986, 21. Translator's note: This passage is from the most recently published French-English translation of van Gennep's work: Arnold van Gennep, *The Rites of Passage,* translated by Monika B. Vizedom and Gabrielle L. Coffee, Chicago 1960, Kindle edition, loc. 434.

14. Ibid., 183 (translation from Vizedom translation, loc. 2887).

15. Sylvia M. Schomburg-Scherff, "Nachwort." In: ibid., 39.

16. In contrast, William Faulkner's novel *A Fable* ascribes coincidence, not choice, in establishing the Unknown. His exhumation troops are both unwilling and degenerate, and the sergeant must prevent them from taking the first available body. Faulkner's approach to the subject often alludes to the symbolic constructions of the Unknown Soldier and at the same time, in an odd manner, attacks the purpose of this procedure—or, more precisely, undermines it and gives it a new meaning.

17. One exception to this is the Polish Unknown Soldier. In this case, a list of cemeteries was presented beforehand and a random choice was made from among them. Lwów (Lemberg) was chosen, so that at least this origin is known about the Polish Unknown. See Christoph Mick, "Der Kult um den 'Unbekannten Soldaten' im Polen der Zwischenkriegzeit." In: *Nationalisierung der Religion—Sakralisierung der Nation,* edited by Martin Schulze-Wessel, Stuttgart 2006.

18. On the contradictory data on the number of British exhumed, see Michael Cavaghan, *The Story of the Unknown Warrior, 11 November 1920,* Preston 1995, 17. Cavaghan adheres to the version of Brigadier General Watt, the former supreme commander of the British troops in France and Flanders, which the British Imperial War Museum also considers to be correct.

19. Ackermann, "'Ceux qui sont pieusement morts,'" 301.

20. Cavaghan, *The Story,* 19 (quoted here in the original English).

21. The eight French coffins were exchanged several times in order to make any conjecture on the origin impossible. See Ackermann, "'Ceux qui sont pieusement morts,'" 311.

22. Cavaghan, *The Story,* 20.

23. Ibid., 23.

24. Ackermann, "'Ceux qui sont pieusement morts,'" 282. André Maginot was minister of pensions at the time. The fact that at the outbreak of the war he stepped down as undersecretary of state in the Ministry of War and served as a sergeant during the war made him very popular among veterans. Later, as minister of war, Maginot initiated the fortifications on France's east border, which after his death were named after him.

25. *Le Figaro,* 11/11/1920, 1. The newspaper spelled the last name of the infantryman "Tain" instead of "Thin" and described the way he appeared during the selection: "Completely pale, his lips closed, the soldier Tain took a humble bouquet from the sacred field and slowly, his eyes fixed on the caskets, circled them two times, stopped in front of the third one in the group on the left, and laid down the bouquet of red, white, and blue" (quote translated from original French). Ackermann makes reference to the fact that Thin chose the sixth coffin by adding the numbers of his regiment, the 132nd. Ackermann, "'Ceux qui sont pieusement morts,'" 283.

26. Ibid. Translator's note: This quotation is my translation of Ackermann's translation of the *Le Figaro* article.

27. Inglis, *Grabmäler,* 412. According to other accounts, Brigadier General Wyatt also chose the British Unknown "blindly," that is, with a blindfold over his eyes. Cavaghan points out that Wyatt himself, in a statement in which he intended to correct the different versions about the process, did not maintain this. In any case, one can presume that the interpretation that he chose "blindly" fulfilled the later need for some kind of ennobling selection. If Wyatt had chosen the Unknown with a blindfold on, then it would not have been him, but fate or at least coincidence that had made the choice. This would meet the need for an intermediary figure other than Wyatt, someone specifically suited for the selection, not through his position as supreme commander but through his or her personal story, as the son of a man missing in action, a widow, an orphan, or a disabled veteran. Specifically, it is obvious here that these intermediaries, from a symbolic perspective, are connected with the Unknown; one could say they became intermediaries because they could be thought of as possible family members or at least comrades.

28. See Ackermann, "'Ceux qui sont pieusement morts,'" 301.

29. Therefore the coffin was brought to London in the same train car that had transported Edith Cavell and Captain James Fryatt; see Cavaghan, *The Story,* 40f. Cavell and Fryatt were held up as martyrs by the British and Allied propaganda, and their execution by the Germans was seen as proof of the atrocities committed by the German Imperial Army. As a nurse in Belgium, Cavell had helped smuggle Allied soldiers into neutral Holland. Fryatt, as a cargo captain following orders from the British Navy, tried to ram a German U-boat that had halted his ship, the *Brussels.* Cavell and Fryatt had become symbolic figures for propaganda, and judgments as to their execution, which from the German perspective was legal under international law, remained controversial.

30. Marshal Foch, accompanied by General Weygand, visited the train carrying the Unknown on his own initiative. See Cavaghan, *The Story,* 27.

31. See Ackermann, "'Ceux qui sont pieusement morts,'" 284; *The Times,* 12/11/1920 (supplement), and the Association Press Report "Service at Tomb Is Heroic as Dead Is Laid Away," 11/11/1921, www.arlingtoncemetery.net/wwi.unk.htm.

32. Ackerman, following Roland Barthes, speaks of a myth: "Never can a myth take hold from rational considerations or be ordered through legal methods by politicians.

Even the founders of the cult do not have to pretend that they can do this: they do not invent, but rather arrange something that exists independently from them." Ackermann, "'Ceux qui sont pieusement morts,'" 310f.

33. "Armistice Day." In: *The Times*, 11/11/1920, 15: "To one group of the people these rites, we believe, will be particularly acceptable—to the widows, the parents, and the other nearest relatives of the great host who have died, and more especially of those who have died without a name."

34. Adrian Gregory, *The Silence of Memory: Armistice Day 1919–1946*, Oxford, Providence 1994, 25f.

35. "The Unknown Warrior. What We Know of Him. His Achievements in the War. The Empire's Pride." In: *The Times*, 11/11/1920, 15.

36. See Paul Fussel, *The Great War and Modern Memory*, London, Oxford, New York 1977.

37. Victor Tuner, "Prozess, System, Symbol: Eine neue anthropologische Synthese." In: *Das Schwein des Häuplings. Sechs Aufsätze zur historischen Anthropologie*, edited by Rebekka Habermas, Berlin 1992, 142.

19

The First World War on the Internet

Gundula Bavendamm

Memory, commemoration, and their role in our understanding of history have definitely become popular subjects. Studies of historical events depicted from the perspective of memory research can be assured of finding an audience. In some circles of the public sphere, especially among those who are curious about culture, there is a strong desire for the kind of information that might help to explain the exact process through which a linkage is developed between the present and an event in the past.

The First World War is a case in point. In 2004, ninety years after the beginning of the war, Germans remember the "seminal catastrophe" of the twentieth century with an intensity that had once been incomprehensible. Museums, scholarly history, book publishing houses, the press, and television have taken this opportunity to prod and encourage commemoration of the First World War. An important contribution in this area has come from the German Historical Museum (Deutsches Historisches Museum). Located in Berlin, this national German museum of history not only offers a large special exhibition on the First World War but also takes strong interest in the culture and practices of remembrance. Its exhibit *Der Weltkrieg, 1914–1918: Ereignis und Erinnerung* (The World War, 1914–1918: Event and Remembrance) focused less on the historical events themselves than on the question of western and eastern European traditions of remembrance that evolved from the war experience of

This chapter represents the state of research in 2004. Taking into account the issue treated in this chapter and the strong dynamics of the internet, this text must be considered a historical commentary from a present-day perspective.

1914–1918. The seventy-six thousand visitors and some five hundred guided tours indicate a broad public interest in both subject matter and concept.

In exploring the phenomena and culture of remembrance, it has become increasingly important to consider not just the traditional intermediary institutions and media such as museums, historiography, and the press, but also the internet. While it is not in the scope of this essay to present a complete inventory of all internet sites concerned with the First World War, selected examples will be cited to demonstrate how various forms of digital world war commemoration are conveyed by organizations and by private individuals on publicly accessible sites. Although this chapter will also touch on eastern European perspectives, it will primarily address examples from this author's language areas of German, English, and French. It will focus on the institutions and individuals hosting internet sites on the subject of the world war, the manner in which the sites are constructed and designed, and the kinds of services offered to visitors to these sites. It will also explore the question of differences based on nationality as well as forms of expression that may be unique to virtual remembrance of the First World War.

There is little in the way of reliable research available on the above topics at present. For some time, however, in the sphere of academic historical research, the internet has become an acknowledged source of meaningful information. This is evidenced by recent introductory-level materials that can be found on the internet, such as handbooks and specialized glossaries.[1] Some preliminary efforts of this kind have also come from the area of world war research. That the digital medium has found increased acceptance among historians is further evidenced by the growing number of discussions on individual internet sites, data banks, and other online offerings. Much of this is disseminated through H-Soz-u-Kult, the largest and most important information and communications platform in the German language for history and professional journals, both digital and printed.[2]

As an overall phenomenon, the remembrance of the First World War on the internet is a part of the collective memory of those nations that had been involved in this conflict. The term *collective memory* was introduced by the French sociologist Maurice Halbwachs in the mid-1920s.[3] By *memory,* Halbwachs meant the long-term memory of a group that is constructed with the help of signs (meaning texts and images) and through certain practices of remembrance such as rituals. According to Halbwachs's pioneering concept, collective memory is a social phenomenon, something fabricated by humans. Nations and societies, then, do not *have* memory—they *construct* it themselves.

What is true for collective memory is also true for the internet. As a socially defined data bank and communications medium created by people, for people, the internet is not isolated or static. Through the constantly changing, decentralized structure of the World Wide Web, data locations change regularly. The attempt to locate information for a second time is, therefore, always accompanied by uncertainty. The manner in which the First World War is documented and discussed on the internet is a reflection of the current interest our society has in this subject. In this digital medium, for instance, one might observe new trends in world war research. In 2004 the server located at Berlin's Humboldt University, Clio-online, which is dedicated to history, opened a subject-matter portal intended as a platform for cultural and historical world war research.[4]

Researchers interested in the First World War encounter websites in considerable quantities. Worldwide public organizations such as research institutes and museums as well as private associations and individuals offer websites on this topic. The dominance of British and American websites both in terms of quality and quantity reflect a strong interest in and a collective awareness of Germany's role in initiating the two world wars.[5] Specific gateways and guidance through the history of the First World War are offered by lists of subject-relevant sites that have been assembled in a web catalogue.[6]

The example of First World War research illustrates that the internet involves the two essential manifestations of collective memory: *communicative memory* and *cultural memory*. Both terms were introduced into the discussion by the cultural scholars Aleida and Jan Assmann.[7] The term *communicative memory* refers to a time period of memory that at most encompasses three generations, covering a period of about eighty to one hundred years. The material involved in communicative memories is essentially conveyed through oral everyday communication. It bears characteristic traits of a firsthand account passed on verbally by someone who experienced or witnessed a historical event. Even on the internet it can be observed that the First World War is on the verge of disappearing from the horizon of communicative memory. It is not rare to see private discussions on the websites of how the growing distance from a historical event—often emphasized through the death of grandparents—inspires many amateur historians to delve into this war, digitize the results of their work, and post it on the internet.

The internet is also associated with *cultural memory*.[8] Cultural memory is based on a society's preexisting canon of elements of remembrance that are considered to be extensively authoritative. Cultural memory aspires to authenticity. What can be called the guardians of cultural memory are professionals or specialized institutions that filter out of the mass of historical sources anything deemed worthy to be part of the collective memory. These are mostly aspects of the past that, when seen in retrospect, bolster one's own national identity and stabilize it in a positive way. In this category are public museums or memorial sites that impart known information about the First World War.

German-Language Internet Sites

German-language internet sites dedicated to the First World War are greatly underrepresented. Their rarity is obvious at first glance through the previously mentioned international web catalogue.[9] While the English-language web indexes may often contain links that are false, incomplete, or obsolete, German historical scholarship is almost not present at all. All the more reason to appreciate the current subject-matter portal Erster Weltkrieg (First World War), which has been in existence for some time now, thanks to support from well-known institutions.[10]

Yet, on the internet sites of German-language history and German military museums, the First World War leads a rather shadowy existence.[11] One notable exception is the Deutsches Historisches Museum, or DHM, whose previously mentioned special exhibit on the First World War is documented in detail on the internet.[12] It provides information on the topic itself as well as on the design and contents of the exhibit. At one time there was also a virtual tour of the exhibit, but this is no longer available. Beyond this special offering, detailed textual information about the First World War can be accessed from the site Lebendiges Museum Online, or LeMo (Living Museum Online).[13] It is illustrated with images of relevant objects from the DHM collections. There is the option of accessing the subject either chronologically or according to the subject matter. Especially useful are the biographies of numerous state officials, politicians, and military officers of the world war era.

On the home pages of the Wehrgeschichtliches Museum, or WGM (Military History Museum) in Rastatt and the Bayrisches Armeemuseum, or BAM (Bavarian Army Museum) in Ingolstadt, the First World War is given very little attention.[14] Both museums focus on the military history of the early modern era and of the nineteenth century, but both possess large contemporary-style exhibit halls addressing the First World War. The Heeresgeschichtliches Museum, or HGM (Military History Museum) in Vienna presents the First World War in only slightly more detail on the internet.[15] Here, the exhibit halls dedicated to world war history are presented in a virtual tour. Several of the museum's "cult objects" have a direct connection to the First World War.[16]

Like museums, memorial sites also function as custodians of the collective memory. They, too, present themselves primarily on the internet, contributing to the digital transmission of world war remembrance. When memorial sites are spoken of in German-language areas, however, it is usually in reference to memorials dedicated to victims of the National Socialist regime and the Holocaust. In Germany there is no memorial of significance dedicated primarily to the First World War. The tradition of the Unknown Soldier was never able to take root here.[17] There is no monument comparable to the Arc de Triomphe in France or the Cenotaph in Britain. The reasons lie in the responsibility that Germany bore for the outbreak of the war in 1914, the fact that the German national territory was only marginally affected, and the German defeat in 1918. The Zentrale Gedenkstätte der Bundesrepublik Deutschland für die Opfer des Krieges und der Gewaltherrschaft (Central Memorial of the Federal Republic of Germany for the Victims of the War and Dictatorship), founded in 1993, has ceased all effort to foster remembrance of the fallen of the First World War. Search results for the Neue Wache (New Guardhouse) Unter den Linden are not only scarce, no official website for this memorial even exists. The federal government sites limit information on it to a few explanations and a copy of the words spoken at its dedication. It is unlikely that many people still recall that the Neue Wache had once been revamped according to a design by Heinrich Tessenow, and that in 1930–1931 it was declared a memorial site for the fallen of the First World War.[18]

Among the few associations in German-speaking areas dedicated to the First World War is the Volksbund Deutsche Kriegsgräberfürsorge e.V., or VdK (German War Graves Commission).[19] On its homepage the organization offers an online grave search that extends back to the First World War. Using various search criteria one can look for soldiers who fell in the First or Second World War. The problem in searches related to the First World War is that the individual's date of death is required. Unlike the fallen of the Second World War, there is usually no date of birth available. The Historiker 1914–1918 (Historians of 1914–1918), founded in 2002, have responded to this and are in the process of updating the VdK data bank. This, however, does not appear to have ignited much enthusiasm among VdK members.[20]

As in English-speaking countries, private individuals from German-language areas are also doing research on the First World War. It is obvious that these are usually not professional academic historians in pursuit of their special interests, but it would also be an oversimplification to say that this circle of amateur historians hosts websites only about weapons technology and military matters.[21] In fact, websites focusing on the First World War that glorify war appear to be the exception.[22] There are many private sites that reflect family or local historical interests in the First World War. What is striking about these privately operated sites is that their owners feel compelled to defend their interest in the First World War, as if expecting to be accused of having morally objectionable intentions. There is also an expressed need to prevent the memory of the war from fading. The operator of the site Frontflieger (Front Flyer) distances himself from all forms of hero worship and asserts that the members of the aviation troops of the First World War were forced by circumstances into service to their country, which is not necessarily the case for that military branch.[23] The operators of another website proclaim themselves dedicated to exposing the horror of war and to issuing a warning to "irresponsible violators of the peace."[24]

On private sites some surprising historical documentation has been achieved. For several years Hinrich Dirksen researched the subject of war experiences of world war fighters from the area around his East Frisian homeland.[25] What led him to this research, he writes, was the death of his grandmother. This had stirred his awareness that the family history associated with the First World War had now faded, no longer part of the family's oral tradition.[26] He began to organize the documents she had passed on, learned to decipher the Sütterlin writing style, and over the course of two years researched the war experience of his great-grandfather Harm Dirksen.[27] In 1998 Harm Dirksen's great-grandson began a bicycle tour in the region around Passchendaele, where Harm Dirksen had fought. The stages of this trip can be retraced on his website, with the help of photos and a reference map.[28] His search for the trail of his ancestor simultaneously became a search for the trail of the First World War. Several times Dirksen placed his photos from 1998 next to historical photos of the same area, showing how the areas had changed over the years while still being recognizable as battle areas of the First World War. Out of Dirksen's work an archive of the war biographies of East Frisian soldiers of the First World War has grown. The biographies are illustrated wherever possible with original documents, providing a trove of research material for micro-historical investigations.[29]

Another site, hosted by B. Abendroth, shows extensive photographic documentation of monuments to soldiers of the First World War, encompassing not only Germany but also other European countries.[30] This site, however, leaves a less than positive impression. The text entitled "My Motivation" clearly reveals that the author is someone who has pondered the horrific results of hatred and violence and questioned the meaning of war. She distances herself from revisionism and glorification of war. On the other hand, Ms. Abendroth, a conservative "patriot," also uses the visual structure and content of her website to conduct a melodramatic, folksy, homeland death cult with striking undertones of German nationalism.

English- and French-Language Internet Sites

The largest share of digital information on the First World War is available on English-language internet sites, and to a lesser extent on French-language sites. As in the case of German-language sites, there are comparatively few offerings of a scholarly nature, as the internet is primarily a platform for clubs and amateur historians. One offering from Britain is that of the Commonwealth War Graves Commission (CGWC), the British equivalent of VdK.[31] The roots of this organization extend as far back as the First World War. In 1915 the Graves Registration Commission was created as a part of the army; in 1917 it became the Imperial War Graves Commission and in 1919 the Commonwealth War Graves Commission. Most of the burial sites from the First World War in Belgium and northern France are Commonwealth sites. They are still designed uniformly according to criteria defined during the First World War: each grave is marked with an individual gravestone and the gravestones are of uniform design, not differentiated by military rank, race, or religion. Like the VdK, the CWGC also offers the opportunity to search online for the grave sites of fallen soldiers of the First World War. The Debt of Honor Register lists 1.7 million men and women of the Commonwealth troops who died in both world wars as well as the 23,000 cemeteries, memorial sites, and other sites where they are commemorated.

The modern and professionally designed websites of the Royal British Legion reflect the magnitude of British military remembrance fund-raising efforts.[32] As Great Britain's leading charity organization, it offers financial, social, and emotional support to former and current members of the Commonwealth troops.[33] It was founded in 1921 to represent the interests of veterans of the First World War and today has five hundred thousand members.

The Royal British Legion is the self-proclaimed central custodian of the collective memory of the war dead of the British nation. Every year on 11 November it leads the moment of silence; on Remembrance Sunday (the second Sunday in November) at the Cenotaph in Whitehall there is a religious service, parade, and memorial ceremony. The organization also sponsors the annual Poppy Appeal, a nationwide donation campaign. The legion organized the first Poppy Day in 1921, a tradition going back to the initiative of an American secretary of state who, at the end of the war, inspired by the famous poem about poppy flowers by the Canadian John McCrae, came up with the idea of selling poppies to help war veterans.[34] In 1922 a factory was established in Richmond where disabled veterans assembled simply designed artificial poppies. The Poppy Appeal of 2001 brought in donations totaling 21.1 million pounds for the benefit of eligible recipients. In 2004 the Richmond factory produced more than 38 million artificial poppies, 98,000 wreaths, 730,000 memorial crosses, and other objects of remembrance. Some of these products are offered for purchase online.[35] The selection ranges from model airplanes to wine and whiskey bottles with poppy imprints all the way to poppy seeds for one's own garden. The British Legion is steadfast in its marketing of the poppy motif, which is ever present on its website.

The website of Imperial War Museum (IWM) is an example of the extent to which museums can take advantage of the internet.[36] It offers practical information as well as insights into the concept and structure of individual exhibition areas, such as its gallery dedicated to the First World War.[37] Online research into the IWM collection has now become available. Organized according to subject matter, the website provides access to information on selected topics and related images. A keyword search such as "trench warfare," for instance, currently brings up a list of fifty-four hits comprised of books, audio documents, paintings, texts and also, to a limited extent, images of three-dimensional objects.[38]

An example of innovative and creative use of the internet can be seen in the web pages of the Belgian World War Museum's In Flanders' Fields.[39] For the most part these are designed to be interactive and are meant to be viewed and explored at a leisurely pace. From the main menu the visitor can choose different approaches to learning about the First World War, including through a timeline of the era using keywords, through the stories of individual participants, or through specific topics, such as "chemical warfare." It is also possible to take a virtual tour of the exhibit halls.

National memorial sites in France and the Commonwealth countries also have their own internet offerings that focus on remembrance of the First World War. One is the Australian War Memorial in Canberra. The citizens of Australia, like Canadians and New Zealanders, derive their national identity from the experience of the world war of 1914–1918; their memorial sites for the war dead therefore represent a kind of pilgrimage destination. A highly respected institution, the Australian War Memorial is exceptional in its use of the internet as a medium for information and communication.[40]

The Australian War Memorial in Canberra is both museum and memorial site, a double function that was conceived of in 1916. In Canberra, one can view the exhibit halls as well as visit the tomb of the Unknown Soldier.[41] The roots of the museum's collection extend back to the year 1917, and its permanent exhibits include a gallery dedicated to the First World War.[42] The collections are accessible online to a large extent, presented in a very user-friendly way. The memorial's commitment to the role of guardian of the collective memory of its nation is clearly apparent on its internet site. An online visitor can access information on the facility's separate Remembrance Area, and under the topic heading "Commemoration" extensive information on the national culture of remembrance can be found, such as descriptions of Remembrance Day in honor of the Armistice of 11 November 1918.[43] Texts of official speeches from earlier Remembrance Days are also available, as are photos of the ceremonies.[44] With a suitably equipped PC, one can listen to the melody of the "Last Post."[45] The Roll of Honour, which lists the names of more than one hundred thousand fallen soldiers, is accessible through a separate data bank. School classes can register online for a visit to the memorial site.[46] The website provides access to a great deal of additional information and services that can only be touched on here, such as a biographical data bank, a research center for family history, and an extensive online shop for souvenirs of all kinds.

Participation in the First World War is also an essential part of Canadians' national identity. The internet sites of the official and national organizations are informative, up to date, and user friendly. The umbrella organization of the archives and libraries has an exemplary online display that provides access to original documents pertaining to the history of the Great War.[47] The site offers a data bank of war journals, which can be selected according to the geographical area of the battles. There are also war recollections by individuals illustrated with original documents and photographs that are fully available bibliographically. Also addressed are more general issues, such as the mobilization of the

Canadian home front, which are accompanied by a wealth of materials. The Canadian Ministry for Veterans Affairs also maintains its own site devoted to Canada's role in the First World War.[48]

A detailed description is provided of the 1917 battle of Vimy Ridge, the first military operation the Canadian Corps planned and carried out under its own leadership, which holds a significant place in the collective memory of Canadians. Rounding out the offerings is a data bank of interviews with veterans and individual documents such as wartime diaries, letters, and poems.

For the French, some of the most important memories come from Verdun and its surrounding area. The combined Mémorial de Verdun, which is both museum and site of commemoration, offers extensive online documentation.[49] Here one can take a virtual tour through the museum portion of the building and find information about the museum and its services prior to visiting. For those seeking further knowledge, a description of the events of the battle for Verdun is available. Especially informative are the detailed texts written by known professionals in the field that focus on the culture of remembrance in its relationship to Verdun, its evolution, and its various levels of meaning. Moreover, in the online dossiers one can access information on specific topics such as the destruction of human life, architecture and nature in the "red zone," or the fate of those with facial injuries.[50]

In the English- and French-language areas there are numerous clubs and other organizations that have taken up researching the history of the First World War, some of which have developed over time into semiprofessional organizations. Through offerings such as trips to former battlefields, or by making extensive documentation available on the internet, they contribute to keeping alive the memory of the First World War.

One of these groups is the Association 1914–1918, a French organization founded in 1990.[51] It is intended as a national platform for everything concerning the history of the First World War, and today has about three hundred members. The members organize battlefield tours and aim to establish an international network of those interested in the world war. The association's newsletter, which is also accessible online and includes a list of its authors, appears about every three months. Further offerings are a mailing list and a discussion forum that is frequented by international visitors. Documents and sources on the website can be particularly useful for amateur historians doing family history research. Texts and original photos are included as well as information on the relocation of individual French units with bibliographical details provided for further research. In addition there is a comprehensively annotated collection of links.

One of the largest and best known private organizations concerned with the history of the First World War is the Western Front Association.[52] It was founded in 1980 by military historian John Giles and today has more than sixty-five hundred members worldwide. The organization has supported many remembrance and research projects. In 1995 it campaigned in support of the Royal British Legion's efforts to revitalize the tradition of the moment of silence on 11 November, a practice that had existed since 1919. Today, even when the 11th of November falls on a workday, much of Britain puts down its work for that moment in honor of the dead of the First World War. The organization sponsors an annual function and publishes two periodicals each year. The home page offers many references for further information on remembrance of the First World War, with a primary focus on the western front. It offers a virtual experience of the most important monuments and remembrance sites of the region. One particularly notable item is a map room, where many maps of battle areas on the western front are available for viewing online, each of which can be enlarged.[53]

Lastly, the Great War Society must be mentioned. Founded in 1987 by a research group at the Hoover Institute for War, Peace and Revolution, the society now has numerous branches.[54] This is another association whose desire is to promote discussion, learning, and research on the First World War by both professionals and amateurs. To this purpose seminars on world war topics take place in various locations in the US as well as study trips to former battlefields. The organization's website is intended to support research and strengthen networking among the members. The site works with design elements similar to those of commercial websites. The website provides a broad spectrum of offerings and services, with a mini-portal providing easy access to special topics, such as the Italian front. The organization publishes an online newsletter and each month a "Veteran of the Month" is presented. For students and researchers a separate portal is available, in which bibliographical lists and addresses of publishers can be found. In addition there is an annotated collection of links.

Many amateur historians in English-language areas are committed to First World War research. Among these was Mike Iavarone, originator of a comprehensive internet resource called Trenches on the Web that is listed in almost all web indexes. Since his death it has been managed by the Great War Society.[55] The site offers a search machine, a discussion forum, an online newsletter, and tips for battlefield tours in northern France. The reason for the popularity of the site becomes clear upon reading the entries under the title "Legends and Traditions." This area contains yarns and stories about the First World War. A mini-documentation of "Hitler's War Service," for instance, will no doubt satisfy some visitors' thirst for the sensational.

Another devotee of First World War research is Tom Morgan of Great Britain. The grandson of a world war soldier, Morgan discovered the subject at age seventeen. For years he researched the biographies of participants in the First World War and traveled to the former battle areas in France and Belgium. In 1996 Morgan posted on the internet a seven-day journal in which he recorded his impressions of a tour of the former battlefields in the Somme region. From these modest beginnings, the world war platform Hellfire Corner was created.[56] Under the topic heading "Latest News," interested visitors can find current information as well as chats and rumors from the (semiprofessional) milieu of world war enthusiasts. One focal point of the site is practical information and tips for planning and carrying out individual battlefield tours. Here one finds numerous trip reports and tour recommendations by individuals who have made the trips to former battle areas, even to far away theaters of war such as Gallipoli. There are also articles and reports containing information on the history and current condition of world war memorial sites and military cemeteries. A further subject heading, "Individual Lives—Research and Remembrance," underscores the connection between research work and the culture of remembrance. Amateur historians on the trail of their ancestors post biographical texts here on the net, which are based for the most part on extensive research.

First World War Remembrance in Eastern Europe

In the eastern European–language areas the remembrance of the First World War is also fostered via the internet, but to a considerably lesser extent than in countries such as Great Britain, the US, or Australia. This imbalance reflects the marginal status of the topic in the collective consciousness of eastern European nations.[57]

Here, too, the digital medium is neither more nor less than a reflection of the structures and guiding themes of societal interests. In eastern Europe in general, the memory of the First World War stands in the shadow of the Russian Revolution and the continued interstate wars that accompanied the founding of the Soviet Union, especially in the Baltic areas.[58] It was not until the end of the East-West conflict and the breakup of the Soviet Union that a gradual transformation took place.[59]

An impressive example of a Polish internet site on the First World War is a photographic montage of the destruction in the city of Kalisz.[60] This is of particular importance because there is much less awareness of the excesses committed against the civilian population in eastern Europe than of the wartime atrocities on the western front. In the national consciousness of the Poles, the almost complete destruction of this unprotected city by German troops in August 1914 represents a major trauma. It is still remembered today as a pogrom. According to details found on this website, 95 percent of the medieval inner quarter of the city fell victim to artillery bombardments and arson. Then came the executions by shooting. After a mass exodus from the city, the number of inhabitants fell from sixty-five thousand to five thousand.[61] The city council of Kalisz planned to rebuild in 1916 but met with resistance from the

German occupiers and the reconstruction could not be carried out until after 1918. The internet site was established in 1995, on the eighty-first anniversary of the destruction of the city, using photographs to document the destroyed parts of the city before and after their restoration. While the text is mostly written in Polish, there are abstracts available in English, French, and German. The nucleus of the material consists of a data bank of black-and-white photographs. A photo of 1914–1915, for instance, is compared to one from 1995, underscoring the amount of devastation and the impressive restoration efforts. A city map allows a virtual orientation within the city, giving precise locations of the individual photos.

Commemoration of the Russian Expedition Corps in France has also begun to develop.[62] On the websites of the Pedagogical Information Center of the Champagne-Ardennes Region, one finds an internet site on the military cemetery of St.-Hilaire-le-Grand, which was established for the Russians who fell in battle in the Champagne region, and which is also a memorial site.[63] The cemetery, which was completely renovated in 1998, includes 489 gravesites with the remains of 915 fallen soldiers. There are also an Orthodox chapel, a memorial monument, and two ossuaries located there. The website is illustrated with numerous photos, and the French-language texts are informative and generally easy to understand.

Further, the Association du souvenir du corps expéditionnaire en France (Association in Honor of the Russian Expeditionary Corps in France) is dedicated to the remembrance of the Russian soldiers who fought in the world war on the side of the Allies.[64] On the website's opening page is a discussion of "the treason of Brest-Litovsk," the treaty, also instigated by the German General Staff, that the Bolsheviks signed as a price for their Revolution. The operators of the site maintain that this betrayal must not be allowed to erase the memory of three years of bloody fighting and the heavy losses suffered by the Russian Expeditionary Corps. The site offers several short texts about the corps and conditions on the western front in 1916. Moreover, one can access photos both from today and from that period. Every Easter the organization conducts a memorial ceremony at St.-Hilaire-le-Grand. Color photos of the ceremony of 2004 are posted on the net.[65]

An organization dedicated to remembrance of the Russian Legion is also present online. The Russian Legion came into being during the October Revolution, when a part of the Russian Expeditionary Corps joined the Bolsheviks and some of its officers decided to continue to fight on the side of the Allies. The legion, officially recognized by the French government in December 1917, fought through to the end of the war on French territory in the area of Lorraine. In memory of the legion, a reenactment group (Reenactment Legion, or RL) was formed.[66] Its website provides texts on the history of the Russian troops in France as well as a very comprehensively annotated list with related historical and contemporary photos and postcards. The requirements for membership in the organization are outlined in detail. These include respect for the uniform of the world war soldier of all parties involved, and the applicant must be a member of the Great War Society. Another requirement is owning a complete set of reenactment equipment, the components of which can be acquired through the RL, which produces and sells historically correct replicas of the uniform pieces. One of the site's unique offerings is the ability to download audio files of historical songs and marches from the Russian Legion.

Steps toward European World War Remembrance on the Internet?

The virtual sphere of the internet has unlimited potential. Through the decentralized structure of the World Wide Web, one can easily surf across barriers posed by language or subject matter. It is also conceivable that in future a kind of world war remembrance could appear on the internet that extends beyond the forms and contents of remembrance handed down and characterized by nationalities. Might the internet evolve into an experimental laboratory for a European culture of remembrance?

There are organizations and projects dedicated to concepts of this sort. One of these bears the cumbersome name of Deutsche Erinnerungskomitee Argonnerwald, 1914–1918 e.V. (German Remembrance Committee of the Argonne Forests, 1914–1918).[67] This organization works to foster the memory of the First World War in the region between the western edge of the Argonne Forest and Verdun. It works in close cooperation with the national French forest authorities, one French club, and one German-French club. Because of its international sphere of influence, the organization has two seats, one in Germany and one in France. The members conduct research in archives and make the results available locally. The website is simple in design, although presented in three languages. Its self-described purpose is to honor the fallen of both sides and to convey the horror of the war to later generations, with the goal of contributing to international understanding.

Certain other types of organizations, while they may function well on a local level and operate through close personal contacts, do not necessarily carry over to larger contexts. One example of this is an internet project sponsored by the European Union, Wege der Erinnerung (Paths of Remembrance), designed for school pupils and university-level students.[68] Over the course of one year, six museums and research facilities from six countries researched and posted to the net documents related to remembrance sites of each participating country with the intention of attracting visitors to a virtual expedition. Yet, as Susanne Brandt noted in her critique of the website, "Despite European desires, there remains a narrow, dominating national perspective."[69] Verdun, for instance, was shown only from the French perspective, even though at this site the Germans and the French had previously exchanged gestures of reconciliation. As the reviewer notes, because of the particular sensitivities of each of the countries involved, it became a difficult process to agree on the content of the text and wording of individual phrases.[70] Still, the ambitions for the project reach beyond these issues, and in the future eastern European institutions and memorial sites are to be added.

An overall more successful and attractive project is the website the Color of Tears sponsored by UNESCO.[71] Here, prestigious European museums display the works of fifty-four painters whose artworks reflect First World War themes. After reading an introductory text, the visitor may choose between two paths: alphabetically according to the name of the painter with cross-references to the respective works, or thematically according to works whose titles are keyed to descriptive phrases or slogans. Each work is accompanied by a description of the painting. The images can be enlarged and can be viewed in very good color quality. The website has a sophisticated design and provides a very interesting introduction to avant-garde art of the world war years. In this case, too, however, the ambition to reflect a broad European perspective is only halfway fulfilled, as the examples consist only of works by western European artists.

Finally, there is a project by students in the Department of Romance Languages and Literatures at the Technical University of Chemnitz.[72] It represents a reflection on death in the First World War and is illustrated with high-quality images as well as both personal and official forms of remembrance. The starting point consists of five images arranged in the form of a cross. From here the visitor can select different groups of images related to one another, each of which expands the theme of the site. The students chose the red poppy as their symbol, arguing that although originally the poppy had been a commemoration symbol for the victors, they feel that a focus on the First World War can reach beyond the model of "victor and vanquished." Here, the poppy flower supposedly stands for a transnational remembrance of those who died in the years 1914–1918. As well meant as this may have been, in the interest of historical accuracy it must be said that the students have misinterpreted the meaning of the poppy. The poppy, which even during the war was used as a symbol of remembrance, was never intended as an emblem of victory. From the beginning the red flower stood for the collective mourning over the millions of losses from one's own ranks.

Perspectives

Today public and private life are unimaginable without the World Wide Web. The internet offers a potentially limitless reservoir of information not only on historical events and topics but also on the standards and strategies of our present conduct in relationship with the past. It is no surprise, then, that this digital medium also plays an ever-increasing role in the remembrance of the First World War. Although it is not a primary influence on opinion, a role still occupied by various print media and television, it is nevertheless making a growing contribution to the collective memory of the nations that were at war and those that were affected by the war.

Public institutions such as museums, memorial sites, associations, and even private individuals are working to document and analyze the First World War. What is striking, however, is that academic scholarship is rarely represented online. Internet sources about the First World War appear to be primarily the domain of private associations and amateur historians. Digital world war remembrance therefore must be classified as a realm of communication and data storage rather than of cultural memory. Amateur research and the need to remember and to issue warnings often seem to go hand in hand.

Most websites on the First World War are in English, French, and German, which is a reflection of the significance of the First World War to the collective memory of each of these language areas. The few websites that were discussed here relating to eastern Europe are not representative and therefore cannot be cited as benchmarks.

In comparing the internet examples from various western European countries, several noticeable differences are evident. First of all, no unbroken tradition of remembrance of the First World War was ever developed in Germany. This stems from the facts, as noted above, that to a great extent Germany was responsible for starting the war, little fighting took place on German territory, and Germany ultimately lost the war. Moreover, for Germany, the Second World War and the Holocaust are still the central focal points of work on collective memory and will remain so for the foreseeable future. As is reflected on the internet, remembrance of the world war is much more immediate in countries such as Great Britain, Australia, and France. For these countries, the events of 1914–1918 are commemorated primarily by memorial sites and museums but are also the focus of many semiofficial organizations. Their collective memory is cultivated at centralized locations, places that are laden with symbolic meaning and highly charged with emotion. The related institutions use the internet as an important medium to promote their efforts and to disseminate information. The internet plays a fundamental role, above all, in countries with a relatively large area and small populations, such as Australia and Canada. One need not travel to Canberra to honor one's ancestors who fought and died during the First World War—one can do so with a click of the mouse from home.

Several of the internet websites discussed here, especially those in English, reveal some important differences with German-language sites. For instance, unlike in Germany, their approach to the study of military history in general, and of the First World War in particular, does not seem encumbered by a fear of confronting the subject. Moreover, they show that memory, memorializing, and commerce are not mutually exclusive. The design of many websites often recall commercial websites with their bold colors, images, and moving elements. The motto “War Sells” appears true in this case. Private operators of websites pertaining to the First World War also usually explain how and why they developed such a keen interest in the subject. The tone of these explanations seems more credible than on many German internet sites. Still, it is not the purpose of this essay to explore the concept of peoples’ fascination with the First World War, or their significant investment of time on their home pages.

The advantages of the World Wide Web as a medium for data storage and communications are simultaneously its disadvantages. While there is quick access to up-to-date information and a decentralized network of the URL addresses, there are also problems, such as the quick obsolescence of some information, difficulty in retrieving information, and the tendency to become deluged in a river of data. Such benefits and problems are also true of internet sites devoted to the First World War. Websites that are regularly managed can provide up-to-the-minute information more easily than a book or professional periodical. Informal communication in the “community” of amateur historians, in particular, runs for the most part via the internet. Anyone interested in family history related to the First World War will make faster progress here than with the German War Graves Commission. Moreover, large world war websites offer an orientation guide for beginners through their catalogues of lists and subject portals. Nevertheless, such sites cannot replace the text of a carefully researched, well-written, and well-organized introduction to the subject. And then there is also the aggravation of incomplete, false, and obsolete web addresses.

A further major advantage of the internet is the ability to experience the memorial sites visually. With advanced technology, the numbers and quality of images posted on the internet are increasing. For many interested visitors, the only way, or the only desired way, to visit the former battlefields of the First World War is online. For others, it is quite usual to visit a place online, then visit it in person. Information on the internet will spark their interest and provide the motivation to spend time in a museum or personally travel to actual historical sites.

One question posed earlier was whether there would someday be an internet-supported European world war remembrance. It appears, in fact, that the internet has awakened the hope that we might overcome the limitations and sensibilities of individual national perspectives and cultivate the remembrance of the years 1914 to 1918 from more of bird’s-eye perspective. Prestigious institutions and facilities have shown interest in offering financial support to such projects. The websites presented here, however, demonstrate that it is a long path to this form of remembrance. None of the projects are pan-European to the extent that they include both eastern and western Europe. Very often it is the language barrier that badly hinders European-wide remembrance of the First World War. The wording of a text on the internet, for instance, can ignite sensitivities, especially when dealing with political correctness and nuances of meaning. Further, the short-term goals of such projects seem counter to a long-term transformation of consciousness. Finally, lack of both motivation and historical knowledge hinders the development of a European perspective of the First World War. The front that divides national memorial areas, each with its own symbols of remembrance, will not be easy to cross, even in the digital age.

Notes

1. See, e.g., Stuart Jenks and Paul Tiedemann, *Internet für Historiker. Eine praxisorientierte Einführung,* 2nd ed. Darmstadt 2002; Waldemar Grosch, *Geschichte im Internet: Tipps, Tricks und Adressen,* Schwalbach i.Ts. 2002; *Gedächtnis und Erinnerung. Ein interdisziplinäres Lexikon,* edited by Nicolas Pethes and Jens Ruchatz, Reinbek 2001, 283–86; *Internet-Handbuch Geschichte,* edited by Stuart Jenks and Stephanie Marra, Cologne 2001; Christian von Ditfurth, *Internet für Historiker,* 3rd ed., Frankfurt 1999; Peter Horvath, *Geschichte online. Neue Möglichkeiten für die historische Fachinformation,* Cologne 1997 (= *Historische Sozialforschung,* supplement 8); Gerhard Paul, *Bilder des Krieges. Krieg der Bilder. Die Visualisierung des modernen Krieges,* Paderborn 2004, 151f.

2. On the rapid development of the fields of social and cultural history since 1996, see Humanities-Net-Sozial-und Kulturgeschichte (H-Soz-u-Kult), *Bilanz nach 3 Jahren.* Edited by Rüdiger Hohls and Peter Helmbeger, Cologne 1999 (= *Historische Sozialforschung,* 89; special issue, "Historical Social Research"). Individual reviews not included here. The scope of the H-Soz-u-Kult applies, for instance, to the digital organ for reviews—*sehepunkte* (perspectives)—or for the newsletter of the Arbeitskreis Militärgeschichte e.V. (Military History Study Group).

3. Maurice Halbwachs, *Das kollektive Gedächtnis,* Frankfurt 1985.

4. See www.erster-weltkrieg.clio-online.de.

5. *Internet-Handbuch,* 95; Ditfurth, *Internet für Historiker,* 205.

6. See, e.g., www.bib.byu.edu/~rdh/wwi/links.html (an international list of links organized by country by the Harold B. Lee Library at Brigham Young University, Utah; www.erster-weltkrieg.clio-online.de (thematically organized Web index); www.worldwar1.com (Reference Library 1914–1918 supersearch).

7. See *Gedächtnis und Erinnerung,* 329–32 (with further references provided under the heading "Kulturelles Gedächtnis" [Cultural Memory]).

8. On cultural memory, see Jan Assmann, *Das Kulturelle Gedächtnis. Schrift, Erinnerung und politische Identität in frühen Hochkulturen,* Munich 1992; *Mnemosyne. Formen und Funktionen der kulturellen Erinnerung,* edited by Aleida Assmann and Dietrich Harth, Frankfurt 1991; *Kultur und Gedächtnis,* edited by Jan Assmann and Tonio Hölscher, Frankfurt 1988.

9. www.bib.byu.edu/~rdh/wwi/links.html; www.erster-weltkrieg.clio-online.de; www.worldwar1.com.

10. www.erster-weltkrieg.clio-online.de.

11. For an introduction to the German-language museum landscape on the internet, see www.webmuseen.de; for an international link index to military museums, see the website of the Arbeitskries Militärgeschichte e.V. at www.akmilitaergeschichte.de.

12. See www.dhm.de. The DHM supports the largest museum server in Germany. Daily about thirty thousand visitors use this service and access around 150,000 pages. See also www.dhm.de/ausstellungen/der-erste-Weltkrieg/index.html.

13. See www.dhm.de/lemo/. Of the thirty thousand visitors to the DHM pages, about 50 percent use LeMo.

14. See www.wgm-rastatt.de. The Militärgeschichtliches Museum (MHM—Military History Museum) in Dresden is presently being renovated according to plans by Daniel Libeskind. In conjunction, there will be a new concept for the permanent exhibitions. For information on the MHM, see the website of the Militärgeschichtliches Forschungamt, Potsdam, www.mgfa.de.

15. See www.hgm.or.at.

16. Among these are items pertaining to the assassination at Sarajevo: the bloodstained uniform jacket of Franz Ferdinand, the automobile in which the Austro-Hungarian crown prince was murdered, and a chaise longue where the dying man was lain.

17. On the "creation" of the Unknown Soldiers, see the essay in this volume by Rainer Rother.

18. Tessenow built the original one-and-a half-story interior area with an inner courtyard as a memorial hall with a circular skylight. On the history of the monument, see *Mahnmahl Mitte. Eine Kontroverse,* edited by Michael Jeismann, Cologne 1999; *Die Neue Wache unter den Linden. Ein deutsches Mahnmal im Wandel der Geschichte,* edited by Christoph Stölz, Berlin 1993; Hermann Hoepker-Aschoff, *Die Neue Wache als Gedächtnisstätte für die Gefallenen des Weltkrieges,* Berlin 1931.

19. See www.volksbund.de. A journal that presently covers 1919 to 2002 shows the domestic political events of that time in relationship to key dates in the history of the Volksbund. This provides a helpful synopsis of the aftereffects of the First World War in the politics and society of the Weimar era and beyond. The Volksbund began in 1919 as a citizens' initiative, which had the goal of caring for the graves of German prisoners of the First World War outside of Germany.

20. See www.historiker 14–18.de/results_mich_7_03.htm.

21. *Internet-Handbuch Geschichte,* 95.

22. The website www.stahlgewitter.com makes a dubious impression. Its journal of the First World War is limited to the months of August–December 1914 and the period between 4/11 and 18/11/1918. Propaganda photos without commentary, such as the "Hanging of Spies" on the eastern front, are placed next to the sometimes depressing pictures of dead German and Allied soldiers. The 1917 texts "Training for Shock Troops" and "Instruction Pamphlet on the Gas War" are quoted verbatim. There is no sort of self-identifying information offered by the site managers.

23. See www.frontflieger.de.

24. See www.weltkrieg.husfeld-online.de/.

25. See www.forum 14–18.de/.

26. "My interest in this war began in 1996, when my ninety-three-year-old grandmother closed her eyes for the last time and I inherited a shoebox of photos and about thirty postcards from the field from her father, who died in 1915." See ibid.

27. See www.forum14–18.de/harm.htm.

28. See www.forum14–18.de/tour1.htm.

29. See www.forum14–18.de/men.htm.

30. See www.kriegerdenkmal.com.

31. See www.cwgc.org/cwgcinternet/search.aspx.

32. See www.britishlegion.org.uk/index.asp.

33. Currently this is about 13 million people, about 20 percent of the British population. Each year, three hundred thousand people turn to the British Legion for support.

34. See www.britishlegion.org.uk/who/poppy_history.asp.

35. See www.britishlegion.org.uk/helups/shop_latest.asp.

36. See www.iwm.org.uk.

37. See http://london.iwm.org.uk/server/show/ConWebDoc.1471.

38. For detailed discussion of the website's offerings, see http://hsozkult.geschichte.hu-berlin.de/rezensionen/type=rezwww&id=44.

39. See www.inflandersfields.be.

40. See www.awm.gov.au.

41. Since 1941, remembrance also applies to the fallen of the Second World War, and since 1952 it also now includes the Australians who fell in all wars.

42. See www.awm.gov.au/virtualtour/ww1.htm.

43. See www.awm.gov.au/virtualtour/commemorative.htm; www.awm.gov.au/commemoration/remembrance/index.htm.

44. See, e.g., www.awm.gov.au/commemoration/remembrance/2003/photos.asp.

45. In Australian military tradition the end of the day's routine is marked with a bugle playing this sequence of notes. This melody is also played at military funerals and religious memorial services, signifying that the soldiers have found their final rest.

46. See www.awm.gov.au/commemoration/wreath/index.htm.

47. See www.collectionscanada.ca/firstworldwar/index-e.html.

48. See www.vac-acc.gc.ca/general/sub.cfm?source=history/firstwar.

49. See www.memorial-14-18.com. A review of the site is available at www.hsozkult.geschichte.hu-berlin.de/rezensionen/type=rezwww&id=41.

50. The red zone refers to a surface of about 120,000 hectares designated as the front line of the First World War. The terrain was considered no longer cultivatable because of extreme destruction. The French government bought up the area and reforested it. On the red zone of Verdun, there are eight completely destroyed villages, the so-called *villages détruits,* which are purposely not being rebuilt and whose former locations are now memorial sites.

51. See www.association14-18.org.

52. See www.westernfrontassociation.com.

53. See www.westernfrontassociation.com/thegreatwar/maproom.php. The comprehensive and well-organized, although not annotated, list of links is a helpful starting point for further internet research on the First World War.

54. See www.worldwar1.com/tgws2.htm.

55. See www.worldwar1.com.

56. See www.fylde.demon.co.uk/welcome.htm.

57. Due to the language barrier, unfortunately no websites in Cyrillic writing will be explored.

58. For a web directory on this topic, see www.barnsdle.demon.co.uk/russ/rusrev.html.

59. See the essay by Kristiane Janeke in the present volume.

60. See www.infokalisz.internetdsl.pl/ka11914/.

61. German-language research literature on Kalisz is almost nonexistent. An outline of the city history can be found on Wikipedia; the official site for the city is www.kalisz.pl.

62. During the First World War, beginning in 1916, four Russian brigades fought with about forty-five thousand soldiers on the French side. See Jamie H. Cockfield, *With Snow on Their Boots: The Tragic Odyssey of the Russian Expeditionary Forces in France during World War I,* Basingstoke 1999.

63. See http://crdp.ac-reims.fr/memoire/lieux/1GM_CA/cimetieres/russes/saint_hilaire.htm. See also www.russie.net/france/cim-hilaire.htm.

64. See http://ascerf.free.fr.

65. Further, there is a discussion forum and a reserved area for club members. Further offerings for downloading are few. All that is available is a video titled *La Marseillaise.*

66. See www.members.aol.com/begemot/legion/.

67. www.argonnerwald.de/index-de.htm.

68. See www.wege-der-erinnerung.de. In addition, see the discussion by Susanne Brandt, "Gemeinsamer Weg im nationalen Alleingang? Ein europäisches Projekt zu Erinnerungsorten des 20. Jahrhunderts." In: *Zeithistorische Forschungen/Studies in Contemporary History,* online ed., 1 (2004), 3, http//www.zeithistorische-forschungen.de/16126041-Brandt-3-2004.

69. Ibid, 3.

70. Ibid., 5.

71. See www.art-ww1.com/d/visite.html. See also the discussion by Aaron Cohen at http://hsozkult.geschichte.hu-berlin.de/rezensionen/type=rezwww?id=38.

72. See www-user.tu-chemnitz.de/~ubrt.

20

Prologue to the "War of Annihilation"?

The Eastern Front of the First World War and the Problem of Continuities

Rüdiger Bergien

What motivated German soldiers to brutalize and plunder Soviet civilians in Kharkov in the fall of 1941?[1] Why did the conservative commander in chief of the 18th Army, Generaloberst (Colonel General) Georg von Küchler, with his Christian upbringing, choose to run a ruthless occupation policy on the outskirts of Leningrad, one that "consisted only of starvation, expulsion, and exploitation?"[2] How did it happen that the members of the civilian administration of the White Ruthenian General Commissariat, who were primarily members of the middle class and had not been open supporters of National Socialism at home, arrived in the east and mutated into racist members of the "master race"?[3] These kinds of questions about the war and occupation practices of the German Reich in the Soviet Union during the Second World War have not been answered satisfactorily, even ten years into a period of renewed research efforts.[4]

One approach to understanding the violence and crime between 1941 and 1945 is through the discourse of "mentalities."[5] This approach argues that the conduct of officers, soldiers, and civil servants is traceable back to what is termed collective dispositions.[6] These dispositions, or basic attitudes of individuals in a social system, are imprinted by the social and material living environment and through experiences that are personally or socially conveyed.

Authors such as Vejas Gabriel Liulevicius and Eberhard Demm have treated this subject in such a way as to posit the war on the eastern front of the First World War in a causal relationship with the German war of extermination during the Second World War.[7] According to their thesis, the actions by the Wehrmacht soldiers in Kharkov become more plausible when their cause is not blamed solely on National Socialistic ideology or on the militarization of German society during the previous years. Instead, what need to be taken into account are the experiences from the "Era of the World Wars."[8] This, in Liulevicius's interpretation, places one's focus inevitably on the first war fought by German soldiers in the twentieth century in central eastern and eastern Europe. The experience of the "forgotten front" of the First World War, according to Liulevicius, had a defining influence on the conduct of the German war of extermination during the Second World War.

What is known as the new cultural history is largely associated with sociology of knowledge posited by Nikolaus Buschmann and Horst Carl.[9] It includes the concept of *Erfahrungsbegriff* (experience), a term that refers to both an individual and a societal dimension of experience. Sociocultural parameters, according to Buschmann and Carl, "precede subjectively experienced reality. . . . Reality proves to be a social construct, which is reproduced and modified via experience."[10] Liulevicius argues that reality, as it was experienced by the Germans in Kharkov in November and December 1941, had been filtered and defined by "the German concept of the east" passed down from the First World War.[11] This image was a social construct, radicalized by experiences on the "forgotten front" during the First World War and postwar period, and gathered by those who would later become the German military elite of the Second World War.[12] One of these was Georg von Küchler, who led the siege of Leningrad and who had been a general staff officer in the "Courland Brigade" during the conquest of Riga.

The idea that that the two German wars in the east are linked in terms of their history of mentalities has found resonance in scholarly historical research. The new interest in the battles that began in 1914 in the area between the Baltic and the Black Seas, which is one focus of the present volume, is to a large extent a result of this thesis of continuities. For this reason the new interpretation of the Second World War prevalent during the 1990s, which used the war of extermination as a focal point for analysis, also inevitably drew on the war in the east. In other words, without the exhibit entitled *The War of Extermination* there would have been no collected volume under the title *The Forgotten Front*.

This approach to researching the eastern front of the First World War leaves room for skepticism. There is no doubt that the history of mentalities approach helps in understanding the motives of the perpetrators of the war of extermination as well as the passivity of its many bystanders. And certainly one must look for the origins of the concept of the "east" that the German soldiers who would later become the perpetrators and co-perpetrators had already assembled in their own minds, and investigate the role played by the war experience between 1914 and 1918. Yet, as someone has pointed out, "The problem with the concept of mentalities . . . is its vagueness."[13] Therefore, although various continuities have been placed into context with experiences, not enough is known at the present time about the significance of each to determine whether they share any common basis.

As long as this shared basis remains undetermined, it seems questionable to refer to the years of 1941–1944 as a continuation of the earlier war in the east, or to adopt the interpretive model of the "war of destruction" of the First World War in a way that turns the "forgotten front" itself into a war of extermination.[14] But if the research on the war in the east of 1914–1918 is to contribute to knowledge about the character and degree of "inner connectedness of the second Thirty Years' War," then some questions need to be addressed clearly. What were the actual experiences of the soldiers of the First World War; which of the direct experiences or developments during the two wars in the east can be considered parallel to one another; and to what extent can a link be found between experiences and continuities?[15]

This essay seeks to address these issues by summarizing the related chapters in this volume and placing them in context with the latest research. This discussion uses Buschmann and Carl's concept of experience, an element of the discourse of sociology of knowledge. The outcomes are divided here into the sections "Military Operations," "Violence and Terror," and "Occupation Government." These headings form the starting point for the reinterpretation of the Wehrmacht's war in Russia.

Military Operations

A historical analysis of operations during the 1914 war in the east must confront the following questions: (1) did the Prussian-German military find itself to be superior to that of Russia to the extent that in 1941 the Germans could justify their belief in the infallibility of Operation Barbarossa? and (2) were the victories at Tannenberg and Gorlice-Tarnów a prologue to the military catastrophe of December 1941?

According to Gerhard P. Gross and Boris Khavkin, the course of military operations in 1914–1915 gave the Germans no cause for hubris. Pointing to the battles at Tannenberg and the Masurian Lakes, Gross notes that, while these were operational victories for the Germans, they nevertheless masked a mistaken strategic decision that would later prove fatal. Fearing a further Russian advance, German leaders transferred divisions from the western to the eastern front, which was exactly how the Franco-Russian plan had predicted they would react. The Czarist Army's "East Prussia Operation" had therefore fulfilled its purpose by dividing the German armies' forces.

Yet even up to 1944–1945 the Prussian-German military elite still maintained its typical attitude of contempt for Russian military leaders. This attitude is one of the threads of continuity that run through the era of the two world wars, but it seems to have been based less on the Germans' actual operational experiences during the First World War than on their concept of the enemy, and this in turn influenced how they interpreted the operations.

Did this concept of the enemy have its basis in the directly experienced reality of the First World War, or was it instead a social construct communicated by key players in society who had never actually seen the "enemy" face-to-face? Christine Beil lends strong support to this thesis with her observations on the concept of "the Russians" created by German war exhibits of the First World War. But the perception held by the average individual German soldier must have differed from this distorted, propagandistic image. Boris Khavkin shows that the Germans had already fought against Masurian soldiers, who were known for their dogged resistance and ability to exploit the terrain for a safe retreat. As Hans-Erich Volkmann points out, this even garnered respect from the so-called terror of Russia, Paul von Hindenburg.

Even with this victory, however, these experiences did nothing to change the German concept of the Russian enemy. As Peter Hoeres notes, even in 1941 these experiences were not part of the calculations. Instead they were erased from memory many times over with remarkable parallelism during the border wars in June and July 1941 against the backdrop of operational victories. In 1942–1943, even when the German Reich had gone on the defensive, the Russian enemy was never acknowledged as having equal status. Instead, Germans now rationalized their defeats through stereotypical references to the Soviet "mass army." An old term from the era prior to 1914, *Dampfwalze*, or Russian steamroller, experienced a rebirth.[16] Thus, the German experiences on the eastern front that were related to operations were not handed down as a collective learning experience.

Nevertheless, was it not true that despite their spirit of resistance, the Russian soldiers of the First World War met with one defeat after the other? Wasn't the German sense of superiority vindicated merely on the basis of territory they conquered? Boris Khavkin holds the opposite to be true. From the Baltic Sea to the Black Sea, the Czarist Army, despite bad equipment, not only withstood the military power of four enemy powers but also won significant victories—in Galicia in the fall of 1914, for instance—and repeatedly undertook offensive operations that eventually resulted in the collapse of Austria-Hungary in the fall of 1918.

In his chapter, Igor Narskij supports Khavkin's revisionist depiction of the Russian Army from the viewpoint of experiential history. That Russian soldiers were backward and lacked the aptitude for a technological mass war (something the later German Army High Command, OKH, still alleged in an official brochure in early 1941), Narskij exposes as a largely after-the-fact construct of Soviet historical writing, which tended to ascribe experiences from the Russian Revolution and Civil War to the first years of the First World War.[17] According to Narskij, Russian soldiers were no more "premodern" than German or Austro-Hungarian infantrymen. One can infer from this that research on the Czarist Army has become subject to *conceptions of experience* as defined within the discourse of sociology of knowledge. In other words, directly experienced reality is not inevitably processed into a learning experience but instead can be distorted by after-the-fact collective interpretations.

This also applies to the German sense of superiority over their most important ally on the eastern front in 1914–1918, Austria-Hungary, for which many German officers had nothing but disdain. The quality of the Austro-Hungarian Army, however, was certainly not the reason for Germany's failed war in the east.[18] The military elite of multiethnic Austria-Hungary did attempt to portray its own units as weaker than they were. The practice of "flirting with one's own weaknesses" was part of the ploy to encourage the German High Command (OHL) to transfer more German units to the east. Actually, the Austro-Hungarian Army accomplished more than had been expected of it. But the German officer corps in particular had formed a mental image of the Austro-Hungarian ally that conflicted with historical reality. Instead, as Günther Kronenbitter demonstrates, the Germans complained about this ally in the attempt to divert attention from their own failures. This strategy, incidentally, operated both ways.

Even in 1914–1915, members of the German military elite displayed an exaggeratedly high opinion of themselves, something that would rear is head once more in 1940 with devastating results. Thus, one cannot credibly argue the Germans had directly experienced superiority in the area of operations that then cleared the path to the war of extermination. They did not directly experience superiority as much as they inferred this experience of superiority, and at the same time they refused to accept their enemy as their equal in battle.[19]

Violence and Terror

While the experiences in operations during the First World War may have had only a small influence on the thinking that led to the war of extermination in 1941, the concept of the enemy that had formed in the minds of the Germans during the years between 1914 and 1918 played an important part. Further investigation might even prove that this concept of the enemy is the dominating continuity between the two wars in the east to a much greater extent than any direct historical experience; and this phenomenon might also be something unique to the Germans.

In his research into cultural life in Russia during the First World War,

Hubertus F. Jahn shows that in Russia there was no specific image of "the German," unlike during the Great War of the Fatherland, the Second World War. For Russia, the enemy was embodied in images of its ruling figures, particularly Wilhelm II. In terms of the issue of continuities, however, one must ask to what extent the Russian concept or image of the Germans in the First World War functioned as a kind of plot element to the extent that it contributed to a brutalization of the conduct of war. Was the First World War in the east actually the prologue to the later war of extermination? And did it have built into it those things that would become the signature of the German-Soviet war—terror and violence? Or can we believe Andreas Hürter, who describes the terror as a product of "criminal ideology and state leadership," something that had not been present in the Kaiser Reich, and thus constitutes a line of distinction between the two eastern fronts?[20]

It must be pointed out here that in terms of quantity, intensity, and especially the ideological motivation behind the terror, the war of extermination of the Second World War differed from the First World War in its dimensions. Still, whatever has been said about terror and violence between 1914 and 1918 comes from a state of research on the subject that has not fully matured. Work by John Horne and Alan Kramer—whether or not one agrees with their results—has shown how little is known about the crimes committed during the Great War even ninety years after it began.[21] On the other hand, research into German "war atrocities" in Belgium and western France has been discussed in scholarly circles with an intensity unmatched for any First World War subject since the controversy over the Reizler diaries.[22] In view of this discussion, the desiderata in the research of the eastern front becomes all the more important. Today it is no longer remembered that there were acts of brutality on the eastern front that paralleled German war crimes in the west, possibly claiming a similar number of victims. First there were the rampages by the Russians in East Prussia between August 1914 and early 1915, and then the terror tactics used by both the Russians and the Austro-Hungarian Army against the civilian population in Galicia in fall 1914 and summer 1915.[23]

When the fighting spilled over into the civilian population, this marked the beginning of the lifting of restraints in the conduct of the war, something that would also mark the German war of extermination twenty-five years later. One might presume that the terror tactics represent a further line of connection between the two eastern fronts, even considering gaps in the research. But in each war, the terror tactics could also have been motivated by different factors. During the First World War aggravating factors may have included the overextending of the soldiers and the fear of *Franctireurs* (irregulars or snipers) and traitors. During the war of extermination, however, a greater role was played by the racial and ideological concept of the enemy, one that had already shown signs of existing during the First World War but later became further radicalized.

Other researchers suggest that the causes of the war of destruction from 1915 to 1918–1919 were essentially the same as those of the war of extermination of 1941–1944. Michael Geyer, for instance, believes the causes were a "genocidal character" in the German conduct of war during the entire era of the world wars, an interpretation that Isabel Hull adopts in her study on the German conduct of their colonial wars.[24]

The chapters in the present volume take a somewhat different view of the situation. Here the violence is viewed less as the result of a deep-seated national military culture than as an outcome of the special character of the eastern front and the relationship between the two multiethnic empires involved.[25] As Jörg Baberowski argues, because national borders and ethnic settlement areas were not clearly identified in the Russian Empire or in Austria-Hungary, loyalty conflicts, distrust, repression, and finally terror, were an inherent part of the system.

In both wars on the eastern fronts the use of terror unquestionably represented a continuity, not only on the German side but on the Russian-Soviet side as well. In either case, the question arises as to the collective mindset and attitudes that influenced the willingness to exert extreme brutality in either war. What was it that led soldiers to commit acts during the first weeks of the First World War that lay outside their individual and social range of experience? One explanation is offered in John Horne and Alan Kramer's work on the "*Franctireur* Complex," the fear of attacks by irregulars. This paranoia had been inculcated into the collective memory of the German military institution and was an effective part of the military enculturation process of every new cohort of recruits. But what was it that led Russian troops in the summer of 1915 to lay waste to Galicia in a way that, as Piotr Szlanta shows, greatly exceeded anything required by the scorched-earth strategy? As these works suggest, although the larger complex of motivations include a collective mindset plus "past experience," an even more important cause may be found in political motives and a worldview imprinted with ideology.

Ideologies, as Baberowski maintains, played an important part even during the First World War. The devastation of the border region of the Russian Empire by czarist troops, he writes, stemmed from what he terms a "nationalist cleansing." The Russian terror policy in the border region of the empire was based on the lessons learned by that point by the Russian generals over the course of the war. As a multiethnic empire, Russia saw that it was too weak to withstand the homogeneous nation-state of Germany. It "therefore would have to stop being a multiethnic empire," a notion that ultimately meant brutal treatment, expulsion, and deportation of minorities such as Poles, Germans, and Jews.[26]

Along with the perception of the enemy, nationalism, and ideologies—which, by their very nature, can turn soldiers into perpetrators—other factors came into play. These are less ascribable to mentalities than to the realities of the actual situation, which produced stress, fear, and physical overloading. In his essay on German geopolitics prior to the Second World War, Hew Strachan underscores these kinds of influences. The German military elite in 1940, he writes, had deluded themselves into thinking that they had defeated Russia militarily in the First World War. Thus, for the second time, they planned a war that was geographically beyond Germany's reach. It was this overextending of the Wehrmacht in the land war in Russia, Strachan argues, that increased the tendency toward extreme brutality. The inadequate logistics of the German east army of 1941 led to the necessity of living off the land. In like manner the low numerical strength of the German Army in relationship to the European Soviet Union had a radicalizing effect on the resolution to suppress any attempt at resistance with brutality, further legitimized by a criminal ideology.

Strachan starts from the premise that these factors also played a role in German "war atrocities" in Belgium (and, analogously, may also have influenced the conduct of the Czarist Army in East Prussia). Added to this was an operation plan that was divorced from reality, which placed the military leaders and soldiers involved under immense pressure, and this had just as much share in the terror and brutality as "soft factors" such as collective experience. In view of these insights, the attempt to interpret continuities stemming from collective experience still appears difficult to justify.

War-related terror tactics also include brutality measures by the military against the civilian population in the rear areas away from the battle front. By 1941 such tactics were employed by both the Germans and the Soviets. The level of brutality, even in the context of military operations, far exceeded anything required by the operational intent. In their studies on besieged Leningrad, Johannes Hürter and Robert Ganzenmüller have shown that the deliberate devastation and starvation strategy of the Wehrmacht was not sufficiently justified militarily.[27] Such barbarism was not unique to the German conduct of war during the Second World War. It was also witnessed—although to a less horrific extent—on the "archaic" eastern front of the First World War. Between 4 and 7 August 1914 the Polish border city of Kalisz, mentioned in the chapters by Gundula Bavendamm and Piotr Szlanta, was almost completely destroyed by German artillery bombardment and arson. A pointless action from a military standpoint, it still stands in the Polish collective memory as a great trauma. In Germany it has been forgotten.

The enemy population of East Prussia was not the only group of victims of belligerent conduct by the occupiers; it even affected German citizens living there. Even as early as the First World War, traditional conventions of military conduct—mercy to strangers and protection of one's own civilian population—had begun to fall away. Hans-Erich Volkmann points out in his chapter that for more than a decade, German operations plans had designated East Prussia as an area that could be sacrificed if need be for the sake of military superiority in the west.[28] The military elite had obviously never planned evacuation measures or any defense efforts by the militias. This demonstrates that even during extremely peaceful periods, military "necessity" took precedence over the welfare of the German population of the eastern province. Moreover, in the 1920s, Joachim von Stülpnagel's "ethnic war plans" called for the devastation of broad portions of the German border area. This shows that the German population now represented a disruptive factor in operations planning rather than a group that needed defending. This is one line of continuity between the First World War and the manner in which the war was conducted in 1944 and 1945.[29] In the collective memory of the German military institution, operational thinking was purely in terms of military success.

The Occupation Government

A government willing to sacrifice its own population for the sake of a strategic advantage was not at all likely to hesitate in subjugating the eastern European neighbor peoples in a quasi-colonial exploitation system. In his chapter in this volume, Liulevicius emphasizes that the Germans did so on *both* eastern fronts. Liulevicius, as previously mentioned, is among the strongest proponents of the thesis of continuity between the two eastern fronts. He refers to the "Land of Ober Ost," the German occupation government in eastern Europe between 1915 and 1918, as a military state that claimed the right to totalitarian control. The ostensible plan of the military state was to introduce German orderliness and to civilize the country. The actual plan was to exploit it. But was there a significant impact that had a connection to the eastern front of the Second World War? If, following the short period of Ober Ost's existence, the German concept of the east had retained its defining characteristics, and if twenty-five years later the structural conditions had still been in place for the establishment of a distinctly more radical terror and exploitation regime by the Reich Commissariat Eastland, then the impact would have been a more significant one. The experiences that the members of the German occupation apparatus underwent between 1915 and 1918 could therefore be said to have been a basis for the German occupation terror of the years 1941 to 1944.

Liulevicius reconstructs the experience of the occupation primarily through letters, journal entries, and firsthand accounts of officers and members of the government of Ober Ost. His characterization of the historical reality of the German occupation in Ober Ost during the First World War is a convincing one and is further supported in a chapter in this volume from a neighboring discipline, literary scholarship. Literary scholar Eva Horn points out here that the only well-respected literary description of the German war on the eastern front, Arnold Zweig's novel *The Case of Sergeant Grischa,* depicts the German military state of Ober Ost in a manner that reads like a literary version of the images developed by Liulevicius.[30] Zweig, as Horn notes, describes the German government of the east as "a kind of war by other means" carried out against the native population. Zweig's work has an undeniable source value in that after his deployment on the western front of June 1917, the author served in the press section of the German High Command until the end of the war. He became familiar with the inner workings of the government of Ober Ost and was able to provide a view of the occupation regime "from its underside" in a way that Liulevicius's study could not.[31]

In his study *War Land in the East,* Liulevicius offers insights primarily from members of the German military and bureaucratic elite.[32] A point of criticism has been the one-sidedness of his source basis, first of all because it focuses on a "concept of the German east" of only a small group. Second, it provides little discussion concerning the actual motives behind German governing practices and exploitation of the east in the manner of a colony. (As Ulrike Jureit has recently pointed out, personal documents such as diaries and letters make a statement primarily about "the individual's identity and construction of meaning" and thus are informative only to a limited extent on the overall motives of the government of Ober Ost.)[33]

Third, it is an open question as to whether this "German image of the east" actually was part of the complex of motives of the men who a quarter century later created the Reichskommissariat (Reich Commissariat). Or was the radicalization of German government authority, such as in its conduct of the war of annihilation, to be interpreted in the context of a total societal militarization or an ideologically based idealization of race and the "fight for a way of life?"[34] Criticism of this kind of construction of continuities targets first of all a concept of experience that places the after-the-fact recollections of a relatively small group on the same plane with "the" German experience of the east. Moreover, it targets a concept that overlooks the interactions of "experience" and further elements of collective dispositions that the members of the government of the Reich Commissariat brought with them to the east.

Liulevicius's thesis has definitely furthered the state of research in this area. Nevertheless, his argument could be strengthened by an expanded source basis and through the laborious process of individual case analysis. One such case is Bernd Wegner's analysis of Fall Blau (Operation Blue), the German offensive on the southern flank of the eastern front in summer 1942. Liulevicius draws on the planning process for this offensive in support of his thesis of an experience-based continuity.[35] Wegner does show that there was very likely an experiential and historical connection between Fall Blau in 1942 and the German Caucasus expedition of 1918, namely, the Caucasus oil fields. It was not Hitler in fact who first understood their crucial importance but Ludendorff. In the summer of 1918 he ordered the German advance on these oil fields, which was halted when the war ended. Fall Blau, the 1942 offensive by Army Group

South, was intended to finish what had been started and disrupted in 1918.[36] This operation, Wegner shows, lay in the hands of men whose store of experience included the 1918 expedition.[37] Thus, there is evidence showing that experiences of the First World War did influence the conduct of operations in the Second World War. It is remarkable, however, that Wegner supports his argument by citing individual, not collective, experiences associated with the planning of Fall Blau. He apparently did not ascribe critical importance to the latter.

During the First World War the German Empire was not the only power to establish a repressive occupation regime in eastern Europe. The Russian government of the occupied portions of Galicia may have been a close second in terms of its system and duration, although not in its radicalism and inhumanity. In the context of Russia's Russification policy, as described by Jörg Baberowski, the eastern part of Galicia was incorporated into the Russian Empire and decreed original Russian territory. The population of Eastern Galicia was then forced to convert to Orthodox Christianity. Like Ober Ost, this too has a line of continuity that can be traced forward to the Second World War. The Russian annexation of Galicia was a sign of the Russians' glance westward, a tendency similar to the westward expulsion of the Polish by the Germans in the Second World War. The forced conversion of the Eastern Galicians to the Orthodox religion also found its echo in the later forced conversion to Socialism, the new social order.

In the occupation policy—and, as was shown in the previous section, in the use of terror tactics—it has been shown that a line of continuity can be drawn between the two world wars. This can also be shown for the conduct of war in the "Eurasian heartland" (Hew Strachan). Yet, considering that the civilian and military elite was completely replaced between 1917 and 1941, can one say that these continuities were determined by experience?[38] It is hardly likely. In the Soviet Union's war between 1941 and 1945, the most profound influences came from situational and geopolitical factors.

Even though comparisons can provide a modest appraisal of the occupations in both world wars, there cannot be an adequate description of the general and specific factors of the German and Russian-Soviet occupation governments without a view from the underside of the populations in question. This type of approach has proven effective in the works of Bernhard Chiari, who addresses the everyday life of the civilian population during the war in the occupied area of the Soviet Union.[39] While he shows that in the governing practices of Ober Ost the people of eastern European were reduced to simple objects of expansive organization plans, it is doubtful that this necessarily carried over to the later Reich Commissariat of Eastland of the Second World War.[40] Chiari refers more than once to its parallels with the Russian-Soviet occupation policy. This would suggest the need for a closer look at the structural conditions that stem from the demands of a total war.[41] In either case, answers can only be provided based on further knowledge of the everyday life of the populations of Ober Ost and Eastern Galicia.

On the Construction of Continuities

Lines of continuity do exist between the wars on the "forgotten front" of the First World War and the "war of extermination" of the Second World War. Of this, recent research leaves little doubt. "For succeeding generations the experience of the war remains present and presents a paradigm for action."[42] Thus, it is hardly surprising that in 1941 on the German side, there was already an image of the east and of the Russians, and these stereotypes could be sensed in the personal testimonials of the officers of the first eastern front.

This image of the east, as shown in the preceding synopsis, was constructed from only a portion of the total experience. For the most part, it was derived from a concept of the enemy that had either been present in 1914 or construed relatively independently from the events on the eastern front. One can perhaps go so far as to argue that this discourse on the enemy, which came into being in Germany only as a result of the war situation with Russia, had more of an impact on the perception of the enemy than the experiences of the soldiers on the front.

This brings the discussion back to the concept of experience, or *Erfahrung,* in the sense of a learning experience. Presently in scholarly historical research, the term *Erfahrung* is often invoked to fill in gaps in historical knowledge. According to the theoretical premise, the terms *Erfahrung* (experience) and *Erfahrungsgeschichte* (history of experience) are distinctly different from *Erlebnis* (direct experience). Direct experience is something one lives through: a small adventure, as it were. This adventure does not become a learning experience (for a culture or society) until it is conveyed socially, presented in the context of a socially prestructured sphere of learning, and becomes part of an existing body of knowledge.[43]

Thus, if the direct experience of the eastern front had a shocking effect on an individual due to its strangeness, the total learning experience of the east is nevertheless defined by means of collective interpretive patterns and is constructed socially. From a general historical perspective, Reinhart Koselleck argues that more attention ought to be given to the predisposition of the social consciousness of the participants who contribute to the reconstruction of learning experiences.[44] Therefore, the history-of-mentalities approach to interpreting the past, when dealing with the "war of annihilation," should not be confined to the war experience of the First World War: instead, where possible, it should also draw on the perceptions of the east in Imperial Germany going back to the nineteenth century.

So far the only named continuities traced between the two eastern fronts are perceptions of the enemy, terror tactics, and repression by the occupation forces. These more visible continuities become doubtful if one posits that there is a genuine causal relationship between the learning experience gained during the first war on the eastern front and the manner in which the second was conducted. First of all, it must remain an open question as to what definite characteristics were present in the collective attitudes of those who perpetrated the war of extermination. Certainly both collective and individual experiences were factors. Yet nothing consistent can be said about German military men's conduct in the Second World War that has anything to do with their respective eastern war experiences. During the Second World War, the Baltic fighter Georg von Küchler did in fact proceed with the plan to starve Leningrad as ordered. His predecessor, however, General Wilhelm Ritter von Leeb, who had experienced the First World War in the east on the general staff of the 11th Bavarian Infantry Division, opposed it. In his opinion it was a senseless way to wage war, and he pressured Hitler to dismiss him from duty.[45]

On the basis of the present state of research, there is little to provide a solid grounding for a future interpretation of the First World War in eastern Europe based on the theoretical approach of *Erfahrungsgeschichte,* or history of experience. First of all, the primary resources on the experience of the eastern front are mostly limited to personal testimonials by the military and bureaucratic German elite. As Jutta Nowosadtko has pointed out, when all "individuals belong to the same 'social camp,'" there is a narrow range of learning experiences.[46] The letters and memoirs of German officers express an extremely unified concept of the east, revealing only a small glimpse of "the" German eastern front experience.[47]

Second, there must be some investigation into areas outside of the range of learning experiences of the military officers. Demanding though it may be, considering the dearth of material to work with, an attempt to construct a view from "beneath" the world war and the occupation government will never reveal anything of substance about the practices of the dictatorship and the everyday war experience in the "war land on the eastern front" unless one includes the eastern European population itself.[48]

Third, one would have to ask whether in the historiographical construction of the First World War German eastern front too much weight is being placed on the participants' personal interpretations and too little on the structural conditions surrounding their actions.[49] Two examples suggest this is the case. First, Russian war crimes in East Prussia prompted German propagandists to invent the term "Russian-Mongolian conduct of war" as an incitement to aggressive action, in the same vein that the Allies used the term "bloodthirsty Huns." One must then ask, did the term "Russian-Mongolian war conduct" from the First World War have any basis in fact that led to German hatred of the Slavs? Or was this an example of stereotyping that fell under the heading of fighting a battle with all available means?

The second example was that the members of the government of Ober Ost promoted their governing actions with nationalistic euphemisms such as "German work" and "orderlinesss." Was this a first step toward the kind of radical nationalism that was later practiced in the Reich Commissariat of the Eastland? Or was it merely an attempt to give meaning to German work related to the war effort?

In order to be able to distinguish between the structural and the ideological influences on the actions of the protagonists, our range of vision must be broadened to include the conduct of war and the demeanor of the occupation government of the other powers that waged war in the east. Only a comparison of German and Austro-Hungarian terror measures of Ober Ost against the Russian occupation in Eastern Galicia will enable the identification of unique national qualities of the conduct of war in eastern Europe of 1914 to 1918. This is the prerequisite for addressing the issue about the line of continuities running between the German wars in the east from 1914 to 1918 and from 1941 to 1944.

Notes

1. Andrej Angrick, "Das Beispiel Charkow: Massenmord unter deutscher Besatzung." In: *Verbrechen der Wehrmacht. Bilanz einer Debatte,* edited by Christian Hartmann, Johannes Hürter, and Ulrike Jureit, Munich 2005, 117–24, here 119.

2. Johannes Hürter, "Konservative Mentalität, militärischer Pragmatismus, ideologisierte Kriegführung: Das Beispiel des Generals Georg von Küchler." In: *Karrieren im National-sozialismus. Funktionseliten zwischen Mitwirkung und Distanz,* edited by Gerhard Hirschfeld and Tobias Jersak, Frankfurt, New York 2004, 239–53, here 247.

3. See Bernhard Chiari, *Alltag hinter der Front. Besatzung, Kollaboration und Widerstand in Weissrussland 1941–1944,* Düsseldorf 1998, esp. 59–72.

4. For a concise summary of the state of research on the so-called war of annihilation by the Wehrmacht, see the collected articles *Verbrechen der Wehrmacht;* on the debate prompted by the Wehrmacht exhibitions, see Hans-Ulrich Thamer, "Vom Tabubruch zur Historisierung? Die Auseinandersetzung um die 'Wehrmachtsausstellung'" In: *Zeitgeschichte als Streitgeschichte. Grosse Kontroversen nach 1945,* edited by Martin Sabrow, Ralph Jessen, and Klaus Grosse Kracht, Munich 2003, 171–86.

5. The term *mentalities* refers here and in future to "a state of consciousness that is informal, unconscious, or preconscious," which is shared by members of a group. See Wolfgang Reinhard, *Lebensformen Europas. Eine historische Kulturanthropologie,* Munich 2004, 20f. See also Ute Daniel, *Kompendium Kulturgeschichte: Theorien, Praxis, Schlüsselwörter,* Frankfurt 2001, 221–29.

6. Ulrike Jureit, "Motive–Mentalitäten–Handlungsspielräume. Theoretische Anmerkungen zu Handlungsoptionen von Soldaten." In: *Verbrechen der Wehrmacht,* 163–70, here 167.

7. Eberhard Demm, "Das deutsche Besatzungsregime in Litauen im Ersten Weltkrieg—Generalprobe für Hitlers Ostfeldzug und Versuchslabor des totalitären Staates."

In: *Eberhard Demm, Ostpolitik und Propaganda im Ersten Weltkrieg,* Frankfurt 2002, 329–39; Vejas Gabriel Liulevicius, *Kriegsland im Osten. Eroberung, Kolonisierung und Militärherrschaft im Ersten Weltkrieg,* Hamburg 2002. For a critical view of their positions, see the essay by Peter Hoeres in the present volume.

8. See Bruno Thoss, "Die Zeit der Weltkriege—Epochen als Erfahrungseinheit?" In: *Erster Weltkrieg–Zweiter Weltkrieg: ein Vergleich. Krieg, Kriegserlebnis, Kriegserfahrung in Deutschland,* published under the auspices of the Militärgeschichtliches Forschungsamt, edited by Bruno Thoss and Hans-Erich Volkmann, Munich 202, 7–30.

9. On the new cultural history, see the explanations and definitions in Daniel, *Kompendium Kulturgeschichte,* 7–25, esp. 17–19.

10. Nikolaus Buschmann and Horst Carl, "Zugänge zur Erfahrungsgeschichte des Krieges: Forschung, Theorie, Fragestellung." In: *Die Erfahrung des Krieges: Erfahrungsgeschichtliche Perspektiven von der Französischen Revolution bis zum Zweiten Weltkrieg,* edited by Nikolaus Buschmann and Horst Carl, Paderborn 2001 (= *Krieg in der Geschichte,* 9), 11–26, here 18.

11. Liulevicius, *Kriegsland im Osten.*

12. See Hans-Heinrich Wilhelm, "Personelle Kontinuitäten in baltischen Angelegenheiten auf deutscher Seite von 1917/19 bis zum Zweiten Weltkrieg." In: *The Baltic in International Relations between the World Wars,* edited by John Hiden and Aleksander Loit, Stockholm 1988 (= *Acta Universitatis Stockholmiensis. Studia baltica Stockholmgiensia,* 3), 157–70; Johannes Hürter, "Kriegserfahrung als Schlüsselerlebnis? Der erste Weltkrieg in der Biographie von Wehrmachtsgeneralen." In: *Erster Weltkrieg–Zweiter Weltkrieg,* 759–71, here 771.

13. Hürter, *Konservative Mentalität,* 240.

14. This term comes from Michael Geyer, "Gewalt und Gewalterfahrung im 20. Jahrhundert—Der Erste Weltkrieg." In: *Der Tod als Maschinist. Der industrialisierte Krieg 1914–1918,* edited by Rolf Spilker and Bernd Ulrich, Bramsche 1998, 240–57.

15. Hans-Ulrich Wehler, "Die 'Urkatastrophe.' Der Erste Weltkrieg als Auftakt und Vorbild für den Zweiten Weltkrieg." In: *Der Spiegel,* no. 8, 16/2/2004, 82–89, here 89.

16. The image of German superiority over the "Slavic mass armies" was firmly rooted in the minds of the German military elite, even after the collapse of 1945. This is attested to in a presentation by former general Theodor Heusinger, the chief of the operations section in the OKW (High Command of the Wehrmacht) and later the inspector general of the Bundeswehr, to a panel of experts of the Bundestag in 1952. In the context of planning for additional military troops for German defense, Heusinger explained: "The plus that comes from twelve German units . . . this plus in the valuation of the European defense in my opinion must not be underestimated. . . . I have such rock-solid confidence in the German people and the German character that I believe there is hope that a new troop will also acquire a similar degree of strength and ability to fight the Russians that the old troops had." *Der Bundestagsausschuss für Verteidigung. Der Ausschuss zur Mitberatung des EVG-Vertrages. Juli bis Dezember 1952,* published under the auspices of the MGFA (Militärgeschichtliches Forschungsamt), edited by Hans-Erich Volkmann, Düsseldorf 2006 (= *Der Bundestagsausschuss für Verteidigung und seine Vorläufer,* 1), 597.

17. "The ordinary soldier . . . is no longer the 'good Mushik' familiar to us from the world war . . . [his] intelligence and understanding of technology have grown." Quoted

in Jürgen Förster, "Zum Russlandbild der Militärs 1941–1945." In: *Das Russlandbild im Dritten Reich,* edited by Hans-Erich Volkmann, Cologne 1994, 141–63, here 145.

18. See Lothar Höbelt, "'So wie wir haben nicht einmal die Japaner angegriffen.' Österreich-Ungarns Nordfront 1914/15." In: *Die vergessene Front. Der Osten 1914/15,* edited by Gerhard P. Gross, Paderborn 2006, 87–119.

19. See the essay by Hew Strachan in this volume.

20. Hürter, "Kriegserfahrung als Schlüsselerlebnis?" 771. This kind of argument is also made by Jörg Baberowski, Peter Hoeres, and Hans-Erich Volkmann in their essays in this volume.

21. John Horne and Alan Kramer, *Deutsche Kriegsgreuel 1914. Die umstrittene Wahrheit,* Hamburg, 2004.

22. For a positive evaluation of the work by Horne and Kramer, see the reviews by Steffen Bruendel in: H-Soz-u-Kult, 25/9/2003, http://hsozkult.geschichte.hu-berlin.de/rezensionen/2003-3-182; a critical view by Peter Hoeres in: *sehepunkte,* 4, 7/8, 15/7/2004, http://www.sehepunkte.historicum.net/2004/07/6108.html.

23. On the brutalities committed by Austro-Hungarian and Russian troops in 1914–1915 in Lwów (Lemberg), which were primarily anti-Jewish, see Christoph Mick, "Ethnische Gewalt und Pogrome in Lemberg 1914 und 1941." In: *Osteuropa,* 53 (2003), 1810–29, here 1811–14. For a comprehensive discussion of the involvement of the civilian population in the conduct of war, see John Horne and Alan Kramer, "War between Soldiers and Enemy Civilians, 1914–1915." In: *Great War, Total War: Combat and Mobilization on the Western Front,* edited by Roger Chickering and Stig Förster, New York 2000, 153–68.

24. Geyer, *Gewalt,* 249; Isabel V. Hull, *Absolute Destruction: Military Culture and the Practices of War in Imperial Germany,* Ithaca, London 2005. Hull argues that even as early as in the German colonial wars in the first decade of the twentieth century the characteristics of a conduct of war had developed whose aim was not victory but the destruction of the enemy. During the First World War in Belgium this turned into, in the words of John Horne and Alan Kramer, a "German way of war." See also Horne/Kramer, *Deutsche Kriegsgreuel,* 243.

25. Dirk Schumann expresses a skeptical view of the link between the German atrocities (*Kriegsgräuel*) in the west in 1914 and the war of extermination (*Vernichtungskrieg*) beginning in 1941 in "Gewalterfahrungen und ihre nicht zwangsläufigen Folge. Der Erste Weltkrieg in der Gewaltgeschichte des 20. Jahrhunderts." In: *Zeitgeschichte Online,* May 2004, http://www.zeitgeschichte-online.de/md=EWK-Schumann, 5.

26. Michael Geyer also expresses this view in "Urkatastrophe, Europäischer Bürgerkrieg, Menschenschlachthaus–wie Historiker dem Epochenbruch des Ersten Weltkriegs Sinn geben." In: *Der Weltkrieg 1914–1918. Ereignis und Erinnerung. Ausstellungskatalog,* edited by Rainer Rother, Berlin 2004, 24–33, here 28.

27. Johannes Hürter, "Die Wehrmacht vor Leningrad. Krieg und Besatzungspolitik der 18. Armee im Herbst und Winter 1941/42." In: *Vierteljahrshefte für Zeitgeschichte,* 49 (2001), 377–440; Ganzenmüller, *Das belagerte Leningrad.*

28. See also Terence Zuber's chapter in the German edition of this book.

29. See Wilhelm Siest, "Die Reichswehr und der Krieg der Zukunft." In: *Militärgeschichtliche Mitteilungen (MGM),* 45 (1989), 81–92; Michael Geyer, "Der zur Organisation erhobene Burgfrieden." In: *Militär und Militarismus in der Weimarer Republik,* edited by Klaus-Jürgen Müller and Eckhardt Opitz, Düsseldorf 1978, 15–100.

30. Arnold Zweig, *Der Streit um den Sergeanten Grischa,* Potsdam 1928.

31. Jost Hermand, Arnold Zweig, "'Der Streit um den Sergeanten Grischa' (1927). Eine systemkritische Analyse." In: *Von Richthofen bis Remarque: Deutschsprachige Prosa zum I. Weltkrieg,* edited by Thomas F. Schneider and Hans Wagener, Amsterdam, New York 2003 (= *Amsterdamer Beiträge zur neueren Germanistik,* 53), 195–205, here 196.

32. Liulevicius, *Kriegsland im Osten.* See the review by Steffen Bruendel in: H-Soz-u-Kult, 13/5/2004, http://hsozkult.geschichte.hu-berlin.de/rezensionen/2004-2-102.

33. Jureit, "Motive," 165.

34. Bernhard R. Kroener, "Kampf als Daseinsform." In: *Der Nationalsozialismus und die deutsche Gesellschaft, Einführung und Überblick,* edited by Bernd Sösemann, Stuttgart, Munich 2002, 312–28.

35. Bernd Wegner, "Der Krieg gegen die Sowjetunion 1942/43." In: *Das Deutsche Reich und der Zweite Weltkrieg,* vol. 6; Horst Boog, Werner Rahn, Reinhard Stumpf, and Bernd Wegner, *Der globale Krieg. Die Ausweitung zum Weltkrieg und der Wechsel der Initiative 1941–1943,* Stuttgart 1990, 761–1102, here 761–78.

36. On the Caucasus operation of 1918, see also Winfried Baumgart, "Das 'Kaspi-Unternehmen'—Grössenwahn Ludendorffs oder Routineplanung des deutschen Generalstabes? Ein kritischer Blick auf die deutsche militärische Intervention im Kaukasus am Ende des Ersten Weltkrieges, Teil 1–2." In: *Jahrbücher für Geschichte Osteuropas,* 18 (1970), 47–126, 231–78.

37. Wegner, *Der Krieg gegen die Sowjetunion,* 768f.

38. As shown in the essay by Kristiane Janeke in the present volume, the memory of the experience of the First World War in the early Soviet Union was much more suppressed and dismantled by the state.

39. Bernhard Chiari, "Grenzen deutscher Herrschaft. Voraussetzungen und Folgen der Besatzung in der Sowjetunion." In: *Das Deutsche Reich und der Zweite Weltkrieg,* vol. 9/2, *Die deutsche Kriegsgesellschaft 1939 bis 1945. Ausbeutung, Deutungen, Ausgrenzung,* published under the auspices of the Militärgeschichtliches Forschungsamt, edited by Jörg Echternkamp, Munich 2005, 877–976; Chiari, *Alltag hinter der Front.*

40. Bernhard Chiari sees a diametric contradiction in the "perception of the native population as 'colonial peoples' and often as 'subhuman' or 'creatures'" during the Second World War and points to the fact that in 1941 the German authorities turned down most of those who applied for the civilian government of the occupied territory in the Soviet Union on the basis of their experience in Ober Ost. They were supposedly looking for a "different type" for the upcoming "difficult tasks" (Himmler). Bernhard Chiari, "Geschichte als Gewalttat. Weissrussland als Kind zweier Weltkriege." In: *Erster Weltkrieg–Zweiter Weltkrieg,* 615–31, here 626f.

41. Chiari, *Alltag hinter der Front,* 303–5.

42. Nicolaus Buschmann and Aribert Reimann, "Zugänge zur Erfahrungsgeschichte des Krieges: Forschung, Theorie, Fragestellung." Wege zu einer Erfahrungsgeschichte des Krieges." In: *Die Erfahrung des Krieges,* 11–26, here 9.

43. Nikolaus Buschmann and Aribert Reimann, "Die Konstruktion historischer Erfahrung. Neue Wege zu einer Erfahrungsgeschichte des Krieges." In: *Die Erfahrung des Krieges,* 261–71, here 262; Jutta Nowosadtko, "Erfahrung als Methode und als Gegenstand wissenschaftlicher Erkenntnis. Der Begriff der Erfahrung in der Soziologie." In: ibid., 27–50, here 41.

44. Reinhart Koselleck, "Der Einfluss der beiden Weltkriege auf das soziale Bewusstsein." In: *Der Krieg des kleinen Mannes. Eine Militärgeschichte von unten,* Munich 1992, 324–43, here 326.

45. Wilhelm Ritter von Leeb, *Tagebuchaufzeichnungen und Lagebeurteilungen aus 2 Weltkriegen.* Edited by Georg Meyer, Stuttgart 1976 (= *Beiträge zur Militär und Kriegsgeschichte,* 16), 69–72. Leeb's advanced age may also have motivated to him to make this decision. The disagreement with Hitler did not prevent him from accepting a generous endowment. See Gerhard L. Weinberg, "Zur Dotation Hitlers an Generalfeldmarschall Ritter von Leeb." In: *MGM* 26 (1979), 97–99.

46. Nowosadtko, *Erfahrung als Methode,* 41.

47. This statement is not meant to diminish the value of the work accomplished; it is evident that particularly the younger members of the officer corps of the First World War played a prominent role in conducting the "war of annihilation." But based on this resource, the image of the experience of the east is rather one-dimensional.

48. Chiari, *Grenzen deutscher Herrschaft;* Chiari, *Alltag hinter der Front.*

49. See Buschmann/Carl, *"Zugänge zur Erfahrungsgeschichte,"* 20.

Contributors

Jörg Baberowski, Dr. phil., is professor of history at Humboldt University, Berlin.

Gundula Bavendamm, Dr. phil., is director of the Foundation for Flight, Expulsion, and Reconciliation of Refugees (Stiftung Flucht, Vertreibung, Versöhnung), Berlin.

Christine Beil, Dr. phil., is a historian and journalist working in Eppelheim, Germany.

Rüdiger Bergien, Dr. phil., is a research fellow at the Center for Contemporary History (Zentrum für Zeitgeschichte), Potsdam.

Stig Förster, Dr. phil., is a professor (ret.) at the University of Bern.

Col. Gerhard P. Gross, Dr. phil., is head of the Department of German Military History before 1945 at the Bundeswehr Center of Military History and Social Sciences (ZMSBw), Potsdam.

Peter Hoeres, Dr. phil., is a professor at the University of Würzburg.

Eva Horn, Dr. phil., is professor of culture and literary studies (Kultur- und Literaturwissenschaft) at the University of Vienna.

Hubertus F. Jahn, Dr. phil., is senior lecturer in east European history at the University of Cambridge.

Kristiane Janeke, Dr. phil., is a historian and curator working in Berlin, Germany.

Boris Khavkin is professor (ret.) of history at the Academy of Military Sciences, Moscow.

Günther Kronenbitter, Dr. phil., is associate professor of history at the University of Augsburg/Bern.

Vejas Gabriel Liulevicius, PhD, is professor of history at the University of Tennessee, Knoxville.

Birgit Menzel, Dr. phil., is professor of Slavic studies at Johannes Gutenberg University of Mainz.

Igor Narskij, Dr. phil., is a professor at Chelyabinsk State University, Russia.

Rainer Rother, Dr. phil., is art director of the German Film Archive (Deutsche Kinemathek), Berlin.

Hew Strachan, Dr. phil., is professor (ret.) of history at the University of Oxford.

Piotr Szlanta, Dr. phil., is associate professor at the University of Warsaw.

Hans-Erich Volkmann, Dr. phil., is a professor (ret.) at Albert Ludwig University of Freiburg.

Index